Studies in the History of Law and Justice

Volume 18

The purpose of this book series is to publish high quality volumes on the history of law and justice. Legal history can be a deeply provocative and influential field, as illustrated by the growth of the European universities and the *Ius Commune*, the French Revolution, the American Revolution, and indeed all the great movements for national liberation through law. The study of history gives scholars and reformers the models and courage to question entrenched injustices, by demonstrating the contingency of law and other social arrangements. Yet legal history today finds itself diminished in the universities and legal academy. Too often scholarship betrays no knowledge of what went before, or why legal institutions took the shape that they did. This series seeks to remedy that deficiency.

Studies in the History of Law and Justice will be theoretical and reflective. Volumes will address the history of law and justice from a critical and comparative viewpoint. The studies in this series will be strong bold narratives of the development of law and justice. Some will be suitable for a very broad readership.

Contributions to this series will come from scholars on every continent and in every legal system. Volumes will promote international comparisons and dialogue. The purpose will be to provide the next generation of lawyers with the models and narratives needed to understand and improve the law and justice of their own era. The series includes monographs focusing on a specific topic, as well as collections of articles covering a theme or collections of article by one author.

More information about this series at http://www.springer.com/series/11794

Cristiano Paixão · Massimo Meccarelli
Editors

Comparing Transitions to Democracy. Law and Justice in South America and Europe

 Springer

Editors
Cristiano Paixão
School of Law
Universidade de Brasília
Brasília, Brazil

Massimo Meccarelli
Department of Law
Università di Macerata
Macerata, Italy

ISSN 2198-9842   ISSN 2198-9850 (electronic)
Studies in the History of Law and Justice
ISBN 978-3-030-67504-2   ISBN 978-3-030-67502-8 (eBook)
https://doi.org/10.1007/978-3-030-67502-8

This Springer imprint is published by the registered company Springer Nature Switzerland AG
The registered company address is: Gewerbestrasse 11, 6330 Cham, Switzerland

Contents

Editors and Contributors

About the Editors

Cristiano Paixão is Professor of Legal History and Constitutional Law at the University of Brasília Law School. He received his Doctor in Law degree from Federal University of Minas Gerais, with postdoctoral studies in historiography at Ecole des Hautes Etudes en Sciences Sociales de Paris and modern history at Scuola Normale Superiore di Pisa. He was a Visiting Professor at Macerata University School of Law and at the Master's Program in Constitutional Law at Seville University, and has published extensively about constitutional history. He was a member of the Brazilian Amnesty Committee (Ministry of Justice) and was one of the coordinators of the Anísio Teixeira Memory and Truth Commission (University of Brasília). His main research interests are constitutional history, law and literature, and interdisciplinary studies in law.

Massimo Meccarelli is Professor of Legal History at the University of Macerata (Italy) and Affiliate Researcher of the Max Planck Institute for European Legal History (Frankfurt am Main). He was Visiting Professor at: Universidad Autónoma de Madrid, Johann Wolfgang Goethe-Universität in Frankfurt am Main, Universität Wien, and Universität Luzern. He is author of several works on history of legal thought, history of justice, historiography, and methodology of legal history. His most recent research interests are law and diversity, legal pluralism, constitution making process, time and law, and law and humanities.

Contributors

Leonardo Augusto de Andrade Barbosa Center for Continuing Education and Professional Development (CEFOR, Chamber of Deputies), Brasília, Brazil

Alfons Aragoneses Department of Law, University Pompeu Fabra, Barcelona, Spain

Claudia Paiva Carvalho Instituto de Pesquisa e Planejamento Urbano, Universidade Federal do Rio de Janeiro, Rio de Janeiro, Brazil

Cath Collins Ulster University, Belfast, Northern Ireland

Maria Pia Guerra School of Law, University of Brasília, Brasília, Brazil

Francesca Lessa Department of International Development and the Latin American Centre, University of Oxford, Oxford, UK;
Observatorio Luz Ibarburu, Montevideo, Uruguay

Massimo Meccarelli Department of Law, University of Macerata, Macerata, Italy

Antonella Meniconi Department of Literature and Modern Cultures, University of Rome, La Sapienza, Italy

Juliana Neuenschwander Magalhães School of Law, Federal University of Rio de Janeiro, Rio de Janeiro, Brazil

Carla Osmo Federal University of São Paulo, São Paulo, Brazil

Cristiano Paixão School of Law, University of Brasília, Brasília, Brazil

Douglas Antônio Rocha Pinheiro School of Law, University of Brasília, Brasília, Brazil

Filipa Raimundo ISCTE-Lisbon University Institute, Lisbon, Portugal

Gabriel Rezende Instituto Brasiliense de Direito Público, Brasília, Brazil

Chapter 1
The Transition to Democracy: A New Object of Study for Legal History

Cristiano Paixão and Massimo Meccarelli

How is the experience of transition after dictatorship important for modern democracies? Is it possible to write a history of these transitions? And, if so, would such a history include different stories of the varied experiences of transition, each one necessarily localized and incommensurable? Or is it instead possible to consider "transition to democracy" in a more general sense, as a framework and a unitary category, an object as such, susceptible—like "dictatorship" and "democracy"—to analysis by legal sciences? The idea for this book stems from these basic questions, which urge us to reflect on the problems of democracy by considering the history of those problems.

This book collects contributions from scholars with different disciplinary and regional backgrounds, with the aim of bringing together diverse research on its subject. Focusing on the problem of transitional justice, but also including other thematic paths—such as constitutional frameworks, political actors, issues of gender, international relations, and international law—the chapters offer comparative perspectives on experiences in Latin America and Europe, in countries that share a common history, a certain cultural proximity, or both.

Rather than presenting an exhaustive picture, the book endeavours to expand the interpretative possibilities for the issue of transition to democracy by synthesizing different approaches. From this interweaving, the book also purports to consider the simultaneity of the different historical times subsumed by transition: social and individual time (of the victims and executioners, for example), as well as the time of politics, law, culture, etc. These historical times concern different aspects of civil

C. Paixão (✉)
School of Law, University of Brasília, Brasília, Brazil
e-mail: cristianop@unb.br

M. Meccarelli
Department of Law, University of Macerata, Macerata, Italy
e-mail: massimo.meccarelli@unimc.it

© Springer Nature Switzerland AG 2021
C. Paixão and M. Meccarelli (eds.), *Comparing Transitions to Democracy. Law and Justice in South America and Europe*, Studies in the History of Law and Justice 18, https://doi.org/10.1007/978-3-030-67502-8_1

coexistence, each with its own evolution and trajectory, but for all, the transition to democracy nevertheless represents the binding moment of common collapse, a unitary process that brings the disparate times into contact with each other, producing an overall acceleration—and, at the same time, a distortion—in their tempo.

1.1 The Problem of Transitional Justice

The subject of transitional justice is plural, manifold, and complex. To a certain extent, the phrase "transitional justice" itself is somewhat misleading. If understood as a single prescription—a uniform set of actions or reparations necessary in a post-dictatorship context—the phrase would be almost useless for understanding the numerous processes for the shift from authoritarian regime to constitutional democracy. Still, one cannot neglect the fact that the authoritarian experiences of the twentieth century—with their different forms and durations—nevertheless tasked political communities with taking specific measures in order to address the legacy of the arbitrariness, violence, and disregard for human rights that characterized those experiences.

Dealing with the complexities of transitional justice means gathering historical data that covers many different aspects of the measures instituted to address that legacy, such as: to what extent were such measures effective? How efficiently did those measures respond to the demands of the victims and of civil society more broadly? What were the reactions of those members of the authoritarian regimes who remained part of either the institutional-bureaucratic framework or the police and security forces? Indeed, there is a field of study related to understanding transitional justice in this sense, with governmental and non-governmental organizations dedicated to the issue and research groups and specialized journals focused on the topic.

Many of the experiences and approaches from the field of transitional justice appear in this book. In some cases, the authors collected in this volume incorporated multiple of these approaches in their discussion of the many issues connected to transitional justice. In other cases, the issues discussed required the authors to go beyond the lenses of transitional justice, leading to a broader and more coherent perspective toward the transitional phenomena per se.

As regards the demand for justice, some crucial aspects must be highlighted. The first one encompasses the so-called "right to the truth," whose attributes, limits, and forms are developed by some of the authors gathered here. As Carla Osmo points out, this right is the outcome of a construction that emerges from the case law of the Inter-American Human Rights System, whose decisions had undeniable (and diverse) impacts on the reparation policies in the South American countries that experienced authoritarian regimes. Alfons Aragoneses, in turn, discusses the stages of the struggle for the "right to the truth" in the Spanish experience. In the Brazilian case, two authors (Paixão and Magalhães) analyze the results of work by truth commissions that took place from 2012 onward.

Another topic treated in this volume is the role of the judiciary in transitional cases. How was the standard of competence for judging the facts, people and processes of the transitional experience determined? Solutions range from military courts (Raimundo) to extraordinary judicial bodies (Meniconi). Some countries created and consolidated a new institutional framework according to the demands of transitional justice in their cases, as we can see in the articles by Carla Osmo and Felipa Raimundo.

In those cases, an additional issue then emerges, one related to engagement in legal debate with regard to problems of transitional justice. The chapter by Massimo Meccarelli outlines the importance of such legal debates in the construction of the theoretical framework for a new criminal law system under democratic constitutional order.

One interesting advancement in political transitional processes is also the mobilization of civil society actors, a phenomenon especially common in South American countries (and even in Europe), analyzed here by Francesca Lessa, Cath Collins, and Alfons Aragoneses.

Other recurring topics in transitional policies are addressed in some of the articles collected here from interdisciplinary perspectives. Filipa Raimundo and Antonella Meniconi, for instance, analyze collaborationism. Lessa and Carvalho (on the Latin American cases), Paixão (on the Brazilian case), and Meniconi and Aragoneses (on the European cases) develop ideas related to the impunity toward agents of the authoritarian regimes' security forces who violated human rights. Carla Osmo, Cath Collins and Filipa Raimundo tackle the topic of institutional reforms in countries that have undergone transitional justice.

Another frequent topic in transitional justice is amnesty. In this volume, several authors address different aspects of this issue: first, the regimes' strategies for preventing the criminal prosecution of agents of the military and security forces; second, the appeal for reconciliation among political actors; and third and most important, the disputes in the present regarding choices made in the past. In addition to these three factors, several authors attend to decisions about who is included and excluded under amnesty policies, as well as other consequences of amnesty in law, politics and international relations. (Meccarelli, Meniconi, Osmo and Collins, among others)

1.2 Limitations of Transitional Justice

This book uses a broader concept of transitional justice than is usually indicated by the term. What is conventionally called "transitional justice" is only one among many possibilities (Rezende) for approaching the phenomena related to the transition from authoritarian regime to democracy. One of the purposes of this book is to perform a critical analysis of the narratives around transition, including the concept of transitional justice itself.

Thus, a number of the contributions published in this volume highlight a remarkable feature of some of the processes of transitional justice: the silenced voices. In this vein, some of the chapters here underscore the issue of selectivity in transitional justice measures. What demands on behalf of gender, race, and minorities in general have been left out? Claudia Paiva, Alfons Aragoneses and Cristiano Paixão address these questions.

Juliana Magalhães emphasizes other methods of silencing and selectivity, by confronting the issue of how indigenous people issues were handled in the Brazilian case. Similarly, Maria Pia Guerra analyzes urban uprisings in Brazil to initiate a discussion of the political players that have been included (or not) in the initiatives related to transition. In the section on theoretical and methodological studies, Douglas Pinheiro presents new possibilities for observing the political and juridical processes of transition.

1.3   Constitutional History and Transitional Processes

A consistent theme in this book is the role that transitional processes play in politics and law. Whenever transitions are triggered, the political and legal systems are affected differently. The duration of political time is different than that of legal time. Transformations can be faster in politics, while institutional structures can be resistant to changes or adapt to them gradually. Therefore, it is of utmost importance to observe and take note of what kinds of constitutional reforms are required by transitional processes, as well as how some of the pre-transitional constitutional arrangements can persist under democratic regimes. The articles by Leonardo Barbosa, Cath Collins, Alfons Aragoneses, and Filipa Raimundo take on this topic through specific cases in Brazil, Chile, Portugal, and Spain.

Another important topic under discussion here is the fact that some of the constitutions written during transitions (and which, in many cases, are seen as an important phase of those transitions) were written based on a political agreement or "pact." To what extent do such political agreements—those made during transitions—influence the contents of the constitutional provisions? In some transitional cases, actors from the fallen political regime gain gain political capital from influencing the constitutional provisions. How, then, does such influence affect the transitional process per se or the democratic credentials of the new regime? Those are the questions raised by Cristiano Paixão and Alfons Aragoneses and Gabriel Rezende, among others.

1.4   The Scope of the Transitional Process

A further issue that emerges from the chapters in this book is related to the spaces in which the transitional processes occur. The phenomenon of transition to democracy does not manifest only at the national level. And while the point of contact between the constitution and the transition is also relevant at the state level; even that additional spatial consideration does not fully address our problem.

Rather, if we consider a multiple spatial scale, it is possible to grasp contours of transitional dynamics that are sure to be of interest and that otherwise would not emerge. If we assume, for example, a regional and comparative focus—one that is capable of synchronically observing multiple national experiences or of analyzing phenomena of a transnational nature at the level of wide-open spaces—we can cast a different light on the major questions related to frameworks for the accountability of dictatorships (Lessa) and the social actors involved in them (Lessa), the relevance of gender to the dynamics of transitional justice (Paiva), and the institutional dialectics between international and state jurisdiction (Osmo).

Similarly, spaces within individual national realities can also be relevant areas of study. As Alfons Aragoneses' essay on the Spanish case shows, it is the actions of local institutions, both legislative and judicial, that redefine the social and political meanings of the transition in relation to options taken at the national level.

1.5 Temporal Dimensions of the Transitional Process

We can also highlight, in the set of papers that make up the book, the growing complexity of the temporal planes in which the transition experiences occur and unfold. It is clear that the time that characterizes the phenomenon at the heart of this book is never a homogeneous time, a point that is essential for understanding certain elements and perspectives related to experiences of transition to democracy.

In this volume, the studies on cases of transitional justice in the relatively recent Latin American democracies demonstrate that the process unfolds via different times of implementation. The comparative perspective adopted by Francesca Lessa shows some examples of different tempos, in the Latin American Countries, in the offering of reparations for victims of human rights violation. For example, there are selective approaches to, or delays in, the prosecution of certain classes of crimes, as in the case of racial crimes (Paixão) or sexual crimes (Paiva). More generally, it seems that the very right to difference—and the rights of minorities—appears to have been neglected in the experiences of transitional justice in post-dictatorial democracies. One reason for this outcome rests, as Douglas Pinheiro explains, precisely on the fact that these experiences of transition have relied on a linear temporality—"marked by a presentist hegemonic contemporaneity and whose boundaries as to past, future, and other alternative presents are rigidly built"—as well as on a normative temporality, "highlighting majoritarian life projects in democracy and rendering subaltern identities and experiences impossible." The consequence of this approach has been an overlapping of multi-temporal social realities that reproduce the mechanisms that exclude access to rights, thereby reducing the level of relative discontinuity between democracy and the dictatorship, particularly with respect to dictatorship-era policies of control.

Conversely, it is possible to approach the transition process with an attitude that accounts for the multi-temporality of social realities (i.e., non-linear and non-normative temporalities). Allowing for this multiplicity of social realities in turn offers the possibility of a different performativity with regard to the construction of social cohesion, one that has a more inclusive character and is based on ethics of care, as well as ethics of justice.

Accounting for the complexities of the temporal dimensions of the transition process are also crucial from a methodological perspective. Taken as a kind of analytical key, transition can result in two kinds of research. On the one hand, focusing on transition highlights the descriptive value of investigating the period between a before and an after, that is, of identifying a segment of the diachronic sequence in which to observe the unfolding of the law.

On the other hand—and this volume seems to offer more evidence in service of this second approach—the time of transition appears relevant in and of itself, as an ascriptive time with his own attributive force in relation to the contents and configurations of the law (Meccarelli). This analytical perspective is one that seems capable of highlighting additional aspects of the legal experience, as well as of the phenomenology of law itself.

This last point applies both to the transition process and to the stages that follow. In other words, it is possible to examine the experience of the transition in its prospective value, that is, with an eye toward gaining an analytical point of view that makes it possible to launch future investigations that explore more profoundly the complex relationship between democracies and former authoritarian regimes.

1.6   Transition and Its Unfoldings

This last reflection introduces us to some considerations regarding the question of outcomes of the transition process. While a definitive consideration of outcomes is beyond the scope of this volume, it is nevertheless possible to reflect on the relationship between (the problem of) memory and the configurations of law (Aragoneses). Moreover, it is possible to consider the consequences of the transition in terms of the way that the experience of the dictatorship casts a shadow over democratic life (Collins).

Although they take different forms and have different dimensions, the experiences analyzed in this volume—those in which the authoritarian regime has played a role in regulating the question of its own overcoming (such as Brazil, Argentina, Chile, Uruguay, Spain), as well as those in which democracy is enforced through political and institutional discontinuity with the previous regime (Portugal, Italy)—suggest that dictatorship evinces a kind of resilience. Its burdens emerge in fragmentary (though no less problematic) ways and in relation to different aspects of political life and social coexistence. Think, for example, of the persistence of certain policies of repression or discrimination (Paiva, Pinheiro) or of the permanent presence of sectors of the ruling class (Meniconi, Raimundo), or even of the issue of the individual and collective impunity (Lessa, Aragoneses). And the list goes on.

It is interesting to note that it is precisely the impossibility of fully severing the link between the democratic regime and the former authoritarian regime (from which the democracy seeks to distinguish itself) that highlights the provisional and necessarily inconclusive status of the transitions (Paixão, Rezende).

Indeed, it is almost as if the work of democracy consists precisely of the continuous re-elaboration and re-stipulation of its own otherness, with respect to a past that has been rejected, but which does not cease to affect the present time. It is almost as if the problem of democracy consists of taking seriously the attributive force of the transition itself, by performing the task of producing the synthesis necessary for sustaining the projects of the future.

Cristiano Paixão in Professor of Legal History and Constitutional Law at the University of Brasília Law School. Doctor in Law degree from Federal University of Minas Gerais, with post-doctoral studies in historiography at Ecole des Hautes Etudes en Sciences Sociales de Paris and in modern history at Scuola Normale Superiore di Pisa. He was a visiting professor at Macerata University School of Law and at the Master's Program in Constitutional Law at Seville University, and has published extensively about constitutional history. He was a member of the Brazilian Amnesty Committee (Ministry of Justice) and was one of the coordinators of the Anísio Teixeira Memory and Truth Commission (University of Brasília). His main research interests are constitutional history, law and literature, and interdisciplinary studies in law.

Massimo Meccarelli is Professor of Legal History at the University of Macerata (Italy), and affiliate researcher of the Max Planck Institute for European Legal History (Frankfurt am Main). He was visiting professor at: Universidad Autónoma de Madrid, Johann Wolfgang Goethe-Universität in Frankfurt am Main, Universität Wien, Universität Luzern. He is author of several works on history of legal thought, history of justice, historiography and methodology of legal history. Most recently research interests: law and diversity, legal pluralism, constitution making process, time and law, law and humanities.

Part I
Brazil

Chapter 2
"Where the Silences Are Mute": Political Transition, State Violence, and the Racial Question in Contemporary Brazil

Cristiano Paixão

Abstract Different temporalities are involved in the observation of politic transitions from the point of view of constitutional history. Victims of the authoritarian regime, the successive generation of victims, the social movements, and the legal courts are involved in a web of social practices and narratives which connect past, present, and future. Our intent in this chapter is to discuss the silence that has prevailed over the repression of the Black Movement during the Brazilian military dictatorship. We emphasize the violations committed against Black citizens by security and police forces in Brazil and the attempts that are being made by social activists, Legislative bodies and Truth Commissions to obtain social visibility and concrete reparations. In the concluding remarks, we propose a reflection on a possible "politics of time" connected to the silences and acts of resistance along Brazilian constitutional history.

2.1 Introduction

One of the key issues for understanding the processes of political transition is related to the visibility of the victims. Authoritarian regimes use repressive mechanisms on a constant, almost routine basis. Throughout their history, such regimes have left a trail of people, families, and groups affected by the repressive power of the state. When a regime change occurs, particularly when democracy is returned or established, processes geared toward revising the past tend to occur alongside the changes in government. Historically, there are many examples of these revisions, which have occurred at various points during the transition to democracy, in a wide variety of dictatorial contexts: in South America in the 1980s and 1990s; in the Iron Curtain countries after the collapse of the Soviet Union; and in South Africa after 1995, in an experience that has become paradigmatic for the consolidation of the field of "Transitional Justice" (see Andrieu 2012; Hayner 2011; Olsen et al. 2010; Berg and Schaefer 2012; Rotberg and Thompson 2000; Cassin et al. 2004).

C. Paixão (✉)
School of Law, University of Brasília, Brasília, Brazil
e-mail: cristianop@unb.br

© Springer Nature Switzerland AG 2021   11
C. Paixão and M. Meccarelli (eds.), *Comparing Transitions to Democracy. Law and Justice in South America and Europe*, Studies in the History of Law and Justice 18,
https://doi.org/10.1007/978-3-030-67502-8_2

In all of these cases, and in those that will no doubt occur in the future, certain decisions need to be made by the bodies conducting the transitional process, regardless of whether that body is a truth commission, parliament, civil society, or political parties: Who are the recipients of the reparation initiatives? Who has suffered as a result of the regime's actions? In many cases, the answers to these questions are not unequivocal and will depend on the decisions made by those who were most affected; on the seriousness of the violations committed; and on the proportioning of measures for institutional reform, reparation, the detailing of past events, and the construction of memory (to use the canonical structures of Transitional Justice).

In making these choices, several factors come into play: the degree to which the victims (or some portion of them) are able to be represented by the structures responsible for conducting the transition, the transformation of the regime's legal framework (which may or may not be accompanied by constitutional change), and the resilience of the perpetrators of the human rights violations, among others. These distinctions become salient, of course, during the transition processes themselves, in the "present tense" of these actual processes. But they have another dimension, which involves historical factors. In the choices made during the transitional processes, it is possible to observe several layers of temporality. In any given political community, groups that were excluded or discriminated against at an earlier historical moment may continue to suffer such exclusion during the transitional processes. That means that their exclusion may be pre-existing in relation to the repressive regime itself and thus needs to be analyzed through a broader historical perspective.

In the present article, I intend to deal with an issue associated with the temporal dimensions of the Brazilian political transition: the silence that has prevailed over the repression of the Black Movement during the military dictatorship. In my analysis, I shall discuss aspects related to Brazilian constitutional history, as well as historical circumstances that relate to police violence in contemporary Brazil.[1]

2.2 Dictatorship, Repression, Resistance: The Black Movement in Question

After a long and difficult negotiation that included many branches of the Brazilian government—the Human Rights Secretariat, the Justice Department and the Military—the Brazilian Congress approved Law No. 12,528 in 2011, which created the National Truth Commission.[2] The Commission was established in May 2012. In an interesting development that was not part of the original plan, local truth

---

[1] I thank Massimo Meccarelli, Claudia Paiva Carvalho, Raphael Peixoto de Paula Marques, Douglas Pinheiro, Maria Pia Guerra, Leonardo Barbosa, Nina Schneider, Renato Bigliazzi and José Otávio Guimarães for suggestions and discussion. I thank Rebecca Scott and Beatriz Mamigonian for introducing me in the study of slavery history in Brazil. I am also thankful to Hilary Levinson and John Milton for reviewing the English version.
[2] BRASIL, Lei n° 12.528, de 18 de novembro de 2011. Diário Oficial da União, 18 nov. 2011, edição extra.

commissions were established throughout Brazil, in states, cities, universities, and professional and trade union bodies, all with the purpose of investigating human rights abuses committed during the dictatorship. As of February 2014, there were around 67 truth commissions operating in Brazil (Schneider 2019: 345–348). The National Truth Commission delivered its final report in December 2014, a long and well-documented report with many recommendations, including the creation of a follow-up government department for implementing and overseeing the concrete adoption of the measures proposed in the report.[3]

Despite the efforts of the National Truth Commission, Brazil remains a country with an extremely high number of victims of state violence. Torture is routine in police stations and prisons; the homicide rate is alarmingly high, as is the number of victims of police shootings. And there is a remarkable racial bias in the numbers of victims: Black people—especially Black young men—are more likely to suffer state and police violence than white people. This situation, which persists even with a democratic and egalitarian Constitution that establishes racism as a felony, presents a series of historical questions.

At this point, it is interesting to raise a question regarding the choices made by the Brazilian National Truth Commission. The final report is divided into several chapters, and the massive human rights violations—acts of disappearance, executions, torture—are the core of the report. Nevertheless, the Commission chose to create a series of "specific" chapters to emphasize certain repressive actions by the regime. As a result, there are sections devoted to violations committed against homosexuals, the clergy, the military who opposed the regime, peasants, indigenous peoples, university students and teachers, as well as other groups. However, there is no chapter on the violence against and persecution of Black people and Black movements.

In fact, there is only one paragraph, in the section that discusses civil resistance to the military regime, in which the creation of the Unified Black Movement and some of its activities are briefly mentioned. No episodes of persecution are quoted, and no movement leaders are named; nor is there any account of the forms of Black resistance. The minimal amount of attention paid to the repression of Blacks is especially noteworthy when we consider the length of the Final Report of the National Truth Commission. Volume II, which contains the thematic texts in question, is 416 pages. Together with the other two volumes, the Commission's Report has 3,388 pages. The term "Black" is seldom used in the Report and usually only in reference to the physical characteristics of those who have died or been disappeared for political reasons (such victims are mentioned in Volume III). The only occasion on which the expression appears with explicit political connotations is when it is associated with the Black struggle in the paragraph just described.[4]

Just one single paragraph in 3,388 pages.

---

[3] The report is available at: http://cnv.memoriasreveladas.gov.br/.

[4] BRASIL, Comissão Nacional da Verdade, Relatório, Volume II, pp. 394–395. See Brasil. Comissão Nacional da Verdade, Relatório Final, Volumes I, II e III. 10 de dezembro de 2014. Available at: http://cnv.memoriasreveladas.gov.br/.

The silence that emerges from this reading the Final Report of the National Truth Commission is not surprising. The absence, in this document, of any narrative about the regime's persecution of Black people—and, more specifically, any narrative of the movements in which the Black population organized itself—is a fact that reveals a historical difficulty. For most of the twentieth century, the myth of "harmony between races" was very influential both in academia and in society as a whole. A very broad formulation—which cannot be detailed here, but which finds its most potent example in the work of Gilberto Freyre—successfully promoted a vision of harmonious coexistence between the races in Brazil (Pesavento 2004: 177–191; Ventura 2000: 356–358).

Obviously, such a narrative does not hold today. It is important, however, to trace the repercussions of this narrative through the long struggle of Black populations for recognition. One of the main motivations for the emergence of Black movements in the second half of the twentieth century and for the emergence of artistic manifestations focused on the identity of Black people (as in theater, music and literature) was precisely the need to construct a narrative that challenged the powerful image of a multiracial Brazil that existed in harmony and without conflicts (Bertulio 1989: 48–52).

Moreover, it is interesting to note that the founding of the Unified Black Movement occurred in a public act on the steps of the Municipal Theater of São Paulo in 1978 (Kössling 2007: 63, 180, 232). This date coincides with a period in which the number of demonstrations against the military regime increased (Kucinski 2001: 73–131; Sader 2010; Antunes 1992: 13–97; Alves 1984: 200–266). Thus, it is reasonable to ask: Is there any relationship between the organizing of the Black Movement and the authoritarian practices of the dictatorship?

Like all authoritarian regimes, the Brazilian military dictatorship was very worried about cultural manifestations in civil society and extensively censored popular song lyrics, plays, film productions, and television shows (Paixão and Carvalho 2016: 336–348; Fico 2010: 187–193). In the written manifestations of the military leaders who prepared the coup d'état, it is possible to find clear criticisms of a certain "anarchy" that permeated Brazilian social relations at the time, whether in labor relations or in the ranks of the armed forces. As is well known, the coup was supported by civilian sectors (Ferreira and Gomes 2014; Alonso and Dolhnikoff 2015; Toledo 2001). Some of the most important demonstrations immediately preceding the coup d'état were the so-called "Marches of the Family with God for Liberty," a series of marches held in large Brazilian cities with strong connotations of family, religion and property (Presot 2010: 71–96).

Thus, throughout its rule, the military was concerned about the place of culture in society. This point is important for understanding the repression established against Brazil's Black population during the dictatorship. However, for this repression to be adequately gauged, it is necessary to consider the various temporalities involved in the repressive practices against Black people. When we notice the National Truth Commission's silence on the subject, other silences appear—and they refer to the very formation of Brazil as an independent country.

Two years after political independence, then Emperor Dom Pedro I put into effect the first Brazilian constitution. Among the striking characteristics of the 1824 Constitution are the provisions for a moderating power (exclusively that of the Emperor), the adoption of Catholicism as the official religion, the monarchical principle, and the refusal of federalism. Moreover, the Constitution of 1824 contains no references to slavery, which was widespread at that time and figured as an essential element in the political, social, and economic structure of a Brazil that had just proclaimed its independence from Portugal. On no occasion does the text of the Constitution use the words "*escravo*" [slave], "*escravidão*" [slavery], or "*negro*" [Black].[5]

This does not mean, however, that political actors of the day did not care about the many consequences of slavery. The fear of a slave revolt was always present, given the significant number of men and women in conditions of slavery and their proportion relative to the free population (Chalhoub 2011: 218–250). In addition, there remained as a kind of specter an alert to rural producers who relied extensively on slave labor: the Haitian Revolution, a slave-led movement that resulted in the revolutionary takeover of political power and the emancipation of the slave population. Thus, one of the main concerns of the local elite that led and forged the post-Independence social and political structure in Brazil was to avoid the unleashing of a revolution along the lines of what had happened in the former colony of Santo Domingo (Duarte and Queiroz 2016). The 1824 Constitution was one of the instruments for avoiding this possible outcome, and it was in force—not by chance—until the end of the monarchical regime and was overthrown only one year after the liberation of the slaves. (That these two events happened in succession underlines the deep interdependence between the political regime of the empire and the persistence of slavery.)

Brazil abolished slavery on May 13, 1888. The liberation of Black slaves was not accompanied, however, by any policy for the inclusion of this population in the labor market (Alonso 2018: 358–364; Schwarcz 2012: 61–65). What was implemented, in fact, was a policy that encouraged European immigration to Brazil, and the marginalization of Black people continued, even though the end of slavery had been decreed. The social and economic condition of the Black population was therefore precarious (Loner 2012; Schwarcz and Starling 2015: 323–325, 342–345). They were also excluded from political life in general, since the Brazilian republican constitutions established a ban on voting by illiterates, which was the situation for most of the black population. The constitutions of 1891 and 1934 contained yet another exclusion clause: it was not possible for beggars to vote, nor could anyone vote for them.[6]

---

[5] BRASIL. Constituições do Brasil: de 1824, 1891, 1934, 1937, 1946 e 1967 e suas alterações. Brasília: Senado Federal (Subsecretaria de Edições Técnicas), 1986, pp. 17–35. Obviously, this is a silence that speaks: slavery was one of the main features of Brazilian economic system under the Empire. So it was present in Brazilian legal and political system on that period. We are just emphasizing the silence on the constitutional text.

[6] For illiteracy, see Article 70, § 1, 2, of 1891 Constitution, and Article 108, "a", of 1934 Constitution. For beggars, see Article 70, § 1, 1, of 1891 Constitution, and Article 108, "c", of 1934 Constitution. Both Constitutions are in the book mentioned in note 5.

Of course, the black population has built forms of resistance on the political and cultural level, but such resistance has had to take place on the margins of official public life. In the 1930s, two nongovernmental bodies, the Black Front and the Black Legion, were created by activists. In the 1940s, an important organization appeared in Rio de Janeiro: the Black Experimental Theater, led by the activist Abdias Nascimento, who created the organization in response to the absence of black people in theatrical and literary narratives in Brazil.[7] In the years that followed, the black population remained active, through various organizational structures and hubs, especially in cities (Bertulio 1989: 52–56; Domingues 2018: 237–243). These cells were active until the unification of the Black Movement in 1978.

In addition to breaking the legality and interrupting the mandate of a legitimately elected president of the Republic, the military dictatorship also impacted a moment of growing cultural change in Brazil. Between the late 1950s and the early 1960s, the country underwent major transformations: increasing industrialization, expansion of the population into central Brazil through the construction of the new capital of Brasília, the increased role of urban life, and a growing intensification of cultural and artistic movements. The force of this cultural mobilization can be seen, for example, in the formation of the neo-concrete movement in visual arts and literature, in "*Cinema Novo*," in the prevalence of popular forms of expression in the theater, and in the harmonic transformations in popular music, among others (Fausto 2007: 514–715; Schwarcz and Starling 2015: 412–436).

With the March 1964 coup and the subsequent stabilization of military power, it became clear that artists, social activists, and cultural producers would be affected by the authoritarian regime. Many of them were exiled, some were arrested, and censorship was institutionalized. These actions were not the only form of repression against the Black population, but they were some of the most obvious.

In summing up the human rights violations committed against the Black population during the period of the military dictatorship, it is worth mentioning the description contained in the Final Report of the Truth Commission of the State of Rio de Janeiro:

> Blitzes, arbitrary arrests, home invasions, expropriation of their places of residence (through removals), physical and psychological torture, and living with the latent threat of extermination groups marked the reality of Black men and women, mainly the inhabitants of favelas, in the outskirts of Rio de Janeiro, and in the Baixada Fluminense surrounding the city. It was the implementation by the State of a criminal policy rooted in Brazilian slave-owning colonialism.[8]

In addition to the practices described in the excerpt above, several documents in archival collections in Brazil, carefully analyzed by researchers such as Thula Pires

---

[7] It is interesting to note that these movements had many differences in political orientation and acted in plural contexts. For a deeper account of the experience of these (and many other) organizations, please see Domingues (2007).

[8] BRASIL, Comissão Estadual da Verdade do Rio de Janeiro, Relatório Final, p. 128. Available at: http://www.memoriasreveladas.gov.br/administrator/components/com_simplefilemanager/uploads/Rio/CEV-Rio-Relatorio-Final.pdf.

and Karin Kössling, show that the military regime directly monitored the activities of the groups that already existed in the big cities, particularly in Rio de Janeiro, through the regime's agents in the intelligence service.

Two records in particular are crucial to understanding this repressive movement. The first one involves Brazilian international politics. Reports by the institutions of repression reveal the regime's concern for possible contact between Black Brazilian leaders and international movements from countries such as Angola and Mozambique that were fighting for their independence from Portugal (Kössling 2007: 129–132, 138). Another focus of the regime was the possible connection between representatives of Black movements in Brazil and American activists, especially the Black Panthers. The archives investigated by Thula Pires contain a considerable number of reports detailing missions to monitor and observe the activity of Black leaders in Brazil, including the use of infiltrated agents in the assemblies and meetings of Black political groups (Pires 2018).

The second record highlighted here is at the cultural level. The archives of the institutions of repression show a concern on the part of the regime's agents and police for new cultural manifestations and demonstrations in Rio de Janeiro. In the cultural supplement of a July 1976 edition of the *Jornal do Brasil*, one of the country's most important newspapers, there was a four-page article by journalist Lena Frias on the "Black power movement" in Rio, which described the huge soul music parties that attracted large numbers of people, the clothing of young Black people who sought to establish new trends, and the difficulties that such young people faced, because of the considerable police repression, in organizing these parties (Frias 1976: 1, 4–6; Alberto 2009).

The article eventually caught the attention of the dictatorship's repressive system, and the documents of the period clearly show the regime's fear that the cultural mobilization of Blacks would take on a political dimension.[9] Leaders were called to testify, and the activities of the collectives began to be closely followed; their meetings were monitored, and agents of the regime attempted to infiltrate the collectives. In this way, the preoccupation with a "foreign influence" on the Brazilian Black population was reproduced through cultural symbols.

From 1978 on, the Black Movement began to unify, and the struggle against the regime strengthened. Until power was finally returned to civilians, in March 1985, the dictatorship directly monitored the activity of Black leaders. Even under civilian rule, the institutions of repression remained in operation and continued to suppress the actions of their targets, while reports documenting the activities of the Movement continued to be produced.[10]

However, with democratization in 1985, the Black Movement had a new agenda: the struggle for rights in the national Brazilian constituent assembly.

---

[9] BRASIL, Comissão Estadual da Verdade do Rio de Janeiro, Relatório Final, pp. 133–135.

[10] BRASIL, Comissão Estadual da Verdade do Rio de Janeiro, Relatório Final, pp. 135–137.

2.3 Democratization, the Constitution, and the Racial Question

The first public demonstration for the convening of a national constituent assembly took place in July 1971, in the so-called "Recife Charter," a document approved by the Brazilian Democratic Movement Party (MDB), which was the only opposition party permitted by the regime. There is, however, an earlier occurrence of such a request. In December 1967, during its Sixth National Congress, the Brazilian Communist Party (PCB) approved a declaration that called for "the abolition of the exception laws introduced by the military coup that took power in 1964, the establishment of democratic freedoms, the holding of elections, the adoption of a democratic constitution and the amnesty of political prisoners." This claim, which obviously had no public impact, is historically rich in meanings, bringing various positions together in a single demand: it classifies the laws of the regime as "laws of exception," supports democracy, and demands the elaboration of a new constitution (Paixão and Barbosa 2008: 120).

Starting in the second half of the 1970s, the agenda for convening a constituent assembly took center stage in the struggle for a return to democracy. At the initiative of relatives of persecuted politicians who had been forced to live in exile, amnesty committees were established and eventually brought together into a National Committee in 1978. The Committee's main demands were the end of arbitrary arrests, the restoration of civil and political freedoms, and permission for those who had been exiled to return to Brazil. The agenda, in other words, was a democratizing one, and its call for amnesty was given a slogan: "broad, general and unrestricted." These committees emerged during a period in which the emergence of the role of civil society in political debate was growing and other bodies, whose aim was to denounce the regime's arbitrariness, were being established. It was also a period of important strikes in factories and other urban institutions, increased prominence of the Catholic Church in grassroots church communities, and growth of neighborhood associations in large cities. In this historical period between 1976 and 1980, in other words, it is possible to say, using the expression conceived by Eder Sader, that "new actors entered the scene" (Sader 2010).

Among these same actors, an idea was taking shape that this type of transformation could only take place through the convening of a constituent national assembly. From 1977 on, this idea was especially salient within the Brazilian Bar Association, which, led by its president Raymundo Faoro, launched a campaign for the convening of a constituent assembly. This movement spread among unions, social movements, and a large part of civil society. One of the best expressions of this movement can be found in the text of the Charter resulting from the First National Conference of the Working Class (Conclat), which marked the creation of the Central Workers' Union (CUT) in 1981. Conclat brought together a wide range of demands and propositions related to social issues, individual and collective rights, trade union structure, economic policy, labor judges, social security, and land reform. However, for the purposes of this article, it is the first topic of the Charter that most attracts attention: the "enacting of a Constitution that guarantees the fundamental rights of the working class" (Paixão 2016: 39).

In the first half of the 1980s, there was an attempt by the organized opposition to overcome the authoritarian cycle via a social movement for direct and free presidential elections. The regime, however, defeated the proposal in the House of Representatives (Grinberg 2014). The opposition then attempted to overthrow the regime from the inside—that is, by using the rules established by the military for the election of the president. For that reason, the first civilian president after 21 years of military dictatorship was indirectly elected by an electoral college made up of representatives, senators, and delegations of state assemblies. The chosen candidate, Tancredo Neves, did not take office because he was hospitalized with a serious illness and died in April 1985. Instead, José Sarney, the candidate for vice-president, took office. He was a civilian who had supported the military regime but broke with the dictatorship to be part of Tancredo Neves ticket (Ferreira 2018).

In February 1987, the work of the National Constituent Assembly (ANC) began. Unlike most similar situations in other parts of the world (and in the Brazilian tradition itself), the ANC did not start with a previously written text, but rather opted for the gradual construction of a draft by thematic blocks, which was made possible by the division of the Assembly into eight thematic committees (each divided into three subcommittees). This process ensured greater internal democracy in the Assembly and made the process less controllable and, to some extent, unpredictable (Paixão 2011: 164–165).

Social participation was intense and relevant: initiatives such as the presentation of popular amendments, the holding public hearings, and intense scrutiny and analysis by the press transformed the ANC into a permanently dynamic space for building a new constitutional text (Paixão and Barbosa 2008: 130–131). It is in this context that discussion on the racial question can be found.

Debate over the rights of the Black population in Brazil took place mainly in the Subcommittee on the Black Population, Indigenous Populations, and Persons with Disabilities, and Minorities, which was part of the Social Welfare Commission. The work of the Subcommittee was intense: many public hearings were held, with testimony from civil society representatives. One such testimony was given by Joel Rufino dos Santos, a historian, writer, and important leader in the Black Movement.

His testimony offers an in-depth analysis of the causes of the various factors that account for racism in Brazil. It is a true microcosm insofar as it contains a narrative of the exclusions and violations of the human rights of the Black population that have been committed throughout history. Initially, Joel Rufino presents what he considers the "remote, historical" cause of Brazilian racism:

> As a person accustomed to dealing with history, thinking history, I must mention two or three reasons for Brazilian racism. One of these reasons, one of these causes, is slavery, the fact that our country has known a slave regime for four-fifths of its existence. And you can see that it was not 50 years, not 100 years, not 200 years, but 4/5 of the 500 years of

the existence of Brazil. This is undoubtedly the most remote and most historical cause of Brazilian racism.[11]

Rufino then goes on to emphasize economic issues, particularly the modality of capitalism adopted in Brazil—a system that is exclusionary and anchored in a colonialist view of the country that emphasizes the prevalence of the conception of a white nation. To illustrate this point, Joel Rufino mentions the work of Clóvis Moura, one of the pioneer intellectuals in the affirmation of Black resistance throughout history:

> I really like a definition of a friend of ours whom I regret is not present here, Clóvis Moura, who, from the time we were children, was already writing about black people and was already studying the Black issue.... I really like an expression of his when he says the following: "White Brazilians are those who were chosen to mirror the color of the settlers." With this, he delves into an analysis of racism and the way in which Brazilians see themselves. That is to say, white in Brazil does not have the purely biological, purely genetic, meaning, and this meaning is even secondary. It has an anthropological, sociological, psychological, even symbolic meaning. White in Brazil is that which is chosen as a model, the European white, and therefore, he emphasizes, conceals the Black side, because, arguably, what Brazil is, is a country of Blacks, whites, Indians and other ethnic groups.[12]

Rufino concludes this part of his testimony by recognizing the importance of the moment, that is, this moment in which the constituent assembly can establish new normative bases for Brazilian society and confront racism. For Rufino, that moment was an opportunity to "make a call to the members of the constituent assembly whose task it is to think Brazil, to re-constitutionalize the Country as a whole, so that they realize and understand that one of the aspects of the Brazilian crisis is precisely this vision that we have of Brazil."[13]

After the completion of the public hearings and external missions, the Subcommittee then produced its pre-project, which was extensive and innovative. In addition to the assertion that Brazil is a multiethnic society, which is already stated in the first article of the report, it also stipulated "compensatory measures" for citizens or groups of citizens "to guarantee their equal participation in access to the labor market, education, health and other social rights."[14]

These articles, however, do not appear in the final text of the Constitution, which was finally enacted on October 5, 1988. Not that the Constitution is entirely silent on the racial question: there are two important devices that deserve to be highlighted here. In Art. 4, VIII, it stipulates that Brazil, in its international relations, is governed by the principle of the repudiation of racism. Further on, in Art. 5, XLII, racism

---

[11] BRASIL, Diário da Assembléia Nacional Constituinte, Suplemento ao n° 63, 21 de maio de 1987, p. 136.

[12] BRASIL, Diário da Assembléia Nacional Constituinte, Suplemento ao n° 63, 21 de maio de 1987, p. 136.

[13] BRASIL, Diário da Assembléia Nacional Constituinte, Suplemento ao n° 63, 21 de maio de 1987, p. 136.

[14] BRASIL. Anteprojeto da Subcomissão dos Negros, Populações Indígenas, Pessoas Deficientes e Minorias, Relator Constituinte Alceni Guerra. *Diário da Assembleia Nacional Constituinte*, Suplemento ao n° 103, 24 de julho de 1987, pp. 150–165.

is classified as "a non-bailable crime, with no limitation, subject to the penalty of confinement, under the terms of the law."[15]

But even among these clauses there is something striking: The Constitution of 1988 is entirely silent with regard to Black people. The Portuguese term *negro* (equivalent of Black in Portuguese) is not present in the constitutional text. In the preliminary draft by the Subcommittee on Black Peoples, Indigenous Populations, Persons with Disabilities, and Minorities, there was—in addition to the above-mentioned devices—a specific section, made up of six articles, entitled "Black People."

There is a kind of subtle filter in the language used. For example, in the draft by the Subcommittee, there was an article that guaranteed "the definitive title of ownership of the lands occupied by the remaining black communities of the Quilombos."[16] This property designation was eventually ensured in the final text of the Constitution, but with different wording: "Final ownership shall be recognized for the remaining members of the ancient runaway slave communities who are occupying their lands and the State shall grant them the respective title deeds."[17]

This ambiguity in language stands out in the constitutional text. There is no doubt that the 1988 Constitution allowed for an unprecedented opening in terms of social participation and the recognition of rights, as evidenced by its broad catalog of fundamental rights and its strong democratizing content. Racial discrimination was clearly repudiated. Land ownership by remaining Quilombos was also assured. And yet, on the other hand, the Portuguese word *negro*, which was prominently featured in the preliminary draft of the Subcommittee on the Black Population, Indigenous Populations, and Persons with Disabilities, and Minorities, disappears from the text of the Constitution.

2.4 Police Violence and Race: The Case of the Mothers of May

Throughout the present article, various dimensions of silence with regard to the racial question have been shown: in the text of the constitutions, in the final report of the National Truth Commission, and in the specific case of the 1988 Constitution. There is, however, yet another absence of speech that is even more striking.

Police violence has always been a problem for the Brazilian Black population. Nowadays, under democracy, this phenomenon seems to be even more present. To understand this dimension of the silence, it will be useful to present some information

---

[15] The 1988 Constitution is available at: http://www.senado.leg.br/atividade/const/con1988/con 1988_atual/ind.asp (including all 105 Constitutional Amendments, the last one enacted on 12 December 2019). For an English version of the 1988 Brazilian Constitution (up to Constitutional Amendment no. 72/2013), see http://www2.senado.leg.br/bdsf/item/id/243334.

[16] BRASIL. Anteprojeto da Subcomissão dos Negros, Populações Indígenas, Pessoas Deficientes e Minorias, Relator Constituinte Alceni Guerra. *Diário da Assembleia Nacional Constituinte*, Suplemento ao n° 103, 24 de julho de 1987, pp. 150–165.

[17] 1988 Constitution, Temporary Constitutional Provisions Act, Article 68.

on homicides in Brazil. The data are from 2016, according to a report issued by IPEA (a branch of the federal government specializing in social and economic analysis). According to the report, in 2016, there were 62,517 homicides in Brazil. More than 50% of the victims were young people. In 2016, 33,590 young people (ages 15–29) were killed. Moreover, there is a racial pattern to these homicides. Young Black men in Brazil are 2.7 times more likely to be victims of homicide than young white men. If we consider the total number of homicides, giving no consideration to the age of the victims, we find the same pattern: 71.5% of the people murdered Brazil were Black (*pretos*) or brown (*pardos*).

Furthermore, we can also consider the number of deaths caused by police forces. It is somewhat difficult to calculate the exact number of victims, as some States do not give accurate information to the Central Authority. However, using the consolidated data, we can be certain that 76.2% of the victims of police killings between 2015 and 2016 were Black.

Taking a broader perspective, the numbers make an even greater impression: there are 30.3 deaths as a result of intentional violence per 100,000 inhabitants. In the last ten years alone, 553,000 people in Brazil have lost their lives to intentional violence.[18]

This is an alarming situation, one that fails to receive attention from the mainstream media and politicians. There are NGOs and research groups dedicated to this subject, but it has not been a priority for past or present state and national governments.

In this context, it is useful to discuss a specific event that produced a social reaction, one that is connected to police violence and clearly demonstrates the silencing strategies that suppress the voice of the victims. In May 2006, the inmates of the São Paulo prisons led a violent revolt. In response, the police forces retaliated against many poor neighborhoods, ostensibly looking for supporters of the riots. Police forces killed around 450 people[19] in seven days, most of who had no relation to the prison revolts and did not take part in criminal gangs. These deaths follow the same patterns of the police violence throughout Brazil: most of the victims were young men who lived in poor neighborhoods, and more than half were Black.[20]

In attempt to attract the attention of public authorities and society at large, a group of mothers decided to create the Mothers of May Truth Commission. The Commission has no legal or official recognition, nor does it receive public funds;

---

[18] All numbers collected in: BRASIL. Atlas da Violência 2018. Ipea e Fórum Brasileiro de Segurança Pública. Available at: http://www.ipea.gov.br/portal/index.php?option=com_content&view=article&id=33410&Itemid=432.

[19] There is some disagreement about the number of murders connected to the police response. According to the "Condepe Report," a document issued by a Committee of Human Rights Department of the Federal Government, there were 505 civilian victims. According to an independent report written by a group of researchers from Harvard University, there were 219 deaths directly connected to the police response. Most available sources, including press reports, indicate around 450 deaths. See BRASIL, Secretaria de Direitos Humanos – Conselho de Defesa dos Direitos da Pessoa Humana, Relatório sobre os Crimes de Maio de 2006, pp. 1–22. Available at: https://www.mdh.gov.br/inf ormacao-ao-cidadao/participacao-social/old/cndh/relatorios/relatorio-c.e-crimes-de-maio. See also Delgado et al. (2011).

[20] BRASIL, Secretaria de Direitos Humanos – Conselho de Defesa dos Direitos da Pessoa Humana, Relatório sobre os Crimes de Maio de 2006, p. 3.

rather, it is a kind of spontaneous initiative by victims' family members. Its leaders take part in legislative committees and are assisted by NGOs. It is interesting to note that the victims' relatives chose to shape their movement by using the category and name of the Truth Commission, implying a claim for recognition of the violence perpetrated by the State against its citizens.[21]

Another attempt to bring events to light, this time through a state legislative body, is also interesting and revealing.

On February 29, 2012, at the request of the Mothers of May Truth Commission, a bill was presented to the Legislative Assembly of São Paulo State. The aim of the project was to create "Mothers of May Day," which would be included in the official state calendar. The entire justification for the bill is based on the pain of the mothers who lost their children, as can be seen in the following excerpt:

> The natural order of life is for children to see their parents depart. However, contemporary society lives a different reality: millions of children lose their lives, while their parents weep as they remember the whole trajectory and perspectives of their beings. A paradigm marked by the traumatic experience of having the life of their children brutally mown down, as a result of a lack of security capable of containing the increase in marginality.
>
> Parents, especially mothers, befittingly fight for their rights to justice, and want to mark the memory and indignation of the acts that occurred in May 2006. In this context, it is imperative to remember, as a form of protest, the so-called "May Crimes. These, in turn, in an appalling way, dominated the scene provoking fear and terror in society before the inefficiency of Public Security.[22]

The bill received a favorable report from two committees of the Legislative Assembly. The Constitution and Justice Committee and the Education and Culture Committee both voted to approve the original text of the bill, without amendments. The bill was voted on by the Legislative Assembly on March 9, 2013. It is important to reiterate that it was approved without changes.

The bill was then sent to the State Governor's approval. There was also no opposition from the State Executive. The sanctioned bill was enacted into law and published by the official State Press on April 6, 2013.

Surprisingly, however, the text of the law, as published, does not contain any mention of the events that occurred in 2013. In Article 1, the law is limited to the provision that "Mothers' May Day is included in the Official State Calendar, to be celebrated annually on May 12, throughout the State."

---

[21] It is interesting to note that in the United States, another country affected by racial problems and police violence, two cities decided to create truth commissions aimed at addressing human rights violations. These commissions were created in Greensboro and Chicago. In the first case, the commission was established by a grassroot organization. In the second, it was sponsored by the mayor and the city council. For a deeper account of these experiences, please see Williams (2009), Ghoshal (2015), and Taylor (2014).

[22] BRASIL, Assembleia Legislativa do Estado de São Paulo, Projeto de Lei n° 91, de 2012, *Diário da Assembleia Legislativa*, 29 de fevereiro de 2012, p. 22. All documents concerning the bill can be found at: https://www.al.sp.gov.br/propositura/?id=1066961.

What is most disconcerting, however, is the way the law is described in its actual text. In Brazil, as a rule, legislative documents contain an *ementa*, a succinct description the law's aims. The text of the *ementa* is highlighted in the legal inscription. In the case analyzed here, the *ementa* is as follows: "State Law No. 14.981, of April 5, 2013 - *Include the event in the State Tourist Calendar.*"[23]

2.5 Concluding Remarks: Race, Silence and Social Time

The narrative hitherto undertaken has revealed a superposition of silences. From the deliberate absence of a treatment of the Black slavery issue in the 1824 Constitution to the extreme "filtering" of the word *negro* from the final text of the 1988 Constitution, a pattern is perceived: a difficulty in uttering the word.

We can also note that in the final report of the National Truth Commission—a document produced through a commission created by a federal law, after years of research and the analysis of sources, with the objective of establishing a comprehensive narrative on the dictatorial period in Brazil—there is a volume entitled "thematic texts," whose aim is to highlight particular forms of human rights violations by the military regime. The topics chosen for this volume were: "human rights violations in the military environment," "violations of workers' human rights," "violations of the human rights of peasants," "violations of human rights in Christian churches," "violations of the human rights of indigenous peoples," "human rights violations in the university," "the dictatorship and homosexuality," "civilians who collaborated with the dictatorship, and "civil society's resistance to serious human rights violations." In sum, among these thematic texts, there is no account of the human rights violations against the Black population in Brazil. The word *negro* hardly appears in the text of the report, and when it does, it takes on a political connotation on only one occasion, in just one paragraph. And that is all: a single paragraph in 3,388 pages.

It is possible to see this pattern expanding to other manifestations of public power, too. For example, we can note that, in the context of the state reaction to a series of prison riots in the state of São Paulo, police and security forces were responsible for the deaths of hundreds of people. In accordance with the general trend of police violence in Brazil, more than half of the victims were Black people. When the state legislature approved a bill whose aim was to establish a "memorial date" (the expression used in the bill) commemorating the deaths resulting from police violence—an act that would also constitute a clear recognition of the struggle of the Mothers of May—a state of silence seemed to prevail. Although an examination of the processing of the bill will show that it was approved in all the legislative committees to which it was submitted and that it was not vetoed by the State Governor, when the law was published, there was no longer any mention of the events that led to the adoption of

---

[23] BRASIL, Estado de São Paulo, Lei n° 14.981, de 5 de abril de 2013. Diário Oficial do Estado de São Paulo, volume 123, número 64, 6 de abril de 2013, p. 1.

the norm. Only the implementation of an "event in the State Tourist Calendar" was included.

Memory, in all its forms, is established through ambivalence and difference. Ambivalence involves the tenuous but essential relationship between the act of remembering and the act of forgetting (Weinrich 2004). For every social, political, and institutional act of memory, there are many silences that result from forgetfulness. In addition, memory is always precarious, fragile, and conflicting. When they decide on the recipients of policies involving memory, governments and parliaments are placed between different—and often directly contradictory—claims (Connerton 2009).

Here, memory is adopted as a tool for observation. We find that the struggles, demands, and forms of resistance to oppression that have been developed by the Black population have been silenced, across diverse social and political situations: in a constitutional text, in an official document of a truth commission, in a legislative text. Moreover, along with these findings, the racial bias of police violence in contemporary Brazil continues.

Up to the present stage of the research, which is still underway, it has been possible to demonstrate the complexity of this silence: from the silenced history of the effects of slavery to the (also silenced) cultural effervescence of the Black Movement in the 1970s to the absence of the utterance of the word *negro* in the Constitution—which is still in force—to the silence of the National Truth Commission on the repression and human rights violations against the Black population during the military dictatorship, a silence that speaks volumes. Clearly, this lack and its unspoken words have persisted.

The silence, however, stems from an act of writing. In the context of the varied forms of life for the black population in Brazilian history, there are experiences to be recovered, understood, known and reconstituted through various narratives. This recovery is the responsibility of contemporary history. Obviously, for these experiences to be included in historical narratives and social discourses, memorial laws or official declarations will not be enough. As noted in recent literature, imposing a "duty of memory" could mean an "abuse of memory" (see Michel 2018; Todorov 2000).

These points make the need for historical research on the subject even more important. Why are there such silences? What are the subtle ways in which these silencing operations are enforced and allowed to persist?

In sum, there are practices, languages, and political experiences that remain silenced, that are not discussed and addressed via the institutional and legal forms of recognition. Silence occurs in time and constitutes time.

When we discuss the temporal dimension in modern society, we take in account the multiple aspects of the connections between individuals, social groups, and the presence of the past. Societies can react to the past in many ways, including the selection of certain events in history for commemoration (as in holidays, for instance), the construction of memorials for remembering events or groups, and the exclusion of some facts from public debate (which can, in turn, stimulate people to forget parts of national or local history), among others. There is always selectivity in the so-called politics of memory. For an act of remembrance, there is also an act of forgetting. As happens in the usual manner of all political communication, memory is also the object of a struggle, a fight. There is no such thing as a "neutral" commitment to memory (Gensburger and Lefranc 2017; Huyssen 2003).

But there is silencing. In this essay, our intent has been to highlight the "cluster" of silences involving the history of the Black population in Brazil. In the aftermath of abolition to the description of the military dictatorship, and including constitutional history, we have been able to identify this pattern of silence. In a provocative analysis, Jacques Rancière (2018: 13–47) emphasizes the relationship between time, politics, and narration. The concept of time should not be limited to the moment, or to the dividing line between past and future; rather, the act of narrating involves a presence, or not, in time. The same choices we pointed out in the context of memory, that same selectivity, can be noted here: being "part of time,"—that is, participating in history—is directly connected with the narrative of things past. Silence, in the way we use the word here, means exactly that: a denial of participation in history, a denial of other possibilities for writing the history – both at the same time.

The official narratives reveal some layers of the past and conceal others. Though absent in the constitutional narrative and in the official descriptions of political repression, the Black population of contemporary Brazil continues to be present in the staggering numbers of social and police violence. An important first step is to understand the relationship between these silences, these choices, and the temporal dimensions of law, politics, culture, and historical research (Meccarelli 2017: 209–219). In a famous elegy, the Italian poet Giacomo Leopardi refers to the "superhuman, infinite silence" as a powerful metaphor for the absence, the void, and the inhuman, but contrasts it with the voice of "the wind rustling through these leaves" (1964: 116). So, silence could also be a starting point, an impulse for research. According to Octavio Paz's precise description (1988: 106), we may find, in this investigation, "a silence that springs from another silence," without having to remain "in the silence where the silences are mute."

References

Alberto, P.L. 2009. When Rio was *black*: Soul music, national culture, and the politics of racial comparison in 1970s Brazil. *Hispanic American Historical Review* 89 (1): 3–39.

Alonso, A. 2018. Processos políticos da abolição. In *Dicionário da escravidão e liberdade*, ed. Lilia M. Schwarcz and Flávio Gomes, 358–364. São Paulo: Companhia das Letras.

Alonso, A., and M. Dolhnikoff (org.). 2015. *1964: do golpe à democracia*. São Paulo: Hedra.

Alves, M.H.M. 1984. *Estado e oposição no Brasil (1964–1984)*. Petrópolis: Vozes.

Andrieu, K. 2012. *La justice transitionnelle: de l'Afrique du Sud au Rwanda*. Paris: Gallimard.

Antunes, R. 1992. *A rebeldia do trabalho: o confronto operário no ABC paulista – as greves de 1978–1980*. Campinas: Editora da Unicamp.

Berg, M., and B. Schaeffer (eds.). 2012. *Historical justice in international perspective: How societies are trying to right the wrongs of the past*. Cambridge: Cambridge University Press.

Bertulio, D. 1989. *Direito e relações raciais: uma introdução crítica ao racismo*. LLM Dissertation, Federal University of Santa Catarina, Law School.

Brasil. Ata da 10ª Reunião Ordinária da Subcomissão dos Negros, Populações Indígenas, Pessoas Deficientes e Minorias Diário da Assembléia Nacional Constituinte, Suplemento ao n° 63, 21 de maio de 1987, pp. 120–143.

Brasil. Comissão Nacional da Verdade, Relatório Final, Volumes I, II e III. 10 de dezembro de 2014. Available at: http://cnv.memoriasreveladas.gov.br/.

Cassin, B., O. Cayla, and P.-J. Salazar (dir.). 2004. *Vérité, reconciliation, réparation*. Paris: Seuil.

Chalhoub, S. 2011. *Visões da liberdade: uma história das últimas décadas de escravidão na Corte*. São Paulo: Companhia das Letras.

Connerton, P. 2009. *How modernity forgets*. Cambridge: Cambridge University Press.

Delgado, F.R., R.E. Dodge, and S. Carvalho. 2011. *São Paulo sob achaque: corrupção, crime organizado e violência institucional em maio de 2006*. São Paulo: International Human Rights Clinic – Human Rights Program at Harvard Law School and Justiça Global.

Domingues, P. 2007. Movimento negro brasileiro: alguns apontamentos históricos. *Tempo* 12 (23): 100–122.

Domingues, P. 2018. Frente negra/Legião negra. In *Dicionário da escravidão e liberdade*, ed. Lilia M. Schwarcz and Flávio Gomes, 237–243. São Paulo: Companhia das Letras.

Duarte, E.C.P., and M.V.L. Queiroz. 2016. A Revolução Haitiana e o Atlântico Negro: o Constitucionalismo em face do Lado Oculto da Modernidade. *Revista Direito, Estado e Sociedade* 49: 10–42.

Fausto, B. (org.). 2007. *História Geral da Civilização Brasileira, Tomo III, vol. 11, O Brasil republicano: Economia e Cultura (1930–1964)*, 4a ed. Rio de Janeiro: Bertrand Brasil.

Ferreira, J. 2018. O presidente acidental: José Sarney e a transição democrática. In *O Brasil republicano, vol. 5: o tempo da Nova República – da transição democrática à crise política de 2016*, ed. Jorge Ferreira and Lucilia de A. N. Delgado, 1a ed., 27–71. Rio de Janeiro: Civilização Brasileira.

Ferreira, J., and A. Castro Gomes. 2014. *1964: o golpe que derrubou um presidente, pôs fim ao regime democrático e instituiu a ditadura no Brasil*. Rio de Janeiro: Civilização Brasileira.

Fico, C. 2010. Espionagem, polícia política, censura e propaganda: os pilares básicos da repressão. In *O Brasil republicano, vol. 4: o tempo da ditadura – regime militar e movimentos sociais em fins do século XX*, ed. Jorge Ferreira and Lucilia de A. N. Delgado, 4a ed., 167–205. Rio de Janeiro: Civilização Brasileira.

Frias, L. 1976. Black Rio: o orgulho (importado) de ser negro no Brasil. *Jornal do Brasil*, Caderno B, July 17th.

Gensburger, S., and S. Lefranc. 2017. *À quoi servent les politiques de la mémoire?* Paris: Presses de Sciences Po.

Ghoshal, R. 2015. What does remembering racial violence do? Greensboro's truth commission, mnemonic overlap, and attitudes toward racial redress. *Race and Justice* 5 (2): 168–191.

Grinberg, L. 2014. Por um "futuro visível do país": a campanha das diretas na *Coluna do Castello*. In *Não foi tempo perdido: os anos 80 em debate*, ed. Samantha V. Quadrat, 34–56. Rio de Janeiro: 7 Letras.

Hayner, P.B. 2011. *Unspeakable truths: Transitional justice and the challenge of truth commissions*, 2nd ed. New York and London: Routledge.

Huyssen, A. 2003. *Present pasts: Urban palimpsests and the politics of memory*. Stanford: Stanford University Press.

Kössling, K.S. 2007. As lutas anti-racistas de afro-descendentes sob vigilância do DEOPS/SP (1964–1983). PhD Dissertation, São Paulo University, Department of History.

Kucinski, B. 2001. *O fim da ditadura militar*. São Paulo: Contexto.

Leopardi, G. 1964. *Canti – introduzione e commento di M. Fubini*. Torino: Loescher.

Loner, B.A. 2012. Trajetórias de "setores médios" no pós-emancipação: Justo, Serafim e Juvenal. In *Escravidão e liberdade: temas, problemas e perspectivas de análise*, ed. Regina C.L. Xavier, 417–442. São Paulo: Alameda.

Meccarelli, M. 2017. Rights in times of crisis: An interdisciplinary issue for legal studies. In *Reading the crisis: Legal, philosophical and literary perspectives*, ed. Massimo Meccarelli, 209–219. Madrid: Dykinson.

Michel, J. 2018. *Le devoir de mémoire*. Paris: Humensis.

Olsen, T., L.A. Payne, and A.G. Reiter. 2010. *Transitional justice in balance: Comparing processes, weighing efficacy*. Washington, DC: United States Institute of Peace Press.

Paixão, C. 2011. Direito, política, autoritarismo e democracia no Brasil: da Revolução de 30 à promulgação da Constituição da República de 1988. *Revista Iberoamericana de Filosofía, Política y Humanidades* 26: 146–169.

Paixão, C. 2016. Mundo do trabalho entre passado e futuro: das greves de 1978/1980 à Assembleia Nacional Constituinte de 1987/1988. In *Como aplicar a CLT à luz da Constituição: alternativas para os que militam no foro trabalhista*, ed. Márcio T. Viana and Cláudio J. Rocha, 36–43. São Paulo: LTr.

Paixão, C., and L.A. Barbosa 2008. Cidadania, democracia e constituição: o processo de convocação da Assembléia Nacional Constituinte de 1987–1988. In *Cidadania e inclusão social: estudos em homenagem à Professora Miracy Barbosa de Sousa Gustin*, ed. Flávio H.U. Pereira and Maria Tereza F. Dias, 121–132. Belo Horizonte: Fórum.

Paixão, C., and C.P. Carvalho. 2016. Cultura, política e moral: as diversas faces da censura na ditadura militar brasileira. In *O Direito Achado na Rua vol. 8: Introdução crítica ao direito à comunicação e à informação*, ed. José Geraldo de S. Junior et al., 336–348. Brasília: FAC-UnB.

Paz, O. 1988. *Libertad bajo palabra*. Madrid: Cátedra.

Pesavento, S.J. 2004. Negritude, mestiçagem e lusitanismo: o Brasil positivo de Gilberto Freyre. In *Intérpretes do Brasil: ensaios de cultura e identidade*, ed. Gunter Axt and Fernando Schüler, 177–191. Porto Alegre: Artes e Ofícios.

Pires, T.R. 2018. Estruturas Intocadas: Racismo e Ditadura no Rio de Janeiro. *Direito & Práxis* 9 (2): 1054–1079.

Presot, A. 2010. Celebrando a "Revolução": as marchas da família com Deus pela Liberdade e o golpe de 1964. In *A construção social dos regimes autoritários: legitimidade, consenso e consentimento no século XX – Brasil e América Latina*, ed. Denise Rollemberg and Samantha V. Quadrat, 71–96. Rio de Janeiro: Civilização Brasileira.

Rancière, J. 2018. *Les temps modernes: art, temps, politique*. Paris: La Fabrique.

Rotberg, R.I., and D. Thompson (eds.). 2000. *Truth v. justice: the morality of truth commissions*. Princeton and Oxford: Princeton University Press.

Sader, E. 2010. *Quando novos personagens entraram em cena: experiências e lutas dos trabalhadores da Grande São Paulo 1970–1980*. 5a reimpr. Rio de Janeiro: Paz e Terra.

Schneider, N. (ed.). 2019. *The Brazilian truth commission: Local, national and global perspectives*. New York and Oxford: Berghahn (forthcoming).

Schwarcz, L.M. 2012. População e sociedade. In *História do Brasil Nação (1808–2010), vol. 3: a abertura para o mundo (1889–1930)*, coord. Lilia M. Schwarcz, 35–83. Rio de Janeiro: Objetiva.

Schwarcz, L.M., and H. Starling. 2015. *Brasil: uma biografia*. São Paulo: Companhia das Letras.

Taylor, G.F. 2014. Chicago Police torture scandal: A legal and political history. *CUNY Law Review* 17 (2): 329–381.

Todorov, T. 2000. *Los abusos de la memoria*. Barcelona: Paidós Ibérica.

Toledo, C.N. (org.). 2001. *1964: visões críticas do golpe – democracia e reformas no populismo*. Campinas: Editora da Unicamp.

Ventura, R. 2000. Um Brasil mestiço: raça e cultura na passagem da monarquia à república. In *Viagem Incompleta: a experiência brasileira (1500–2000)*, ed. Carlos G. Mota, 2a ed., 329–359. São Paulo: Editora Senac.

Weinrich, H. 2004. *Lethe: The art and critique of forgetting*. Ithaca: Cornell University Press.

Williams, J.E. 2009. Legitimacy and effectiveness of a grassroots truth and reconciliation commission. *Law and Contemporary Problems* 72: 143–150.

Cristiano Paixão in Professor of legal history and constitutional law at the University of Brasília Law School. Doctor in Law degree from Federal University of Minas Gerais, with post-doctoral studies in historiography at Ecole des Hautes Etudes en Sciences Sociales de Paris and in modern history at Scuola Normale Superiore di Pisa. He was a visiting professor at Macerata University School of Law and at the Master's Program in Constitutional Law at Seville University, and has published extensively about constitutional history. He was a member of the Brazilian Amnesty Committee (Ministry of Justice) and was one of the coordinators of the Anísio Teixeira Memory and Truth Commission (University of Brasília). His main research interests are constitutional history, law and literature, and interdisciplinary studies in law.

Chapter 3
Political Transition, Continuities and Permanences: The Rights of Indigenous Peoples and Political Transition in Brazil

Juliana Neuenschwander Magalhães

Abstract It can be said that Brazilian Transitional Justice was characterised as a complex of measures that simultaneously allowed the construction of memory and forgetfulness about the military dictatorship in Brazil. A political memory and, at the same time, a legal oblivion. In our view, this Brazilian option has prevented a real transition, accentuating and deepening the authoritarian continuities, a hypothesis that we will demonstrate in this article, regarding the serious violations of human rights suffered by the Indigenous Peoples during the military dictatorship in Brazil. These violations, which were silenced for a long time, were the most forgotten, and yet, possibly, those that generated the largest number of victims, with characteristics of true ethnocide.

3.1 Introduction

When we talk about political transition, we intend to point out both the change of political regime and the period of time when this change happens, which involves the activation of political and legal mechanisms of past elaboration, through processes of accountability, reparation, construction of memory and search for truth. The notion of transition is paradoxical, because one can only think of transition in the face of a regime change that has already occurred, but at the same time one can only observe such a change when the transition has already occurred. This paradox is constitutive of transition, which refers at the same time to a past to be overcome and to a future to be constructed, because it is both the time for the elaboration of the past and that for the projection of the future.

In this intermediate time, a society may find a new destiny free from the bonds of authoritarianism, or, on the contrary, the past may return without anything having been learned from it. Each social context, each transitional experience, chooses its own paths of transit between one regime and another. Transitional models do not

J. Neuenschwander Magalhães (✉)
School of Law, Federal University of Rio de Janeiro, Rio de Janeiro, Brazil
e-mail: juliananeue@direito.ufrj.br

© Springer Nature Switzerland AG 2021
C. Paixão and M. Meccarelli (eds.), *Comparing Transitions to Democracy. Law and Justice in South America and Europe*, Studies in the History of Law and Justice 18, https://doi.org/10.1007/978-3-030-67502-8_3

guarantee anything, do not avoid retrogressions or ensure democratic peace. The future remains always contingent and open. But this does not mean that it does not project itself onto and out of the experiences of transition that, with their pretensions of rationality, despite the future being uncertain, allow the subsequent trajectory to be able to be oriented by the results that are being obtained (Luhmann 1997: 176).

Therefore, observing the transitional periods is relevant. The process of elaboration of the past and of memory in the context of political transitions constructs the bearings of the future's horizon for after the transition. Transitional justice processes turn to an elaboration of the past, so that there is learning of what should not happen again. Thus, the transition can last a "huge instant", we can say, like João Guimarães Rosa, because "what is real is neither upon the exit nor the arrival, it is available to us in the middle of the crossing" (Rosa 2006).

The political transition in Brazil has been a long crossing: "slow, gradual and secure" as proclaimed in the period of democratic openness. It can be said that it is very far from being a true "reckoning" with the past of the longest dictatorship of South America (1964–1985), adopting politics of memory of the dictatorship, on the one hand, and legal oblivion on the other. The first civil governments, when they inaugurated the "New Republic" from 1985, were reluctant to "reckon" with the dictatorship. Under the Sarney government (1985–1989), the first efforts to make public the human rights violations, including torture, murders and forced disappearances, were unofficial, with the *Brasil: nunca mais* (Brazil: Never Again) report, drafted under the auspices of the Christian churches under the leadership of Cardinal Dom Paulo Evaristo Arns and Pastor Jaime Wright. Only in December 1995, under the government of Fernando Henrique Cardoso (FHC) and under pressure from the Commission of Relatives of the Dead and Disappeared for Political Reasons (CFMDRP), the Brazilian State acknowledged its responsibility for the death of 136 political militants and established the creation of the Commission on Political Deaths and Disappearances, also providing indemnification to the families of the victims (Law 9140/95). In 2007 the report entitled "Right to Memory and Truth" was published. Under the FHC government, the Amnesty Commission was created, whose role was to declare amnesty and decide on indemnifications for the victims of the military dictatorship regulated by Law 10550/2002. The Amnesty Commission under the Lula and Dilma Rousseff governments expanded its field of activity, inserting itself in the work of memory and adopting the practice, on behalf of the Brazilian State, of asking for forgiveness of those persecuted by the military dictatorship. In those years, the notion of amnesty ceased to mean only "forgetfulness" to mean "lest it be forgotten, lest it should ever happen again".

Notwithstanding such efforts, in 2010, in the ADPF n. 153 judgement, the Federal Supreme Court (STF) was called upon to examine the consistency of the Amnesty Law (Law 6683/79) with the Federal Constitution and stated that it did not violate any fundamental constitutional principle. In the narrative that prevailed in the Court, the central argument was that the Amnesty Law of 1979 should be interpreted in ight of the time, since the so-called Amnesty Law conveys a political decision at that time - the moment of the conciliated transition of 1979. In the same decision, the

Minister Carmem Lúcia, current President of the STF, referred to the amnesty as a true "armistice".

Only under the government of Dilma Rousseff in 2011 was it determined that the Armed Forces would cease to celebrate the anniversary of the 1964 Coup d'état every 31st March. Rousseff also instituted the National Truth Commission (CNV), created by Law 12528/2011 and set up in 2012 to examine and clarify the grave human rights violations committed during the dictatorship, "in order to realise the right to memory and historical truth and to promote national reconciliation." The establishment of the CNV consisted of a milestone that could lead Brazil to a genuine political transition involving all aspects of such processes, such as reparation, reconciliation, memory and accountability. In December 2014 President Roussef was presented with the Commission's extensive final report, which in more than four thousand pages described the State's behaviour during the military dictatorship in violation of the rights of students, military personnel, artists, peasants, Indians, homosexuals, religious people, workers, describing the *modus operandi* of a regime that made torture a State practice.

The CNV Report exposed as a novelty the fact that 8,530 Indians suffered human rights violations during the long period between 1946 and 1988 investigated by the Commission. It should be remembered that previous documents did not refer to the Indians as victims of the dictatorship. In the famous "Brasil: Never Again" report, which became the biggest bestseller of non-fiction in the late 80s, there is a radiography of the main targets of the State's repressive apparatus—military personnel (especially those who had been faithful to President Goulart), trade unionists, students, politicians, journalists, religious people—but there is no reference whatsoever to the persecutions suffered by the Indians, perhaps the most invisible victims of the military dictatorship. Curiously, the Epilogue of the aforementioned book is, precisely, a saying of the Indian Kelé Maxacali, of the Mikael village in Minas Gerais, in the year 1984:

My father told me; I'm going to tell my son

When he dies? He tells his son. It's like this: nobody forgets.

The CNV Report, due to the greatness of its numbers and the gravity of the facts, reveals that the Indians were not only victims of the dictatorship, but were the greatest and most invisible victims of the regime. The last book of the CNV's extensive report has the biography of the 434 people who were killed and disappeared in Brazil during the period from 1946 to 1988. Among them are not any Indian victims, although the CNV itself, in the chapter titled "Violations of Human Rights of Indigenous Peoples", nominally identified at least two indigenous leaders killed in the 1980s: Marçal de Souza and Angelo Kretà. Indians total the astonishing number of 8,530 dead, but they do not have names, records or photographs. They are victims who are "approximated", "estimated" and indiscernible.

The Indians, indiscernible in the forests they inhabit, recluses in tribes that were often not even contacted, or segregated on the outskirts of large cities, were not persecuted as individuals, but because they were Indians. It is important to remember that the indigenous movements had a strong impetus from the end of the 60s onwards, experiencing their zenith between the 80s and 90s, just when the so-called political transition began. Ailton Krenak, says about this period: "I think there was a discovery of Brazil by the whites in 1500, and then a discovery of Brazil by the Indians in the 1970s and 1980s. What is important is the latter. The Indians discovered that, although they are symbolically the owners of Brazil, they have nowhere to live in that country. They will have to make that place exist day by day" (Cohn 2015: 19).

During that period, several indigenous assemblies were held, and in the late 1970s the Union of Indigenous Nations (UNI) was founded, a council of tribes representing all indigenous nations in Brazil in defence of their interests and needs. Mário Juruna was elected as the first and so far the only indigenous federal deputy, having been responsible for the creation of the Indian Commission. In the Constituent Assembly of 1987, the participation of the indigenous movement was intense and relevant, in the Subcommittee on Blacks, Indigenous Populations, Persons with Disabilities and Minorities (Carneiro da Cunha 1987; Cohn 2015). The demands of the period were mainly for the recognition of the Indians' right to live on the lands traditionally occupied by them, with the demarcation of the indigenous lands.

Only more recently, during the period of the National Truth Commission, we find references to the dictatorial period and the relationship between the developmentalism undertaken by the military in government, the advancement of agricultural frontiers, and the expropriation of indigenous lands. There was a new perception, also on the part of the Indians themselves, that there is a relationship between the rights violations, the authoritarianism and developmentalism of the military dictatorship period. In an interview given to *Nau* magazine in 2013, Ailton Krenak mentioned that in the period in which throughout the Southern Cone had "a commanding general", the developmentalism produced what Shelton Davis called "Victims of the Miracle," with Brazil becoming a building site (Cohn 2015: 243; Davis 1978).

That interview occurred precisely during the period of the National Truth Commission's work and, therefore, that sharpened perception of the relationship between the dictatorship, developmentalism and indigenous rights violations can also be attributed to the activation of the transitional mechanism of search for memory and truth. But even when that perception is activated, as can be gathered from Ailton Krenak's speech, it is curious to notice that no distinction is made between the conduct of the State under dictatorship and under democracy. Krenak made a very strong criticism of President Dilma Rousseff's developmentalist politics, comparing it to that of the Geisel government (1974–1979).

That comparison, undoubtedly somewhat rhetorical, reveals that for the Indian there is no difference between the attacks they suffered during the dictatorship and the violations suffered in democratic times. Living in "stateless societies", to the Indians only one thing matters: the land. There is a nexus of life between the Indian and the land, between the Indian and nature, because all the beings of the forest are part of the same "humanity" (Viveiros de Castro 2014). There is a relationship that is not of "property" in the sense of the right of those who live in State societies, but of reciprocal belonging. We can not fall into the mistake, as pointed out by Roy Wagner, of thinking or imagining a culture for people who do not conceive of themselves (Wagner 2012). Like Wagner, we can think that doing the same with the law is also a mistake, which applies to the forms designed for transitional justice in relation to the Indians.

It is possible, therefore, to observe the complexity of the theme proposed here. In addressing the violation of the rights of Indigenous Peoples and the political transition in Brazil, it becomes relevant to know whether the persecutions that the Indians suffered during the dictatorship should be treated as something specific to the military period or, on the contrary, they were only the continuity of the process of extermination that Indigenous Peoples have suffered in Brazil since the time of discovery. If we look at the more than five hundred years of persecution, extermination and dispossession of the Indigenous Peoples, it may seem that there is nothing new in the conduct of the military regime against the Indians, historical victims of colonialism and greed for their lands.

Nevertheless, even recognising that the Indians were victims of the colonisation process itself and of the territorial conquest in Brazil, doesn't eliminate the fact, described in detail by the CNV and other relevant documents, such as the Figueiredo Report (1968), that the Indians were also direct victims of the military dictatorship. In this step the question becomes that of knowing whether there is something specific and directly related to the characteristics of the military regime in the persecution of the Indians in Brazil between 1964 and 1985. It is important to enquire about the specificity of the persecution of the Indians during the dictatorship, both as regards the history of extermination and despoliation that they suffered, as well as the rights violations suffered by the other victims of the regime of exception that was implanted in Brazil between the mid-1960s and the mid-1980s.

Knowing these very characteristics of the persecution of the Indians during the dictatorship is relevant for the construction of memory of the dictatorship, both for the elaboration of transitional justice mechanisms that take account of the indigenous question, and for the Brazilian indigenous movement itself to rethink the relationship between the indigenous question and the political directions of the Brazilian State. It can be assumed that the absence of an understanding of the nexus between the dictatorship and the violation of the the Indians' rights has contributed to the denial that such rights continue to be infringed today, more than 30 years since the end of the military dictatorship in Brazil. The very notion of a "timeframe" ("*marco temporal*") adopted by the Federal Supreme Court since 1998 ends up obstructing the realisation of transitional justice in relation to the Indians, since there can only be one possible reparation for damages in relation to the Indigenous Peoples who were killed and expelled from their lands: the recognition of the right to the lands they had traditionally occupied, even though they were no longer there on 5 October, 1988, the date of the promulgation of the Federal Constitution.

Considering this actuality of the indigenous question, in this article, I intend to (1) make an historical-legal outline of the extermination of the Indigenous Peoples to demonstrate how, from the colony to the present day, the law has functioned as a way of "including the exclusion" of the Indian in Brazil; (2) describe the persecution of the Indians during the military dictatorship as an "organised extermination policy" or a State-administered extermination; (3) investigate whether, in the case of the Indigenous Peoples, one can speak of a "political transition" capable of addressing the historical violations of the rights of the Indians, from the "discovery" to the present day.

3.2 History of the Rights and the Extermination of the Indians in Brazil

The extermination of the Indians in Brazil is due to the colonising process itself and occurred through the expulsion, dispossession, enslavement and murder of the Indians, in the wars of conquest waged by the invading white man, but also through the spread of plagues and diseases. In the words of the indigenous leader Ailton Krenak, the 500th anniversary of the arrival of the Portuguese ships in Brazil signifies the beginning of the disappearance of the Indians: "We were 900 tribes only here in this part that today they call Brazil. From the 16th century until today, at the end of the 20th century, we have been reduced to 180 tribes; 720 ethnic groups have been wiped out by the sword, disease, violence, brutality, and social and cultural breakdown" (Cohen 2015). It is an indisputable fact that over these five centuries the extermination of the Indians has been practiced with the connivance or explicit support of the State, although it has been masked by policies that have oscillated between segregationist, integrationist or preservationist. These policies have been legally designed by norms that have recognised the rights of the Indians to their lands, but which have contemporaneously supported policies that have interrupted the life and cultural cycle that binds the Indian to those lands. In other words, the law has included the Indians as subjects of rights in order to, in the next instant, legitimise aggressive policies of invasion and despoliation of those lands.

In 1532, upon decreeing that the Indians were human (*Sublimis Dei* Leaflet), Pope Paul III inserted this new part of humanity into the "divine economy" (Carneiro da Cunha 2012: 40). Based on this economy of a scale of beings, in which the creatures closest to God our found at the highest levels, the Christianisation policy was created, which was entrusted to the Society of Jesus, which arrived in Brazil in 1549. The efforts to include the Indians in the social hierarchy by way of Christianisation coexisted, however, with a policy of extermination carried out in the so-called wars of conquest, which from the year 1550 were waged by the Europeans against the Indians, expelling them from their lands, enslaving them, and forcing them to live in villages under the tutelage of missionaries (Carneiro da Cunha 2012: 15). In those wars the Indians themselves were used as contingent troops to destroy other tribes. It was during that period that occurred the massacre perpetrated by the governor Mem de Sá, which at the end of 1550 reached the Tupinambá and Tupiniquin Indians of Bahia and Espirito Santo, with the help of the latter to overthrow the former (Almeida 2013). In that campaign Mem de Sá destroyed more than 60 villages, while one Jesuit affirmed that the number reached 160. That massacre was told by Mem de Sá himself as such: "The night I entered Ilhéus I went on foot into a village that was seven league from the town. (…) and before morning, at two o'clock I went on the hillside and destroyed and killed all those who wanted to resist, and upon coming back I came burning and destroying all the villages that remained behind … so that no Tupiniquim remained alive" (*apud* Almeida 2013: 67).

The history of Indian law in Brazil began only in the following century, almost two hundred years after the arrival of the Portuguese in 1680, when Portugal recognised, in the Royal Charter of 1st April, the right of the Indians to *remain on their lands*, without being disturbed and "*not moved from places against their will*". But in spite of this and other laws, such as the Charter of 7 June, 1755, the Jesuit-run Indian settlement policy still perdured, with the segregation of the Indians in villages close to the villages inhabited by the Portuguese, which favoured the transmission of diseases, as well as the invasions and plundering of the lands inhabited by Indians, actions that had the explicit support of the Crown (Araujo 2006). Thereby, between 1650 and 1825 the Indian population was halved from 700,000 to 360,000 individuals (Azevedo 2008).

The Indian settlement policy practiced by the missionaries subsisted until the "Directory of the Indians", created by the Marquis of Pombal in 1757 and abolished in 1798, a period in which administration of the indigenous villages ceased to be religious and became secular. The Directory aimed to "assimilate physically and socially the Indians into the rest of the population" and to break the isolation in which the Jesuits kept the Indians on their missions (Carneiro da Cunha 2012: 75). With the Directory already repealed, but unofficially in force, the Royal Charter of 2 December, 1808 declared as vacant the lands that had been "won" from the Indians in the so-called "Just Wars" undertaken by the Portuguese government against the Indigenous Peoples who did not submit to its dominion in Brazil. The objective here was clearly to make Indian lands bartering chips, because the fact that the indigenous lands were deemed unoccupied allowed them to be granted to whomever the Portuguese Crown wished, since vacant land was assumed to be land of the public domain without any specific destination (Araujo 2006: 25).

In that direction, since 1832 the lease and sale of indigenous lands has been permitted. In 1845 the "Regulation on Catechism Missions and Civilisation of the Indians" (Decree 426 of 24/7/1845) provided for the removal and assembly of villages, corroborating the legalisation of the despoliation. The regulation, by establishing "new" political and administrative guidelines for the settlements, made that policy even more explicit, with the deportation and concentration of the Indians in places close to the cities where the settlers lived, which allowed them to take advantage of the indigenous labour force. In those forced settlements, several ethnic groups were gathered together that were often traditional enemies, often causing the Indians to end up killing each other (Carneiro da Cunha 2012: 77).

Between 1798 and 1845, during the so-called self-government of the Indians, there was some resistance to invasions and plundering. It is worthy to note the episode in 1821 and 1822, in which the chief of the Gamela de Viana Indians of Maranhão obtained from the provincial magistrate the demarcation of the village lands (Carneiro da Cunha 2012: 92–93). In 1850 the so-called "*Lei de Terras*" secured once again the territorial right of the Indians, reaffirming the "*indigenato*", on the basis of which, later, villages that had been abandoned by the Indians were considered vacant. The "*Lei de Terras*" opened space for an extremely aggressive policy regarding the Indian lands. If the pombaline settlements had favoured the permanency of "civilised people" together with the Indians, one month after the promulgation of the "*Lei de Terras*" the Empire ordered the incorporation of the lands of Indian villages living "dispersed and confused with the mass of the civilised population" (Carneiro Cunha 2012: 79). After that, municipalities, provinces and the Empire started to wage disputes over the indigenous lands. At first those lands were treated as vacant by the Empire that declared in 1858 that any leases of those lands made by the Local Councils should be considered void. But from 1875 the Local Councils began to be able to sell to the tenants the lands of the extinct Indian villages and to use them for the foundation of towns or villages. More than that, since it was up to the presidents of the provinces to attest that the lands had been abandoned, many began to do so without the abandonments having actually occurred (Araujo 2006: 28).

In this way, there has been the conjunction of the policy of segregation of the Indians in small spaces (settlements), practiced since colonial times, with the tendency to transform the indigenous lands into vacant lands. This strategy, practiced by the whole Empire and also by much of the Republic, was intensified when the republican Constitution of 1891, in its article 64, transferred to the states the vacant lands, until then in the hands of the central administration. As soon as the states were declared by the Constitution of 1891 "owners" of the vacant lands, they arranged to grant them to individuals. It should be noted that, although the Constitution of 1891 deals with the individual rights of Brazilian citizens, it completely omits the rights of the Indians, like the imperial Constitution of 1824.

Yet the successive republican constitutions of 1934, 1937 and 1946 recognised the rights of the Indians, referred to as "savages" (that is, as those who were born and live in the jungle). The Constitution of 1934 was the first of an historical series of constitutions to affirm that "the possession of the lands by the savages found on them, permanently located, shall be respected, however alienating the lands is prohibited" (art 129). In addition, it established, adopting an integrationist bias, the Union's competence to legislate on the "incorporation of the savages into the national communion". In the Constitutions of 1937 and 1946 protection is again limited to possession, and in 1946 not only alienation, but transfer more generally, is prohibited. Again, notwithstanding that prohibition, there are reports of various land titles being granted by the states during that period, causing situations such as the expulsion of the Krenak Indians from their lands in 1957.

Throughout the second half of the twentieth century a new mentality concerning the political-juridical treatment of the indigenous question began to be outlined, influenced by Candido Rondon's ideas, such as the pioneering establishment of the right to difference (Ribeiro 1995: 147), the proposal of a "compensatory right", by which the Indians had the same rights as other Brazilians, rights that could not be demanded of them as duties, in a kind of "affirmative action". Rondon inspired intellectuals such as Darcy Ribeiro and *sertanistas* (bushmen or specialists in the undeveloped interior of Brazil) like the Villas Bôas brothers, who, following his ideas, dedicated themselves to the study of and coexistence with the Indigenous Peoples.

In 1961, thanks to the work begun in the 50s by Darcy Ribeiro and the Villas Bôas brothers, the Xingu National Park was created. The "preservationist" intention of the Villas Bôas brothers, however, contrasted with that adopted by the Brazilian Indian Protection Service (SPI) and later, during the military dictatorship, by the National Indian Protection Foundation (FUNAI) created in 1967. Both SPI and FUNAI were guided by the developmentalist and strongly integrationist idea of the integration of the Indians into "national communion". Although SPI and FUNAI had as their main objective the protection of the Indians, neither of them was able to prevent the genocide of the Indians practiced by the Brazilian State during the military dictatorship.

On the contrary: corruption and deviations of purpose contaminated these institutions. According to the CNV Report, the Parliamentary Commission of Inquiry (CPI) about Indians established in 1977 concluded that FUNAI followed the practices of SPI, modernising them and justifying them in terms of "national development". It emphasises that FUNAI instilled in those practices a business management approach (Indigenous Income, Community Development Finance Program, etc.). The CNV Report also affirms that "in the actions of the airforce major Luis Vinhas Neves, General Bandeira de Mello and Romero Jucá, for example, there were cases of grave human rights violations associated with the extraction of wood and minerals, colonisation and infrastructure works" (Brasil/CNV 2014).

3.3 The Policy of "Organised Extermination" of the Indians Under the Military Dictatorship

What are the specific characteristics of the persecution suffered by the Indians under the military dictatorship? According to the CNV's numbers, the greatest victims of the dictatorship are the Indians. They are also the most invisible and indiscernible, as has already been pointed out above. But it is curious to note that official demographic data indicates that the indigenous population grew over the years of the dictatorship, which may seem to contradict the CNV's data. When the military coup occurred in 1964 it was estimated that there were between 70,000 and 110,000 "settled" Indians, who lived on demarcated lands under the jurisdiction and control of the Union. As Rubens Valente recalls, not considered were the thousands of Indians who lived in the forests and on the banks of rivers, called "wild" or "hostile" (Valente 2017: 9). In 1980, still under the dictatorship, it was verified that there was an unprecedented growth in the indigenous population, counted as 210,000 individuals (0.19% of the total population).

That "population growth" appears to contrast with the high number of Indians killed by the military regime, a fact that can be explained, paradoxically, by the same reason that led to the expulsions and deaths of Indians. This is because the capitalist expansion and the advance of the agricultural frontier towards the Amazonian region made possible finding tribes that had been uncontacted because they had been "hostile" or even unknown. Therefore, the conquest of the Amazon led to an increase in the number of Indians in Brazil as new tribes were found.

It is therefore again this encounter with the white man that caused the death of thousands of Indians. In the context of the strong capitalist expansion that marked the period, the Indians were seen and treated as an obstacle to development, thus they were denied any right, including that which had been recognised since colonial times, to remain on the lands of which they were the original inhabitants. In that process of expansion of capitalism toward the rainforest, the Indians "fell" as much as the trees. The indigenous parks and reserves were, on account of the developmentalist wrath, shrinking in size, to the extent that it was no longer possible to preserve the cultural integrity of an indigenous nation. Land conflicts continued, under the absolute omission of the State, and even with its active participation in the defence of the interests of land-grabbers, farmers and business groups that, with the elimination of the Indians, sought to make way for their business activities, especially agriculture, livestock production and mining.

In the same period, between the 60s and 70s, in Brazil and in other countries with indigenous populations (Canada, United States) there was a series of legal advances in the treatment of the indigenous question. These considerable normative advances also reflected those achieved in the field of International Law, such as the International Covenant on Economic, Social and Cultural Rights, adopted by the United Nations General Assembly in 1966 (and ratified by Brazil only in 1992), which provided the "inherent right of all peoples to enjoy fully and freely their natural wealth and resources". In this context favourable to the (at least formal) recognition of the rights of the Indians, the Brazilian Constitution of 1967 treated the lands of the "savages" as "assets of the Union", guaranteeing their usufruct, including the exploitation of the natural resources. This mechanism fulfilled the role of both establishing a greater control over the territory by the Union (revealing a concern even about national security, since many Indian lands are in frontier zones) and moving away from the practice of the States, since the Constitution of 1891, of expropriating and subdividing indigenous lands. Constitutional Amendment No. 1 of 1969 made a determination about the lands inhabited by the savages in article 198, declaring them inalienable and recognising the Indians' permanent possession of them, as well as declaring the right to exclusive usufruct of their natural resources and all their uses (Constitutional Amendment No. 1/1969, article 198).

The Indian Statute of 1973 consisted of a step forward in the recognition of indigenous rights, although it retained certain traits of authoritarianism, such as the provision of tribal emancipation decided by the President of the Republic, as well as the insistence on the idea of "the integration of the Indians into national communion". The drafting of the Indian Statute fell to the Minister of the Federal Supreme Court, Themistócles Cavalcanti, for whom the Indian was considered "a human being, equal to any of us, with the same rights and possibilities, with the freedom to live in their *habitat*, but to perfect their conditions of existence, always admitting better possibilities for their communication with 'our world'" (Chaves 1979: 117). Still in force today, the Indian Statute uses the expressions Indians and savages as synonyms and is founded on the purpose of "preserving their culture and integrating them, progressively and harmoniously, into national communion." The Statute has extended to the Indians and the Indigenous communities the protection of Brazilian laws in the same terms as they apply to other Brazilians, defending indigenous practices, customs and traditions (Indian Statute, Article 1). The Statute also contains advances in the treatment of the rights of the Indians to their lands, affirming that possession precedes the demarcation of the lands, which does nothing more than acknowledge it. Octavio Ianni observes in this regard the curious distinction made in both the law that created FUNAI and in the Statute, between *Indian* and *national*: "these laws distinguish and contrast 'tribal communities' or 'indigenous communities' and 'national society' or 'national communion'. After all, who is the Brazilian? The way in which the Indian is defined ends up transforming them into a "special 'other', apart, different, strange, foreign" (Ianni 1986: 200). It is important to note here that the expression "national communion" came from the 1934 Constitution.

In practice, the dictatorship treated the indigenous question as a kind of anthropological gardening exercise: the Indians were placed in reserves that tended to progressively reduce their lands, making the reserved Indians end up as semi-imprisoned Indians, unable to maintain their culture on the tiny tracts of land (Ianni 1986). In view of this, anthropologists have since sought to demonstrate the "misleading ambiguity" present in the legal and bureaucratic apparatus of the State aimed at "protecting" or "integrating" the Indians. "The very fact of the reduction of the Indian to a reserve or park is already a first and basic expropriation involving both the land and the culture" (Ianni 1986: 210).

Under the mantle of the integrative and protective doctrine, as well as an awareness of the necessity to preserve the culture of Indigenous Peoples, juridically guaranteed, the developmentalist impulse of the military dictatorship once again made the legislation work as a dissimulation of the widespread violation of the rights of Indigenous Peoples. According to the sociologist Octavio Ianni, from 1964, with the implantation of an extensive capitalist development policy in the Amazon, the interests and rights of the Indians who inhabited that region were disregarded, as if the Indians were not there from the beginning (Ianni 1986: 199; Davis 1978: 103–104).

Thus, what took place under the dictatorship in Brazil was a *destructive protection of the Indigenous communities*, "in the sense that it propitiates, organises and accelerates the expropriation of its labour force, culture and land" (Ianni 1986: 210). The bishop of the Catholic Church in São Felix, Araguaia, Pedro Casaldáglia, described this policy as an "*aggressive acculturation policy*". I propose to identify the peculiarity of the extermination practised against the Indians under the dictatorship as an *organised extermination*. This is the differential of the persecution that the Indians suffered during the years of the military dictatorship in Brazil. Despoliations, forced evictions and deaths are related to a developmentalist State project supported by the regime's military and authoritarian apparatus. The violation of the Indians' human rights is a constant in the history of Brazil, before, during and after the dictatorship. In fact, however, there was something specific to the military dictatorship. This extermination was militarised, organised and bureaucratised.

In the Figueiredo Report, commissioned by the Ministry of the Interior in 1968 and containing more than 7,000 pages and 30 volumes, many violations of the Indians' rights are reported, chronicling the occurrence of torture, mistreatment, abusive detention, forced appropriation of indigenous labour and misappropriation of riches from indigenous territories by officials of various levels of the Indian protection body, the SPI. According to the CNV, the Figueiredo Report pointed to widespread corruption, including at the highest echelons of state governments, as well as to the omission of the judicial system regarding the protection of the Indians' rights. This Report also includes the list of beneficiaries of indigenous lands at the time, as well as their links to politicians, military personnel, judges and civil servants (Brasil/CNV 2014: 207). The denunciations of violations committed against Indigenous Peoples and corruption in the indigenous body led to four Parliamentary Commissions of Inquiry (CPI)—in the Senate, the CPI of 1955, and in the House of Representatives those of 1963, 1968 and 1977. The denunciations were also analysed by the Russell Tribunal, which judged and condemned Brazil in the cases of Waimiri-Atroari, Yanomami, Nambikwara and Kaingang de Manguerinha (Brasil/CNV 2014: 202).

In describing the forms of violation of Indigenous Peoples' rights under the dictatorship, the Report of the National Truth Commission indicates two different attitudes of power that settled in Brazil with that year's Coup. Firstly, until 1968 with the issue of AI-5, the Union established conditions propitious to the despoliation of indigenous lands, behaving mainly in an omissive way, "covering up local power, private interests and failing to control corruption in its cadres" (Brasil/CNV: 198). In the 60s the despoliation was consolidated of the lands of the Xetá Indians, who had been kept in separation and forced deterritorialisation, to be later abandoned in several indigenous posts (Brasil/CNV: 226). In 1967 the Public Ministry of Paraná based on Law n° 2.889/1956 qualified the extermination of the Xetá as the crime of genocide. Secondly, from the issue of AI-5 until 1988, with the promulgation of the Federal Constitution, "the Union's protagonism in the grave violations of the Indians' rights is evident, without any lethal omissions ceasing to exist, particularly in the area of health and in the control of corruption" (Brasil/CNV: 198–199).

As an example of this organised and bureaucratised persecution, one can cite the case of the Krenak Reformatory, a joint prison and concentration camp (an expression used by the Russell Tribunal), where Indians were imprisoned on irrelevant grounds, forced into labour and were also victims of torture and maltreatment. The CNV gathered evidence linking the Krenak Reformatory to torture centres (Brasil/CNV 2014: 239). The surveillance of the reformatory was carried out by the Indigenous Rural Guard (GRIN), which recruited Indians along the Araguaia and Tocantins rivers, as well as from Minas Gerais, to act as a police force in the indigenous areas. Subsequently, GRIN was accused of committing arbitrary acts, beatings, and abuses of all kinds). According to Rubens Valente, the GRIN Indians received military training and had classes in physical torture (Valente 2017: 74).

Between 1973 and 1974 the Avá Canoeiro Indians, in the region of the Araguaia River, were captured by agents of the State, when women suffered sexual abuse before being transferred to an enemy tribe's territory. The Indians were also victims of the repression against the Araguaia Guerrillas, when the Brazilian Army subjected the Aikewara people (known as Suruí do Pará) to a kind of "house" arrest, similar to that experienced by the Krenak people, when a prison was set up on their lands (Brasil/CNV 2014: 239–240). The Report also describes the expropriation of the Arara ethnic group, as well as the massacre of the Kayapó and the Waimiri Atroari, in which war tactics were used between 1960 and 1980, among many other rights violations suffered by the Indians over the period. It is worth mentioning the Waimiri Atroari account:

> Kramna Mudî was a Kiña village that was located on the western side of BR-174, on the lower Alalaú River [...]. In the second half of 1974, Kramna Mudî welcomed the Kiña people to their traditional festival (...) At noon, a rumble of a plane or helicopter approached. The people left the ancestral long house to see. The children were all in the courtyard to see. The plane spilled a dust. All but one were hit and died. (*apud* Brasil/CNV 2014: 235)

Many other examples and reports may be cited here, although the objective of this article is much more to discuss the Indians' rights and the political transition than to collect reports of rights violations suffered by the Indians under the dictatorship. The cases recollected above reveal, however, the specificity of the violation of Indigenous Peoples' rights under the Brazilian military dictatorship. During the dictatorship, the Indian came to be seen as an obstacle to the developmentalist enterprise of the State. The idea of insertion of the Indian in national communion was part of an expropriation strategy. According to Octavio Ianni, "to transform tribal property into property that is occupied, illegally occupied, a latifundium, a farm, or commercial, is always the first and last step in transforming the 'Indian' into 'national'" (Ianni 1986: 215). Moreover, as the CNV recalled, the military regime operated a true historical inversion. While traditionally the Indians had been employed in the conquest and defence of Brazilian territory, as in the case of the Paraguayan War, during the military regime they were treated as virtual enemies. "From defenders of Brazil's borders, they become suspects, virtual internal enemies, under the allegation of being influenced by foreign interests or simply due to their territory having mineral wealth, being situated on the frontiers or in the way of some development project" (Brasil/CNV: 205). In the words of General Breno Borges Fortes, during the 10th Conference of American Armies held in Caracas, "the enemy is indefinite, he uses mimicry and adapts himself to any environment, using all means, licit and illicit, to achieve his goals. He masquerades and disguises himself as a priest or teacher, a student or peasant, a vigilante defender of democracy or an advanced intellectual, [...]; goes to the field and to schools, to factories and churches, to cathedra and magistrature [...]" (Brasil/CNV 2014: 205). The enemy, invisible and indiscernible, are the Indians, the first inhabitants of Brazil and owners of the lands invaded by the Portuguese in 1500.

3.4 Political Transition Between Continuities and Permanencies and the Paradox of the Inclusion of the Exclusion of the Indians in Brazil

It is worth repeating that the political transition in Brazil has been in "slow motion" (Brito 2013: 235). With regard to the extremely grave violations of Indigenous Peoples' rights, the gains made by the indigenous movement in the 80s and 90s, with the Constitution of 88, have met with strong resistance and, in recent years, have receded.

The grave facts narrated first in the Figueiredo Report and later in the CNV Report, even though they have been investigated by Parliamentary Commissions and by the Russell Tribunal, have not been made known and have not sensitised society to the fact that the Indians were victims of the military dictatorship. During the 80s and 90s, even when the indigenous movement gained considerable momentum in the context of the realisation of ECO92, and counted upon the support of Prince Charles, the singer Sting and the former French first lady Danielle Mitterrand, there was no mention of the need to "reckon" with the violations suffered by the Indians during the military dictatorship. At that time, the central theme was the preservation of the Amazon Rainforest ("the lung of the world") and, as a corollary of this, the preservation of the Indians as guardians of the rainforest. The debate was not deepened about the expansionist and capitalist dynamic that fueled the devastation of the Amazon and the extermination of the Indians as a legacy of the dictatorship and political authoritarianism.

The indigenous movement gained strength and actively participated in the constituent process that resulted in the Federal Constitution of 1988. The redemocratisation, although it has been a gradual and slow process incapable of elaborating the past of the military dictatorship, leaving many scars and continuities, had as a benchmark the constituent process that resulted in the Federal Constitution of 1988. The Constituent Assembly was set up by a constitutional amendment to the Constitution of 1967/69 as a kind of bridge that would lead the Brazilian nation, with no greater traumas, from dictatorship to democracy. The new constitution was originally not projected as a founding moment for the exercise of popular sovereignty, but much more as a artifice that would prevent a genuine rupture with the old regime. What happened was that, throughout the constituent process, the Constitution was "occupied" by social movements and protest. The intense popular participation of movements such as those of street children, women, environmentalists and also Indians resulted in a Constitution that, although very far from the reality of Brazil at that time, projected a Country of men and women, Indians and non-Indians, whites and blacks, locals and foreigners, free and equal.

The Constitution of 88, a normative framework of political transition, in the chapter titled "The Indians", recognises the Indians' right to their social organisation, customs, languages, beliefs and traditions, as well as "the original rights over the lands they traditionally occupy" (art. The Constitution defines "traditionally occupied" lands as those inhabited by the Indians on a permanent basis, those used for their productive activities, those indispensable for the preservation of the environmental resources necessary for their well-being and those necessary for their physical and cultural reproduction, according to their practices, customs and traditions. In this way, it recognises not only the originariness of the Indians' rights to the lands they inhabit, but also the vital and cultural nexus that binds the Indian to the land.

The Federal Constitution has not performed any miracles, since the land conflicts and despoliations of the lands have never ceased to occur, this being the reality of social forces in the Brazilian countryside. However, at first, the Judiciary and especially the Federal Supreme Court (STF), proceeded to adopt the constitutional text as a normative and political framework. In the 1990s we can highlight the position of Minister Francisco Rezek in the case of the Krenak Indians of Minas Gerais, judged in 1993. Rezek acknowledged the "indubitable immemorial presence of the Krenak and Pojixá Botocudos in the disputed area", based on numerous documents that, since 1918, attested to the presence of these Indians in the location already in the 1910s. Rezek further argued that the defendants themselves acknowledged in the records that the Krenak occupied the disputed lands and had been brutally transferred from them in the 1950s and 1970s. Analysing the anthropological data, the rapporteur rejected the defendants' arguments that the Krenak were an extinct ethnic group, demonstrating how these people, who at one point were reduced to two individuals no longer of reproductive age, later regrouped. The thesis of the "abandonment of the lands" by the Indians in 1958 was rejected, based on the provisions of the constitutions of 34, 37 and 46, prior to such date, which had already transferred such lands to the Union. Thus, "the unshakeable fact remains that, if land abandonment occurred in 1958 (…) such fact is totally ineffectual for the purpose of transferring the ownership of the same lands that had already been integrated into the Union's patrimony". Consequently, the STF declared "radically void" the title deeds granted to the defendants by the State of Minas Gerais. Another example is the decision, dated 1998, in which the Panará Indians obtained reparation, since in the 1970s they had suffered forced evictions and unhealthy contact that decimated half of their population (Brasil/CNV 2014: 199). However, four years after the decision in the Krenak case, in the judgment of *Recurso Extraordinário* no. 219983-3/98, the STF decided a similar question in a completely different way. In that case, the court established in an unprecedented way the timeframe of the Constitution of 1988 for the recognition of the Indians' right to the lands inhabited by them. The rapporteur of the case, Minister Marco Aurélio, concluded that "items I and XI of article 20 of the Federal Constitution do not cover situations where, "in memorable times, the lands were occupied by Indigenous Peoples". In an argument reminiscent of the position of Minister Cordeiro Guerra in 1980, the Rapporteur pointed out that a "different conclusion would imply, for example, allege that the whole of Rio de Janeiro consubstantiates Union land, which would be a real absurdity".[1]

By establishing the timeframe ("*marco temporal*") of the 1988 Constitution for the localisation of the right of the Indians to the lands where they live, the STF broke both

---

[1] Marco Aurélio Melo, *voto*, RE 219.983-3/98, Grifo nosso.

with its own tradition and that of Brazilian constitutionalism, respecting the series of Brazilian constitutions from 1934 to the present day, including authoritarian ones, that recognised the rights of the Indians to the lands which they inhabited. This right, as described above, has its philosophical foundation in the fact that the Indians were the original inhabitants of the lands they used to call Pindorama, of which they were legitimate owners or masters. Until 1998 even in the case of extinct Indian settlements, those original rights were recognised. In 2010 when the Raposa Serra do Sol case was judged, the STF issued Summula 650/2010, which determines that the extinct Indian settlements or even the lands occupied by Indigenous Peoples in the remote past are not Union assets. Based on Summula 650/2010, which has no binding effect, the STF denied the Indians rights over the Limão Verde Indigenous Land. For the STF, the concept of "lands traditionally occupied by Indians" does not encompass those that were owned by natives in the remote past.

The use of the notion of a "timeframe" with the application of Summula 650/2010 excludes any possibility of transitional justice in relation to the Indigenous Peoples who were exterminated or expropriated during the military dictatorship. It is not possible to speak of transitional justice if the Indians can not recover their original right to the lands where they lived until they were expelled and persecuted by the military regime. As long as the Federal Supreme Court does not reverse its position on the timeframe, all efforts toward transition justice in relation to the Indians will be futile.

Many efforts have been made in this direction, especially after the release of the CNV Report. We can mention the historic judgment in September 2014 by the Amnesty Commission of the Ministry of Justice in the case of the Aikewara (the Suruí of Pará), which recognised the action of repression and exception on the part of the Brazilian State against "the whole of an indigenous community" and officially asked for forgiveness, "this being the first conquest by the indigenous movement towards a new benchmark in the concept of Transitional Justice" (Brasil/CNV 2014: 199–200). The *Ministério Público Federal* (MPF, the Federal Prosecution Service) has created a Working Group and has been taking a series of measures aimed at bringing justice to the Indians who have been stripped of their territories and their right to live their traditional culture fully and freely. The mechanisms of reparation suppose that individuals had their lives interrupted by the military dictatorship. Very recently the MPF has filed a lawsuit claiming a high level of indemnification for the Waimiri-Atroari people for the tragedy of their destruction by the Brazilian state under the military dictatorship.[2] But again we ask ourselves (Neuenschwander Magalhães 2016), like Roy Wagner and also Viveiros de Castro, if it is not a mistake to think of the Indians' expectations of reparation based on our own expectations.

---

[2] MPF. Ação civil pública "Povo Krenak" N. 0064483-95.2015.4.01.3800. http://www.mpf.mp.br/mg/sala-de-imprensa/docs/acp-reformatorio-krenak.pdf/view. MPF. Pedido de anistia política ao povo Krenak. http://www.prmg.mpf.mp.br/instituicao/arquivos%20/requerimento-anistia-krenak.

3.5 Final Considerations

The retrogression in the recognition of the Indians' rights to their lands, especially when it is captained by the STF, the same STF that reaffirmed the official interpretation and validity of an amnesty law condemned by the Inter-American Court of Human Rights, shows there exists a connection between the absence of true transitional justice in Brazil and the grave violations of the rights of Indigenous Peoples that still continue today. The STF thus places itself in the sad situation both from a legal and philosophical point of view, of grave social and democratic regression, reiterating the form of inclusion of the exclusion of the Indians in the reparatory process inherent to the memory of the military dictatorship. That is why, even today, after more than 30 years since the beginning of the transition, we seek to denounce the project "of a repressive citizenship process, euphemised as 'social inclusion' whose perverse effect, if not the ill-concealed objective, is to reduce the intractable indigenous multiplicity (…) to an homogeneous, obedient and hopeful workforce, a welfare-dependent poor (woefully, even more so), an eternal candidate for some 'qualification' (Viveiros de Castro 2015: 15). As a Krenak Indian, Douglas, said, for them the dictatorship began long before the 60s (Demeter 2017: 52). We could add: for them, the dictatorship continues long after it has ended.

References

Araújo, V. (ed.). 2006. *Povos indígenas e a "lei dos brancos": o direito à diferença.* Brasília: Ministério da Educação, Secretaria de Educação Continuada, Alfabetização e Diversidade; LACED/Museu Nacional.

Almeida, M.R.C. 2013. *Metamorfoses indigenas. identidade e cultura nas aldeias coloniais do Rio de Janeiro.* Rio de Janeiro: FGV/Faperj.

Azevedo, M.M. 2008. Diagnóstico da população indígena no Brasil. *Ciência e Cultura* 60 (4).

Arquidiocese de São Paulo. 1985. *Brasil nunca mais: um relato para a história.* Petrópolis: Vozes.

Brasil/CNV. 2014. *Relatório da Comissão Nacional da Verdade, vol.2.* Violação de Direitos Humanos dos Povos Indígenas. Brasília: CNV.

Brito, A. B. 2013. "Justiça transicional" em câmara lenta: o caso do Brasil. In *O passado que não passa*, ed. Antônio Costa Pinto and Francisco Carlos Palomanes Martinho, 235–260. Rio de Janeiro: Civilização Brasileira.

Carneiro da Cunha, M. 1987. *Os direitos dos índios. Ensaios e documentos.* São Paulo: Editora Brasiliense.

Carneiro da Cunha, M. 2012. *Índios no Brasil. História, direitos e cidadania.* São Paulo: Claro Enigma.

Carneiro da Cunha, M. 2014. O STF e os índios. Disponível em http://www1.folha.uol.com.br/fsp/opiniao/196246-o-stf-e-os-indios.shtml.

Chaves, A. 1979. Indio. *Revista de Informação Legislativa* 62: 117–132.

Cohn, S.C. (ed.). 2015. *Ailton Krenak.* Rio de Janeiro: Azougue.

Dallari, D.A. 2000. Terras indígenas: a luta judicial pelo direito. In *Conflitos de direitos sobre as terras Guarani Kaiowá no estado do Mato Grosso do Sul*, ed. Conselho Indigenista Missionário, Comissão Pró Índio de São Paulo, Procuradoria Regional da República da 3a Região. São Paulo: Palas Athena.

Davis, S. 1978. *Vítimas do milagre: o desenvolvimento e os indios do Brasil*. Rio de Janeiro: Zahar Editores.

Demétrio, A. 2017. *A (In) justiça de transição para os povos indígenas no Brasil*. Unpublished master's thesis, Pontificia Universidade Católica do Paraná, Curitiba.

Ianni, O. 1986. *Ditadura e Agricultura. O desenvolvimento do capitalismo na Amazônia: 1964–1978*, 2a ed. Rio de janeiro: Civilização Brasileira.

Kehl, M.R., and D. Pieri. 2015. STF na ponta da flecha. *Folha de São Paulo*, April 19.

Luhmann, N. 1997. *Die Gesellschaft der Geselschaft*. Frankfurt am Main: Suhrkamp.

Neuenschwander Magalhães, J. 2013. *A formação do conceito de direitos humanos*. Curitiba: Juruá.

Neuenschwander Magalhães, J. 2014. Los límites del multiculturalismo en las sociedades multiculturales: formas de inclusión y exclusión. *Forum Historiae Iuris - Erste europäische Internetzeitschrift für Rechtsgeschichte* 1: 1.

Neuenschwander Magalhães, J. 2015. Diversidade Cultural e Justiça de Transição. *Quaderni Fiorentini* 44: 1137–1163.

Neuenschwander Magalhães, J. 2016. La costruzione giuridica della diversità. Per un dialogo tra antropologia e diritto a partire dal prospettivismo multinaturalista. In *Diversità e discorso giuridico. Temi per un dialogo interdisciplinare su diritti e giustizia in tempo di transizione*, org. Massimo Meccarelli, 41–74. Madrid: Universidad Carlos III de Madrid.

OIT. Convenção no 169 sobre Povos Indígenas e Tribais em Países Independentes. http://www.planalto.gov.br/ccivil_03/_ato2004-2006/2004/decreto/d5051.htm.

Ribeiro, D. 1995. *O povo brasileiro. a formação e o sentido do Brasil*. São Paulo: Companhia das Letras.

Rosa, J.G. 2006. *Grande sertão: veredas*. Ed. Comemorativa. Rio de Janeiro: Nova Fronteira.

Souza Filho, C.F.M. 1998. *O renascer dos povos indígenas para o direito*. Curitiba: Juruá.

Valente, R. 2017. *Os fuzis e as flechas. História de sangue e resistência indígena na ditadura*. São Paulo: Companhia das Letras.

Viveiros de Castro, E. 2014. *A inconstância da alma selvagem*. São Paulo: Cosac Naif.

Viveiros de Castro, E. 2015. Alguma coisa vai ter que acontecer. In *Encontros*, ed. Ailton Krenak, 8–19. Rio de Janeiro: Azougue.

Wagner, R. 2012. *A invenção da cultura*. São Paulo: Cosac Naif.

Juliana Neuenschwander Magalhães is Professor of Sociology of Law, Legal History and Human Rights at the Federal University of Rio de Janeiro and researcher of CNPq. She received her LLM from Federal University of Santa Catarina, JSD from Federal University of Minas Gerais and JSD from Università degli Studi di Lecce. She was research scholar at the Max Planck Institute for European Legal History (Frankfurt am Main) and was visiting professor at Birkbeck College, University of London. Her main research interests are sociology and history of human rights, system theory and law and politics.

Chapter 4
Unemployed People in Street Protests: Theories of Political Transitions and the Limits of the Brazilian Democratization

Maria Pia Guerra

Abstract Theories of political transitions have traditionally oscillated between top-down, institutionalist analysis and bottom-up analysis influenced by theories of new social movements. This chapter takes as its point of departure a political conflict at the end of the military regime in Brazil—the looting waves of 1983—in order to analyze social exclusions promoted by the political transition and later reinforced by its theoretical accountings. The narrative depicts three descriptive categories representing distinct levels of exclusion: looters, who contested a consensual transition; unemployed people, isolated by historical poverty and the local associativism; and impoverished criminals, entrenched in long-term institutional mechanisms. The result is a portrait of the people on the fringe of the transition.

4.1 Introduction

The literature of political transitions has traditionally oscillated between top-down, institutionalist analysis and bottom-up analysis influenced by theories of new social movements. This chapter takes as its point of departure a political conflict at the end of the military regime in Brazil—the looting waves of 1983—in order to analyze social exclusions promoted by the political transition and later reinforced by its theoretical accountings.

The chapter is divided into five parts. The first part presents two of the main explanatory currents about transitions in Latin America: transitology and the theory of the new social movements. The aim is to indicate potentialities and limits of the traditional analyses in relation to popular groups. The second part describes a case of protests and looting that occurred in 1983, in São Paulo, a case that is representative of the social tensions of the period. The aim is to introduce the event, which will be discussed in detail in the parts that follow. Thus, the third, fourth and fifth parts detail three descriptive categories representing distinct levels of exclusion: looters

M. P. Guerra (✉)
School of Law, University of Brasília, Brasília, Brazil
e-mail: mpguerra@unb.br

© Springer Nature Switzerland AG 2021   49
C. Paixão and M. Meccarelli (eds.), *Comparing Transitions to Democracy. Law and Justice in South America and Europe*, Studies in the History of Law and Justice 18,
https://doi.org/10.1007/978-3-030-67502-8_4

and troublemakers, who contested a consensual transition; the unemployed, isolated by historical poverty and the local associativism; and the impoverished criminal, entrenched in long-term institutional mechanisms. Finally, the final remarks debate the connections between these social exclusions and the theoretical models of understanding the transitional processes. If social exclusions are historically constructed, this means that narratives concerning the past and the future also constitute those exclusions. The result is a portrait of the people on the fringe of the transition.

4.2　Debates on the Latin American Political Transitions

Processes of democratization have long been under discussion among social scientists. In the background of enquiries concerning the factors and causes of regime change lie fundamental questions about what constitutes or initiates a political macro-process, what the relationship is between liberal democracy and popular sovereignty, how to found democratic societies, or even what constitutes a democracy at all.

Since the wave of democratizations in Latin America in the 1970s and 1980s, a series of studies, coming from distinct theoretical traditions, have sought to explain the phenomenon. One of the prevailing explanatory lines, represented by O'Donnell and Schmitter (1986), stressed the strategic interaction between political actors. They assumed that transitions are highly unpredictable processes that occur when past structural and behavioral parameters lose the ability to predict the outcomes of one's actions. As decisions are made based on inadequate information and short-term horizons, individual political skills become more important than they would be in normal times (O'Donnell and Schmitter 1986: 4).

This "theory of abnormality" has the quality of putting into perspective the structural determinants of previous analytical traditions, seeking the roles played by each class, social group, or institution in specific historical processes (Collier 1999). However, it ends up promoting another restriction: that of an analysis centered on the State and political elites, to the detriment of other collective actors not strategically oriented.[1] For O'Donnell and Schmitter (1986), these non-institutional social groups would emerge at the beginning of liberalization—when the mitigation of censorship and repression lowers the cost of popular participation—but would decline with the rise of the new democratic government, supplanted by formal channels of political representation (Schmitter 1993: 6). In a similar vein, Stepan (1988) argues that non-institutional social groups arise because of the lack of adequate political instruments for representation, which then replace the non-institutional social groups when they

---

[1] The process of liberalization as described by these authors has three phases. First, members of the authoritarian group conflict over issues concerning the regime consolidation and split into factions that vie for power. Second, the faction aligned with the liberalization gains prominence and starts the abertura, even though it places itself in a risky position, since the revocation of any emergency acts restores the freedom to organize and protest to oppositional groups. Third, authoritarian elites negotiate the terms of their departure with moderate political elites. Non-institutional social groups, though considered relevant, remain exogenous elements.

are reestablished. In either sense, social movements would thus be rather temporary, or at least insufficient for the consolidation of democracy (Avritzer 2000: 70).

Those findings present significant limitations, considering that this period marks what was heralded as a "rebirth of civil society" in Latin America. A multiplicity of actors and interests entered the public sphere in the 1970s and 1980s, such as workers, women, and students, as well as small-scale community movements that demanded housing, food, or a better cost of living. In this context, another series of studies, inspired mainly by theories of new social movements, sought to understand the particularities of those movements. Despite the pluralistic nature of this effort, it is possible to list common features (Alonso 2009). As with much of transitology studies, this series of studies rejected deterministic explanations connected with historical materialism. Movements could not be identified with a singular class, such as workers, because they constitute themselves in a process of collective identity construction, subject to constant redefinition (Sader 1988: 42). Contrary to the European theories of the new social movements that inspired these studies, however, the theories on Latin America recognized in the movements of the region a combination of post-material and material demands, connecting sociocultural patterns and the economic scarcity that had previously united the workers' movements. The demand for political citizenship was coupled with the demand for social citizenship (Almeida 1983).

Developed by authors who were also frequently engaged in militancy, these theories "took on utopian overtones" (Forewaker 2001: 4). Starting from the premise that society could organize itself autonomously, via direct action, into spontaneous groupings detached from state and political parties (Doimo 1995: 48), these authors produced romanticized interpretations that understood these movements as opportunities to transform the entire political culture. With an eye toward a kind of grassroots democracy, they developed an extensive bottom-up literature. However, in spite its recognition of the inadequacies of the institutionalist approach, this literature did not go far enough in terms of deepening the theoretical understanding of democratization, since the top-down and bottom-up approaches never really met each other in the middle. At least initially, this literature had a significant analytical omission in terms of its failure to draw connections between institutional changes and popular participation (Collier 1999: 9).

In 1980s Brazil, when the process of decompression (political liberalization) from above seemed to bypass or ignore the movements and their promises of transformation, some of the new social movements' scholars were frustrated to recognize that "the growth of the social movements was actually not as extensive as initially envisioned" (Cardoso 1989: 5) and, further, that these social movements had not fulfilled the "expectations that militants and scholars had about their transforming potential" (Jacobi 1987: 20). As Cardoso noted, "the assumption that these organizations act as a single agent capable of renewing the entire political system has also become untenable" (1989: 5), whether that was because the state had become more receptive to their aims, because some of the movements' members increasingly joined political parties, or because the fragmentation of the social movements did not lead to the expansion of a common cause. Authors such as José Álvaro Moisés and Francisco

Weffort—who had maintained the potential of popular participation and dedicated their theoretical efforts to reconstructing civil society (Weffort 1988) and understanding urban protests (Moisés and Allier 1977)—reoriented their analysis in the late 1980s toward the need for rebuilding the state and democratic institutions that formally distribute power (Moisés 1988: 60; Weffort 1996).

A practical and analytical turn occurred in Brazil with the drafting of the Federal Constitution of 1988. The constituent process, the most democratic and participatory in the history of Brazil, galvanized distinct social sectors into pressure groups through mechanisms such as national campaigns to develop "popular amendments," i.e. petitions or suggestions that came directly from the citizenry (Michelis 1989). The constituent assembly became a "national unanimity" (Bastos 1985: 147), a term that, though it's viewed with some skepticism nowadays, indicates the intensity of the social mobilization. This process produced at least two significant consequences. First, it consolidated a "language of rights," similar to that of other Latin American countries. When vocalized as rights, demands for housing, land, or health lost the quality of petition and began to reverberate as requests for major social change (Forewaker 2001: 5). Second, bearing in mind ideas of popular democracy, the process allowed for the inclusion in the constitutional text of several mechanisms for social participation, especially mandatory councils and conferences in sectorial public policies. Finally, a new round of practices and studies occurred during the 1990s and 2000s, when these councils were institutionalized. As a consequence of that institutionalization, a recent body of literature has emerged, working to definitively overcome the approaches that divided social movements from institutional politics and seeking to understand these and other forms of popular participation within and outside of the state (Avritzer and Ramos 2016).

However, a few challenges remain. Firstly, it is important to understand the role played by associativism in the construction of democracy. Avritzer, in contrast to the extant literature on transitology, argues that associations play an important role in the transformation of political culture. Even if we conclude that Brazilian elites have changed very little over time, it would still be possible to recognize that there are, in Brazil, "two political cultures differentiated by the changes and continuities that might prevail at the level of Brazilian civil and political societies" (Avritzer 2000: 70). The emergence of collective forms of action renewed the stock of democratic practices, particularly at the level of civil society, by deepening democracy in a variety of ways: training citizens for political action, promoting accountability, and stimulating distributive policies, etc. (Avritzer and Ramos 2016).

Diniz (1992), on the other hand, with a more pessimistic tone, criticized the results of the democratization process with respect to the political representation of capital and labor. In spite of the incorporation of innovative social rights and mechanisms, the transition maintained the fragmented and corporatist means through which entrepreneurs access state bodies. In a similar pessimist tone, Boito (2002) has criticized the persistent corporatist form by which the state deals with unions.[2] The

---

[2] In a different perspective, Coslovsky, Pires and Bignami (2017) argues "labor unions have combined the corporatist authority they gained under state control with the autonomy they acquired

result is the difficulty, if not the unfeasibility, of constructing national democratic policies. Moreover, in more recent years, the Brazilian political and institutional scenario seems to have undergone a change in the meaning of social control, moving from social participation through councils and conferences, as in the early moments of democratization, to social participation as accountability, assigned mainly to state bodies such as the Judiciary and the *Ministério Público* (Avritzer and Marona 2017; Arantes and Moreira 2019).

In this sense, it is important to understand the margins of the Brazilian transition, or the limited inclusionary features of social participation and associativism during transition. Weffort (1996: 22) criticized the process of democratization for creating a dual system, formed by integrated and marginalized groups. For those groups with social and economic rule—and other organized segments of society—that are inside the power structure, there is a competitive political regime. For those marginalized by social, political, and cultural conditions that transform them into non-organized masses, police repression remains. Although, following Avritzer, it is possible to argue for the existence of distinct patterns of action, this classification does ring a bell with regard to the forgotten people of the Brazilian transition (Benvindo 2017).

This article will analyze a street protest at the epicenter of the Brazilian democratization. It points to some constitutive features of Latin American social movements, such as the combination of political and social demands. It signals several limits of the transitional literature, particularly with regard to excessive institutionalism and narrow-minded isolation between bottom-up and top-down lines of thinking. It also reveals the limits of the transition itself, or how certain social groups have continued to be marginalized by institutions and society. In this sense, this article covers an event that serves as a symbol of the limits of the Brazilian political transition.

4.3　Street Protests During the Brazilian Political Transition: The Case of Looting in São Paulo (1983)

In the late 1970s and early 1980s, a series of street protests in Brazil's largest regional capitals made the transitional process even more troublesome. These protests, especially the wave of looting in São Paulo, Rio de Janeiro, and the Northeast in 1983, allow us to understand exclusions promoted not only by the military regime, but also by the transition and the Constituent Assembly themselves.

As noted above, in addition to changing forms of government, new political and economic factors gave unforeseen contours to the hitherto controlled decompression promoted by the military regime and paved the way for the emergence of new political relations.

The first factor concerns the emergence of new social movements, which reinforced the wide-ranging expectations for social transformation related to the end of

---

under democratization to devise new modes of action and to safeguard existing regulations". See also Davis and Faletti (2017).

the military regime. The presence of people occupying the streets, at least with this intensity, was a novelty in the Brazilian political scene. Thus, the way they might come to be incorporated into public life could signal specific openings or closures for the coming years.

The second factor concerns the major economic crisis that deteriorated the Brazilian population's living conditions and limited the possibilities of the military and civilian government for responding to social demands. In 1983, about 25% of the metropolitan population of the city of São Paulo was unemployed, and about 43.2% survived on only the minimum wage (Munhoz 1989). This was the same challenge faced by many other Latin American countries, where the democratization processes overlapped with a new international economic orientation that limited the available financial resources for the universalization of social rights.

The third factor, circumscribed to the states of São Paulo, Rio de Janeiro and Minas Gerais (the most populous in Brazil), concerns the combination of military government at the federal level and the presence of a civilian oppositional government in those influential states in the early 1980s. The 1982 elections for governors weakened the military regime. They brought to power, for example, André de Franco Montoro, the first opposition governor elected in the state of São Paulo since 1964, whose campaign platform promised, among other projects, the reform of the government apparatus and the implementation of a human rights policy against the dictatorial arbitrariness. In this sense, his project seemed to meet with those of social movements that opposed the dictatorial government. However, a further deepening of the economic crisis imposed additional challenges for the regional government, leading not only to an increase in demonstrations, but also to a rise in the crime rate and, as a consequence, to an evolving sense of social disorder that bolstered the resistance, both in civil society and in the military milieu, to governments inclined toward liberalization.[3] That is to say, the crisis emphasized the very limits of the project of the electoral opposition. Montoro's impasse is thus a symbol of the impasses of the Brazilian transition: how far could it go toward guaranteeing equality and restoring the social order?

4.4 Looters and Troublemakers: Political Citizenship in the New Republic

From April 4 to 6, 1983, just two weeks after the inauguration of the civilian and opposition Governor Franco Montoro, a wave of looting took place in the city of São Paulo. The riot began at a regular demonstration of the "Movement against Unemployment and High Cost of Living" in Santo Amaro, a popular and crowded district where unemployed people traditionally sought work. As the movement's leaders addressed bystanders at the square, a small group headed for a truckload laden with oranges from the public food company COPAL and began launching them

---

[3] O Palácio dos atônitos. 1983. Veja, April 13th, p. 39. Also Caldeira (2000).

at police officers and shop windows. As the first person shouted "Take everything!!," the mob got out of control. As described by a well-known newspaper: "The artillery of fruits at 10 am on the 4th of April 1983 was the first violent sign that a huge gunpowder barrel was about to explode in the largest Brazilian city. Within 48 h, São Paulo lived under the impression that peace was murdered in the streets".[4] What was left behind was impressive: looted commercial areas, public facilities, cars destroyed, 375 people detained, dozens of people injured, and one fatality, supposedly killed in retaliation by a burglary victim in retaliation.[5]

The wave of looting did not achieve the same positive support in mainstream media as other social movements had, such as the religious organizations that denounced torture and the communities that demanded public utilities (Serbin 2001; Moises 1982). In the State of São Paulo, the newspapers emphasized from the very beginning the dangers of social collapse. Assuming the existence of a moral economy that guides collective action and institutional responses (Thompson 1971), such an economy in Brazil was oriented toward rejecting violent movements. The Catholic Church, for example, only emerged as an opposition leader to the regime after having adopted a doctrine of non-violent resistance and moderating her radical positions over the course of the 1970s. As Zirker (1999: 275) points out, "The dictatorship's Achilles tendon, its fragile sense of legitimacy, had been stretched upon the breaking point by modest acts of nonviolent resistance." During this wave of looting, according to Napolitano (1995), this aspect of the Brazilian transition manifested itself as an opposition between the looter and the orderly citizen, the same one who, in the following years, would participate in a consensual way in other street protests, such as the movement for direct elections for the presidency (*Diretas Já*).

Critics of the act of looting yet recognized the existence of a perilous economic situation that subjected individuals to difficult choices. Thus, left-wing newspapers and journalists reported that "hunger rebellion shakes São Paulo",[6] noting the "claims to collect a historical social debt".[7] Even more conservative positions emphasized social penury as the true promoter of disorder because "What promotes the explosion is not the fuse, but the existence of the explosive".[8] However, in general, critics focused on the illegitimacy of violence. As noted by the influential Cardinal Dom Evaristo, "the current economic situation is urgent, but it is the government's responsibility to prevent a peaceful and orderly movement from descending into plunder, aggression, and disorder".[9] Furthermore, "Fraternity is the solution. Violence is the way to chaos".[10]

---

[4] Negros dias de abril. 1983. Veja, April 13. p. 28.

[5] Negros dias de abril. 1983. Veja, April 13. p. 27. Also Silva (2017).

[6] Rebelião da fome sacode São Paulo. 1983. Tribuna do Povo, April.

[7] É cobrança de dívida social. 1983. Folha de São Paulo, April 8th, p. 13.

[8] Freitas, Jânio. 1983. O caos visto por trás. Folha de São Paulo, April 7th, p. 5.

[9] Evitar o desespero: apelo contra a violência em geral formulado pelo Cardeal Dom Evaristo durante a páscoa. 1983. Folha de São Paulo, April 5th, p. 2.

[10] Fraternidade é a solução. Violência é o caminho para o caos. 1983. Folha de São Paulo, April 6th.

The burden of illegitimacy seems to have weighed heavily on those who were present. A series of interviews conducted by Stroh a few years later reveals some ambiguity and hesitation regarding the episode. On the one hand, a few of them rejoiced at breaking the rules of social conduct: "I sincerely laughed at people leaving with bundles of things in their arms, it was the greatest euphoria, you realize the guys' joy at having things. I laughed at the way the guys went into the supermarket as if it was theirs. They said, it's ours, naturally."[11] On the other hand, others sought to dissociate their conduct from criminal self-indulgence or mere disorder, either for fear of possible criminal charges or of moral condemnation: "I mean, I myself didn't do anything, I didn't steal anything, I only broke a few windows" (Stroh 1989: 117). Or another: "the important thing is that nobody was drunk, no one had been drinking" (Stroh 1989: 121). A similar sense of hesitation was reported by a mainstream newspaper. This account, however, adds a new distinction, between peaceful individuals and an irrational crowd in fury.[12] Thus, the paper reported: "it was as if a herd of cattle threatened to enter their house".[13]

Violence demanded a firm response from the government, one that would solve the economic situation and, especially, control the disordered population (Ferreira 2009, 34). The violence of the multitude granted the state the authorization to act with "vigor," in the name of order. As a journalist said: "There are times when violence is sacred, because the law (...) has to be an Ordination, an order'".[14] Governor Montoro had previously sought to differentiate himself from the repressive dictatorial regime.[15] He resisted sending the police to repress the looting, a fact noticed by newspapers as an initial omission in the face of vandalism.[16] However, from the moment the movement became associated with crime and disorder—and especially when the depredations approached rich neighborhoods (Stroh 1989: 134)—state bodies were granted, albeit informally, the authorization to resort back to their former

---

[11] In detail: "They simply said: we took it. There was not much concern with a moral issue, of never having done it" (Stroh 1989: 147). "I myself did not loot, but everyone said it was a wonderful feeling. That it is a pleasure to leave carrying all that from inside" (Stroh 1989: 147). "When we passed by the store, there was no other way, a guy said like that: 'you know what, I'm going to take a sack of rice home.' Then the other one said 'I'm going to take a little cookie.' You know that it is even a pretty nice thing to see? The manager came in and said he could not, etc., but then came another guy with a packet of cookies. The guys took everything" (Stroh 1989: 124). "Break it all. If the poor man can't, the rich man can't either. Only the rich have the right? The poor have the right, too" (Stroh 1989: 145).

[12] O saque, uma loucura. 1983. Estado de São Paulo, April 5th.

[13] Negros dias de abril. 1983. Veja, April 13. p. 28.

[14] Queiroz, P. 1983. Democracia, governo de deuses. Folha de São Paulo, April 7th, p. 2.

[15] Pimentel admite demora para agir. 1983. Folha de São Paulo, April 8th, p. 13.

[16] Um dia de tumulto e omissão policial. 1983. Estado de São Paulo, April 5th. Stroh's interviewees confirmed that delay, stating that the police were initially restrained from use violent means, either because the crowd far exceeded the number of police officers present or because they had been ordered not to "beat anyone." In the words of an interviewee: "The lieutenant came and negotiated with us. He said: 'we are not going to hit you, you can do the demonstration, you can continue the movement. We are not allowed to beat you up.' We agreed and to some extent, they kept their promise, until 11 a.m." (Stroh 1989: 120).

patterns of repression.[17] Although the boundary between direct action and criminal insurrection is tenuous, and the allegation of vandalism and violence had also been used by the military regime (Serbin 2001), the mark of lawlessness pushed away not only conservative organizations, such as the Trade Association of São Paulo (Stroh 1989: 132), but also some leftist politicians and organizations, which identified in the looting the infiltration of right-wing militants.[18]

Perhaps the construction of the looting as illegitimate—and, as a result, the silence around it in the years to come—can be clarified in comparison to another street protest of the same period, the *Diretas Já*. Beginning at the end of 1983, a series of rallies throughout the country asked for a constitutional amendment that would establish direct elections for the presidency. The rallies grew as the indirect elections approached and galvanized a significant share of the Brazilian population. On January 12, 1984, the Curitiba rally had 40,000 people; on April 10, the Rio de Janeiro rally registered more than one million, and on April 16, the rally in São Paulo registered about one million and a half, forcing television broadcasters to finally carry out extensive coverage of the movement (Bertoncelo 2007: 163).

The demand for direct elections took on great symbolic strength, functioning as an open bond that allowed social groups as distinct and antagonistic as politicians, businessmen, artists, unions, and local associations to associate with each other (Mendonça 2004: 60). Opposition politicians tried to capitalize on the social mobilization to acquire political resources they could use in Congress, while also taking into account an eventual rejection of the amendment, with indirect elections as usual (Rodrigues 1999). This ambiguous position—the attempt to please civil society while, foreseeing the defeat of the amendment, also working to ensure a future personal political victory—explains why Franco Montoro and Tancredo Neves, the governor of Minas Gerais and the presidential candidate under indirect elections, moderated their opposition to the regime and opposed the March rally in São Paulo, even as they showed signs of support for the movement and amendment (Bertoncelo 2007: 155). However, a striking social mobilization coupled with a certain carnivalesque autonomy from the state removed the politicians from control of the situation. The movement was taken over by an active and engaged civil society that political elites had failed to perceive clearly, and even though the amendment was rejected in the end—resulting in the indirect election of President Tancredo Neves and former ally of the military regime Vice-President José Sarney—*Diretas Já* had already changed the course of the transitional process, burying the legitimacy of the military government and affirming the participation of civil society in democratization.

---

[17] As an interviewee said: "The police came in and beat us up. The lieutenant told us: 'Sure you should be beaten up, you guys lost control of the movement'" (Stroh 1989: 125). Governor Montoro had provided buses so that demonstrators in front of the government headquarters could return to Santo Amaro. However, the buses were plundered, which generated a reaction from the police. As reported by Veja magazine, "Military police soldiers beat passengers on all the buses that arrived in Largo May 13 with broken windows" (Negros dias de abril. 1983. Veja, April 13. p. 28).

[18] Brizola aponta relação entre distúrbios e atentados terroristas. 1983. Folha de São Paulo, April 8th, p. 14.

Diretas Já produced two effects on the transitional process. On the one hand, though it was not the only one of its kind, it was the first mass movement in decades that took place in public space and was welcomed for its political strength. It revealed a new kind of political actor and offered a new place for his expression: the streets (Bertoncelo 2007: 199). By suppressing the images of an apathetic and amorphous society, it laid the foundations for social participation both in the constituent assembly and in the New Republic. On the other hand, however, *Diretas Já* was generally described in association with a non-confrontational type of politics, through a narrative constructed with the support of mainstream media. As described by Napolitano (1995), Diretas Já's citizens, unlike the looters, joined a "festival of democracy." Thus, the newspaper *O Estado de São Paulo* exalted "the great civic celebration in the best Carioca style, where irreverence and joy came altogether with a sincere public cry with a political nature".[19] In the same vein, the newspaper *Folha de São Paulo* explained, "in none of these concentrations, at any moment, did the slightest manifestation of anger, incivility, lack of control occur; these multitudes possess the maturity and tranquility of those who fight for a new destiny".[20]

From the lootings to *Diretas Já* the transitional process constituted the image of an orderly citizen, present in the streets, but ready to join in consensus. Both protests were connected, in their own way, to institutional politics, a fact that signals the limits of an institutionalist understanding of politics. *Diretas Já* confronted parliamentary and governmental negotiations by re-signifying the idea of direct elections. The wave of looting, as one can tell by observing whom the looters acted against, confronted both the market—through establishments that sell basic goods—and the state, insofar as the looters criticized the absence of social and economic policies to reduce famine (Sader 1987). Looters ransacked supermarkets and shops. They invaded police stations to rescue those who had been arrested (Ferreira, 2009: 19). They destroyed public and state utilities and equipment (Sader 1987). They also destroyed the gates of the state government building, just after they had destroyed, on their way there, a statue in honor of the then-President Figueiredo's father (Stroh, 1989: 135), with chants of "Down with Figueiredo! We want jobs!" (Ferreira 2009: 40). Although the looting was not directly connected to electoral politics, they certainly reacted against poverty and pointed out those whom they considered guilty, a posture that seems to have bewildered analysts:

> What cannot be accepted is that the same population that massively voted for the opposition candidates now contests the order only twenty days after the inauguration of new leaders. What seems unlikely is that those who broke the thresholds of the Bandeirantes Palace were truly workers, when the government cannot be blamed for the economic recession caused by other levels of power in other times.[21]

The lootings and the *Diretas Já* created a new form of participation in public space and even in institutional politics. The difference lies on the narratives concerning social order and the way those perceptions reinforced a preference for a consensual

---

[19] Festa e batucada - e a cidade para. Estado de São Paulo, April 11th, p. 7.

[20] Freitas, Jânio. 1984. A ordem das multidões. Folha de São Paulo, April 11th, p. 5.

[21] Santayana, Mauro. 1983. A serviço do caos. Folha de São Paulo, April 7th.

transition. If, on the one hand, both these movements opened up possibilities for public collective action, preparing the grounds for significant social participation at the Constituent Assembly, on the other hand, *Diretas Já*, widely acclaimed in the face of the dangers of social collapse that arouse from lootings, narrowed the forms of legitimate contestation. It was not able, however, to either solve the social and economic issues that gave rise to lootings or provide means to politically articulate the most affected groups, as one can see by the efforts to constitute a social movement for unemployed people. Even though the transition was shown as a consensual process, nonconsensual and even violent social tensions abound.

4.5 Looters and the Unemployed: Social Citizenship in the New Republic

The wave of looting in 1983 reveals a deadlock for the Brazilian transition. The renaissance of civil society coincided with—and was even the product of—a severe local economic crisis and a new global context of neoliberal ideas, which clashed with the expectation of social inclusion that was developed in the process of transition. The task of reconciling political and social citizenship was carried out in an adverse context (Almeida 1983).

The dictatorship developed a conservative type of Welfare State during its twenty years in power. Like other welfare regimes, it consolidated and expanded a national and institutional system created in the 1930s, funded by a diverse range of public means and revenues and organized by professional and bureaucratic bodies selected according to criteria of competence, with the aim of appointing specific clientele from each field to regulate the market and establish a collective consumption base (Draibe 1994: 274). During the 1960s and 1970s, the regime advanced the process of institutional centralization and extended the groups under protection. Social achievements were impressive, granting the regime popular legitimacy. Between 1970 and 1980, social security coverage increased from 2.3 to 5.3 million people. In the same period, the number of hospital admissions increased from 2.9 million to 11.7 million and the number of clinical consultations from 44 to 179 million. Between 1960 and 1980, the percentage of children in the aged 7 to 14 in school soared from 45% to a surprising 80%, supported by the creation of a nutrition program for about 17 million school-aged children (Fagnani 1997).

Other features of the system, however, had conservative contours that were clearly in evidence in the 1980s: the regressiveness of the financing mechanisms and their reduced redistributive character. The main sources of funding—except for health, food and transport policy—were social contributions, such as the FGTS, based not on income or on the circulation of general goods, but on the wages of employees. This fiscal structure resulted in a logic of "financial self-sustainability" for social policies, which were limited in at least three ways: first, by surcharging workers' payments; second, by not collecting enough funds, since the system was based on Brazil's traditionally low wages; third, by giving the system excessive cyclical sensitivity, which means that in times of crisis they were immediately restricted by the rise in unemployment. Moreover, the regressiveness existed not only in financing, but also in the supply of services. In social security, the access to the contributory system and special sub-systems was more beneficial to certain professional and corporatist categories. In the health system, the focus on hospitalization strengthened the hospital market to the detriment of preventive medicine. In housing, middle classes were preferred for they had a lower rate of default (Fagnani 1997: 192).

Between 1968 and 1973, a period known as the economic miracle, the average rate of GDP growth was 10.2% and almost 12.5% between 1971 and 1973, in contrast to an average rate of about 7% from the post-war period to the early 1960s (Lago, n.d.). Economic growth overall benefited workers and the social security system, as consequence of the increase in the wage bill. In 1974, with the slowdown of the economy, the first challenges appeared. The government under President Ernesto Geisel (1974–1979) sought to revive the economy and revise some of its policies, rationalizing administrative management and extending social security coverage. For example, he created new nutrition programs and granted everyone the right to medical care in emergencies (Fagnani 1997: 210). However, the deepening of the economic crisis and the tendency toward regressive economic measures greatly damaged state revenues. The high rates of inflation produced a violent distributive conflict and became the main driver of union action and strikes, as the result of a policy of state control over monetary correction (Noronha 2009). Between 1982 and 1984, total federal social spending fell by 27% in real terms. The impact was even greater on extra-fiscal revenues—and thus on social policies based on social contributions— which fell by 30%, compared with the 17% for fiscal revenues (Fagnani 1997: 212). In 1983, it is estimated that in the metropolitan region of São Paulo, about 30% of the population, already affected by low wages, was unemployed.

In this scenario of economic and social crisis, looting cycles erupted in São Paulo, Rio de Janeiro, and the Northeast of the country. It is significant that the looting of 1983 was initiated by an attack on the COPAL orange truck; COPAL is the state body responsible for food policy. The small margin of social protection gained in the previous decade was rapidly being torn apart. Thus, the first measure announced by the government was the food bonus, since, at least initially, unemployment insurance proposals were rejected for lack of resources.[22]

It is also in this period that the notion of the *unemployed* begins to emerge, not as a transitory and involuntary situation, but as a lasting condition, an effect and a structural element of the economic system (Guimarães 2009). Since the 1980s, even in advanced capitalist countries, long-term and recurrent unemployment has become a challenge to the state social protection system. Since then, the dichotomy of long-term occupation and occasional unemployment has been blurred, giving rise to atypical forms of work interspersed with long periods of non-occupation. In Brazil, this new model for work intensified on propitious terrain. First, because of the absence of a solid historical experience of protection, workers at the margin of the

---

[22] Um caldeirão fervente. 1983. Veja, April 13, p. 37.

economy were left more vulnerable. And second, because of the labor market regime that was historically established in the country: instead of a single structured market, in Brazil, one can see the creation of at least two sectors, formal and informal, as well as different work statuses. Among these different statuses are registered employees, unregistered employees, regular workers, "*bicos*," and self-employed workers (Guimarães 2002: 113). The occupational trajectory of poor urban Brazilian people in the 1980s already alternated among self-employment, paid employment, and unemployment (Valladares 1991: 106). The similarity with the regime that would later be instituted in Europe is such that some authors nowadays have pointed to a possible "Brasilianization of the West" (Beck 2000: 2).

Paradoxically, in the Brazil of the 1980s, the regime that consolidated permanent and recurrent unemployment was also the one that made it difficult to create a collective identity for its sufferers. That is because an identification with the idea of being unemployed depends, at least to some extent, on a distinction between employment and unemployment. As these boundaries were always blurred in Brazil, other forms of identification, such as the homeless and the landless, seemed more effective (Guimarães 2005). The process of constructing the figure of "the unemployed" in Brazil benefited from the 1983 looting episode and, subsequently and in even greater part, from the organization, in the months that followed, of the movement of the unemployed people. In fact, "the unemployed," along with "the protester," seem to have been the central characters presented by the looting episode.

In order to scrutinize the above-mentioned link between the looting episode and the construction of a social and political citizenship proper to the New Republic, it is interesting to return to the relationship between the looters and the unemployed movement. The variety of groups involved in the looting shared with the movement the social cost of unemployment and underemployment. The very choice of dates, the first days of the month, when workers receive wages and buy basic goods, already reveals the proximity with poverty and the worsening of the living conditions of the population (Zaluar 1985). However, although the looting started during a demonstration of the movement of the unemployed people, there was no direct connection between the two. When Governor Montoro, after some hesitation, decided to negotiate with the leadership, he did not obtain any results. The looters were not an organized movement, but a mass of people in agitation: "it had no leadership", "there was no convocation" (Stroh 1989: 134). Furthermore, to be perfectly accurate, the looting seems to have started not together with, but rather in opposition to, the movement, as indicated by an interviewee of Souza:

> One of the tactics was to distribute pamphlets in the region indicating that there would be job selection in the candy-making company, Adams candy, Adams chewing gum. So with that (this was done over the weekend), ... on Monday there were about five, six thousand people looking for a job, believing the pamphlet that had been made. When they arrived there was no job, it was not what they expected. Then the guys felt cheated, demanded explanations. (Stroh 1989: 110)

The origins of the unemployed people's movement can be found in the neighborhood movements, which occupy a prominent place in the Brazilian transition process. Until the early 1970s, there were still "friends of the neighborhood societies" in São Paulo and other cities: long-lasting groups that had lost much of their political strength under the strict control of the military regime. There were also "mothers' clubs," groups housed by the Catholic Church for aid and assistance activities. After 1972, some of these clubs, under the coordination of Catholic pastoralists, gradually rejected the earlier pattern of wealthy women offering assistance services and restructured themselves under the motto of "organization by us." The meetings combined labor-intensive activities traditionally reserved for women with debates about personal and social issues in light of biblical texts, a dynamic that served to re-signify aspects of domestic and political life (Sader 1988: 208).

These clubs unfolded under the Cost of Living Movement. In Doimo's analysis (1995: 96), this movement was as a large political umbrella, which house a number of organized segments in addition to the mothers' clubs, such as students' groups, Women for Amnesty, and clandestine left-wing organizations, with the support of the Catholic Church. The movement allowed for changes in the type of political influence it engendered, in comparison with former groups whose pattern of action consisted of demanding specific public utilities or services. Since the reduction in the cost of living could not be achieved in the same way as the construction of a school, a kindergarten, or a health center, members—on the one hand—had to cling to new forms of political motivation. On the other hand, they could extend and grow to amass more people. For Sader (1988: 214), this shift was a positive sign of transformation, from a clientelistic form of action into a one that confronted authorities. They instituted a "day for the fight against the cost of living," bringing petitions to authorities and assemblies. In 1975, for example, the movement organized a survey on the increase in basic good prices that compared the city outskirts with central neighborhoods. To carry out the survey, members of the movement visited various establishments and over two thousand homes, resulting in a petition to President Geisel signed by 1,250,000 people who presented themselves as "mothers in despair" (Monteiro 2015: 51).

In 1979, the movement changed its name to the Movement Against Scarcity (MAS). It suffered, however, a depletion, which can be explained by a retreat from the Catholic Church in the face of an increased presence of radical leftist groups, whose political ideas were less attuned to the specific needs of the cost of living (Monteiro 2015: 104). Its decline coincided with the diversification of countless neighborhood and sectorial movements linked to demands for housing, health, and unemployment.

The Movement against Unemployment was one of those movements that, especially in São Paulo, benefited from former members of the MAS and from the institutional support of the Catholic Church. In 1981, the National Conference of the Working Classes (I Conclat) included among its resolutions the creation of committees to combat unemployment. In the same year, the bishops of the State of Paraná issued a general appeal to parishes to reflect on the reality of unemployment. In 1983, after the wave of looting in São Paulo, Cardinal Dom Evaristo Arns issued a manifesto to all parishes calling for a Mass for the unemployed in the central square of the Sé. In that same year, the Unemployment Solidarity Association of São Paulo already had 168 "solidarity groups" (Doimo 1995: 107).

Stroh (1989: 159) links the emergence of this movement, at least in São Paulo, to a public acknowledgment of the existence of unemployment, which came about as the result of debates that took place during the 1982 electoral campaign for governor. Not only was the issue intensely discussed, it was one of Franco Montoro's most important campaign promises, including, in particular, a call for the creation of 400,000 jobs, a number that became a reference point for local movements. The issue was featured prominently in mainstream regional and local media, especially after the wave of looting, in a move that combined solidarity with unemployed people who were living in scarcity with an overall concern for the risk of social rupture.

It was, however, a long road from the existence and public recognition of unemployment to the creation of an unemployed movement. Constituting the experience of famine as a shared condition and the identification of employment as a political demand was extremely difficult. In this sense, Stroh emphasizes the difficulties of self-identifying as an unemployed people and, consequently, the challenges of forming and constituting a political movement. The social basis for the movement was comprised of individuals whose work history was compromised by unemployment, poverty, and social marginality. As the looting episode revealed, the proximity to illegality and illegitimacy made for an ambiguity that limited the possibilities of positive collective identification. That ambiguity similarly deterred the trade union movement, as noted by a union leader interviewed by Stroh (1989: 171): "In reality, what we realized is that nobody believes in the unemployed people, neither a party nor a union." It limited the possibility for communal solidarity, as demonstrated by one of Souza's interviewees (2010: 109): "the unemployed people don't mobilize because everyone is depressed, a guy is out of the production line, he doesn't feel good about being unemployed, and you have no place where you could call him to a meeting because the union is more concerned about those who can afford the monthly fee." That same ambiguity also deterred other popular movements, whose organizational logic presupposed notions of internal democracy and active participation. In the words of another interviewee: "It's not easy. You can't think it's like a factory, where you have discipline. You don't have it. These guys are moving around trying to cope with life (*Esse pessoal tá de trânsito na vida*). They live much more on courage and daring and scorn the organization as a slow-moving thing" (Stroh 1989: 172).

With regard to the movement in São Paulo, the months following the looting episode were very fruitful for the process of self-identification. On September 5, 1983, after the wave of protests, a few leaders decided to settle a camp for about 800 people in the Ibirapuera Park, which was widely visited by the middle and upper classes in the city of São Paulo. The camp lasted for sixty days, and although it was under strict surveillance, it was not immediately repressed by the police, a fact that confirms a change in security policy under Montoro. Regional authorities tried to negotiate a solution, even as they imposed clear limits on the demands and political inclusion of the protesters. On the one hand, they promised jobs for the campers and temporarily provided food baskets—a policy that had a paradoxical effect on a movement constituted under the motto of autonomy, since it required enrollment and, as a consequence, fostered the movement's organization (Stroh 1989: 169).[23] On the other hand, the regional authorities fenced in the camp, thereby limiting the circulation of campers throughout the park.[24]

As the camp continued, new forms of social hostility replaced the initial social support that had been granted the protestors, possibly due to an overall level of empathy for those who had suffered the effects of the economic crisis.[25] Being asked about the relationship between campers and the state assembly officials working in an adjoining building, a camper said:

> "At first we noticed that they were disgusted with us. (…). One day we noticed that the cups of coffee had been swapped for disposable cups. When we asked the reason, the coffee girl said there was an outbreak of hepatitis in the Assembly. I soon demanded an explanation if it was because of us. We said that we were all dirty with mud, but we had no disease. We had a big argument, but they did not put the cups back. (Stroh 1989: 186)

The act of limiting circulation throughout the park and promoting certain hygiene measures produced a new distinction, between groups that were more or less politically included, even though they all opposed the military regime. This case reveals that underneath the description of a consensual transition and alongside the image of protests as violent social disturbances was also the image of people made invisible. Though they were differentiated by their means and methods, looters and unemployed people met again on the fringe of the Brazilian civil society.

The members of the Movement against Unemployment were gradually redirected to other movements that had collective identities considered more appealing than the identity of "the unemployed" (Guimarães 2002: 114). Once the Catholic Church embraced the task of organizing those various movements under the umbrella of her grassroots associations—and especially through her ecclesial communities (Comunidades Eclesiais de Base)—the movements merged to create the Peasant Movement (Movimento dos Sem Terra) in 1984.

It is worth noting, however, that the looting, the constitution of a movement, and the intervention of the Catholic Church did have an important effect on institutional politics. In those years, state authorities created the first relevant analytical tools for understand the dimensions of these social problems, most notably the Employment and Unemployment Survey, which was carried out by renowned data gathering agencies (Jardim 2009: 126). The survey changed its research methodology to cover both overt and hidden unemployment, which affects individuals who are dissatisfied with precarious work and have sought employment in the last twelve months. During that same period, state authorities instituted unemployment insurance. On February 27, 1986, as part of the Cruzado Plan for Economic Stabilization (which exchanged currency and frozen prices and revenues), the federal government instituted a provisional benefit for unemployed people (Decree N. 2283/86). Later, the

---

[23] A similar argument, related to Argentina, can be seen in Garay (2016).

[24] From an interviewee: "The mayor had the camp fenced so that we couldn't move around the park. He delimited the area as if we'd taken the right of possession. We were suddenly squatters, that is, we took the land from city hall. That was the sense we gave it" (Stroh 1989: 194).

[25] Demitidos terão ajuda de campanha. 1983. Folha de São Paulo, April 4th, p. 12.

Federal Constitution of 1988 granted this benefit a stable funding base through the creation of an employee support fund that supports several other programs in this sector.

Since the 1990s, so-called unemployment sociology in Brazil has been developing theoretical studies on this subject. However, in contrast to what happened for example, in Argentina (Garay 2016), political movements that organize unemployed people remain scarce. Although Brazilian unions have, for the last two decades, been seriously concerned about increasing unemployment and under-employment rates, their reactions has been very limited, confined, for example, to the creation of supply programs for workers (Souza 2010). The constitution of "the unemployed" as a political actor faces the same coordinating challenges now as it faced in the 1980s.

4.6   Looters and Criminals: Notes on Legal Instrumentalization

Taking a look at one last feature of the looting episode—the often poorly analyzed judicial system—helps us to understand how the criminal and the worker met. The judiciary, called to respond after the arrest of a few looters, had to evaluate the legality and legitimacy of the participants in the looting episode and their forms of action, as well as the new ideas of *rights* developed during the transitional process.

Two suspects—Delvor Rodrigues and Benedito de Lima—were arrested during the April lootings, suspected of having participated in the looting of a clothing store in Santo Amaro. The police arrived at the crime scene only 30 min after the shop was looted, so no one was arrested during the criminal act. However, Delvor and Benedito were in the vicinity carrying a large number of items, which raised suspicions about their conduct. They were arrested *in flagrante delicto*—caught in action—after being recognized by two of the store employees, who were also taken as witnesses to the police station.

The arrest led to a criminal case (Criminal Case N. 453/1983). The prosecutor claimed that the suspects were guilty of aggravated theft because the crime had been committed in a situation of particular misfortune for the victim—Article 155 (4) (IV), Article 25 and Article 44 (II) (k), Criminal Code. The aggravating factor corresponded to the riot and was defined as "taking advantage of the misfortune of the store owners, considering that groups of unemployed people and idlers vandalized and looted local stores and supermarkets".[26] The criminal complaint replicated the commissioner's report, which argued that "the suspects were participating in the demonstration taking place in Santo Amaro when they decided to enter the establishment, which was already being looted by other rioters (idlers)".[27] After eight days in prison, the defense

---

[26] Delvor Rodrigues and Benedito de Lima v. the State of São Paulo. 25ª V. Cr., São Paulo, Brazil, 1983, p. 2.

[27] Delvor Rodrigues and Benedito de Lima v. the State of São Paulo. 25ª V. Cr., São Paulo, Brazil, 1983, p. 26.

asked for the suspects' release on the grounds that the suspects had a good criminal record and stole (if the charges were proven) only items of low value. Moreover, the defense argued that even if they were convicted, they would be entitled to *sursis*, a kind of sentence where detention gets converted into non-involving deprivation of liberty measures.[28]

Recognizing the defense's arguments, the judge released Delvor and Benedito the following day. In his ruling, rendered on April 12, he prelimi rejected the complaint and acquitted the suspects, thereby closing the case at an early stage of the process. The main reasons for this decision were neither that this was a first-time offense nor the possibility of *sursis*, but the inability of criminal law to effectively account for collective turmoil: "It is known that in these riots is rather difficult, if not impossible, to recognize people (…). Given what happened (…) I come to the conclusion that it will be fruitless for any lawsuit to determine the liability of each of the accused".[29] Modern criminal law rests on individual responsibility. It has been historically founded in an individualistic perspective of human action and, therefore, has few tools for understanding and accounting for collective actions and movements. Thus, the ruling noted that the legal system would be unfit to establish limits for collective political processes. Politics should find another way.

However, other aspects of the criminal process reveal a less explicit—albeit even more effective—way of involving the legal system in the process of constituting a society. In their opening statements, the two suspects were asked about their current occupational status. Delvor Rodrigues answered he was unemployed, and Benedito de Lima replied that he was employed by a civil construction company. Benedito presented a statement confirming that he was *tarefeiro*—paid per task—a common form of work that exempts contractors from the compliance with labor laws. Though his statement signaled his condition as a precarious worker, it was enough to relieve any suspicion of his propensity for disorderly life or activities.

The boundaries between criminal and labor law were also blurred with regard to the witnesses. Antônio Brisola Neto, one of the witnesses of the event, declared that he was a police officer who worked part-time for the Besni store during his off-hours. This type of part-time contract, known as a *bico*, though irregular before police corporations, was very common for police officers generally, who tended to be very underpaid. A kind of precariousness therefore accompanied this witness, too: in the store he was a private security worker, hired for his police skills and his license to carry weapons. In the police corporation, he was a public employee formally subject to disciplinary measures and even dismissal, even if there was an informal agreement of non-punishment. In the streets, he was a low-paid worker, afflicted by the worsening living conditions under the economic recession. In the criminal proceedings, his position became equally ambiguous. Although initially registered as witness to the incident, he had his position switched back and forth between "representative of the

---

[28] Delvor Rodrigues and Benedito de Lima v. the State of São Paulo. 25ᵃ V. Cr., São Paulo, Brazil, 1983, p. 18.

[29] Delvor Rodrigues and Benedito de Lima v. the State of São Paulo. 25ᵃ V. Cr., São Paulo, Brazil, 1983, p. 31.

interests of the victim" and, simply, "victim". By the way, the case files themselves equivocated with regard to the definition of who was the victim: the detention report and the release report named police officer Antônio Brisola, without clarifing his status as mere representative; the technical expert opinion named the Besni store; and the Commissioner's report even created a hybrid concept of *firm-victim*.[30] At no time did the storeowner's name get mentioned. Thus, the property owner was someone invisible to (and made invisible by) the criminal process.

The agents' positions in the criminal proceedings mirrored their positions in the labor market and, with respect to the suspects, mirrored their positions and forms of private life. Thus, official forms filled out by the suspects listed the information considered relevant for evaluating their personal history and were mostly designed to ascertain their profile in terms of whether they led an orderly or disorderly life. After the more usual questions of name, nationality, marital status, age, and address, the forms inquired as to occupation status and level of education. They also requested information on how formalized their family bonds were, an issue more common to the middle and upper classes: "any legitimate, illegitimate and legitimized children"; "has been raised or lived with tutors"; "has propensity for alcohol or other drugs"; "has or had mental illness or psychiatric treatment"; "is married, divorced or in cohabitation"; and "has harmonious marital life." The form also inquired about the existence of any "property owned or rented"; "real estate or bank investments"; "monthly salary"; "reasons for, if applicable, being unemployed"; "existence of relatives or dependents"; "practices of assisting persons or charities"; "prior felonies"; and "former civil and criminal proceedings". The form ended by presuming the guilt of the suspects, asking: "Do you regret having committed the crime of which you are accused or consider that your attitude was premeditated and was within your purposes"?

Combining these criteria, the judicial system signaled the selectivity of its subjects. Through historically constructed standards such as individual liability, criminal law has offered limits to claims of punishment and social control. However, through the use of unorthodox tools and informal practices, the criminal prosecution reaffirmed— for this and other cases, considering the standard forms applicable to all criminal investigations—social control initiatives originated in the labor market and in public security. During the political transition, the Criminal Case N. 453/1983 revealed a long-term social control that was operated by, and within, the law.

4.7 Final Remarks

The political transition transformed Brazilian institutions and society. The emergence of new social actors and new political practices deprived state agents of their expectations for controlling the outcomes of the transition process. Notwithstanding

---

[30] Delvor Rodrigues and Benedito de Lima v. the State of São Paulo. 25ª V. Cr., São Paulo, Brazil, 1983.

the utopian tones of early Latin American theories of the new social movements, the looting episodes of 1983 and the *Diretas Já* pressured institutions to take their citizens into account in the new political arrangements.

The lootings, in particular, signaled the positive aspects and the fundamental limits of both institutionalist and new social movements theories. Contrary to institutionalist theories of transitology, the lootings revealed, first, the limits of political representation. Even though federal military and regional civilian governments were distinct, as one may have gleaned from other institutional responses, the votes in favor of Franco Montoro, an opposition governor, had little value for the mob in action only two weeks after his inauguration—to the surprise of some analysts of the period. Moreover, the looting episode revealed that the interaction between institutional and social spheres is a complex one. This interaction can be seen in the way the rioters and demonstrators of *Diretas Já* rejected institutionality, even as they kept it as a point of reference for their actions. This complex dynamic can also be seen, to a significant degree, in the way the consensual features of the transition—which supported both an elite pact and a more general rejection of violence agreement—were constituted not only through the methodological rationality of political leaders, but also through the political practices of various social groups. This dynamic of interaction marks the political transition from the beginning of the transition through the following period, known as New Republic. To silence the relevance of these protest movements for the process of democratization is to reproduce precisely the standards for top-down governance that characterized the regime being criticized.

Contrary to the first and most optimistic theories of the new social movements, the lootings attested, on the one hand, to the dual nature of these Latin American movements, which identified with both post-material and material demands. On the other hand, the lootings pointed out the limits of creating collective identities in the face of modifications to the contemporary labor market. The unions, structured via cleavages of social class, were not able to encompass the large contingent of people who were on the outer frontiers of formal employment, frontiers that were the product of global and Brazilian economic model. Likewise, the new social movements, constituted under the idea of autonomy and direct action, imposed restrictions on the "people who were just moving around trying to cope with life" and allowed for political demobilization and social marginalization. In part, these limits resulted from the elements of political conflict that always resist being institutionalized, either by state organizations or civil society (Lefort 1983). But they are also the product of a form of associativism based on cleavages segmented by sectorial demands, in which groups preferred, for example, to be constituted not by the idea of unemployment, but by the demand for land and housing. These cleavages, though they remain connected to the challenges of social inequality, only marginally confront the features of the labor system that produce social precariousness. The absence of political responses to unemployment remains to this day.

In the end, the unemployed person, alongside the troublemaker, appeared as a central character of the transition—as the looting episode demonstrates. He exposes the impasses of a democratization that takes place in a context of historical social segregation and severe economic crisis. Democratization strengthened itself insofar as it fostered social expectations for political and economic inclusion. However, in both the judicial system and in redistributive public policies, democratization clashed with the historically institutionalized means of handling the precarious worker who lives on the outer edges of labor, poverty, and legality. It also clashed with the political lines of neoliberal theories, which sought to implement regressive economic solutions and criticized as anachronistic the proposals for the creation of a national, non-conservative welfare state made during the Constituent Assembly. The image of the unemployed person thus represents some of the main impasses in contemporary Brazil. Notably, we see this impasse in the challenge of a recent democracy that has expanded the opportunities for political participation, but kept limited any real possibilities of changing the precariousness of the life of the poor and the inequality of the country as a whole.

References

Almeida, M.H.T. 1983. É tempo de novos direitos. *Novos Estudos* 2.

Alonso, A. 2009. As teorias dos movimentos sociais: um balanço do debate. *Lua Nova, São Paulo* 76: 49–86.

Arantes, R., and T. Moreira. 2019. Democracia, instituições de controle e justiça sob a ótica do pluralismo estatal. *Opinião Pública* 25 (1).

Avritzer, L. 2000. Democratization and changes in the pattern of association in Brazil. *Journal of Interamerican Studies and World Affairs* 42 (3): 59–76.

Avritzer, L., and M. Marona. 2017. A Tensão entre Soberania e Instituições de Controle na Democracia Brasileira. *Dados* 60 (2): 359–393.

Avritzer, L., and A. Ramos. 2016. Democracy, scale and participation. Reflections from Brazilian participatory institutions. *Revista Internacional de Sociologia* 74 (3).

Bastos, M.T. 1985. *Constituinte e democracia no Brasil hoje*, ed. Emir Sader and Raimundo Faoro, 128–146. São Paulo: Editora Brasiliense.

Beck, U. 2000. *The brave new world of work.* Cambridge: Polity Press.

Benvindo, J. 2017. The forgotten people in Brazilian constitutionalism: Revisiting behavior strategic analyses of regime transitions. *International Journal of Constitutional Law* 15 (2): 332–357.

Bertoncelo, E. 2007. *A campanha das Diretas e a Democratização.* São Paulo: Fapesp.

Boito, A. 2002. Neoliberalismo e corporativismo de Estado no Brasil. In *Do corporativismo ao neoliberalismo*, ed. Angela Araujo, 59–88. São Paulo: Boitempo.

Caldeira, T. P. do Rio. 2000. *Cidade de Muros: Crime, Segregação e Cidadania em São Paulo.* São Paulo: Editora 34.

Cardoso, R. 1989. *Popular movements in the context of the consolidation of democracy.* Working Paper 120. Kellogg Institute.

Collier, R. 1999. *Paths toward democracy: The working class and elites in Western Europe and South America.* New York: Cambridge University Press.

Coslovsky, S., R. Pires, and R. Bignami. 2017. Resilience and renewal: The enforcement of labor laws in Brazil. *Latin American Politics and Society* 59 (2): 77–102.

Davis, E., and T. Falleti. 2017. Poor people's participation: Neoliberal institutions or left turn? *Comparative Political Studies* 50 (12).

Diniz, E. 1992. Neoliberalismo e Corporativismo: as duas faces do capitalismo industrial no Brasil. *Revista Brasileira de Ciências Sociais* 20 (7).

Doimo, A.M. 1995. *A vez e a voz do popular: movimentos sociais e participação política no Brasil pós-70.* Rio de Janeiro: Relume-Dumará.

Draibe, S. 1994. As políticas sociais do regime militar brasileiro 1964–1984. In *21 de Regime Militar: balanços e perspectivas*, ed. Glaucio Soares and Maria Celina D'Araujo, 271–309. Rio de Janeiro: Editora FGV.

Ferreira, C. 2009. *Representações de intolerância na imprensa escrita: saques e quebra-quebras em São Paulo*. Unpublished doctoral dissertation. Universidade de São Paulo, São Paulo, Brazil.

Fagnani, E. 1997. Política social e pactos conservadores no Brasil: 1964/92. *Economia e Sociedade* 8: 183–238.

Forewaker, J. 2001. Grassroots movements, political activism and social development in Latin America: A comparison of Chile and Brazil. *Civil Society and Social Movements Programme*, Paper Number 4. United Nations Research Institute for Social Development.

Garay, C. 2016. *Social policy expansion in Latin America*. New York: Cambridge University Press.

Guimarães, N. 2002. Por uma sociologia do desemprego. *RBCS* 17 (50): 103–121.

Guimarães, N. 2005. Brasilializando o ocidente? *Inteligência VII* 28: 92–110.

Guimarães, N. 2009. A sociologia dos mercados, ontem e hoje. *Novos Estudos* 85: 151–170.

Jacobi, P. 1987. Movimentos sociais urbanos numa época de transição: limites e potencialidades. In *Movimentos sociais na transição democrática*, ed. Eder Sader, 11–23. São Paulo: Cortez.

Jardim, F. 2009. *Do desemprego ao desempregado: desenvolvimento das políticas públicas de emprego no Brasil*. Unpublished doctoral dissertation. Universidade de São Paulo, São Paulo, Brazil.

Lago, L. n.d. Milagre Econômico. *Dicionário Histórico-Biográfico Brasileiro*. São Paulo: FGV.

Lefort, C. 1983. *A Invenção Democrática: os Limites da Dominação Totalitária*. São Paulo: Brasiliense.

Mendonça, D. 2004. *Tancredo Neves: da distensão à nova República*. Santa Cruz do Sul: Edunisc.

Michelis, C. 1989. *Cidadão Constituinte: a saga das emendas populares*. São Paulo: Paz e Terra.

Moises, J.A. 1982. *Cidade, Povo e Poder*. Rio de Janeiro: Paz e Terra.

Moisés, J.A., and R. Cusminski. 1988. Sociedad civil, cultura política y democracia. Los obstáculos de la transición política. *Revista Mexicana de Sociología* 50 (3): 37–60.

Moisés, J.A., and V. Martinez-Allier. 1977. A Revolta dos Suburbanos ou Patrão, o Trem Atrasou. *Contradições Urbanas e Movimentos Sociais* 1.

Monteiro, T. 2015. *Como pode um povo vivo viver nesta carestia: o movimento do custo de vida em São Paulo*. Unpublished master's thesis. Universidade de São Paulo, São Paulo, Brazil.

Munhoz, S.J. 1989. *A ordem do "caos" versus o ocaso da ordem: Saques e quebra- quebras em São Paulo – 1983*. Unpublished master's thesis. Universidade de Campinas, Campinas, Brazil.

Napolitano, M. 1995. O protesto de rua nos anos oitenta e a crise do regime militar. *Revista de Sociologia e Política* 4 (5): 161–174.

Noronha, E. 2009. Ciclo de greves, transição política e estabilização: Brasil, 1978–2007. *Lua Nova* 76: 119–168.

O'Donnell, G., and P. Schmitter. 1986. *Transitions from authoritarian rule: Comparative perspectives*. London: Johns Hopkins Press.

Rodrigues, A.T. 1999. Democracia e mobilização social: participação autônoma e instituições políticas na transição brasileira. *Revista de Sociologia e Política* 12: 99–119.

Sader, E. 1987. Movimentos populares na transição inconclusa. *Lua Nova* 13.

Sader, E. 1988. *Quando novos personagens entram em cena*. Rio de Janeiro: Paz e Terra.

Schmitter, P. 1993. *Some propositions about civil society and the consolidation of democracy*. IHS Reihe Politikwissenschaft 10.

Serbin, K. 2001. *Diálogos na sombra: Bispos e militares, tortura e justiça social na ditadura*. São Paulo: Companhia das Letras.

Silva, M. 2017. O motim de 1983 contra a fome e o desemprego em São Paulo. *Projeto História* 58: 344–362.

Souza, D. 2010. *Sindicalismo e desempregados no Brasil e na Argentina de 1990 a 2002*. Unpublished doctoral dissertation. Universidade de São Paulo, São Paulo, Brazil.

Stepan, A. 1988. *Democratizando o Brasil*. Rio de Janeiro: Paz e Terra.

Stroh, P.Y. 1989. *Vai trabalhar vagabundo: a exclusão social e o protesto político dos desempregados em São Paulo.* Unpublished doctoral dissertation. Pontifícia Universidade Católica de São Paulo, São Paulo, Brazil.

Thompson, E. 1971. The moral economy of the English crowd in the eighteenth century. *Past and Present* 50: 76–136.

Valladares, L. 1991. Cem anos pensando a pobreza no Brasil. In *Corporativismo e desigualdade: a construção do espaço público no Brasil*, ed. Renato Boschi, 81–112. Rio de Janeiro: IUPERJ.

Weffort, F. 1988. Por que democracia? In *Democratizando o Brasil*, ed. Alfred Stepan, 483–520. Rio de Janeiro: Paz e Terra.

Weffort, F. 1996. *Qual democracia?* São Paulo: Companhia das Letras.

Zaluar, A. 1985. *A máquina e a revolta: as organizações populares e o significado da pobreza.* São Paulo: Brasiliense.

Zirker, D. 1999. The Brazilian church-state crisis of 1980: Effective nonviolent action in a military dictatorship. In *Nonviolent social movements: A geographical perspective*, ed. Stephen Zunes, Lester R. Kurtz, and Sarah Beth Asher, 259–278. Oxford: Blackwell.

Maria Pia Guerra is Professor of Law at the University of Brasília, Brazil. She obtained her PhD from the University of Brasília. She has been a visiting researcher at the Max Planck Institute for European Legal History (Frankfurt am Main), and a Consultant for the Brazilian Amnesty Commission and the United Nations Development Programme. Her research interests include legal history, constitutional history, transitions, and authoritarian regimes.

Chapter 5
Constitutional Politics During the Early Years of Brazilian Civil-Military Dictatorship: The Constitution as a Tool for Authoritarian Political Transition

Leonardo Augusto de Andrade Barbosa

Abstract One of the most prominent features of the 1964 civil-military dictatorship is the pervasiveness of constitutional law. The leaders of the military coup of 1964, and the government that followed it, envisioned the constitution as a critical tool for social and political reform; as a consequence, between 1964 and 1969, several changes in the rules governing constitutional reform were introduced, along with a new Constitution in 1967, substantially altered by an Amendment decreed in 1969. The overlapping of mechanisms of formal constitutional change and the power of preempting constitutional provisions by decree sheds light on the many contradictions between revolutionary discourse and reformist practices. The failure of the regime's constitutional politics is summarized in the preamble of the Institutional Act No. 5, of 1968, which reads: "the legal instruments provided by the victorious revolution for the Nation's defense, for its development, and for the well-being of our people, are now used as means for challenging and destroying the revolution." The enactment of the fifth Institutional Act in December of 1968 marked the end of a four-year transition from the 1946 constitutional order to the legal and political system that defined the Brazilian civil-military dictatorship. While the conceptual category of "transition" is usually employed to analyze the departure from a dictatorship to a democratic system, this chapter argues that it is also important to understand how constitutional democracies collapse into different forms of authoritarian rule.

I am indebted to the comments of the participants in the panel "Constitutional History, Authoritarian Rule and Transition to Democracy in Brazil and Comparative Perspectives", which was part of the program of the European Society for Comparative Legal History 2016 Conference, in Gdansk. I particularly thank Massimo Meccarelli, who acted as chair and commentator of the panel, for his remarks. I also thank Cristiano Paixão, Maria Pia Guerra, Claudia Carvalho, and all the members of our research group at the University of Brasília Law School, who provided valuable feedback on the first draft of this work. Kristin McGuire copyedited this chapter.

L. A. de Andrade Barbosa (✉)
Center for Continuing Education and Professional Development (CEFOR, Chamber of Deputies), Brasília, Brazil

© Springer Nature Switzerland AG 2021
C. Paixão and M. Meccarelli (eds.), *Comparing Transitions to Democracy. Law and Justice in South America and Europe*, Studies in the History of Law and Justice 18, https://doi.org/10.1007/978-3-030-67502-8_5

5.1 "Legal Instrumentalism" and Political Transition in the Context of Brazilian Civil-Military Rule (1964–1985)

In his review of Brian Z. Tamanaha's *Law as Means to an End* (2006), Adam Vermeule expresses his skepticism about a general critique of "instrumentalism." He argues that many theoretical approaches fit this general description and that we should evaluate the merits of those multiple approaches locally, rather than globally (Vermeule 2006, 2007: 2113). It follows that this discussion of a fragment of Brazilian constitutional history through the lens of "legal instrumentalism" requires a prior explanation of what precisely counts as instrumentalism in this context. When considering the civil-military dictatorship's legal framework, which features assume law as means for an end, and to what extent?

We should note that the authoritarian intelligentsia failed to develop a unified and coherent doctrine, capable of reconciling the many contradictions of the regime's legal and political enterprises. A handful of Brazilian jurists from different generations are renowned for their collaboration with the government and their work to provide legal justification for the policies and legislation of the new regime. In spite of considerable differences in their approaches and intellectual backgrounds, their work unsurprisingly converges on specific points that were crucial to the post-1964 government.

First, it seems fair to assert that most jurists supporting the dictatorship shared a *lack of appreciation for the tenet of separation of powers*, at least in its Madisonian version (Levinson and Pildes 2006). One of their common concerns, therefore, was equipping the Executive branch with powers to effectively *command* the government, that is, to prevail over the Legislative branch, which they depicted as an intrinsically ineffective and anachronist institution, an intellectual trend that was not at all new, even in the 1960s (Schmitt 1988). One of the most eloquent formulations of this belief is found in the work of jurist Carlos Medeiros Silva, who co-drafted the Institutional Act of April 9, 1964. This document was the foundational legal landmark of the regime (Barbosa 2012: 23). According to Silva, "the function of government has become progressively mingled with the enactment of legislation," to an extent that "to govern is no longer to act according to a framework of pre-existing laws," but to "control legislation itself; to govern is, in one word, to enact legislation" (Silva 1964b: 450). This predilection for the Executive branch corresponded to a disregard of the "liberal-minded" connection between parliament, freedom, and democracy— A refusal that entailed recognizing the president as having greater democratic legitimacy than the Congress.[1] This perspective, in turn, relied on a particular *view of the law and the law's role within contemporary societies*.

Writing in 1938, Francisco Campos (the other co-draftsman of the Institutional Act of April 9, 1964) noted that "legislation is no longer limited to defining basic rights: it

---

[1] Ferreira Filho claims that, as the President is chosen through direct elections, he enjoys higher democratic legitimacy than Congress: "[…] it is highly implausible to portray parliaments as a more democratic institution than the Executive branch" (Ferreira Filho 1968: 234).

is a huge *technique for controlling the national life in all its manifestations*" (emphasis added). For Campos, all technological developments that followed the Industrial Revolution were potential legislative matters, including not only "technical issues," but also issues related to making the technical and scientific improvements work in favor of the collective well-being. Further, he believed that parliament was incapable of this work: "parliament has neither the time nor the appropriate organizational structure and work processes for this task, which demands special prerequisites." The legislative branch lacks these prerequisites, he argued, because the recruitment of representatives is based on criteria "completely disentangled from their constitutional attributions" (Campos 2001: 89).

Manoel Gonçalves Ferreira Filho, in a 1968 study of congressional procedures, reasserted this view by arguing that the legislative process is "inadequate." He believed this inadequacy was due to the fact that political representation in Congress is a fiction and to the impossibility of a politically-driven body to perform an activity that is per se "technical" ("as it is the case with legislation"). This technocratic approach to legislation is closely linked to transformations in governmental functions since the 1930s. The welfare state requires government to perform new positive duties, specifically in the steering of the economy, and these activities require the right "choice of instruments," Ferreira Filho argued, because managing the national economy is also a "technical matter."

In Ferreira Filho's view, as government is bound by law, the legislative process had to be reshaped to abide by the rules of technical and scientific expertise. In this case, legislation ceases to be the locus of a decision on the collective good and becomes, rather, "an *instrument* to accomplish certain material goals": "Even outside the particular realm of economy, the general coordination assigned to government, once its functions are no longer restricted to the safeguard of individual well-being, demands legislation to play an *instrumental role*" (emphasis added).[2] Under such circumstances, the legislative process is no longer about deliberative decision-making. It is, at best, an instance bound to *ratify* technically validated "inputs" provided by the Executive branch. In this context, law cannot—or should not—be framed in a non-instrumental perspective, as the result of public discussion, or, more ambitiously, as the collective perception of the common good. Particularly under the 1964 dictatorship in Brazil, the common good was a "given fact" prior to legislative debate, and crystallized in the regime's interpretation of the "national interests."[3] Law was a tool for coordinating and planning social change. In the words of Miguel Reale, "to a certain extent, the 'Law of Planning' [*'direito do planejamento'*] […] corresponds or complements the systematic intervention of the State on the realms of economy and culture."[4]

---

[2] Ferreira Filho blatantly states that "the inadequacy of the legislative process is, in the end, the inadequacy of parliaments themselves to perform the task of enacting legislation." He argued that two of the main shortcomings of the legislative process are its tardiness and the lack of secrecy in its proceedings (Ferreira Filho 1968: 228–232).

[3] See, for instance, the preamble of the Institutional Act of April 9, 1964.

[4] Although Reale emphasizes the role of law in the coordination and steering of social change, he does not endorse a fully instrumental view of law, at least on paper. Reale criticizes the "reduction

This conceptual framework requires law to be *more pervious to politics*. If law is the tool employed by the government to coordinate and steer social development, it should be readily available to those in command. The jurists associated with the civil-military regime of 1964 knew that law could not guarantee a particular social outcome, but that it could stimulate one. Thus, with control of the legislative process, one could at least *make sure to provide the appropriate stimulus* (that is, the legal proposal validated by technical or scientific expertise). So, law should be used primarily as *a tool for controlling and domesticating the lawmaking process* within the legislative branch, mitigating the principle of separation of powers.

The military leaders and their civil collaborators, however, still had to figure out how to make constitutional law abide to their goals. They had neither a fully developed conceptual framework nor a set of institutional practices that could be immediately deployed in the political arena, as we will discuss in the next section. The constitutional experiments of the first years of the civil-military regime of 1964 reveal a kind of "political transition." Although this concept is usually employed to describe how a nation departs from authoritarianism and embraces democracy, this chapter assumes that analyzing the way a dictatorship becomes an enduring regime is equally relevant. Actually, the widespread use of the word "transition" to refer to re-democratization can be misleading. As Thomas Carothers (2002) has pointed out, a general assumption of the "transition paradigm" is that any country moving away from authoritarianism is moving toward democracy. To a certain extent, this view might lead to the rather naïve idea of democracy as a focal point of history. He insists, on the other hand, that:

> (…) aid practitioners and policy makers looking at politics in a country that has recently moved away from authoritarianism should not start by asking, "How is its democratic transition going?" They should instead formulate a more open-ended query, "What is happening politically?" (Carothers 2002: 6)

Carothers poses this more suitable question. And if we are not looking to the future, as policy makers usually do, but to the past, it seems even more important. Historians recognize contingency as a key element for understanding the past. When the first Institutional Act was signed on April 9, 1964, the military and their civil allies did not know exactly where they were heading. Their effort to stabilize Brazilian constitutional politics was dressed up in revolutionary clothes, but apart from political rhetoric, the new regime was committed to reform rather than to revolution. What it

---

of law to administrative schemes," which would result in "a decline of the power of political participation of individuals in the direction of political matters." He argues that it is a big mistake to exclude jurists from the problematic of ends and means, as far as the content of the former and the efficacy of the latter are involved. Relegating jurists to "formalities" overlooks the fact that "legal structures are more than mere conventional configurations, adaptable ad libitum to any kind of planning." Constitutional guarantees should be enforceable against an arbitrary use of the government's power. For that reason, jurists should help to assess the "angle of legislative possibilities" [*ângulo das possibilidades legislativas*]. Reale's assertion, of course, should be read not only as a theoretical observation, but also as a pragmatic defense of the role jurists (including himself) should play in government and of the amount of power they should necessarily share in the advancement of a successful legal culture (Reale 1973: 94–95).

would take to build a long lasting political system was still unclear at that time. In order to understand how a 21-year dictatorship was made possible, one has to take into account the kinds of choices that were made in the early years of the regime, before its legal and political vocabulary had been fully translated into institutional practices.

5.2 Controlling Constitutional Change

The long preamble of the Institutional Act of April 9, 1964, co-written by Francisco Campos and Carlos Medeiros Silva, introduced the landmarks of a new political regime. Although the document, addressed to "the Nation", invoked the constituent power, it refrained from promulgating a new constitution. Instead, it declared that the 1946 Constitution was still in force, even if some of its rules and guarantees were preempted on a temporary basis by the provisions of the Institutional Act.

In order to understand the early developments of Castello Branco's government, it is crucial to keep in mind that, once in power, the military had neither an organized government plan nor a clear political strategy (Fico 2004a: 75). Castello Branco took office on April 15, 1964, after an indirect election. He was appointed to serve the rest of the five-year presidential term initiated by Jânio Quadros on January 31, 1961 and thus had less than two years of presidency ahead of him. (Ultimately, his term was extended for another 14 months in July 1964, by an amendment to the Constitution.[5]) Direct elections for the presidency and state governments were abolished in October 1965, setting the stage for a prolonged period of civil-military rule. Hence for the first year and a half, legislative and constitutional politics evolved in an environment of great incertitude.

Time was a scarce resource for Castello Branco, and the rules governing constitutional change in the 1946 Constitution did not make his life any easier. Although Congress had the power to alter the constitutional text on its own, with no need of ratification by the states, a two-thirds majority in two votes in each House was required in order to immediately pass an amendment. Reaching a lower quorum—a simple majority of votes in each House—would still allow the procedure to continue, but only after a mandatory interstice: the second vote would have to take place in the subsequent legislative year. Moreover, the president did not have the power to propose an amendment to the Constitution. These proposals required the support of one-fourth of the members of either House of Congress.

These procedural complexities were closely linked to relevant political complexities. The new government did not have a safe majority in Congress, let alone the

---

[5] See Emenda Constitucional n. 9, de 22 de julho de 1964, Art. 6°, parágrafo único. The candidate elected in the 1960 presidential run was Jânio Quadros. Quadros served from January 31, 1961 to August 25, 1961, when he resigned. A political crisis followed his resignation, and João Goulart was sworn into the presidency only on September 8, 1961, under an improvised parliamentarian regime (that was repealed in January 1963, restoring his full presidential powers). He was in office until March 31, 1964 (Paixão and Barbosa 2013).

two-thirds majority necessary to approve constitutional amendments without the constitutional interstice. In Brazil, different from many other dictatorships in South America, the 1964 regime kept Congress operating. Afonso Arinos noted in 1965 that, "a revolution does not maintain a working Congress [...] for the sake of kindness."[6] He was right. Both international and domestic circumstances made it difficult to shut down the legislative branch and endorse an open dictatorship. However, in such a scenario, keeping the representatives and senators on a short leash was crucial to the success of the government's reform plan. The Institutional Act allowed the "commanders-in-chief" to suspend political rights for a ten-year term and also to remove from office any elected representative of the legislative branch within the federal, state, or local government, in the name "of peace and national honor."[7] During the 1963–1967 Legislature, sixty-seven representatives (out of four hundred and nine) were removed from the lower House of Congress [*Câmara dos Deputados*], creating a sort of *"rump parliament."*

Simply tipping the political equilibrium within Congress would not do the trick, however; it was necessary to alter the rules of constitutional change themselves. In a short introduction to a book on the 1967 Constitution, Pedro Aleixo wrote: "we need to emphasize that, today, to demand exceptional or extraordinary requirements to reform the Constitution is unacceptable." In Aleixo's view, if a legislative majority was firmly devoted to changing the constitutional text, it was preposterous to prevent it from doing so based on "procedural restraints," or on conditions whose fulfilment "depends on a more or less ponderable political minority" (Aleixo 1967:xxxvi). Aleixo was actually echoing observations previously made by Carlos Medeiros Silva and Miguel Reale. In two articles written respectively in 1964 and 1965, both jurists had criticized the "inertia" and "filibustering" in Congress, which had to be fought, they argued, with "acceleration measures," given the constrained timeframe of Castello Branco's political agenda (Silva 1964a: 474; Reale 1964: 68).

This perspective translated into new rules for constitutional amendment, introduced by Article 3° of the Institutional Act. This provision not only empowered the president to initiate the amendment process in Congress without gathering previous parliamentary support, but also: (a) reduced the necessary quorum to pass amendments from two-thirds of the members of each House to the majority of the members; (b) adopted deliberation in joint sessions of both Houses of Congress for proposed constitutional amendments (avoiding bicameral complications); (c) limited to thirty days the deadline for Congress to deliberate on the president's proposals to amend the Constitution. These rules were reenacted in the Second Institutional Act, in October

---

[6] *Anais do Senado Federal* [The Federal Senate Records], Livro 14, 27 Oct. 1965, 324.

[7] Article 10 of the Institutional Act read: "For the sake of peace and national honor, and without the limitations provided for by this Constitution, the Commanders-in-Chief who have enacted the present provisions may suspend political rights for a ten-year term and remove from office legislative representatives elected within the federal, state, or local government. These acts shall not be reviewable by the Judiciary." On April 10, 1964, one day after the enactment of the Institutional Act, almost forty congressmen were purged from the lower House of the Brazilian Congress (de Azevedo and Rabat 2012: 27–30).

1965,[8] and were valid throughout Castello Branco's presidential term. An important detail: those provisions were applicable *only* to proposals initiated by the president. Proposals initiated by congressmen were subjected to the process provided for in the 1946 Constitution.

With one single exception, the president initiated all fifteen amendments to the 1946 Constitution passed between April 1964 and the adoption of the 1967 Constitution. All of the core constitutional reforms that he proposed would have *failed* to reach the original two-thirds threshold of the 1946 Constitution. Those included the extension of Castello Branco's own presidential term; the modification of the legal regime of political disqualifications (allowing Congress to add by statute to the roll of constitutional enumerated disqualifications); the adoption of new rules governing the 1965 state elections; the reform of the Legislative branch; the reform of the Judiciary; and adjustments in the tax system. The successful (and timely) enactment into law of all those measures depended hugely on the provisions of the first two Institutional Acts, especially those regarding initiative and quorum (Barbosa 2012: 66–67, 81–82). Therefore, even with lighter requirements for passing constitutional amendments, the newly established government had difficulty pushing its agenda through Congress. Not even the forced exclusion of a considerable part of the political opposition inside and outside the Legislative branch resulted in a blank check for the regime to enact legislation. Triumphing in the legislative arena was not always easy, and there was even occasional defeat and defiance, usually triggering violent responses. Those responses were generally effective, but costly, at least from the perspective of the regime's legitimacy in the public eye. Moreover, each of the government's attempts to normalize and stabilize politics through Institutional Acts backfired into more crises.

Between 1964 and 1968 the country was riding a sort of constitutional roller coaster. After the first Institutional Act, while the path of the regime was still unclear, the 1965 direct elections for governor in eleven states were maintained. But, even after all the hard work to craft election law rules that would fit the "revolutionary" needs (benefiting from the lighter amendment requirements and from a purged Congress), and to foster judicial decisions that would enforce those rules "properly," the polls resulted in defeat for the government's candidates in the states of Minas Gerais and Guanabara. The winners were allegedly close allies to Juscelino Kubitschek, a former president and senator removed from office in 1964, but still one of the most popular politicians in Brazil throughout the 1960s (Barbosa 2017).

Defeat in these two crucial states in the 1965 elections fomented upheaval among the so-called military hard-liners, who pushed for radical measures to "secure the revolution," leading to the enactment of the second Institutional Act in October 1965. The Act claimed, "the Revolution is alive, and it will not retreat," a statement that laid the foundations for the doctrine of "permanent constituent power." According to the preamble of the Institutional Act, the constituent power of the Revolution

---

[8] The first Institutional Act was set to expire on January 31, 1966, the date on which Castello Branco's presidential term would originally end. With the extension of the presidential term, the government reckoned it would be hard to carry on with constitutional reforms without it (Barbosa 2012: 81).

"had not been exhausted": it was "inherent to the revolutionary process," and it had to be "*dynamic to achieve its goals*" (emphasis added). In other words, the ability to shape the law—particularly constitutional law—to the contingent interests of the "revolution" was decisive. Just like in the First Institutional Act of 1964, the invocation of the constituent power did not lead to the enactment of a new constitution. Instead, the temporary rules facilitating the amendment of the 1946 Constitution were renewed. Direct elections for president and state governor were abolished, and new purges within all branches of government were authorized. The Second Institutional Act made it very clear that Brazil was not facing a momentary military intervention.

The 1946 Constitution remained in force throughout Castello Branco's term, even with many of its provisions preempted by the rules of the 1964 and 1965 Institutional Acts. Of even greater note, however, is the fact that the last day of Castello's mandate, March 15, 1967, was also the promulgation date of the 1967 Constitution, a Constitution forced upon a purged and controlled Congress, through a highly undemocratic procedure (Barbosa 2012: 109–112). It seems clear that Castello Branco thought of his own term as a period of institutional adjustment and consolidation. Viana Filho, Castello Branco's former Chief of the Executive Office [*Chefe da Casa Civil*], observed, based on the president's hand notes, that the "task of the Revolution" was divided in two separate moments: the first encompassed Castello Branco's mandate, conspicuous for its provisional arrangements and exceptional measures, and the second began after the enactment of a new constitution, "establishing the basic principles of the new regime." After that point, in Castello's own words, any act of government "would have to follow the regular procedures," and there would be a "new period of normality in the country" (Viana Filho 1975: 452). As Thomas Skidmore argued, by March 1967 the Revolution should have accomplished its basic institutional organization (Skidmore 1988: 135). If the "revolution" intended to translate its ideas into functioning institutions, relying on occasional "acts of exception" was not a viable strategy.

> Castelo saw a new constitution as a necessary step towards the consolidation of the victorious movement. It would be not only the institution of a legal order which would express the ideas of the Revolution and compile the rules of the institutional and complimentary acts, but also the conclusion of the revolutionary process. In the end, he embraced Milton Campos's thoughts: "the Revolution shall be permanent as an idea and as an inspiration," but "the revolutionary process shall be transitory and brief," to avoid its "consecration to arbitrariness." This idea fit well with the president's conceptions. (Viana Filho 1975: 452)

The enactment of the 1967 Constitution was, however, not driven only by an ideological or theoretical urge to put an end to the revolution and commit to stability: it was wrapped up in the intricacies of presidential succession. Costa e Silva, one of the leaders of the 1964 coup, secured his nomination for the 1966 indirect election, much to the disgust of Castello Branco (Gaspari 2002: 99–100). Castello Branco did not believe that Costa e Silva was the right man for the job, but he expected—quite naively—that the "furious lawmaking" that marked the end of his own term, especially with the promulgation of the new Constitution, would tie the hands of his successor, reconcile the military doctrine with constitutional aspirations, and prevent inefficient and misconceived economic policies (Gaspari 2002: 273).[9] Skidmore refers to this as the "elitist belief according to which the solution to any problem consists in passing legislation" (Skidmore 1988: 121). It might be more accurate to describe this view as the belief that *crafting* legislation provides the solution to all problems.

The years 1967 and 1968 saw escalating economic, social, and political tensions, involving different actors, such as student movements, labor unions, artists, radicals (inside and outside the Armed Forces), and opposition politicians. The government had been considering "hardening the regime" for a while, at least since July of 1968, and was threatening to declare a state of emergency to control the political crisis (Gaspari 2002: 310–314). The solution, however, was even more bitter. In a fatidic meeting on December 13, 1968, Costa e Silva pushed the Institutional Act No. 5 through the—rather superfluous—Counsel of National Security. If the Second Institutional Act marked the birth of the doctrine of "permanent constituent power," No. 5 was closer to a "declaration of death" of constitutional democracy.

Unlike its previous counterparts, the Institutional Act No. 5 did not come with an expiration date. Its provisions—some that had been included in former Institutional Acts, and others that were brand new—would be permanently available to government (until ten years later, when it was finally repealed). Taken in its full scope, the Act provided the president with the means to circumvent almost any conceivable legal or political obstacle. For instance, it authorized the president to adjourn Congress whenever he deemed necessary; for the duration of the adjournment, the president was granted full legislative powers. The president was also allowed to arbitrarily encroach on states' powers. Habeas Corpus was suspended for those facing charges of crimes against the national security. And, finally, no act of government based on the Institutional Act No. 5 (AI-5) could be challenged in a court of law. The separation of powers, the federative principle, basic rights and guarantees: all the cornerstones of constitutionalism had collapsed.

Ten months after the AI-5, Costa e Silva suffered a near-fatal stroke that cut short his presidential term and put him out of politics for good.[10] Pedro Aleixo, his civil vice-president, was prevented from taking office in a true "coup inside the coup," orchestrated to ensure military command (Barbosa 2012: 136–138). The military chiefs immediately took over and a month later they decreed a comprehensive amendment to the 1967 Constitution, largely based on prior studies prepared by a committee of jurists assembled by Costa e Silva earlier in 1969 (de Araújo and Maciel 2002). The resulting constitutional text read, in Article 182: "The Institutional Act No. 5, of December 13, 1968, remains in force." The enactment of a Constitution that embraced its own exception is the climax of the contradictory constitutional politics of the civil-military regime. It provided the ultimate version of a legal interplay aimed

---

[9] Conventional Brazilian historiography presents Castello Branco as a moderate, legalistic, and liberal-oriented politician. This view, however, is correctly called into question by Carlos Fico (2004b: 32–34).

[10] Costa e Silva died shortly after that, in December 1969. For a short biographical note on Costa e Silva, see Artur da Costa e Silva, https://jk.cpdoc.fgv.br/biografia/artur-costa-silva.

at obscuring the limits between constitutional normality and acts of exception. The ambiguities that marked the first years of the dictatorship's constitutional discourse were rendered immediately obsolete. As president Médici, who was in office between 1969 and 1974, eloquently put it: "I had the AI-5, I could do anything" (Gaspari 2002: 130).

It was not the 1967 Constitution that marked the end of the political transition to a new regime in Brazil, as Castello Branco had believed. It was the blunt statement of Constitutional Amendment No. 1 in 1969, declaring that the Institutional Act No. 5 remained in force. Ironically, the Institutional Act became, simultaneously, the source of the government's authority to decree a new constitution (dressed up as a constitutional amendment) and the final guarantor of the new constitutional order's stability, by allowing government to arbitrarily bypass constitutional principles whenever such a measure were necessary to address legal or political challenges.

5.3   Conclusion: The Failure of the Authoritarian Constitutional Project

The first five years of the 1964 dictatorship shed light on the limits of the regime's constitutional politics and on its ultimate paradox. Despite its claims of a "revolutionary pedigree," the Civil Military dictatorship struggled to advance an agenda dominated by constitutional reform. While declaring that its legitimacy did not flow from Congress but the other way around, the regime insisted—contradictorily—in getting most of its crucial measures approved within Congress. When Congress resisted, it was circumvented, either by forced adjournment, arbitrary purges, or exceptional measures, such as the Institutional Acts. Every step toward the institutionalization of the regime was followed by arbitrary actions in the opposite direction, oriented to the circumstantial needs of the government, rather than to general principles. If the "natural" goal of the revolution was to establish a stable and organized constitutional order—as Milton Campos as well as Castello Branco himself assumed—the regime blatantly failed to do so; if the goal was—more modestly—to impose the government's will while "keeping the appearances" of a functioning constitutional democracy, the AI-5 exposed the fantastic character of such a narrative.

In its attempt to gain complete control over constitutional law—to turn the law into a serviceable tool for the regime's purposes, from its birth to its interpretation within courts—the dictatorship embraced the ultimate denial of the rule of law: the Institutional Act No. 5. This "perfect tool" came to be a "self-defeating" tool, to use Vermeule's expression. It demoralized any attempt to present the constitutional order of the civil-military regime as legitimate law. Limited government becomes a fictional concept if legal boundaries to political power are only valid when convenient or acceptable. Despite its considerable duration, the military regime had sowed the seeds of its own failure during its first years. The conditions of its stabilization were ultimately one of the causes of its collapse.

In the beginning of this paper we suggested that a comprehensive critique of legal instrumentalism is not feasible. The history of the early years of the 1964 Brazilian dictatorship does not provide us with a coherent rebuttal to a particular theory of law. However, it does allow us to understand some of the risks involved in the attempt to use law as a *mere tool* for imposing particular values and political perspectives that are "taken for granted" by those in power (like the ones presented in the Doctrine of National Security, during the civil-military regime). When law is approached as an "empty form" that can be filled with any content whatsoever, detached of any moral assumption and completely available to political power, the result may involve the exclusion, elimination, or stigmatization of conflicting points of view, sometimes with brutal repercussions on those who stand for them. If the law cannot be presented as the result of a fair agreement, on the legislative side, or of a rational application of legal rules, on the judicial side, its ability to provide and reinforce normative expectations is severely endangered.[11]

References

Aleixo, P. 1967. Introdução. In *A Constituição do Brasil ao alcance de todos*, ed. Paulo Sarasate, xxxiii–xl. Rio de Janeiro: Freitas Bastos Editor.

Barbosa, L.A.A. 2012. *História constitucional brasileira: mudança constitucional, autoritarismo e democracia no Brasil pós-1964*. Brasília: Edições Câmara.

Barbosa, L.A.A. 2017. The ballot under the bayonet: election law in the first years of the Brazilian civil-military regime. *Direito GV* 13 (1): 145–170. https://doi.org/10.1590/2317-6172201707.

Campos, F. 2001. *O estado nacional: sua estrutura, seu conteúdo ideológico*. Brasília: Senado Federal.

Carothers, T. 2002. The end of the transition paradigm. *Journal of Democracy* 13 (1): 5–21.

de Araújo, C.E.P., and E.C. Maciel. 2002. A Comissão de Alto Nível: história da Emenda Constitucional n. 1, de 1969. In *A Constituição que Não Foi: História da Emenda Constitucional n. 1, de 1969*, ed. Senado Federal, 31–78. Brasília: Senado Federal.

de Azevedo, D., and M.N. Rabat. 2012. *Parlamento mutilado: deputados federais cassados pela ditadura de 1964*. Brasília: Edições Câmara.

Ferreira Filho, M.G. 1968. *Do processo legislativo: ensaio crítico de direito constitucional comparado, tendo em vista especialmente a Constituição do Brasil, de 24 de janeiro de 1967*. São Paulo: Saraiva.

---

[11] On that particular issue, William Regh reminds us, "modern legal norms require only outward compliance regardless of individual motivation, but they should, at the same time, have a rational basis that also makes it possible for persons to accept them as legitimate and thus deserving of obedience. The need for legitimation is acute, because such norms must be positively enacted without appeal to a higher source of justification, such as a shared religious worldview. In view of this duality, one can see that coercible law can be accepted as legitimate insofar as it guarantees two things at once. On the one hand, as demarcating areas in which private individuals can exercise their free choice as they desire, law must guarantee the private autonomy of individuals pursuing their personal success and happiness. On the other hand, because its enactment must be such that reasonable individuals could always assent to its constraints rationally, legitimate law must also secure the public autonomy of those subject to it, so that the legal order can be seen as issuing from the citizens' rational self-legislation, as it were" (Regh 1996: xxv).

Fico, C. 2004a. *Além do golpe: a tomada do poder em 31 de março de 1964 e a ditadura militar*. Rio de Janeiro: Record.

Fico, C. 2004b. Versões e controvérsias sobre 1964 e a ditadura militar. *Revista Brasileira de História* 24: 29–60.

Gaspari, E. 2002. *A Ditadura Envergonhada*. São Paulo: Cia. das Letras.

Levinson, D., and R. Pildes. 2006. Separation of parties, not powers. *Harvard Law Review* 119: 2311–2386.

Paixão, C., and L.A.A. Barbosa. 2013. Crise política e sistemas de governo: Origens da 'solução parlamentarista' para a crise político-constitucional de 1961. *Universitas Jus* 24: 47–61. https://doi.org/10.5102/unijus.v24i3.2622.

Reale, M. 1964. *Imperativos da revolução de março*. São Paulo: Livraria Martins Editora.

Reale, M. 1973. Direito e Planificação. *Revista de Direito Público* 24: 93–97.

Regh, W. 1996. Introduction to *Between Facts and Norms*. In *Between Facts and Norms*, ed. J. Habermas, ix–xxxvii. Cambridge: MIT Press.

Schmitt, C. 1988. *The crisis of parliamentary democracy*. Cambridge: MIT Press.

Silva, C.M. 1964a. Observações sobre o ato institucional. *Revista de Direito Administrativo* 76: 473–475.

Silva, C.M. 1964b. Seis meses de aplicação do ato institucional. *Revista de Direito Administrativo* 78: 449–452.

Skidmore, T. 1988. *Brasil: de Castelo a Tancredo*. Rio de Janeiro: Paz & Terra.

Tamanaha, B.Z. 2006. *Law as means to an end: Threat to the rule of law*. New York: Cambridge University Press.

Vermeule, A. 2006–2007. Book Review: Instrumentalisms. *Harvard Law Review* 120: 2113–2132.

Viana Filho, L. 1975. *O governo Castelo Branco*. Rio de Janeiro: Livraria José Olympio Ed.

Leonardo Augusto de Andrade Barbosa is Professor of the Master's Degree Program in Legislative Affairs at the Center for Continuing Education and Professional Development (CEFOR, Chamber of Deputies). He is an expert in Brazilian legislative and constitutional matters. He has been a legislative attorney with the Chamber of Deputies (the lower House in the Brazilian Congress) since 2002. He obtained his LLM and JSD from the University of Brasília. He was a Michigan Grotius Research Scholar at the University of Michigan Law School.

Part II
Comparative Perspectives

Chapter 6
Transitional Justice and Sexual Crimes in Latin America: Argentina, Brazil and Chile in Comparative Perspective

Claudia Paiva Carvalho

Abstract This chapter makes a comparative analysis of transition justice responses to sexual crimes in Argentina, Brazil and Chile. In all three countries, the dictatorships incorporated the practice of sexual crimes as part of the repressive strategies for persecuting their political opponents. However, it took a long time for these violations to be recognized and properly addressed. Through an empirical and qualitative methodology, the present chapter investigates the reasons for the delay in addressing these crimes and the different strategies and measures adopted by the new democracies to respond to them. Considering the different stages of development in each country, particular attention is paid to the legal obstacles, on the one hand, and to the legal arguments and strategies developed to seek justice, on the other. We demonstrate that the use of law in transitional justice is not gender neutral and that specific approaches are required to make sexual violations visible and to enable them to be prosecuted and punished.

6.1 Introduction

During the 1980s, the political transitions in Argentina, Brazil, and Chile involved disputes regarding accountability for past crimes perpetrated by the dictatorial regimes.[1] Argentina and Chile established truth commissions to investigate violations of human rights. Argentina also held judicial trials for the crimes committed by the military government. Brazil took some initial steps toward reparations for victims of the regime and held unofficial initiatives to document the violations. All three countries approved amnesty laws to avoid or impair the criminal prosecution of the crimes. In particular, for the purpose of the present research, it is important

---

[1] For a comparison between the dictatorships and political transitions, see Pereira (2010).

C. P. Carvalho (✉)
Instituto de Pesquisa e Planejamento Urbano, Universidade Federal do Rio de Janeiro, Rio de Janeiro, Brazil

© Springer Nature Switzerland AG 2021
C. Paixão and M. Meccarelli (eds.), *Comparing Transitions to Democracy. Law and Justice in South America and Europe*, Studies in the History of Law and Justice 18, https://doi.org/10.1007/978-3-030-67502-8_6

to note one of the common features of these transitions: the silence regarding the sexual violence committed against women.

In all three countries, the dictatorships incorporated the practice of sexual crimes as part of their repressive strategies for persecuting and destroying their political opponents. Nudity during interrogations, sexual torture, and rape were common occurrences within the operation of the security forces (Aucía et al. 2011; Teles 2015; Calandra 2010). However, it took a long time for these violations to be recognized and properly addressed. The present paper aims to investigate the reasons for the delay in addressing these crimes and the different strategies and measures adopted by the new democracies to respond to the sexual crimes perpetrated during the dictatorial regimes.

This analysis is based on research conducted in 2016 that was funded and supported by the Latin American Transitional Justice Network (*Rede Latino-americana de Justiça de Transição*—RLAJT).[2] This original research project involved a nine-country study on sexual crimes and transitional justice, with a focus on two aspects in particular: the judiciary and the archives (Carvalho 2016).[3] Data on Argentina, Brazil, and Chile were used in the present study in order to analyze and compare their respective experiences. The methodology for collecting information was threefold, involving, first, the distribution of questionnaires to human rights organizations from each country (members of the RLAJT) and compilation of their responses[4]; second, semi-structured interviews with actors (victims, lawyers, experts) from each of the countries[5]; and third, document analysis of statutes, reports, judicial decisions, and protocols.

Sexual violence is understood as a gender-based violation, which means that patterns of structural discrimination and gender inequality—which preceded the dictatorships and have continued since their end—influence the practice and meaning

---

[2] The RLAJT is comprised of 17 members from 9 countries (Argentina, Brazil, Chile, Colombia, Guatemala, El Salvador, Mexico, Peru and Uruguay). The members are from human right organizations and research centers dedicated to transitional justice.

[3] The final results of the research were published in the book *Sexual Crimes and Transitional Justice in Latin America: justice and archives* ("Crimes sexuais e justiça de transição na América Latina: judicialização e arquivos"). The book can be downloaded at: https://www.justica.gov.br/central-de-conteudo/anistia/anexos/miolo_crimes-sexuais_final.pdf/.

[4] The questionnaire template is available in (Carvalho 2016). The following representatives and organizations were responsible for the responses Luz Palmas, from *Centro de Estudios Legales y Sociales—CELS* (Center for Legal and Social Studies), in Argentina; the team supervised by Emílio Peluso Meyer, from *Centro de Estudos sobre Justiça de Transição—CJT* (Transitional Justice Studies Center), in Brazil; Boris Hau and Cath Collins, from *Observatorio de Justicia Transicional—OJT* (Transitional Justice Observatory), at University Diego Portales, in Chile.

[5] Among the 13 interviews conducted for the original study, 6 are used in this study. The people interviewed are from the 3 countries and are linked to the political, legal and academic field. Among those interviewed are political activists, former political prisoners, attorneys and victims' representatives, members of the Public Prosecutor's Office, scholars/experts. The semi-structured interviews were conducted from an original script that presented a set of pre-determined questions. This script sought to access the visions of the different actors and their experiences and also compare the processes in each country. The list of people who were interviewed is available at the end of the text.

of the sexual violations. I follow Diniz's definition of gender as a political regime imposed by the patriarchal power (Diniz 2014, 11–12). Therefore, a gender perspective is crucial for understanding the idea that the violence is not practiced within a sexually neutral power structure. The functioning of the law and other institutions also plays a role in strengthening gender hierarchies. The resulting hierarchies make women and girls more vulnerable to sexual crimes and then create obstacles that make it more difficult to address these violations (because it's both more difficult to report them and to bring them to justice). In other words, the difficulties women and girls face in trying to deal with sexual crimes are directly related to gender inequality because the structural subordination of women by men both makes the sexual crimes less serious and turns the crimes themselves into sources of shame and embarrassment.

The paper is divided into two parts. The first part examines the context of the political transitions in Argentina, Brazil, and Chile and the reasons why sexual violence remained virtually invisible during that time. It aims to explain how the legal structures in these countries favored an interpretation of sexual crimes as private and minor violations or as simple side effects of the political violence. The second part of the paper analyses the different paths for transitional justice in each country, with a focus on the attempts to investigate, prosecute, and punish sexual crimes committed during the dictatorships. Specific attention will be paid to the legal obstacles, on the one hand, and to the legal arguments and strategies developed to seek justice, on the other.

6.2 Political Transitions and Silence Surrounding Sexual Crimes

During the 1980s, after long periods of dictatorships, Argentina, Brazil, and Chile went through political transitions that sought to return the countries to democracy. The three countries faced similar challenges in terms of accommodating both political stability and the demands for accountability for past crimes. However, the measures adopted during their transition processes did not adequately address sexual violence.

The governors in Argentina and Chile created truth commissions right after the transitions to democracy had concluded. In Argentina, the National Commission on the Disappearance of Persons (CONADEP—*Comisión Nacional sobre la Desaparición de Personas*) was established in 1984 and published the report *Nunca Más*, which became known as a pioneering initiative in the investigation of State terrorism. As its name indicates, CONADEP focused on cases of enforced disappearance perpetrated by the dictatorial regime. Its main purpose was to prove the existence of a systematic plan for the extermination of opponents carried out by the State from 1976 until 1983. Although many testimonies taken by CONADEP reported the practice of sexual crimes in the clandestine detention centers, those crimes did not receive any special attention.

The investigations conducted by CONADEP provided important evidence for the so-called "trial of the military juntas," in 1985, that convicted five members of the armed forces who had been a part of Argentina's dictatorial government. The prosecution focused on paradigmatic cases that did not involve any sexual offenses. Therefore, the specificities of gender violations remained overshadowed by other offenses:

> the main goal of proving illegal repression overshadowed the individual experiences that, although they were repeatedly mentioned in the testimonies and recovered in historical texts, were clearly seen as secondary compared to the broad scope of the systematic plan for disappearance and extermination. (Balardini et al. 2011, 170)

The justice process in Argentina was interrupted by the approval of the "impunity laws" in 1986 and 1987: the *Ley del Punto Final* (Law 23.492, 1986) and the *Ley de Obediencia Debida* (Law 23.521, 1987). These laws removed the possibility of prosecuting State crimes, except for three offenses that were considered unrelated to the alleged "fight against subversion": the kidnapping of babies, the theft of the victims' personal property, and sexual violence. Even though the prosecution of sexual crimes was explicitly allowed under the "impunity laws," no criminal proceeding was initiated at the time. The topic of sexual violence was not on the agenda of human rights organizations and was not a strong subject of public debate (Barbuto and Fries 2008, 43).

In the case of Chile, the Aylwin government created the National Commission on Truth and Reconciliation (*Comisión Nacional de Verdad y Reconciliación—Comisión Rettig*) in 1990. The Commission faced serious limitations concerning its composition, time constraints, amount of work, and restricted powers. The final report was made public in March 1991 and, as in Argentina, focused on the investigation of murder and enforced disappearance during Pinochet's dictatorship. Among the eight members of the commission, only two were women, and none of them were gender experts, which may have contributed to the lack of attention toward sexual violence and the violations against women (Barbuto and Fries 2008, 72).

During the 1980s in Brazil, the Archdiocese of São Paulo carried out the important work of documenting violations committed by the State during Brazil's repressive regime. The work was based on the examination of proceedings against political opponents brought before the military court and resulted in the publication of the report "Brasil Nunca Mais" in 1985.[6] However, the report did not highlight cases involving sexual violence.

At the institutional level, Brazil only officially recognized its responsibility for the assassination and disappearance of political opponents in 1995, with Law n° 9.140. The same Law established the parameters for compensating the victims' families and created a special commission in charge of deciding reparations claims and conducting investigations into the fate of missing persons. Along with the first commissions in Brazil's neighboring countries, the *Special Commission on the Dead and Political*

---

[6] See Arns (1987). More information about the project "Brasil Nunca Mais" is available at: https://bnmdigital.mpf.mp.br/pt-br/.

Disappeared ("Comissão Especial sobre Mortos e Desaparecidos Políticos") did not address the specificity of sexual violence.

This overview of the measures adopted in Argentina, Chile, and Brazil demonstrates that the primary concern in the first years after the transition was to clarify what had happened to the fatal victims and to locate the whereabouts of those who had been disappeared. This approach reveals an underlying question of choice when it comes to designing responses to past crimes. Because of their limited length, as well as limited human and material resources, the transitional policies had to set priorities for which groups of victims and which types of violations would be their primary focus (Souza Pinto 2013, 156). During the political transitions, a sense of urgency in terms of dealing with the crime of enforced disappearance rendered other violations and victims less important. In this scenario, women were treated as secondary or indirect victims of the repression, as witnesses to their partners' deaths or their children and grandchildren's kidnapping, but not as protagonists of their own stories of violence and suffering (Nagy 2008, 286).

In addition to the practical constraints and to the necessary choices required by transitional policies, the silence surrounding sexual violence also reveals a narrow and excluding view of transitional justice. According to Rosemary Nagy, this traditional approach to transitional justice is connected to a liberal-democratic background that considers human rights violations as individual and homogeneous violations. As a consequence, "predominant views [of transitional justice] construct human rights violations fairly narrowly to the exclusion of structural and gender-based violence" (Nagy 2008, 276). The prevailing "legalist paradigm" structures these conceptions of violence and justice as neutral and universal, which neglects the specificities of gender violence, such as sexual offenses. In this regard, Nagy argues:

> Until very recently women and gender have been glaringly absent from transitional justice programmes. Masculinist determinations of the transitional problem have centred on political violence with, as noted above, an emphasis on 'extraordinary' violations of civil and political rights. This construction disregards and treats as 'ordinary' the private or intimate violence that women experience in a militarised, unequal society. (Nagy 2008, 285–286)

Even sexual violence committed by security forces against women under arrest was disregarded for a long time. There were no official initiatives to investigate sexual violence because it was considered a minor and a private violation. The legal statutes in international and domestic law reinforced such characterizations. In the context of international law, sexual crimes were classified as "crimes against honor," until this understanding was reviewed in the 1990s, when sexual offenses came to be considered war crimes and crimes against humanity (Hagay-Frey 2011).

Domestic laws went through a similar development. For instance, until the reform of the Penal Code in Argentina in 1999, rape and other forms of sexual violence were characterized as "crimes against honesty." The 1999 reform reinterpreted them as crimes against the sexual integrity of the victims. In its turn, the Brazilian Penal Code of 1940 described sex crimes as "crimes against custom." Other penal provisions stated that only an "honest woman" could be a victim of sexual crimes and that, in cases where the victim married the perpetrator, the crime was extinguished. Only under Law 12,015 of 2009 have sex crimes been reclassified as "crimes against sexual dignity." In a study of the Argentinean case, Lorena Balardini, Ana Oberlin, and Laura Sobredo discuss this protection of honor and of customs:

> The crime against honesty—understood as a value worthy of protection—indicates that a man is impressed and affected in his moral integrity by the actions of women related to him. In this interpretation, the law has no intention of defending the victim as a citizen, but rather seeks to protect a certain social order, a set of morals, that is expressed through certain customs, and clearly demonstrates the validity of the hierarchical patriarchal order. (Balardini et al. 2011, 181–182)

Other aspects of the criminal treatment of sexual offenses also demand consideration. For one, rape had a narrow definition, restricted to vaginal penetration to the exclusion of other forms of sexual abuse. This definition is gender-biased, as it protects the inheritance and the descent of the father or husband, not the dignity of the woman (Balardini et al. 2011, 182). It also limits the potential victims, excluding subjects other then women. This concept of rape prevailed in domestic laws until recently. In Chile, a 1999 legislative reform of sexual offenses, set out by Law 19,617, extended the definition of rape to include anal and oral penetration, in addition to non-consensual vaginal penetration. It also recognized that any person, not just women, might be a victim of rape.

The slow pace of legal change is symptomatic of the difficulties that women have encountered in reporting sexual abuses, on both a personal and institutional level. The criminal status of rape reinforced the idea that it was a minor offense that belonged to the intimate sphere of the victims and should be a cause of shame and embarrassment. Under such constraints, most female victims were unwilling to report those violations during the political transitions. Three main reasons explain this silence: (i) the testimonies of the victims were focused on investigating the cases of enforced disappearance; (ii) there was a lack of awareness regarding the meaning and gravity of sexual violence, which was minimized and disqualified; and (iii) people did not want to listen to the victims' narratives of violence.

With regard to the first reason, besides the disregard of sexual crimes by the trials and commissions, the female victims themselves were discouraged to report what had happened to them. They also thought their demands were secondary to the urgent claims of the families desperate to find out what had happened to their missing relatives. The second—and related—reason has to do with the overall lack of awareness of gender-based violence. Former female political prisoners interviewed for this research project stated that, by the time of the political transitions, women neither realized that they had suffered sexual abuse nor that such abuse constituted serious violations. Amelinha Teles, a former Brazilian political prisoner and feminist activist, described the situation in these terms: "I would say that practically all women who were abducted or arrested were victims of sexual assault. Many may not have had the courage to speak out or even the awareness that it was a sexual offense (I think this is relevant, too, that lack of awareness)."

The women were incapable of naming the violence that was inflicted on them. And in comparison to the brutal tortures suffered by other comrades, women who had experienced sexual abuse were made to feel as if their experiences were somehow less grave or as if they had been spared the worst by not being subject to the same kind of torture as their comrades. Many women were accused of being traitors, told that they colluded with repression by "giving in" to sexual harassment so as not to suffer harsher punishments (Balardini et al. 2011, 181; Barbuto and Fries 2008, 48). As a result, in addition to the difficulties of reporting sexual crimes, in general, because of fear or shame, the female victims of the dictatorships felt particularly guilty and stigmatized.

The third reason for the silence around sexual abuse refers to the lack of a system for adequately listening to victims at a societal and institutional level, as the Chilean context demonstrates:

> During the first years of the dictatorship, the women that requested assistance from human rights and welcome centers (…) did not talk about the sexual violence they had suffered, for embarrassment, to protect the 'family name' or because it was not considered so serious as the suffering of other prisoners and because the staff (men and women) that assisted the victims did not ask them about sexual violence to protect them from shame, because it was implied, or to avoid prolonging the pain, because it was important to know quickly where other people were, and the women's testimonies had no room and were kept underreported. (Barbuto and Fries 2008, 85)

By the end of the dictatorships, many people, either from the victims' personal relations, their militancy circle, or the institutional spheres, did not want to—or were unable to—listen to the women's reports on sexual violence (Memoria Abierta 2012, 88). The victims who were willing to speak were met with a lack of interest and of sensibility on the part of their interlocutors. On the one hand, there is a general difficulty, both individually and collectively, in listening to traumatic experiences (Balardini et al. 2011, 172). On the other hand, and especially in the case of sex crimes, many people felt uncomfortable listening to the reports or did not care about them or even thought that by exempting the victims from speaking, they would be protecting them from pain and sparing them from embarrassment or humiliation.

In her interview for this study, Amelinha Teles shared a personal experience on this subject. When she told a fellow political activist about the sexual violence she had suffered, he advised her to remain silent in order to preserve herself, because people would find her guilty for what had happened to her. In the same vein, Beatriz Bataszew, a former political prisoner in Chile and member of the organization *Mujeres Sobrevivientes Siempre Resistentes* ("Surviving women, always resistant"), commented:

> We women have had many opportunities to give testimony, even during the dictatorship, even in the concentration camp. We offered testimony about our comrades who had disappeared. When we gave these testimonies, we were recounting this situation of torture, this situation of political sexual violence or sexual torture. However, the judges who, on this occasion, should have investigated ex officio didn't do so. We also gave testimony to some of the organizations, such as the *Vicaría de la Solidaridad,* that played an important role in our country by protecting victims and offering some judicial support, but it wasn't accepted there, either. After the dictatorship, when someone went to look at these testimonies, they would find that in the part about torture they would talk about degrading treatment and in the part about sexual violence they would talk about humiliating treatment. But in general our statements were erased. This shows that people or institutions didn't even have the ability to

differentiate, and because the accounts must have seemed so atrocious to them, they simply erased them and instead gave them a general label that in their view represented what had happened to us.

Beatriz's narration demonstrates how sexual violence was either minimized or, at best, understood as part of the tortures. Described simply as a case of mistreatment, sexual abuses remained invisible. Such disregard of sexual violence not only reflected the lack of preparation by institutions and their staff, but was also harmful to the victims, according to Susana Chiarotti, who made this point in relation to Argentina:

> [...] when you talk to the victims we interviewed, some of them had already given their accounts to CONADEP and told us that when they recounted these events, those who were listening, the prosecutors, looked the other way and lowered their heads, even [Julio] Strassera, who directed the "trial of the military juntas," as if they didn't want to bother the women, as if they didn't want to make them even more uncomfortable. But somehow, by taking everything they had reported and summarizing it all as torture, they were ignoring the cruel and painful experience that these women had recounted with great effort.

For all of these reasons, the silence on sexual violence during the transitions in the 1980s is directly connected to the way legal texts and institutions have interpreted this violation. The process for overcoming this invisibility ultimately involved a strong mobilization led by feminist movements during the 1990s.[7] They demanded the incorporation of a gender perspective into transitional policies that responded to past abuses. Bell and O'Rourke (2007, 26) have described this effort, noting that the initial focus was on legal efforts to deal with sexual violence:

> Efforts to 'add gender' to transitional justice have been most prominent with respect to the legal treatment of sexual violence in conflict. In the course of the 1990s the major focus of transnational feminist mobilization concerned the need to end impunity for violence against women. This mobilization had a very clear relevance to transitional justice, as it sought to expose the widespread and systematic occurrence of sexual violence in situations of violent conflict. It stood on theorized notions of the relationship of gender to violence, and of the use and limits of law as a tool with which to address such violence.

An important outcome of this mobilization was that the meaning of sexual violence changed at the international level (Chiarotti 2011; Copelon 2000; Gaggioli 2014; Hagay-Frey 2011). The development of international human rights law and the functioning of ad hoc International Criminal Tribunals (from Rwanda and former Yugoslavia) led to the recognition of sexual violence as a serious violation of human rights and as a crime against humanity. The 1998 Rome Statute, which created the International Criminal Court (ICC), confirmed this understanding, alongside specific rules of procedure and evidence that must be observed in cases of sexual crimes.

As to the national contexts in Argentina, Brazil and Chile, beyond the shared silence during transition, these countries faced—and still face—common obstacles in terms of bringing cases of sexual crimes to trial. Nevertheless, in each country, specific political and social conditions were created, and different legal arguments

---

[7] The role played by social and feminist movements is of central importance considering a perspective of "transitional justice from below" (McEvoy and McGregor 2008).

and strategies were developed to address sexual violence. A comparative perspective highlights the similarities and differences between the three transitional justice models in the Southern Cone and thus allows for a historical and legal learning exercise.

6.3 Different Paths for Addressing Sexual Violence: The Uses and Limits of Law

6.3.1 Obstacles and Strategies to Bring Sexual Violence to Court

In the questionnaires that they answered, human rights organizations in Argentina, Brazil, and Chile indicated that, in all three countries, reports of sexual crimes committed by the dictatorships only came to light more than 20 years after the political transitions. One of the general reasons for this delay was the impunity measures, and particularly the amnesty laws, that were approved by the three countries in the 1980s. These amnesties interrupted or prevented justice processes from developing for decades.

The prosecution of past crimes began, or was resumed, in different ways in each country. In Argentina, the National Congress decreed the nullity of the laws of impunity in 2003, and in 2005, the Supreme Court declared the laws unconstitutional in the case "Simón, Julio y otros s/ privación ilegítima de la libertad, etc." In Chile, there has not been a formal repeal of the amnesty law, but since 2004, the Judiciary has consistently dismissed applications for amnesty and waived the statute of limitations for crimes by members of Pinochet's dictatorship. Brazil still struggles to overcome the obstacles that impede access to justice. In 2010, the Supreme Court ruled that the amnesty law is valid, which impairs the prosecution of violations committed during dictatorship. The public prosecution has tried to circumvent that decision in order to bring cases to trial, especially by making the argument that crimes against humanity and permanent crimes (such as enforced disappearance) should be excluded from any amnesty provisions or provisions that enforce a statute of limitations. However, so far, the judiciary has not accepted these arguments.[8]

The different stages of development in the three countries reflect their respective stances with regard to sexual crimes. In Brazil, by 2019, 37 criminal proceedings had been brought to trial, none of them successful insofar and only one related to sexual violence.[9] The first and only complaint of this nature was lodged on December 2016 and was at first rejected by the Judiciary in March 2017, in a decision that will be further considered. Chile has prosecuted and condemned hundreds of perpetrators, but sexual offenses have been mostly absent from judicial account. Some progress

---

[8] More detailed information regarding the transitional justice processes may be seen in Osmo (2016).

[9] Detailed information about the criminal cases may be seen in https://cjt.ufmg.br/acoes-criminais/.

has been made, though, as judicial decisions started to take into consideration the sexual aspects of torture. More recently, in 2019, a first conviction recognized the practice of sexual offenses by intelligence agents during the dictatorship.[10] Argentina has the most advanced case law, which includes more than 200 cases related to State terrorism. Among them, there were 27 convictions for sexual offenses through June 2019.[11]

These numbers reinforce the different paths each country has followed. But they also reveal an important pattern: in all countries, the sexual crimes were disadvantaged compared to other violations. This finding indicates that the prosecution of sexual crimes faces greater and more specific obstacles. Even in Argentina, only a small fraction of the convictions for human rights violations are related to sexual crimes. Carolina Varsky, Coordinator of the Prosecution Office for Crimes against Humanity (*Procuraduría de Crímenes contra la Humanidad*), also pointed out the slow pace of the investigations. According to her, "there are 18 sentences [by 2016], but there are a lot of reported cases on which the investigation does not move forward."

In an interview for this study, the Brazilian prosecutor Marlon Weichert stated that the Judiciary's resistance to prosecuting other cases has also delayed formal complaints about sexual crimes. It is understood that the Judiciary will more readily decide to prosecute other violations, such as enforced disappearance. Since it has not even taken this initial step, complaints about sexual crimes have remained on hold. For strategic reasons, even when sexual violence was part of a case brought before the courts, there was no formal complaint for the sexual offenses. The 37 proceedings initiated as of 2019 dealt mostly with crimes of homicide, of kidnapping, and of concealment of a corpse.[12]

The first and only complaint for sexual offense was filed in December 2016. The complaint reported the sexual violence and rapes suffered by Inês Etienne Romeu while she was being held at a detention center known as "Casa da Morte" (Death House). Inês was the only survivor of this clandestine detention center kept by the Army Intelligence Service in Petrópolis, Rio de Janeiro. The public prosecution was able to identify the direct perpetrator and accused him of committing two rapes against the victim, Inês Etienne Romeu.[13]

In the Chilean context, the Judiciary took until 2019 to recognized sexual violence as criminal conduct practiced by the Pinochet dictatorship. Up to that date, according

---

[10] Observatorio de Justicia Transicional, Universidad Diego Portales, Santiago de Chile. *Boletín informativo n. 52*, marzo y abril 2019.

[11] Information available at: https://www.fiscales.gob.ar/lesa-humanidad/estado-actual-del-pro ceso-de-juzgamiento-ya-suman-226-sentencias-por-crimenes-contra-la-humanidad-de-las-cuales-solo-el-12-identifica-delitos-sexuales-de-manera-autonoma/.

[12] Information on all criminal proceedings is available at the data base held by the *Centro de Estudos em Justiça de Transição—CJT* (Transitional Justice Study Centre) from the Federal University of Minas Gerais).

[13] Brasil. Ministério Público Federal. 2017. 2ª Câmara de Coordenação e Revisão. *Crimes da ditadura militar*. Relatório sobre as atividades de persecução penal desenvolvidas pelo MPF em matéria de graves violações a DH cometidas por agentes do Estado durante o regime de exceção. Brasília: MPF, 217–228.

to Beatriz Bataszew, sexual violence was mentioned by victims' testimony, but there was no judicial answer. The first sentence was held against intelligence agents from the *Servicio de Inteligencia de Carabineros* (SICAR), convicted of aggravated kidnapping with sexual connation due to the practice of rape and sexual abuse against the victims, Ana María Campillo Bastidas and Patricia del Carmen Herrera Escobar. According to the *Observatorio de Justicia Transicional* (Transitional Justice Observatory) in Chile, one of the main factors obstructing access to justice for victims of sexual crimes is the lack of State support. The State program supports the families of non-survivors (victims of execution and enforced disappearance) with legal assistance, but not survivors themselves, such as victims of torture and sexual violence. For this reason, the surviving victims must hire a private lawyer, using their own resources, to file a complaint. Because of this difference in status between the assistance to those who survived and to the families of those who didn't, the Supreme Court used to consider only cases of disappeared or executed victims as "human rights causes" eligible for examination by specialized judges designated to those cases in particular. As a result, Daniela Quintanilla from *Corporación Humanas* highlighted, in her interview for this study, that "the Courts that were beginning to investigate the causes of torture were old criminal justice tribunals that were not dedicated exclusively to this issue, that did not have the appropriate tools for carrying out this investigation."

The efforts to bring cases of sexual crimes to court have involved the mobilization of feminist movements such as *Mujeres Sobrevivientes Siempre Resistentes*. This group of women has organized campaigns and protests to make visible the sexual political violence suffered by female victims during the Pinochet dictatorship. Other organizations, such as *Corporación Humanas*, provide legal assistance to victims. They represent the victims in front of the courts, formulate legal arguments, and seek to influence the judiciary's interpretation of their cases.

In both Chile and Argentina, the participation of organizations as amicus curiae was an important strategy for organizing and disseminating legal arguments based on international norms and case law. In Chile, Women's Link Worldwide submitted amicus curiae briefs to the case of Ana María Campillo Bastidas, in November 2015.[14] In Argentina, CLADEM (*Comité de América Latina y el Caribe para la Defensa de los Derechos de la Mujer*, Latin American and Caribbean Committee for the Defense of Women's Rights) and INSGENAR (*Instituto de Género, Derecho y Desarrollo*, Institute for Gender, Law, and Development) participated as amicus curiae in the "Campo de Mayo" case in February 2010.[15] The arguments emphasized the international obligation of the States to investigate and prosecute sexual crimes

---

[14] Women's Link Worldwide. *Amicus Curiae*. Rol 99-2015 Del 34° Juzgado del Crimen de Santiago, Ministro Instructor Don Mario Carroza Espinoza. Incorporación de la Perspectiva de Género y la Categoría de Crímenes Internacionales a la Investigación del Caso de Ana María Campillo Bastidas. Madrid, noviembre de 2015.

[15] Comité de América Latina y el Caribe para la Defensa de los Derechos de la Mujer (CLADEM); Instituto de Género, Derecho y Desarrollo (INSGENAR). Amicus Curiae. Causa No 4012 "Riveros, Santiago Omar y otros por privación ilegal de la libertad, tormentos, homicidio, etc.". Juzgado Federal en lo Criminal y Correccional no 2 de San Martín. 9 de fevereiro de 2010.

committed during military dictatorships. In addition, the appeal to international bodies also integrates the "strategic litigation" developed by various organizations to influence local policies and law practice (Torelly 2016, 148–149).

When it comes to legal strategy, two main lines of argument have been used in these national contexts: sexual violence may be treated as a form of torture or as an autonomous crime. Equating rape and other forms of sexual violence with torture was a victory for women's human rights in international courts (Chiarotti 2011; Carvalho 2016, 60–62). This equation meant that rape and other sexual violence were recognized as violations that are as serious as torture. The risk of this operation, however, is that it can make sexual violence invisible. If torture is understood as a generic category, it may disregard the specificities of sexual torture against women.

In January 2016, Juan Mendéz, the UN Special Rapporteur on Torture and Other Cruel, Inhuman, or Degrading Treatment, released a report that discusses the gender aspects of torture. The rapporteur recognized that torture is traditionally treated as a practice committed against men, which renders invisible the specificities of violence and suffering caused in women, girls, and other groups that, by sexual orientation or gender identity, don't fit the socially dominant patterns. For those reasons, the rapporteur stressed the need to take into account the gender nature of torture, both for analyzing its causes and consequences (with emphasis on the structural factors of discrimination) and for formulating state responses, especially in providing adequate reparation to victims.[16]

In Chile, the first criminal accusations against perpetrators of sexual violence followed the first legal strategy outlined above and incorporated sexual violence into the practice of torture (or *apremios ilegítimos*, illegitimate pressures, according to the definition of the criminal norm at the time). According to Daniella Quintanilla, the allegations emphasized the sexual nature of the torture, even though there were no repercussions in terms of criminal liability or in punishment. But there has been progress in the case law, as courts have come to recognize sexual violence as a proven fact and to recognize the sexual connotation of the torture. Other complaints brought before the courts took the process a step further by making simultaneous accusations of crimes of torture and rape.

Daniella Quintanilla has sustained that the criminal regulation of sexual violence is disputed in civil society. There is no consensus as to the adequate penal technique, whether sexual violence should be considered a separate criminal offense, an aggravating factor, or a specific form of torture. In November 2016, the government approved law 20.968, which included the crime of torture in the Chilean Penal Code. The new law incorporates sexual violence as a form of torture. During the legislative process, the proposed bill was criticized by the organization *Mujeres Sobrevivientes Siempre Resistentes*, which defended the recognition of sexual violence as distinct from torture.[17] Nonetheless, despite these divergences, Daniella Quintanilla stressed

---

[16] Méndez, Juan. 2016. *Report of the Special Rapporteur on torture and other cruel, inhuman or degrading treatment or punishment.* 5 January 2016, UN Doc. A/HRC/31/57, §68.

[17] The group released a note stating that they "require the criminalization of sexual violence as an autonomous crime, without being subsumed under the concept of 'torture' included in the new

that all women agree that the regulation of torture must not make sexual violence invisible again.[18]

In turn, there is a strong consensus in Argentina that sexual violence should be separated from torture. This consensus represents a claim by the victims, who have demanded that the perpetrators also be judged as rapists (Aucía et al. 2011, 253). This view is also the official position of the Attorney General's Office of Argentina (*Procuración General de la Nación*) which, in 2012 approved instructions to guide prosecutors in investigating and making accusations of sex crimes in the context of State terrorism.[19] These guidelines were prepared by a special unit of the public prosecution office that is dedicated to dealing with human rights violations committed during the military dictatorship.[20] In particular, the instructions include the consideration of sexual violence as a separate crime, according to the specific criminal offenses provided in the Penal Code at the time.

Thus, in Argentina, it is the prosecution's opinion that subsuming sexual violence to torture makes sexual violence less visible, harder to recognize. But that does not mean that sexual violence could not constitute torture; according to the document, "it is not our intention to deny that a classification as torture can be given concurrently with a classification as crimes against sexual integrity, but to affirm that the

---

draft law on torture" (Observatorio de Justicia Transicional. Universidad Diego Portales, Santiago de Chile. *Boletín informativo No 33*, diciembre 2015, enero y febrero 2016. pp. 17–18).

[18] A focus on the gender aspects of torture was emphasized by *Corporación Humanas* in a document that sought to subsidize the work of the *Comisión Asesora para la Calificación de Detenidos Desparecidos, Ejecutados Políticos y Víctimas de Prisión Política y Tortura* (Advisory Commission for the Qualification of Detained-Disappeared, Executed Dissidents and Victims of Political Prison and Torture). *Corporación Humanas* drew attention to the peculiarity of the torture practiced against women during the Chilean dictatorship. According to the text, "there was a type of torture that was exercised disproportionately against the women for the sole fact of being women." As a consequence, the Commission was warned that a restrictive conception of torture, conceived as a generic category, would be inconsistent with the specificities of the injuries suffered and thus unable to provide adequate remedies. (Corporación Humanas, "Minuta sobre violencia sexual como tortura. Comisión Asesora para la Calificación de Detenidos Desparecidos, Ejecutados Políticos y Víctimas de Prisión Política y Tortura"). My thanks to Daniella Quintanilla for making the document available.

[19] Resolution PGN No. 557 of 2012, of the Attorney General's Office of Argentina (*Procuración General de la Nación*), instructs all prosecutors to observe a document prepared by the Fiscal Unit for Coordination and Follow-up of cases for human rights violations committed during State terrorism (*Unidad Fiscal de Coordinación y Seguimiento de las causas por violaciones a los derechos humanos cometidas durante el terrorismo de Estado*), entitled "Considerations on the prosecution of sexual abuse committed in the context of State terrorism" ("*Consideraciones sobre el juzgamiento de los abusos sexuales cometidos en el marco del terrorismo de Estado*"). Resolución de la Procuración General de la Nación 557/2012, Unidad Fiscal de Coordinación y Seguimiento de las causas por violaciones a los derechos humanos cometidas durante el terrorismo de Estado, *Consideraciones sobre el juzgamiento de los abusos sexuales cometidos en el marco del terrorismo de estado*, Ciudad de Buenos Aires. Available at: https://www.mpf.gov.ar/resoluciones/pgn/2012/PGN-0557-2012-002.pdf.

[20] The document was prepared by the *Unidad Fiscal de Coordinación y Seguimiento de las causas por violaciones a los derechos humanos cometidas durante el terrorismo de Estado* in articulation with *Programa del Ministerio Público Fiscal sobre Políticas de Género*.

classification as crimes against sexual integrity cannot be left aside".[21] Rather, it would be a problem to exclude the application of specific criminal offenses and to classify sexual violence under the generic definition of torture, given that "the crime of torture does not express in any way the particular essence that an aggression of a sexual nature contains".[22]

The perspective of the Attorney General's office is also supported at the regional level. At a meeting held in June 2015, Mercosur prosecution offices approved the "Guide for Public Prosecutions in the criminal investigation of cases of sexual violence perpetrated within the context of international crimes, in particular crimes against humanity." The Guide contains the following instruction:

> Article 4. Obligation to investigate crimes of sexual violence
>
> b) Visibility of the facts of sexual violence. Public Prosecutions shall classify crimes of sexual violence as specific sexual offenses, as provided for in the domestic law of each State. If an event can be classified as several crimes, all of those crimes must be made visible.

In her interview for this study, Susana Chiarotti drew attention to another aspect of this issue related to disputes over memory. She highlighted the importance of reporting sexual violence in order to demonstrate the true nature of the repressors, since a substantial part of society still thinks they were well-intentioned Christian people who sought to save the country from the dangers of communism and to restore morality. Chiarotti argues that:

> people can tolerate being told that that a military man has tortured someone, but they can't tolerate being told that he has raped someone, because when you say torture, people imagine a soldier with a cattle prod [*picana*], or a stick that mediates between him and the victim's body, that separates him from the victim's body, trying to obtain information to ensure the country's security. But when you show a man throwing himself on the top of a hooded detainee with her hands tied, the image is that of an animal, and you totally destroy the idea of the good repressor who had to use some excessive force to obtain information to save the country.

6.3.2   Obstacles and Strategies of Legal Procedure

Once sex crimes began to be prosecuted separately, other obstacles emerged. Among them three difficulties may be highlighted: (i) the difficulty in gaining recognition for sexual violence as a crime against humanity and therefore requiring the waver

---

[21] Resolución de la Procuración General de la Nación 557/2012, Unidad Fiscal de Coordinación y Seguimiento de las causas por violaciones a los derechos humanos cometidas durante el terrorismo de Estado, *Consideraciones sobre el juzgamiento de los abusos sexuales cometidos en el marco del terrorismo de estado*, Ciudad de Buenos Aires, 10. Available at: https://www.mpf.gov.ar/resolucio nes/pgn/2012/PGN-0557-2012-002.pdf.

[22] Resolución de la Procuración General de la Nación 557/2012, Unidad Fiscal de Coordinación y Seguimiento de las causas por violaciones a los derechos humanos cometidas durante el terrorismo de Estado, *Consideraciones sobre el juzgamiento de los abusos sexuales cometidos en el marco del terrorismo de estado*, Ciudad de Buenos Aires, 12. Available at: https://www.mpf.gov.ar/resolucio nes/pgn/2012/PGN-0557-2012-002.pdf.

of the amnesty provision and the waiver of any time limits imposed by the statute of limitations; (ii) the difficulty in proving that the specific acts of sexual violence took place, given the clandestine nature of the violations and the lack of available evidence; (iii) the difficulty in proving the authorship of the crime in the face of the traditional conception that only the direct perpetrator of sexual crimes can be held responsible.

International law describes crimes against humanity as particularly severe crimes committed in the context of a widespread or systematic attack against a civilian population, according to Article 7 of the Rome Statute. The courts have recognized that this category of international crimes cannot be time barred or submitted to amnesty provisions, given the seriousness of the violations and the need to avoid the risk of impunity.

In Brazil, in general, the judiciary does not recognize any of the violations committed during the dictatorship as crimes against humanity. The failure to integrate international law into national case law is one of the main reasons why the Brazilian judiciary refuses to prosecute and to punish perpetrators, as Marlon Weichert stated in his interview. Judges generally reject complaints based on the statute of limitations: they consider these claims to be time barred and, further, they consider these crimes to be covered by amnesty provisions. This position is disrespectful to the international condemnations that Brazil has received, and it disregards key concepts and categories from international human rights law, as Emílio Peluso Meyer (2016, 53–54) points out:

> There are several problems related to the lack of understanding with regard to the significance and binding nature of international human rights law and its concepts: crimes against humanity, non-applicability of statutory limitations, the impossibility of applying amnesty are ignored by these decisions that still see an opposition between sovereignty and human rights, with the clear primacy of the former (…).

These same grounds (amnesty and statutes of limitations) were used to reject the first claim regarding the sexual offenses against Inês Etienne Romeu that was filed in 2016. However, the judicial response to this claim did not stick to the usual arguments. The decision not only recognized the grounds for excluding criminal liability, but it also disqualified the victim. Firstly, the judge decided that the victim's testimony, given in 1979, was useless as evidence. He expressly pointed out that the victim's statements were provided "EIGHT YEARS after the time of the crime, according to the complaint." What the judge suggests is that the testimony lost credibility because of the delay. The judge also made explicit reference to the convictions handed down by the military courts against Inês Etienne Romeu during the dictatorship to conclude that human rights could not serve as a "pretext to give advantages to minorities".[23]

---

[23] Federal Court of the Judiciary Section of Rio de Janeiro. Process n°. 2016.51.06.170716-2. Plaintiff: Inês Etienne Romeu. Defendant: Antonio Waneir Pinheiro Lima. Judge: Alcir Luiz Lopes Coelho. Rio de Janeiro, March 6th 2017.

The decision was appealed by the Federal Public Prosecutor's Office and was reversed by the appeal court in August 2019.[24] The appeal court received the complaint and ordered the case to be heard and prosecuted. It is, therefore, the first criminal proceeding in progress that deals with sexual crimes committed by the dictatorship. Despite the fact that the complaint was ultimately received, Ines Etienne case is representative of the deficiencies of the justice system in Brazil to properly address the human rights violations of the dictatorship and especially gender-based violations (Meyer and Carvalho 2019).

In Argentina and Chile, in contrast, the concept of crimes against humanity has gained ground in the case law that addresses human rights violations committed during the dictatorships. In addition, in Chile, Law 20,357 of 2009 defined crimes against humanity and included among them rape and sexual abuse (Article 5, number 8). Although this law does not apply to the crimes of the dictatorship, it explicitly considers sexual violence as a crime against humanity and demonstrates an improved interaction between national and international legal order.

Even though other violations have been recognized as crimes against humanity in Argentina, this recognition was at first denied to sexual crimes. The initial position of the Judiciary was that the sexual crimes could not be considered crimes against humanity because they had not been systematic or widespread. In the case "Circuito Zárate Campana," the Federal Chamber of Appeal argued that the rapes were occasional and isolated events and were not part of the repressive plan of the dictatorial regime (CELS 2015). This same understanding was shared by the Federal Court n. 3 of the Capital, in deciding a criminal action against Jorge R. Videla in December 2009:

> (…) although a great number of women were subjected to these kinds of violations, the dynamics under which these acts were committed, lacking the marks of systematic forethought and the intentionality that would go along with it, do not reflect the inclusion of said violations in the clandestine plan for repression established by the regime.[25]

In response to these arguments, the project *Grietas del Silencio* gathered testimonies from female victims that demonstrated that sexual crimes were not isolated episodes. On the contrary, they were a common and routine practice in detention centers located throughout Argentina. But even if sexual violence had not been committed on a massive scale, to constitute a crime against humanity—according to Article 7 of the Rome Statute—the attack on the whole must be widespread or systematic, not the individual types of violations. In other words, a single act of sexual violence constitutes a crime against humanity as long as it is connected to, or

---

[24] Federal Regional Court of the 2nd Region. Process n°. 0,500,068-73.2018.4.02.5106. Recurrent: Ministério Público Federal. Defendant: Antonio Waneir Pinheiro Lima. Rio de Janeiro, August 14th 2019.

[25] Cause 14.216 / 03 of Federal Court No. 3 of Federal Capital. Date of decision: 30 December 2009. This reference was taken from the following document: Resolución de la Procuración General de la Nación 557/2012, Unidad Fiscal de Coordinación y Seguimiento de las causas por violaciones a los derechos humanos cometidas durante el terrorismo de Estado, *Consideraciones sobre el juzgamiento de los abusos sexuales cometidos en el marco del terrorismo de estado*, Ciudad de Buenos Aires, 5–7. Available at: https://www.mpf.gov.ar/resoluciones/pgn/2012/PGN-0557-2012-002.pdf.

is part of, the "widespread or systematic" attack against a civilian population. In her interview, Carolina Varsky reinforced this understanding:

> even if there is only one case in a clandestine detention center, the systematic character refers to the generalized attack, not to the practice of rape itself. Even if there is only one case it is a crime against humanity, because it was committed within the framework of that systematic plan for the extermination of the opponents to the dictatorship.

The Argentine Public Prosecutor's Office sets out the requirements for deeming acts of sexual violence crimes against humanity. Firstly, it is required that there be a multiple commission of violations (the attack) that affects a large number of victims (widespread) or that was coordinated by a pre-conceived plan (systematic). In the case of Argentine state terrorism, the repression was both widespread and systematic. The connection between the violation and the attack may be proven by the fact that the crime is by its nature and consequences part of the attack or by the accused's knowledge that an attack existed and that his act was a part of it.[26]

Another criterion for determining whether a sexual crime constitutes a crime against humanity is to evaluate whether the context increased the dangerousness of the crime or the vulnerability of the victims. This is not valid for all crimes in this period, but only for crimes shielded by the political repression, that is, crimes that were "favored or facilitated by the existence of the attack, precisely because there is no authority available to avoid them or to punish them." That was the case for sexual violence committed in the clandestine detention or extermination centers, since the torturers had a practically absolute dominion over their victims.[27] In addition, the sexual crimes were tied to the structure of power, as clarified by a victim: "I am sure that if he were to be let loose in the streets, he would not be a serial rapist; he raped women because this was part of his power in that place" (Balardini et al. 2011, 130).

Judicial understanding began to change with the first conviction for sexual offense, in the "Molina Case" judged by the Federal Oral Court of Mar del Plata in June 2010. Officer Gregorio Molina was sentenced to life imprisonment as the direct perpetrator of five rapes and an attempted rape in the clandestine detention center known as "La Cueva." The tribunal considered the rapes to be crimes against humanity, as they "did not constitute isolated or occasional events, but were part of practices carried out within a systematic and widespread plan of repression" ("Molina

---

[26] Resolución de la Procuración General de la Nación 557/2012, Unidad Fiscal de Coordinación y Seguimiento de las causas por violaciones a los derechos humanos cometidas durante el terrorismo de Estado, *Consideraciones sobre el juzgamiento de los abusos sexuales cometidos en el marco del terrorismo de estado*, Ciudad de Buenos Aires, 5–7. Available at: https://www.mpf.gov.ar/resoluciones/pgn/2012/PGN-0557-2012-002.pdf.

[27] Resolución de la Procuración General de la Nación 557/2012, Unidad Fiscal de Coordinación y Seguimiento de las causas por violaciones a los derechos humanos cometidas durante el terrorismo de Estado, *Consideraciones sobre el juzgamiento de los abusos sexuales cometidos en el marco del terrorismo de estado*, Ciudad de Buenos Aires, 5–7. Available at: https://www.mpf.gov.ar/resoluciones/pgn/2012/PGN-0557-2012-002.pdf.

Case").[28] This recognition of sexual violence as a crime against humanity is important for demonstrating that these acts were not individual deviations but part of the repressive plan, and they were motivated not by sexual desires but for the purposes of political domination.

The second difficulty lies in proving the violations. Victims' testimony is, as a rule, the only available evidence, since the crimes were committed clandestinely and were not witnessed by others. After decades, it is also not possible to perform physical examinations to prove sexual assault. Given this situation, the courts in Argentina initially rejected the testimony of the victims as the only evidence and even questioned the credibility of the reports, since it took so long for the victims to raise these issues The paradox, pointed out by Memoria Abierta (2012, 18), "is that the same is not required in the case of torture, which is considered proven by the context of clandestine detention itself." It is contradictory to consider the victims' testimony as sufficient evidence to prove torture, but disqualify it when it comes to sexual crimes (Oberlin 2019, §31).

Based on the rules of evidence set out in international law, national legal strategies have sought to recognize that victims' testimonies are fundamental and credible evidence. Other important rules of international case law establish that: the sexual history of the victim cannot be taken into account; absence of consent may be presumed or inferred from the coercive context in which sexual aggression was practiced; any inaccuracies or gaps in the reports do not undermine the credibility of the testimony, but represent effects of the psychological trauma itself caused by the violation.

Both the document from *Procuración General de la Nación*, in Argentina, and the amicus curiae of Women's Link Worldwide, in Chile, reinforce the use of these criteria for the treatment of evidence in cases of sexual crimes. The criteria seek to influence how courts incorporate and value evidence given the centrality of the victims' testimonies and the almost inexistence of other evidence. It has also been argued that courts cannot impose a higher probative standard for sexual crimes compared to other human rights violations (Memoria Abierta 2012, 23).

The Mercosur Guide assigns to the public prosecutors the task of conducting exhaustive and rigorous interviews with appropriate psychological monitoring (Article 5 (c)). Interview protocols should also incorporate a gender perspective in order to avoid the risk of revictimization.[29] The Argentine prosecution office emphasizes the need for proper training of the legal practitioners, as well as due preparation of the site and the modality of the interviews. In particular, judges and prosecutors ought to

---

[28] Cause No 2086 and its cumulative No 22, Federal Criminal Oral Court of Mar del Plata. Date of decision: 16 June 2010, 111.

[29] See, for instance, Centro Ulloa and CELS. Centro de Asistencia a Víctimas de Violaciones de Derechos Humanos "Dr. Fernando Ulloa". Protocolo de Intervención para el Tratamiento de Víctimas-Testigos en el Marco de Procesos Judiciales. Secretaría de Derechos Humanos del Ministerio de Justicia y Derechos Humanos de la Nación; Corte Suprema de Justicia de la Nación. Buenos Aires, septiembre de 2011. And Centro de Estudios Legales y Sociales. Guia de Trabajo para la toma de testimonios a víctimas sobrevivientes de tortura. CELS; Unión Europea, 2012.

assist the victim with whatever needs she has; to ensure that her testimony is given in an appropriate context so that it is given as freely as possible; to prevent interrogations that distort, coerce or disturb the victim; to provide the necessary security and psychological assistance measures; and if necessary to avoid public exposure, making use of any corresponding technical means (videoconference, Gesell camera, or other similar alternatives).[30]

Due to the difficulties in obtaining direct evidence of sexual crimes, such as physical evidence, crime scene examination, or body examination ("corpus delicti" exam), other means of proof have been added. In the amicus curiae submitted to the Judiciary in Chile, the Women's Link Worldwide supported the use of circumstantial or conjectural evidence, as well as evidence that proves the connection between the crimes and the context. This obligation to take into account the context of the crimes is also a mechanism to relieve the victims from "bearing all the burden of proof in these cases".[31]

Finally, there is the difficulty of pointing out authorship in cases of sexual crimes. Traditionally it has been understood that rape is a crime that can only be committed by the direct perpetrator. Since the perpetrators of sexual crimes in the dictatorships acted clandestinely and most often concealed their identities, it is practically impossible to identify those directly responsible. According to Balardini et al. (2011, 203–204):

Obviously, in cases of state terrorism, determining who committed the specific acts of sexual violence is exceptional. Due to the context in which they occurred, in which the victims were generally deprived of sight, subjected to inhumane living conditions, kept naked, and physically and psychologically abused, all of which greatly increased their vulnerability, and in which the perpetrators intentionally sought future impunity, using false names in order to avoid being identified, (…) the direct perpetrator of these acts can rarely be accurately determined.

Although case law in Argentina has admitted the prosecution of indirect or mediate perpetrators in case of other violations, such as torture, this possibility was not initially admitted in cases of sexual crimes (Memoria Abierta 2012, 19). Both in Argentina and in Chile, victims' representatives have used Claus Roxin's "theory of domination of the fact" ("act domination" or "control theory of perpetration") to hold indirect perpetrators criminally liable for the crimes committed by direct perpetrators through, and within, the military organization.[32] Kai Ambos has explained how the individual criminal responsibility of indirect perpetrators is grounded in this theory:

---

[30] Resolución de la Procuración General de la Nación 557/2012, Unidad Fiscal de Coordinación y Seguimiento de las causas por violaciones a los derechos humanos cometidas durante el terrorismo de Estado, *Consideraciones sobre el juzgamiento de los abusos sexuales cometidos en el marco del terrorismo de estado*, Ciudad de Buenos Aires, 25. Available at: https://www.mpf.gov.ar/resolucio nes/pgn/2012/PGN-0557-2012-002.pdf.

[31] Women's Link Worldwide. *Amicus Curiae*. Rol 99-2015 Del 34° Juzgado del Crimen de Santiago, Ministro Instructor Don Mario Carroza Espinoza. Incorporación de la Perspectiva de Género y la Categoría de Crímenes Internacionales a la Investigación del Caso de Ana María Campillo Bastidas. Madrid, noviembre de 2015, 19.

[32] Resolución de la Procuración General de la Nación 557/2012, Unidad Fiscal de Coordinación y Seguimiento de las causas por violaciones a los derechos humanos cometidas durante el terrorismo de Estado, *Consideraciones sobre el juzgamiento de los abusos sexuales cometidos en el marco del terrorismo de estado*, Ciudad de Buenos Aires, 5–7. Available

(...) the organizational structure of a military apparatus can confer upon its leaders and commanders the power to dominate the acts of their subordinates, who—as direct perpetrators—carry out the crimes conceived and ordered by the commanders. Although the subordinates are criminally responsible, the commanders are in total control since the former are easily replaceable: they are fungible mediators of the act (...). The domination of the system implies the domination of each individual who forms part of the system. (Ambos 2013, 114)

The Argentine public prosecutor also supports the analysis that says that limiting accountability to the direct perpetrator reinforces the idea that sexual crimes require the presence of pleasure or lasciviousness and therefore can only be committed individually.[33] In opposition to this idea, criminal responsibility must be gauged from the control that each co-perpetrator exercises over the execution of the crime. In addition to the direct perpetrator, those who induce, facilitate, and provide means, or do not prevent the commission of the crime, when they have a duty to do so, are also responsible. Whoever exercises force over the victim, whoever dispatches orders, or whoever commands the detention center, for example, are indirect perpetrators.

With this logic, hierarchical superiors and commanders of detention centers are also liable for the sexual crimes practiced for two main reasons. First, they guaranteed the apparatus and the impunity that allowed for the sexual crimes to be committed. Second, they had control over the criminal acts that were practiced under their command, especially considering the vertical and hierarchical organization of the Armed Forces.[34] According to the lawyer Ana Oberlini, if it were not for the repressive context and the material means involved, there would have been no violation (Memoria Abierta 2012, 23).

The Mercosur Public Prosecution Office's Guide to Action provides the same understanding regarding criminal participation:

Article 4. Obligation to Investigate Crimes of Sexual Violence

c) Criminal participation. In criminal proceedings relating to crimes of sexual violence, Public Prosecutors, within the framework of their specific competences and in accordance with the domestic law of each State, shall investigate and promote criminal prosecution to criminally charge all those responsible [...] (direct authors, mediators, co-authors, accomplices, among others).

---

at: https://www.mpf.gov.ar/resoluciones/pgn/2012/PGN-0557-2012-002.pdf. Also Women's Link Worldwide. Amicus Curiae. Rol 99-2015 Del 34° Juzgado del Crimen de Santiago, Ministro Instructor Don Mario Carroza Espinoza. Incorporación de la Perspectiva de Género y la Categoría de Crímenes Internacionales a la Investigación del Caso de Ana María Campillo Bastidas. Madrid, noviembre de 2015.

[33] Resolución de la Procuración General de la Nación 557/2012, Unidad Fiscal de Coordinación y Seguimiento de las causas por violaciones a los derechos humanos cometidas durante el terrorismo de Estado, *Consideraciones sobre el juzgamiento de los abusos sexuales cometidos en el marco del terrorismo de estado*, Ciudad de Buenos Aires, 21. Available at: https://www.mpf.gov.ar/resolucio nes/pgn/2012/PGN-0557-2012-002.pdf.

[34] Women's Link Worldwide. *Amicus Curiae*. Rol 99-2015 Del 34° Juzgado del Crimen de Santiago, Ministro Instructor Don Mario Carroza Espinoza. Incorporación de la Perspectiva de Género y la Categoría de Crímenes Internacionales a la Investigación del Caso de Ana María Campillo Bastidas. Madrid, noviembre de 2015.

6.4 Final Remarks

The use of law in transitional justice is not gender neutral. The analysis of the political transitions in Argentina, Brazil, and Chile shows that these countries' institutions, norms, and legal operators have prioritized certain victims and violations over others. It also reveals that a generic category of human rights violations does not respond to the specificities of sexual violence.

After the return to democracy, cases of sexual violence—when compared to other crimes—took longer to be brought to court, were prosecuted in smaller numbers, and faced more procedural delays, as well as greater obstacles to prosecutions and punishments. Sexual offenses are more severely affected by the impunity measures and probationary difficulties that have traditionally obstructed criminal proceedings in transitional justice. At the same time, there are specific difficulties related to the reporting of sexual crimes. Along with the shame, guilt, and fear of the victims, discriminatory practices in the justice system discourage reports because victims face the risk of suffering new violence.

Argentina, Chile, and Brazil are at different stages in the transitional justice process, particularly in their responses to sexual crimes committed during the dictatorships. A comparison of the different experiences in each country demonstrates the complexity of factors that allow access to justice for these crimes. The mobilization of victims, the work of lawyers and representatives, and the involvement of institutional actors are all important aspects of the struggle for justice. The acceptance by the judiciary of key concepts and categories in international law is also a prerequisite. Where transitional justice has not yet taken this initial step, as in the case of Brazil, the response to sexual crimes is even more deficient or practically non-existent.

In the judicial field, different strategies have been used to overcome the obstacles with regard to legal classification, evidence assessment, and indicating the authorship of sexual crimes. Alongside legal arguments, these strategies involve better training and preparation for the justice system operators. Although these obstacles remain an ongoing challenge, the results of efforts thus far have demonstrated the importance of reversing the invisibility of sexual crimes and of resignifying the societal connotations of these violations previously considered minor. In this respect, the law can also contribute to retelling the stories of these repressive periods by including narratives of subjects and of violations that have long been excluded.

References

Ambos, K. 2013. *Treatise on international criminal law. Volume 1: Foundations and general part.* Oxford: Oxford University Press.

Arns, P.E. 1987. *Brasil: Nunca Mais. Um relato para a história*, 20a ed. Petrópolis: Vozes.

Aucía, A., F. Barrera, C. Berterame, S. Chiarotti, and A. Paolini, eds. 2011. *Grietas en el silencio. Una investigación sobre la violencia sexual en el marco del terrorismo de Estado.* Rosario: Cladem.

Balardini, L., A. Oberlin, and L. Sobredo. 2011. Violência de gênero e abusos sexuais em centros clandestinos de detenção: uma contribuição para a compreensão da experiência argentina. *Revista Anistia Política e Justiça de Transição/Ministério da Justiça* (6) (jul./dez). Brasília: Ministério da Justiça.

Barbuto, V., and L. Fries. 2008. *Sin Tregua: Políticas de reparación para mujeres víctimas de violência sexual durante dictaduras y conflictos armados*. Santigo de Chile: Corporación Humanas.

Bell, C., and C. O'Rourke. 2007. Does feminism need a theory of transitional justice? An introductory essay. *The International Journal of Transitional Justice* 1: 23–44.

Calandra, B. 2010. Un tema "incómodo e indecente". El debate alrededor de la violación sexual en Chile postautoritario. *Studia Historica: Historia Contemporánea* 28: 213–236.

Cánaves, V. 2011. Como la cigarra: notas sobre violencia sexual, jurisprudencia, y Derechos Humanos. *Revista Jurídica de la Universidad de Palermo* 12 (1): 88–110.

Carvalho, C.P. 2016. *Crimes sexuais e justiça de transição na América Latina: judicialização e arquivos./Crímenes sexuales y justicia transicional en América Latina: judicialización y archivos*. Florianópolis: Tribo da Ilha; Belo Horizonte: Projeto Memorial da Anistia; Rede Latino-Americana de Justiça de Transição (RLAJT); Centro de Estudos sobre Justiça de Transição, Universidade Federal de Minas Gerais (CJT/UFMG), Universidade de Brasília (UnB).

Centro de Estudios Legales y Sociales (CELS). 2015. Juzgamiento de la violencia sexual durante la última dictadura cívico militar en Argentina.

Chiarotti, S. 2011. Jurisprudência internacional sobre violencia sexual. In *Grietas en el silencio. Una investigación sobre la violencia sexual en el marco del terrorismo de Estado*, ed. Analía Aucía, Florencia Barrera, Celina Berterame, Susana Chiarotti, and Alejandra Paolini. Rosario: Cladem.

Copelon, R. 2000. Crímenes de género como crímenes de guerra: integrando los crímenes contra las mujeres en el derecho penal internacional. *McGill Law Journal*.

Diniz, D. 2014. Perspectivas e articulações de uma pesquisa feminista. In *Estudos Feministas e de Gênero: ArticulaAÇÕES e Perspectivas*, ed. Cristina Stevens, Susane Rodrigues de Oliveira, and Valeska Zanello, 11–21. Florianópolis: Ed. Mulheres.

Gaggioli, G. 2014. Sexual violence in armed conflicts: A violation of international humanitarian law and human rights law. *International Review of the Red Cross* 96 (894): 503–538.

Hagay-Frey, A. 2011. *Sex and gender crimes in the new international law: Past, present, future*. Leiden and Boston: Martinus Nijhoff Publishers.

McEvoy, K., and L. McGregor. (2008). Transitional justice from below: An agenda for research, policy and praxis. In *Transitional justice from below: Grassroots activism and the struggle for change*. Portland: Hart.

Memoria Abierta. 2012. *"... y nadie quería saber". Relatos sobre violencia contra las mujeres en el terrorismo de Estado en Argentina*, 1a ed. Buenos Aires: Memoria Abierta.

Meyer, E. P. N. 2016. Responsabilização e ditadura. In: Claudia Paiva Carvalho, José Otávio Nogueira Guimarães, Maria Pia Guerra (Org.). Justiça de transição na América Latina: panorama 2015 = Justicia de transición en América Latina : panorama 2015. Brasília: Ministério da Justiça, Comissão de Anistia, Rede Latino-Americana de Justiça de Transição (RLAJT).

Meyer, E.P.N., and C.P. Carvalho. 2019. Sexual crimes and transitional justice before courts in Brazil: Accountability for crimes against humanity. In *Criminal legalities in the global south cultural dynamics, political tensions, and institutional practices*, vol. 1, 1st ed., org. Pablo Ciocchini and George Radics, pp. 190–230. London: Routledge.

Nagy, R. 2008. Transitional justice as global project: Critical reflections. *Third World Quarterly* 29 (2): 275–289.

Oberlin, A. 2019. Respuestas judiciales en Argentina, Chile y Uruguay a las violencias estatales diferenciales hacia mujeres y personas fuera de la cis/heteronormatividad durante el terrorismo de Estado, Amérique Latine Histoire et Mémoire. *Les Cahiers ALHIM*, 38. Available at: https://journals.openedition.org/alhim/7977.

Osmo, C. 2016. *Judicialização da Justiça de Transição na América Latina*. Brasília: Ministério da Justiça, Comissão de Anistia, Rede Latino-Americana de Justiça de Transição (RLAJT).

Pereira, A.W. 2010. *Ditadura e Repressão: o autoritarismo e o estado de direito no Brasil, no Chile e na Argentina*. São Paulo: Paz e Terra.

Roesler, C.R., and L.C.M. Senra. 2013. Gênero e justiça de transição no Brasil. *Revista Jurídica da Presidência* 5 (105): 35–67.

Souza Pinto, G.R. 2013. *Para a democracia: soberania, transição e rastro na Ação de Descumprimento de Preceito Fundamental n. 153*. Dissertação (Mestrado em Direito). Faculdade de Direito, Universidade de Brasília, Brasília.

Teles, M.A. 2015. Violações dos direitos humanos das mulheres na ditadura. *Estudos Feministas* 23 (3): 1001–1022.

Torelly, M. 2016. *Governança Transversal dos Direitos Fundamentais*: Experiências Latino-Americanas. Tese (Doutorado em Direito). Faculdade de Direito, Universidade de Brasília, Brasília.

Interviews

Amelinha Teles, Former political prisoner, Member of the São Paulo's Truth Commission "Rubens Paiva", Brazil, 20 July 2016.

Beatriz Betaszew, *Mujeres Sobrevivientes, Siempre Resistentes*, Chile, 12 July 2016.

Carolina Varsky, Coordinator of the Prosecution Office for Crimes against Humanity (*Procuraduría de Crímenes contra la Humanidad*), Argentina, 18 July 2016.

Daniela Quintanilla, *Corporación Humanas*, Chile, 21 July 2016.

Marlon Weichert, Public Prosecution, São Paulo, Brazil, 12 July 2016.

Susana Chiarotti, Director of the Gender, Law and Development Institute of Rosario, member of the Consultative Council of CLADEM and member of the Committee of Experts on Violence of the OAS, Argentina, 7 September 2016.

Claudia Paiva Carvalho is Professor of Law at the Federal University of Rio de Janeiro (UFRJ), Brazil. Juris Science Doctor (J.S.D) and Master of Laws (LL.M) from the University of Brasília, School of Law. Former researcher of the Latin American Transitional Justice Network (Rede Latino-Americana de Justiça de Transição—RLAJT) (2015–2016) and of the National Truth Commission (2014). Member of the University of Brasília Truth Commission (2014–2015). Her main research interests are constitutional history, constitutional law, human rights and transitional justice.

Chapter 7
Justice Entrepreneurs and the Struggle for Accountability in South America: Comparative Reflections on Transitional Justice and Operation Condor

Francesca Lessa

Abstract In recent decades, numerous South American countries have lived through long-lasting transitions, endeavouring to consolidate democratic governance while simultaneously trying to shed light onto unspeakable state-sponsored atrocities. Some countries were able to successfully investigate the crimes of the recent past, while others significantly lagged behind, even leaning towards impunity. Scholars have explained these varied accountability outcomes with reference to variables such as veto players, international pressure, and judicial leadership. This chapter focuses instead on civil society. Using examples from criminal prosecutions for Operation Condor crimes and broader transitional justice policies across South America, it is contended here, first, that human rights activists have played a fundamental role in accountability processes, acting as a relentless force for truth and justice and developing innovative strategies to counter state-sponsored policies of silence and impunity. Second, the concept of "justice entrepreneurs" is introduced to better analyse the crucial part these actors have played and unpack in detail six sets of strategic actions they have carried out over time. The existence and active mobilisation of justice entrepreneurs represents a necessary precondition for achieving accountability.

7.1 Introduction

South America has lived through long-lasting transitions to democracy since the 1980s. Numerous countries endeavoured, with different levels of success, to consolidate democratic governance in the aftermath of dictatorial rule, while simultaneously also shed light onto the unspeakable atrocities perpetrated during the recent decades of state terror. The panorama in the region four decades after democratic transition is

F. Lessa (✉)
Department of International Development and the Latin American Centre,
University of Oxford, Oxford, UK

Observatorio Luz Ibarburu, Montevideo, Uruguay

© Springer Nature Switzerland AG 2021
C. Paixão and M. Meccarelli (eds.), *Comparing Transitions to Democracy. Law and Justice in South America and Europe*, Studies in the History of Law and Justice 18,
https://doi.org/10.1007/978-3-030-67502-8_7

mixed at best. While some countries have successfully implemented policies to investigate the crimes of the recent past, others continue to significantly lag behind on the matter and, in fact, some of them leaned in favour of impunity. Argentina and Chile have carried out the highest number of prosecutions for past human rights violations in the world. Conversely, despite efforts by local activists and prosecutors, the situation of judicial impunity has remained largely unchanged in Brazil and Paraguay. In a sort of middle ground stands Uruguay, where human rights lawyers and activists have filed over 300 criminal lawsuits for past atrocities, but have achieved justice in just a handful of cases while the majority remains shrouded in impunity.

Scholars have explained these different accountability outcomes with reference to a number of variables, including the role of veto players, civil society demand, international pressure, and judicial leadership (Payne et al. 2015), as well as political will and the role of the military (Skaar et al. 2016). In this chapter, particular attention is devoted to one of these factors, namely civil society, by unpacking in detail the role this actor has played in the quest for accountability. The analysis begins by providing a brief historical background on authoritarian regimes and the so-called Operation Condor, namely the transnational coordination of terror established by South America's dictatorships in the mid-1970s to hunt down and murder political opponents all across the region and beyond. Second, the chapter succinctly considers the transitional justice experiences of Argentina, Brazil, Chile, Paraguay, and Uruguay, as well as judicial efforts to investigate Operation Condor atrocities in a third section.

Choosing to focus of Operation Condor serves two specific purposes. While Operation Condor atrocities can, on the one hand, be considered unique because of their transnational nature and connotations, on the other, they unfolded in parallel to domestic state policies of repression and reproduced common patterns of human rights violations on a regional scale. Additionally, the focus on Operation Condor allows us to transcend the existing transitional justice scholarship, and adopt instead a regional approach to accountability. This proposed shift from the national to the regional lens is an important and long overdue analytical move in this field. Indeed, the dominant tendency in transitional justice scholarship and practice has been to frame discussions and analyses around the state, it being perceived as the "primary means of reflecting on and organising transitional justice approaches" as well as "the cornerstone of transitional justice" (Hazan 2017: 1). Elsewhere, I have critiqued this prevalent state-centric approach, suggesting it limited the potential for analysis in transitional justice scholarship and practice (Lessa 2015). In the chapter, both lenses, the national and the regional, are used to provide a comprehensive discussion of transitional justice dynamics in South America.

Using examples from judicial prosecutions for Operation Condor crimes as well as broader transitional justice policies, the fourth section of this chapter puts forward a two-fold argument. First, it highlights how human rights activists and lawyers across South America have acted as a relentless force to obtain truth and justice for state-sponsored atrocities, developing creative and innovative strategies to counter state-sponsored policies of silence and impunity. Second, the concept of "justice entrepreneurs" is introduced to capture and further elaborate the crucial part played by these actors in the search for justice. While agreeing with most scholars that no single factor (political will, judicial leadership, etc.) is sufficient to bring about account-ability, a necessary precondition is in fact the existence of justice entrepreneurs, actively pushing for that goal.

7.2 South America's Dictatorships and Transitions

Since the mid-1950s, South American countries witnessed increasing numbers of authoritarian spells, accompanied by the consolidation of dictatorial regimes that would remain in power, in some cases, even for twenty or thirty years. Dictatorial rule spread across this region and was characterised by unprecedented levels of human rights violations committed in a systematic fashion against the local population, affecting thousands of people.

Paraguay was the first country to fall to the dictatorship of Alfredo Stroessner (1954–1989), to later be followed by Brazil (1964–1985), Uruguay (1973–1985), Chile (1973–1990), and Argentina (1976–1983). These regimes shared a common ideological foundation in the global backdrop of the Cold War and, especially, the National Security Doctrine (NSD), which closely inspired the philosophies and oper-ations of the dictatorships. The NSD combined anti-Communism and the threat of an internal enemy with a defence of Western Christian values; achieving national security was a fundamental objective that trumped all others, and resulted in serious violations of individual rights by the state (Pion-Berlin 1988). These dictatorships felt they were engaged in sort of a Third World War, against the perceived threat of Communism and subversion. The category of "subversive" was so amply defined that policies of repression in practice targeted large and different sectors of these coun-tries' societies, not only directly aiming at curbing guerrilla and revolutionary armed groups, such as the Argentine Montoneros, the Chilean Revolutionary Left Move-ment (Movimiento de Izquierda Revolucionaria) and the Uruguayan Tupamaros, but also all forms of peaceful political and social opposition, including students, teachers, trade union leaders, journalists, moderate left-wing leaders and political, as well as social activists. Despite local differences, all of these repressive policies were characterised by extreme brutality and encompassed a similar range of human rights violations, which included torture, kidnappings, enforced disappearances, arbitrary executions, illegal detentions, sexual violence, and illegal appropriation of children (King 1989). Complementing the violence unleashed inside each country, in late November 1975, the regimes of Argentina, Chile, Uruguay, Paraguay, and Bolivia, also established "Operation Condor." Brazil joined in 1976, while Peru and Ecuador did so in 1978. Condor was a secret transnational network of intelligence and repres-sive operations set up to eliminate political opponents in exile within South America. Operation Condor effectively established a borderless area of terror and impunity all across this region and beyond, with crimes committed also in the US and Europe (Dinges 2004; McSherry 2005).

Only after the return of democracy in the 1980s and 1990s, the real scale of political repression across South America became clear, with official investigations into past violence establishing it had reached astonishing numbers. In Chile, the final reports of the Rettig (1990) and Valech Commissions (2004–2005, 2011) confirmed a total of 3,214 dead and disappeared, as well as 38,254 victims of political imprisonment and torture (Observatorio Derechos Humanos 2011). In Argentina, at least 9,334 persons disappeared, with some 500 children abducted along with their parents or born in captivity and later illegally adopted by members of the security forces; there were also over 12,000 political prisoners and 2,286 executions (Crenzel 2011: 2). In Uruguay, there were 196 disappearances and 202 political murders (Secretaría de Derechos Humanos 2020), with close to 6,000 long-term political prisoners and uncountable cases of torture and illegal detentions. In Paraguay, the final report of the truth commission identified 19,862 arbitrary detentions, 18,772 cases of torture, at least 59 victims of summary executions, 336 forced disappearances and an overall total of more than 128,000 victims of the military regime (Paraguay Report 2008). Finally, in Brazil, the National Truth Commission (CNV) identified 434 dead and disappeared, of which 210 remain disappeared to date (CNV 2014: volume III). A well-known 1985 civil society report also acknowledged 17,000 victims of the military justice system (USIP 2017). The Amnesty Commission, established in 2002, additionally recognised there had been at least 38,000 victims of other forms of repression, including individuals being unfairly dismissed from employment (Mezarobba 2016).

The first country to transition to democracy was Argentina, in late 1983. The dictatorship, which had been in power for seven years, collapsed in the aftermath of a shambolic defeat in the 1982 Falklands/Malvinas conflict, an event that worsened a pre-existing situation of economic failure, rising international and national allegations of human rights violations, and escalating pressures from politicians, labour unions, the press, and the judiciary to open up the system (Acuña and Smulovitz 1995). On 10 December 1983, Raúl Alfonsín was inaugurated as president. Unlike the implosion of the Argentine military junta, the transition to democracy in Uruguay and Chile, in the early and late 1980s respectively, was negotiated between political leaders and the armed forces, in a context of enduring military strength, especially in Chile, where Augusto Pinochet would remain as Commander-in-Chief of the armed forces until 1998. The statement in the early 1990s by Chilean President Patricio Aylwin that he could only pursue justice '*en la medida de lo posible*' (to the extent possible) well encapsulated the obstacles faced in the shadow of the dictatorship (Barahona de Brito 1997: 176). The Brazilian transition can, instead, be categorised as a "transformation," since it unfolded through a slow and gradual process of political liberalisation (*aberdura*) led from the top, which began in 1974 and culminated in a democratic government taking over in 1985 (Mainwaring 1986). A large degree of continuity existed between the government of President José Sarney and the prior military regime. Differently from the rest of the countries, Stroessner's dictatorship in Paraguay finally came to end in October 1989 due to internal power struggles within the ruling Colorado Party. Army General Andres Rodriguez toppled Stroessner in what has been labelled "a palace coup" rather than a "formal political transition" (Collins 2016a: 153).

7.3   Accountability After Terror

After the return of democracy, the five South American countries struggled with how to redress the unparalleled human rights atrocities suffered under dictatorship. Especially those countries that transitioned in the early 1980s, such as Argentina, Brazil, and Uruguay, had little guidance available on how best to settle accounts with the horrors of the recent past. In fact, it was in South America where transitional justice scholarship and practice began to take shape, when these countries had to find new ways to respond to past crimes. The core challenge laid in striking a difficult balance between two competing, and equally valid, demands. How to provide accountability for state-sponsored atrocities, while simultaneously consolidating a new and often fragile democracy in the shadow of a watchful military?

Across South America and beyond, confronting the past had often meant turning the page. Oblivion and impunity usually dominated. Yet, the unprecedented crimes perpetrated in the second half of the twentieth century ruptured this pattern. Although criminal prosecutions faced numerous obstacles, in all these countries timid steps were taken in favour of accountability, through the creation of truth or investigative commissions, as well as the sanctioning of reparations' policies. Eventually, they all admitted to and recognised the role of the state in perpetrating unspeakable crimes.

Each country tackled the question of the recent past in different ways and at various moments, with ebbs and flows, in the post-dictatorship decades. Although transitional justice encompasses a wide range of tools, the discussion in this chapter focuses on three processes, namely criminal accountability, the search for the truth, and reparations. Moreover, only some of the key developments can be discussed here; a comprehensive discussion of all the transitional justice tools enacted over time falls beyond the scope of this chapter (see Table 7.1—Overview of Transitional Justice Measures by country). As we will see below, the scenario was usually unfavourable to the search for truth and justice immediately after transition in the 1980s and 1990s; meanwhile, starting from the mid-1990s, shifting local, regional and global contexts in favour of international justice and human rights permitted to achieve more progress.

7.3.1   Justice vs. Impunity

The slogan "*juicio y castigo a los culpables*" (trial and punishment to those responsible) was a key claim of the renowned NGO Mothers of May Square dating back to 1982, when Argentina was still under military rule (Pagina12 1999). Criminal accountability remained an essential demand by survivors and their relatives throughout the region. However, the results achieved have been diverse. In the aftermath of transition, Argentina, Chile, and Paraguay conducted a small number of emblematic criminal prosecutions, which were however halted soon afterwards. Conversely, Brazil and Uruguay adopted from the start tight policies of impunity.

Table 7.1 Overview of Transitional Justice Measures by country[a]

Country	Truth Commissions	Criminal Trials	Reparations	Amnesties
Argentina	1984—National Commission on the Disappearance of Persons	250 verdicts 18 trials ongoing 1013 individuals sentenced, 164 acquitted 3448 individuals under investigation	1986—relatives of the disappeared (Law 23.466); 1991—victims of political imprisonment and arbitrary detention (Law 24.043); 1994—victims of enforced disappearances (Law 24.411); 2004—minors who were victims of state terror (Law 25.914)	1983—Law 22.924 of National Pacification (overturned); 1986—Law 23.492 of Full Stop (overturned); 1987—Law 23.521 of Due Obedience (overturned); 1989—Pardons 1002, 1003, 1004 and 1005 (overturned); 1990—Pardons 2741, 2742 and 2743 (overturned)
Brazil	1985—Brasil: Nunca Mais' report (non-gov); 2014—National Truth Commission	None	1995—victims of political assassination and disappearance (Law 9.140); 2002—victims of institutional acts that revoked fundamental rights (Law 10.559)	1979—Law 6.683;
Chile	1990—National Commission on Truth and Reconciliation (Rettig); 1999—Mesa de Dialogo (roundtable dialogue); 2003/2011—National Commission on Political Imprisonment and Torture (Valech I and II)	476 sentences (76 in civil cases and 400 in criminal cases) 2,837 individuals condemned in first instance	1992—families of victims of political violence identified in the final Rettig report (Law 19.123); 2004—victims of imprisonment and torture for political reasons identified by Valech Commissions (Law 19.992)	1978—Decree Law 2.191
Paraguay	2004—Truth and Justice Commission	9 trials completed; 8 condemned	1996—victims of human rights violations during dictatorship (Law 838)	None

(continued)

Table 7.1 (continued)

Country	Truth Commissions	Criminal Trials	Reparations	Amnesties
Uruguay	1985—Parliamentary Commissions; 2000—Peace Commission; 2015—Working Group for Truth and Justice	318 open criminal investigations Verdicts in 15 criminal lawsuits 45 individuals prosecuted or charged	1985—restitution of employment benefits to unfairly dismissed public workers (Law 15.783); 2006—pension and retirement benefits to citizens unable to work for political union reasons (Law 18.033); 2009—victims of state terrorism (Law 18.596)	1985—Amnesty Law 15.737; 1986—Expiry Law 15.848 (overturned)

[a]This table was built by the author using the following sources of information: for Argentina, https://www.fiscales.gob.ar/wp-content/uploads/2020/09/Lesa_infografi%CC%81a.pdf; for Chile, data provided to the author by the Transitional Justice Observatory of the Diego Portales University and www.pjud.cl/documents/396729/0/Poder+Judicial+y+Derechos+Humanos+Min istro+Cisternas.pdf/5fd451d5-b9c9-4bf1-a587-6c78f3f10312; for Uruguay https://www.observato rioluzibarburu.org/reportes/ and https://twitter.com/SitiosMemoriaUY/status/129757029634248 7041; for Paraguay, information provided by the Human Rights Unit of the Attorney General's Office, on file with the author; data from the Transitional Justice Research Collaborative Dataset https://transitionaljusticedata.com/browse

Subsequently, in the 2000s, judicial investigations resumed in Argentina, Chile, and Uruguay, eventually breaking the existing judicial paralysis. Overall, by 2020, Argentina and Chile can be categorised as leaders in criminal prosecutions, not only within South America but also in global terms, while Brazil, Paraguay, and Uruguay remain as laggards.

Argentina's 1984–1985 historic prosecution against the members of the military juntas was unprecedented in the region. Five of the nine commanders were found guilty for crimes such as murder, unlawful deprivation of freedom, and torture (Amnesty International 1987). Subsequent attempts to broaden judicial investigations of the crimes to middle and lower ranking officers were nevertheless met with resistance in a context of rising tensions with the armed forces. As a result, Congress sanctioned two amnesty laws, the 1986 Full Stop Law and the 1987 Due Obedience Law, halting all proceedings. In Chile, conversely, the Pinochet dictatorship had sanctioned in 1978 an amnesty decree to shield all officers from prosecution, with the explicit exclusion of the murder of former Chilean politician Orlando Letelier in Washington, DC in 1976. In fact, one of just a handful of verdicts dictated in Chile in the 1990s related to that emblematic Operation Condor assassination and was upheld by the Supreme Courtin 1995 (Collins 2010). In Paraguay, a small number of prosecutions for cases of disappearances and homicides were held in the 1990s against a handful of symbolic figures of Stroessner's dictatorship, including Pastor Coronel, the chief of the infamous Police Investigations' Department (Collins 2016a). While in Argentina the trial of the commanders could unfold owing to the implosion of the dictatorship, strong civil society pressure, and the election of a president sympathetic to accountability, in Chile instead the small number of criminal proceedings can be explained with reference the limitations faced by the nascent democracy, especially Pinochet's permanence as head of the armed forces. In Paraguay, conversely, one of the main factors behind the occurrence of trials was internal "score-settling" within the ruling Colorado Party, combined with the 1992 discovery of the Archives of Terror, which had provided irrefutable documentary evidence on four decades of political repression (Collins 2016a: 157).

On the other hand, in Uruguay, although hundreds of cases had been filed before the courts in the early and mid-1980s, pressure from the military and the election of President Julio Maria Sanguinetti, who had been one of the architects of the nego-tiated transition, shifted the balance in favour of impunity. Indeed, after numerous back and forth, Parliament ultimately approved an amnesty law, the so-called Expiry Law in late 1986, which suspended all proceedings looking into dictatorship's atroc-ities committed by state agents. This law was systematically applied between 1986 and 2002 to shelve all investigations into past violations (Lessa 2013). In a similar manner, in Brazil, the new democratic administration was drawn from the National Renovating Alliance, the pro-military party during the dictatorship, which kept close ties with the intelligence services and the military, and effectively governed in asso-ciation with elements of the armed forces (Barahona de Brito 2001). This set of political constraints and continuities, combined with the 1979 amnesty law, resulted in a scenario of absolute judicial impunity that lasts into the present.

Starting in the mid-1990s, judicial accountability processes for past crimes force-fully returned to the Southern Cone owing to local, regional, and international factors, including confessions by military officers in Argentina, the detention in London of former General Pinochet on human rights charges, and the identification of illegally appropriated minors in Uruguay. All of these variables, combined with the consolida-tion of international justice at the global level, reactivated mobilisation in this region. In Argentina, efforts by civil society, especially led by the Centre for Legal and Social Studies (CELS) and the Grandmothers of May Square, to overturn the impunity laws and reopen criminal trials were finally successful with prosecutions resuming in 2006. As of December 2020, 250 trials have been completed, with 1013 people condemned and 164 absolved, as well as 3448 currently under investigation (Lesa Humanidad 2020). In Uruguay, starting in 2002, efforts to achieve accountability initially focused on bypassing the amnesty law and the opening of approximately 25 trials (Burt et al. 2013). Later on, due the unrelenting civil society pressure and a condemnatory verdict by the Inter-American Court of Human Rights (IACtHR) in the *Gelman vs. Uruguay* case, Parliament eventually derogated the Expiry Law in late 2011. Nonetheless, factual, rather than legal, impunity persists and the results have been disappointing: verdicts have been dictated in only 15 criminal lawsuits to date and 45 individuals have been prosecuted or charged out of a universe of over 200 active case files pending before the courts (Abella 2021). Attempts to overturn their respective amnesties also occurred in Chile and Brazil, but were ultimately unsuccessful. In Brazil, the 1979 amnesty law remains in force and continues to be systematically applied to prevent prosecutions of past crimes, despite recent challenges both in domestic courts and internationally, including the 2010 condemnatory sentence by the IACtHR in the *Gomes Lund* case. In Chile, on the other hand, a new interpretation of the amnesty eventually took hold, allowing trials to go ahead in a number of crimes: enforced disappearances, extrajudicial executions and, to a much lower extent, torture. As a result, as of late 2020, 476 sentences have been handed down, with 76 dictated in civil cases and 400 in criminal cases (data from the Transitional Justice Observatory). In Paraguay, despite the lack of a formal amnesty, progress in judicial accountability has been limited. Collins (2016a) highlights how 25 new cases relating to disappearances had been filed between 2009 and 2011, but prosecutorial inaction had resulted in a lack of progress.

7.3.2 Finding the Truth

The question '*Donde están*? (Where are they?) is emblematic of the relentless search by relatives of victims of enforced disappearances throughout South America. Trying to establish what has been the final fate of the *desaparecidos* (disappeared) has been one of the main catalyst for mobilization in the region. Since the 1970s, enforced disappearances became the symbol of brutal political violence, of criminal states who illegally detained, tortured, and murdered thousands of their citizens. Terror targeted not only the disappeared, but also their families and societies at large. Disappearances endure into the present, with thousands of families left in a situation of permanent uncertainty and incomplete mourning.

Two trends can be identified in the search for the truth. First, official state-sponsored truth-commissions were frequently established to probe crimes. The timing however differed. In some countries, such as Argentina and Chile, such bodies were created immediately after transition; meanwhile in Brazil, Paraguay, and Uruguay, we see the onset of "late" truth commissions, set up two or even three decades after democratization. Second, civil society had a fundamental role in shedding light onto past atrocities in those countries, as Brazil and Uruguay, where the state was unwilling to initially sponsor investigations.

Argentina established the first truth commission to complete a final report and receive widespread regional and international attention (Grandin 2005). A few days into democracy, in late 1983, President Alfonsín ordered the creation of the National Commission on the Disappearance of Persons (CONADEP). Comprised of highly reputed public figures, it was tasked with investigating the thousands of disappearances occurred during the dictatorship. After working for nine months, interviewing survivors, inspecting sites where clandestine detention centres had operated, and visiting mass graves, morgues, hospitals and prisons, the CONADEP presented its findings to the President in September 1984 (Crenzel 2008). Its famous *Nunca Más* (Never Again) report confirmed the systematic nature of the human rights violations perpetrated and provided an open list of 8,961 disappeared. Similarly, in Chile, soon after taking power, President Aylwin created the National Truth and Reconciliation Commission (or Rettig Commission), to disclose the truth about deaths and disappearances between 1973 and 1990. The February 1991 final report corroborated 2,130 victims of enforced disappearance and extrajudicial execution. Subsequently, owing to the lobbying by associations of former political prisoners that wanted to have the truth about victims of political detention and torture also revealed, President Ricardo Lagos (2000–2006) established the Commission on Political Imprisonment and Torture (or Valech Commission) in November 2003. This Commission officially recognized 28,459 victims of political imprisonment and torture, identified 1,132 detention places, and acknowledged that the torture had been a systematic practice, not the result of individual excesses (Lira 2011). In 2010, some 30 additional cases of disappearances and 9,795 new victims of political imprisonment and torture were added, bringing the final total of dead and disappeared to 3,216 and of victims of political imprisonment and torture to 38,254 (Observatorio Derechos Humanos 2011).

Unlike Argentina and Chile, the new democratic government of Uruguay did not establish a truth commission early on.[1] With no official report forthcoming, a human rights NGO, the Peace and Justice Service (SERPAJ), decided to conduct its own investigation into the atrocities committed between 1972 and 1985, releasing in 1989 its main findings. Entitled *Uruguay: Nunca Más*, the report documented in detail the system of prolonged imprisonment, political repression, and torture set up by the dictatorship (Servicio Paz y Justicia 1992). The establishment of an official truth commission would only take place fifteen years after transition, when in August 2000, President Jorge Batlle (2000–2005) created the so-called Peace Commission. Composed of political and religious figures, it released its final report in April 2003, confirming the disappearance of 26 Uruguayans in Uruguay and over 130 in the region. The Commission's work represented the first official acknowledgement of the state's responsibility for dictatorship crimes. Yet, because of its limited mandate to only probing cases of disappearances, the report accounted for a minority of human rights violations, failing to include a large number of victims of political imprisonment and torture. Likewise, Paraguay was also a late comer in truth-seeking, with the official Truth and Justice Commission being created fifteen years after transition, in October 2004. It was tasked with accounting for the abuses under Stroessner's dictatorship and contributing to criminal prosecutions for those deeds. The nine commissioners worked for four years and delivered their final report in August 2008, in which 19,862 arbitrary detentions, 18,772 cases of torture, at least 59 victims of summary executions, and 336 forced disappearances and a total of more than 128,000 victims of the military regime were confirmed (USIP 2017). Unlike earlier commissions, this one also looked into the economic backdrop of the

---

[1] In the mid-1980s, opposition parties in Parliament successfully set up four investigative commissions to shed light onto the cases of Uruguayans that had disappeared in Uruguay and abroad, as well as specific crimes, such as the murders of politicians Zelmar Michelini and Héctor Gutiérrez Ruiz, the disappearance of teacher Elena Quinteros, and the death by poisoning of Cecilia Fontana de Heber (the wife of politician Mario Heber). These commissions importantly gathered information and testimonies, but had limited resources and powers.

dictatorship, especially the role of "the country's still-powerful quasi-feudal landed elites" (Collins 2016a: 163).

Brazil has established the region's most recent truth commission, which President Dilma Rousseff inaugurated in May 2012. The mandate of the CNV was broad, encompassing cases of torture, disappearances, and murders, and including the identification of perpetrators (Mezarobba 2016). The Commission had seven members and organized its tasks in 13 working groups, dealing with various themes such as gender violence and the Araguaia guerrilla. The final report, released in December 2014, disclosed the names of 377 perpetrators and provided details on 434 deaths and disappearances, and talked about potentially up to 20,000 victims of torture. Similar to Uruguay, in the mid-1980, an unofficial truth investigation had played a fundamental role in fighting silence and oblivion. It was conducted by the Catholic Archdiocese of São Paulo and the World Council of Churches, by using data from files of the military justice system. Released in 1985, the *Brasil: Nunca Mais* (Never Again) report described torture practices and other gross human rights violations carried out during the dictatorship, including a list of 444 torturers and an estimated 17,420 victims of the military justice system (Weschler 1998: 51–52).

7.3.3 Reparations

Policies of reparations were adopted in all the five countries. Nonetheless we focus here only on monetary reparations, even though symbolic reparations, in the form of museums, the transformation of several former detention centres into sites of memory, and memorial plaques have also been established, often by civil society organizations and sometimes by national or local governments.

Argentina and Chile adopted extensive reparations programmes, targeting many of the victims affected by state terror. In Argentina, in 1986, a pension was initially granted to the relatives of the victims of disappearance. In the early 1990s, the Government of President Carlos Menem (1989–1999) expanded reparations to victims of political imprisonment and disappearance. In 1991, benefits were granted to victims of illegitimate detention between 1974 and 1983, while in 1994 compensation was sanctioned by law, worth US$224,000 per person to be received by parents, children, or lawful heirs of individuals who had disappeared or died as a consequence of political repression (Guembe 2006). In the same year, Law 24.321 of Absence by Forced Disappearance created a new legal status with no precedents in national or international law for all persons who had involuntarily disappeared before 10 December 1983 and for whom there was no information on their whereabouts (Smulovitz 2008). Ten years later, President Néstor Kirchner (2003–2007) granted compensation also to minors who had been victims of state terror, in particular, awarding 224,000 pesos to victims of identity substitution (Guembe 2006).

In Chile, a comprehensive policy of reparations was initiated immediately after transition. In 1991, a Programme of Reparations and Comprehensive Health Care for

Victims of Human Rights Violations was set up, providing physical and psychological health care to former political prisoners, relatives of the disappeared, and victims of torture, benefiting thousands of victims over time. In 1992, a lifetime pension was also created for the families of victims of human rights violations or political violence identified in the Rettig Commission's report, together with educational benefits for the disappeared person's children, exemption from mandatory military service, and health care provisions. In December 2004, in the aftermath of the Valech Commission, a reparatory pension and benefits were established specifically for victims of political imprisonment or torture acknowledged by that Commission (Lira 2011).

In Uruguay, similarly to the search for the truth and justice, reparations for victims of human rights violations and their families were delayed for over twenty years. At the time of transition, in 1985, Sanguinetti's government only adopted provisions to facilitate the return and social reintegration of exiles, and restored public jobs to individuals unfairly dismissed under the dictatorship (Barahona de Brito 1997). After much lobbying by victims' groups, twenty years later, in September 2005, under President Tabaré Vázquez, the legal category of 'absent due to enforced disappearance' was finally established. In October 2006, pension rights were also restored to individuals who, for political or trade union reasons, could not work during the dictatorship; a special reparatory pension was also granted to former political prisoners. In September 2009, the systematic practice of repression, torture, disappearances and homicides was officially recognized by the state, together with the payment of a one-off sum to four categories of victims: relatives of victims of enforced disappearance; victims of very serious injuries; children disappeared for over 30 days; children born during their mothers' detention or detained with their parents for over 180 days. Uruguay's late reparations laws were particularly criticized by the UN Special Rapporteur on the promotion of truth, justice, reparation and guarantees of non-recurrence. The Rapporteur highlighted how these laws fail to comply with the notion of integral reparation, obliged victims to select between pension rights and reparatory rights—which are fundamentally different—and did not contemplate all the relevant categories of victims (de Greiff 2014). Despite severe criticisms, no significant reforms have yet been carried out.

In Brazil, a number of reparation policies have been enacted, encompassing initially mainly the relatives of victims of death and disappearances, and later targeting survivors of political persecution as well. As Mezarobba (2016: 111) contends, "reparations have been the principal transitional justice measure used by the Brazilian state, as well as the earliest to be pursued in any systematic fashion." First, in 1995, when Congress enacted Law 9.140 of the Disappeared, this act amounted to the first official recognition by Brazil that grave human rights violations had been committed by the dictatorship. The law recognised that relatives of the dead and disappeared had a right to receive compensation for the crimes suffered. Owing to continued social mobilisation and pressure by survivors, in 2002, Congress enacted Law 10,559, which acknowledged a set of the rights to be granted to the victims of political persecution, including their right to receive financial reparations. Regarding the latter point, the law mainly focused on reparations for loss of earnings, and did not contemplate psychological or moral damages (Mezarobba 2016). In Paraguay, on the other hand, reparations have been marred by difficulties. The main instrument regulating economic reparations is Law 838 of 1996. The beneficiaries are victims (or their direct relatives) of forced disappearance, extrajudicial killings, torture, political imprisonment (for more than a year) committed between 1954 and 1989. A beneficiary is only allowed to make a claim for one type of violation, even if s/he suffered multiple types. The implementation of the policy has been characterised by controversies and delays. On the one hand, the Ombudsman's Office, tasked with overseeing their payment, was not set up until 2001. On the other, the burden of proof was placed on survivors who had to gather documents and proof in order to show that they qualified to receive reparations. Subsequent modifications in 2011 finally put the burden to gather the necessary official paperwork onto the competent authorities, rather than victims themselves (Collins 2016a).

This brief panorama of transitional justice initiatives highlighted the ups and downs in accountability efforts across this region. While all the five countries have adopted some measures to investigate past atrocities, none have completely resolved the question of the past. Undeniably, some countries, such as Argentina and Chile, have been more successful than others, as Brazil, Paraguay, and Uruguay, in settling accounts with past horrors. Yet, many pending issues still need to be address, showing how transitional justice endures for a significant amount of time. And the potential for setbacks is also never too far away. Proof of that is the 2017 verdict by Argentina's Supreme Court, known as 2×1, which aimed to secure the early release of individuals condemned for state terrorism. Fortunately, large civil society mobilisations meant that the judiciary had to retrace its steps. We now turn our focus towards Operation Condor and accountability for those transnational horrors.

7.4   Justice for Operation Condor

The so-called Plan, System, or Operation, Condor was a secret network of transnational intelligence and coordinated repressive policies that was originally set up by Argentina, Bolivia, Chile, Paraguay, and Uruguay in late 1975, to illegally detain, torture, and, most often, murder political opponents all across South America (McSherry 2005). Condor arose out of previous informal and bilateral forms of cooperation between the armed and security forces of Argentina, Paraguay, Chile, and Uruguay dating back to the early 1970s. The network was officially created at a meeting of intelligence and security forces organised by the Chilean National Intelligence Directorate (DINA), which was held in Santiago, Chile, between November 25 and December 1, 1975; 50 officials from across the region participated at that gathering. Later on, in 1976, Brazil formally joined Condor and, in 1978, Peru and Ecuador also did so. By using declassified US documents, scholars have pinpointed three phases to Operation Condor: (1) close coordination and intelligence exchange; (2) joint operations in South America; and (3) targeted assassinations outside South America (Dinges 2004).

The defining characteristic of transnational crimes vis-à-vis domestic political repression relates to the specific nature of the crimes perpetrated, which had one or more of these specific trademarks. First, *complex geographies of crimes*, whereby at least two countries, occasionally more, were responsible for committing atrocities: this normally comprised the country of nationality of the victim being sought and that where the crimes were physically perpetrated. For instance, in the case of the murder in September 1974 of Chilean General Carlos Prats and his wife, Argentina and Chile were both implicated: the first, since Prats had been in exile in Buenos Aires since September 1973, and the second, given that Chile was where Prats had had a long military career and he was being persecuted by the Pinochet's dictatorship. Second, *multinational taskforces*, composed of agents of the country where the victim was located, as well as their counterparts from the victim's country of origin (sometimes, even agents from other interested countries), were in charge of implementing operations. For example, Uruguayan exile Sara Mendez was kidnapped in Buenos Aires in July 1976. When the taskforce broke into her home in the Belgrano neighbourhood of the Argentine Capital, the person leading the operation that night introduced himself to her and stated his full name (he was a well-known Uruguayan colonel). Third, *a crossing of borders*, whereby the perpetration of crimes always entailed a physical or informational exchange. This could take the form of intelligence sharing from one country to the other regarding individuals being targeted, and/or the actual forceful, and usually, clandestine transfer of individuals detained in one country back to their home country. In the case of Uruguayan exile Gustavo Inzaurralde, it was determined that he had been detained together with three Argentines and one other Uruguayan in Asuncion, Paraguay, in late March 1977. A Uruguayan colonel travelled to Paraguay specifically to interrogate him. Subsequently, a document from the Paraguayan Archives of Terror proved that Inzaurralde, together with the other four prisoners, were all illegally flown back to Argentina in May 1977, where they ultimately disappeared (National Security Archive 2007).

The transnational repressive coordination completely disregarded all principles of international law on refugees and the long custom of protecting exiles in South America. Exiles, thinking that they had found safe havens, became victims of death traps abroad (Lessa 2015). Between 1975 and 1978, Condor facilitated the perpetration of disappearances, kidnappings and murder of hundreds of political leaders, activists and refugees. According to the Database on South America's Transnational Human Rights Violations, which I have been compiling since 2017, there were at least 763 victims of transnational repression between 1969 and 1981, i.e. 368 Uruguayans, 184 Argentines, 111 Chileans, 38 Paraguayans, 27 Brazilians, 13 Peruvians, 10 Bolivians, and 12 from other nationalities.[2] Victims ranged from renowned politicians, such as Uruguayans Zelmar Michelini and Héctor Gutiérrez Ruiz, to political activists, guerrillas, and refugees under the mandate of the United Nations High Commissioner for Refugees. A major location of crimes was Buenos Aires, due to the large number of political exiles living there since the 1960s. The

---

[2] See the "Database on South America's Transnational Human Rights Violations," https://sites.goo gle.com/view/operationcondorjustice/database?authuser=0.

clandestine detention centre known as Automotores Orletti, located in the capital's Floresta neighbourhood, was a key detention site from which Argentine, Chilean, and Uruguayan agents conducted Condor-related operations. *Orletti* functioned between May 11 and November 3, 1976. Around 300 people were illegally detained there: the majority were foreigners (Uruguayans, Chileans, and Cubans), many of whom were forcibly returned to their country. Other well-known places of clandestine detention and torture associated with Condor include, in Argentina, the Pozo de Banfield and Pozo de Quilmes; in Santiago de Chile, Villa Grimaldi and Cuatro Alamos; in Uruguay, Punta Gorda House, "300 Carlos," and the building that housed the Defence Intelligence Service (SID) in Montevideo; and in Paraguay, the Police Investigation Department in Asuncion.

7.4.1   Accountability for Transnational Crimes

Beyond mapping the geography of transnational repression in South America, I have also systematically tracked criminal proceedings that probe cross-border atrocities. So far, 40 judicial proceedings, at different stages of the judicial process, have been recorded in Argentina, Chile, Uruguay, Italy, the USA, Paraguay, Brazil, and Peru. Verdicts have been reached in 25 of the 40 cases and 116 defendants have been condemned for the crimes perpetrated against 227 victims.

Initially, there was a tendency to consider all foreign victims of enforced disappearances as potential victims of Operation Condor. While this may well be true in a large number of cases, it is not always so. Many foreigners in fact became involved in local political and/or armed groups after moving to another country, and they were ultimately targeted because of that militancy, rather than their nationality. While nationality is often an important element, it is not the defining one regarding Condor.

As part of my research, I organised two conferences and two workshops on accountability for Operation Condor in Chile and Uruguay, in which judges, prosecutors, lawyers, human rights activists, survivors, academics and policy-makers from Argentina, Brazil, Chile and Uruguay participated. We came to the conclusion that the key condition to be met in order for a case to be considered as falling under Operation Condor is that a *crossing of a boundary must have taken place*.[3] This crossing can take one or more of these three forms: (a) exchange of information about a victim between two countries (the victim's country of origin and the country where the victim is located); (b) the participation of multinational taskforces in the criminal act(s); or (c) the forceful return of the victim(s) from the country of detention to their country of origin.

---

[3] See the Policy Brief "Justice Without Borders: Accountability for Plan Condor Crimes in South America," by Francesca Lessa, November 2016, available in English, Spanish, and Portuguese at https://www.lac.ox.ac.uk/article/launch-of-policy-brief-0.

The existing literature is characterised by a lack of consensus on the number of victims of Operation Condor. Divergent positions have characterised scholarly and journalistic debates on Condor: some publications underestimate the real number of Condor, while others inflate the total, by considering all the victims of repression in South America as victims of Condor too. While, of course, Operation Condor unfolded as part of broader processes of political repression in this region, the term nonetheless should be used to denote a specific set of cases, which must be clearly distinguished from the rest. Being categorised as a victim of Operation Condor does not constitute a higher or more significant category or status. Instead, it simply denotes a specific set of terror practices which are worth underscoring, since they speak of the lengths to which this region's criminal states were willing to go to target particular individuals. In fact, these criminal states suspended the traditional norm of the inviolability of state borders and territorial integrity to establish a transnational alliance of terror to hunt down specific opponents beyond borders. Operation Condor directly persecuted and targeted those exiles who, after having left their home country and relocated elsewhere in South America, continued to nonetheless engage in political activism that clearly focused on their country of origin and often actively worked to denounce the human rights atrocities perpetrated there.

The majority of the victims of Operation Condor were in fact politically active exiles who deliberately tried to undermine the dictatorial regime in power in their home country, by drawing international attention to the crimes committed there and/or supporting and funding local resistance. To a lesser extent, Operation Condor also targeted members of guerrilla or armed groups, whether or not those formed part of the Revolutionary Coordinating Junta[4] (JCR with its Spanish acronym), relatives of victims, or other exiles who were no longer politically active. As Lopez (2016: 92) rightly contends, the existence of the JCR became a "convenient excuse" for South American criminal states to internationalise state terror.

7.4.2   Emblematic Operation Condor Sentences

Criminal investigations into Operation Condor atrocities served a strategic role in the fight against impunity in the Southern Cone. This was especially so in the late 1990s and early 2000s, when human rights activists were endeavouring to find loopholes allowing them to break a scenario of absolute impunity. While nowadays, Argentina and Chile are global pioneers in judicial accountability, going back to the late 1990s, the situation was rather different. In Argentina, the sanctioning of amnesty laws and pardons had quashed the early progress obtained in judicial accountability of the mid-1980s. By the 1990s, only trials for the crime of baby kidnapping could go

---

[4] The JCR was an alliance among left-wing and armed revolutionary groups in South America. It was composed of composed of the Chilean Revolutionary Left Movement (MIR), the Argentine People's Revolutionary Army (ERP), the Uruguayan Tupamaros, and the Bolivian National Liberation Army (ELN). See Lopez (2016).

ahead, resulting in the prosecution of 23 defendants between 1988 and 2005 (Lesa Humanidad 2005). In addition, the so-called "truth trials," unfolding in the late 1990s and early 2000s, were judicial proceedings whereby relatives, witnesses, and military officers were summoned to appear and questioned to gather information on the final fate of the disappeared. There was however no final verdict on the culpability of those responsible for the crimes.

In Chile, similarly, the amnesty decree was applied to halt all judicial investigations into past crimes, until the early days of 1998. This broad interpretation and application of the amnesty finally began to be restricted in 2004. A set of crimes, namely wrongdoing committed after the sanctioning of the law (1978), disappearances, war crimes, as well as crimes against humanity, fell outside the scope of the law and could be subject to prosecution (Collins 2016b). Likewise, in Uruguay, the 1986 amnesty law was methodically applied by the judiciary and different governments in power, stalling all attempts to investigate dictatorship-era crimes. Even those crimes whose investigation was technically permitted under the law, such as economic crimes and disappearances, remained unpunished and were never probed until the mid-2000s (Lessa 2012).

In this scenario, investigations relating to the crimes of Operation Condor were crucial in breaking away from impunity. In these three countries, a group of relentless human rights activists and lawyers successfully combined social pressure and mobilisation with deliberate legal strategies and arguments aimed at bypassing and undermining the obstacles standing in the way of judicial accountability. In Argentina, in November 1999, a group of six women, who were relatives of victims of Operation Condor from Uruguay, Paraguay, Argentina, and Chile, filed a lawsuit accompanied by their lawyers before the courts in Buenos Aires, asking them to investigate seven cases of enforced disappearances and the illicit association of Operation Condor (Lessa 2015). Contending that disappearances constituted ongoing crimes, these women put pressure on the judiciary to carry out investigations into the transnational terror network at a time when the judiciary was still reluctant to look into past crimes. This landmark lawsuit would, as we will discuss below, eventually lead to a historic verdict over fifteen years later. Another case relating to Operation Condor within the Argentine judicial system was particularly important in unlocking the situation of impunity and it occurred before the 2005 nullification of the amnesty laws in Argentina. A former Chilean secret police agent, Enrique Arancibia Clavel, was sentenced to life imprisonment for his role in the 1974 murder in Buenos Aires of exiled Chilean General Carlos Prats and his wife. In reviewing that case in August 2004, the Argentine Supreme Court of Justice recognised for the first time in the country that crimes against humanity should not be subject to statutory limitations, thus reopening the way for all investigations regarding past crimes to resume (Pagina12 2004). In Chile, by the year 2000, victims and relatives had filed over 200 lawsuits against former General Pinochet for crimes such as genocide, murder, and illegal detentions. Eventually, the investigation into Operation Condor remarkably allowed judge Juan Guzman to strip the former dictator of his senatorial immunity for a second time and for a formal indictment to be dictated in December 2004 (Rohter 2004).

Finally, Uruguay is especially illuminating of how Condor crimes contributed to achieving some form of justice in the country. Indeed, impunity was so watertight in Uruguay that not a single criminal trial for past atrocities unfolded in the country for well over 15 years. Owing to this, in June 1999, a group of six Uruguayan and Argentine women, who were mothers and/or wives of Uruguayan exiles who had been illegally detained and disappeared in Buenos Aires in the 1970s, decided to file a case in Rome. They asked Italian prosecutors to investigate the murder of these activists, since many victims of Operation Condor were of Italian descent and the Italian criminal code allowed tribunals to investigate such cases abroad as well.[5] Given the lack of opportunities for justice inside Uruguay, victims' relatives had to turn to foreign courts to obtain some accountability. Eventually, in the mid-2000s, human rights lawyers and activists, sensing a different political scenario due to the election of the first left-wing government in late 2004 in Uruguay, adopted a deliberate policy of strategically litigating a set of crimes falling outside the amnesty's remit, in order to challenge head-on judicial paralysis and passivity (Lessa 2013). In that context, Operation Condor atrocities proved a strategic tool. Indeed, lawyers started contending that the amnesty was inapplicable to those crimes, since they had been perpetrated outside of Uruguayan territory. This innovative argument was eventually accepted and the judiciary began investigations into some emblematic cases of Uruguayans who had been victims of Condor in Argentina and Paraguay (Fried and Lessa 2011). Indeed, the very first sentence to ever be delivered with regard to dictatorship-era crimes in Uruguay was dictated in a Condor lawsuit in March 2009. In *Adalberto Soba* et al., the judge in fact sentenced eight former military and police officers for the murder of 28 Uruguayans, all members of the political party *Partido de la Victoria del Pueblo*, who had been illegally detained in 1976 in Argentina and later murdered.

With the passing of time, several more investigations into Operation Condor opened across the region. Some of them were rather limited in their focus, such as for instance the Operation Condor trial in Chile, which is probing only cases where both victims and perpetrators are Chilean nationals. In other cases, similarly, investigations are strictly defined by either location, relating to crimes committed in a specific site, or in light of affiliation, looking at cases of persecution against members of a defined political party or group. In Argentina, for example, five trials unfolded between 2009 and 2020 to probe atrocities committed in the former detention centre known as Automotores Orletti. In Uruguay, on the other hand, another verdict handed down in 2009 related to the murder of 37 Uruguayans all belonging to the left-wing movement *Grupos de Acción Unificadora*, who were disappeared in Buenos Aires between late 1977 and early 1978.

The so-called Operation Condor trials that took place in the mid 2010s in Buenos Aires and Rome respectively surpassed earlier prosecutions by transcending the focus on individual crimes and delivered a judgement on Operation Condor itself. In the Argentine trial, there was a specific charge of illicit association, which was used to categorise the wrongdoing committed by the transnational network, while the Italian

---

[5] Author email exchange with Silvia Bellizzi, 14 February 2018.

court tackled the nature of Condor indirectly when considering the crimes charged and the role of the defendants. The two verdicts, dictated only a few months apart, were greeted by mixed reactions. On the one hand, the sentenced delivered by Federal Criminal Tribunal 1 of Buenos Aires on 27 May 2016, was hailed as historic and unprecedented, receiving unparalleled attention in both regional and international newspapers, including by the BBC and the New York Times. The tribunal dictated a verdict that encompassed 174 cases of victims (67 from the Automotores Orletti case and 107 from Operation Condor) for crimes of illegal detention, illicit association, and torture. The judges sentenced 15 of the 17 defendants, with sentences ranging from 8 to 25 years, while two accused were acquitted. A particularly significant element in this sentence was the recognition by the tribunal that Operation Condor had constituted a transnational illicit association, which had been deliberately established in order to illegally exchange information and intelligence, and persecute, kidnap, forcefully repatriate, torture, and murder political activists in the Southern Cone. Most of the defendants, 13 out of the 15, were condemned not only for specific crimes of kidnappings, for but also on the charge of illicit association, namely for their role in setting up the transnational criminal enterprise of terror across South America. While the majority of the accused were sentenced for holding high-level ranks and decision-making roles during the dictatorship, two defendants, an Argentine civil intelligence agent and a Uruguayan colonel, were condemned for being directly involved in perpetrating human rights violations.

Similar expectations accompanied the trial in Italy, and the verdict that was read out on 17 January 2017. Nonetheless, much disappointment, especially from victims' relatives and human rights activists in Uruguay, followed soon after the verdict was delivered. While the public prosecution had asked the tribunal to condemn the 27 defendants to life imprisonment for the murder of 43 victims, the judges only finally dictated eight such sentences, and acquitted 19 of the defendants, who were all tried *in absentia* except one. The eight life imprisonment verdicts related to high-level state officials, such as Luis Garcia Meza, Bolivia's president between 1980 and 1981, Juan Carlos Blanco, Uruguay's foreign minister between 1972 and 1976, and Francisco Morales-Bermudez, Peru's president between 1975 and 1980 (*La Repubblica* 2017). The acquittals related to lower ranking officials who had been responsible first-hand for committing the crimes. The clearing of many officials, especially of 12 Uruguayan defendants, many of whom are serving time in Uruguay for crimes committed during the dictatorship, generated much disillusionment within the community of human rights activists and relatives, who had originally initiated this prosecution. So, while on the one hand, the Italian court did recognise the existence of Operation Condor and the role of this transnational machinery of terror in persecuting and murder political opponents in South America by condemning some of the region's highest political representatives that had created the system, it failed to satisfactorily establish the role of middle and lower ranking officers who participated directly in the commission of atrocities. The public prosecution appealed the verdict and on 8 July 2019 Rome's First Assize Appeals Court dramatically overturned the first-instance sentence, condemning 24 out of 25 defendants from Uruguay, Chile, Bolivia, and Peru to life imprisonment. On appeal, the magistrates forcefully showed how the middle and lower ranking officers had provided functional contributions to the murders under investigation, by abducting, torturing and holding victims in secret prisons, and were thus to be considered equally responsible as Operation Condor's intellectual authors (Lessa 2020).

7.5 Justice Entrepreneurs

Unpacking transitional justice measures enacted in these five South American countries, as well as specific prosecutions for Operation Condor, permits to appreciate the decisive role played by human rights activists and lawyers. These actors have been immensely significant in acting as a force for change in spite of all the adversities endured in complex political contexts in the post-dictatorship years. These decades were in fact often characterised by strong pressures in favour of impunity from the cronies of the old dictatorial regimes and their sympathisers, weak or condescending new democratic regimes and political leaders, and frequently passive judiciaries. In an earlier work, I developed the label "advocates of change" to identify those political leaders, human rights activists, as well as committed individuals who have tirelessly worked against impunity and endeavoured to overcome obstacles in the way of justice (Lessa 2013: 228). In this chapter, I introduce the concept of "justice entrepreneurs." I feel the latter better captures the way in which these actors have operated. I was inspired by the work of US sociologist Howard Beckett who coined the term "moral entrepreneurs" and, additionally, by its adaptation to post-transitional contexts by Argentine sociologist Elizabeth Jelin, who generated the category of "memory entrepreneurs" (Jelin 2003: 33). Such actors mobilise their energies for the sake of a cause that they strongly believe in; in the cases of struggles over the memory of a recent past, according to Jelin, they seek social recognition and political legitimacy for their own interpretation of a shared past.

The label 'justice entrepreneurs' describes therefore in a more appropriate way the mobilisation and activism that these individuals and groups undertake. Using the term 'entrepreneur' better represents how these actors take on and manage a project or an undertaking that is especially complicated, difficult, as well as risky. Such a term encapsulates the proactive, strategic, and often pioneering efforts that human rights activists and lawyers have to carry out in their quest for accountability. In the context of transitional societies, justice entrepreneurs then denote those actors (most often human rights activists, victims' relatives, journalists, and lawyers, but also occasionally judges, political and/or religious leaders) who endeavour in every possible way to obtain accountability for past atrocities, whether through judicial or non-judicial means, overcoming innumerable obstacles in the face of contexts often characterised by impunity and silence.

In the earlier pages of this chapter, we have seen numerous examples of the role of justice entrepreneurs across South America. They have carried out at least six sets of strategic actions over time. **First**, in many opportunities, these actors had to *take on tasks and responsibilities that correspond to states* when it comes to human rights violations. When democratic governments were unwilling to conduct investigations into past horrors, they have stepped into the shoes of states in elucidating crimes. That was the case in Brazil and Uruguay in the 1980s, when religious bodies and human rights NGOs produced solid "Never Again" reports detailing the policies of repression during the dictatorship at a time when little information was available on the real scope of the crimes. When transitional justice measures were finally taking place, these activists continued to share the burden of finding evidence to support their legal or reparative claims. This happened for instance in Paraguay, where victims and their relatives had to garner evidence, most frequently from the Archive of Terror, to demonstrate their eligibility to receive reparations for their suffering during Stroessner's rule. In Uruguay, on the other hand, victims and human rights lawyers have to actively feed relevant proofs to ongoing criminal cases. This task normally corresponds to public prosecutors but, due to the inactivity of the latter, these activists have to go to different archives or seek witnesses to ensure progress in the investigations. A team of dedicated human rights lawyers was established since early 2015 within the Luz Ibarburu Observatory to support victims in these efforts, given that very often accessing data in archives is marred with difficulties and is obstructed by those very officials that should guarantee access.

Second, justice entrepreneurs *maintain the spotlight on human rights atrocities* even during the darkest hours. Argentine human rights NGOs, for instance, staged marches and protests throughout the late 1980s and early 1990s when amnesty laws and presidential pardons were being sanctioned by political leaders. Likewise, the relatives' association, Mothers and Relatives of Uruguayan Disappeared Detainees, kept its doors open even in the early and mid-1990s when impunity had firmly consolidated in Uruguay. They shifted their focus from justice to truth, focusing their efforts in the search for the missing children of the disappeared, and conducted numerous activities abroad within the framework of the Latin American Federation of Associations of Relatives of Disappeared Detainees.

Third, these entrepreneurs *resort to unused mechanisms or even invent new ones* when all doors seemed shut. The day after the Expiry Law was enacted in Uruguay in 1986, activists announced they would call a referendum to derogated the law by resorting to a little used article of the Constitution (article 25). Even though the result of the referendum, which was eventually held in April 1989, was unfavourable to the cause of justice, the preceding campaign helped disseminate knowledge about past horrors to society at large for years, in clear opposition to state-sponsored policies of silence and oblivion. Similarly, the right to truth was vehemently advocated by the CELS in Argentina in since the mid-1990s. This led in the late 1990s to the establishment of truth trials, a sort of hybrid mechanism that combined features of criminal trials and truth commissions, to continue investigations into the final fate of the *desaparecidos*.

Fourth, justice entrepreneurs *create innovative and ingenious legal arguments*, thereby putting pressure on the judiciary and shaking judges as well as prosecutors from apathy and passivity. In the early days of January 1998, two months before Pinochet was about to become Chile's first life senator, a criminal lawsuit was filed before Santiago's Appeals Court against the former dictator. The Chilean Communist party, together with his lawyer Eduardo Contreras, alleged several crimes, including genocide, murder, kidnapping, and illicit association. For the first time, the lawsuit was accepted and a judge nominated to probe the allegations. Soon after, this original case grew exponentially, encompassing hundreds more allegations of human rights violations; this ultimately led to Pinochet being stripped of his immunity from prosecution in several cases. In Argentina, too, in late 1999, a pioneering legal claim was filed against the top-officials responsible for Operation Condor, using the argument that disappearances constituted ongoing crimes that the courts had to investigate notwithstanding the existence of amnesty laws. This prosecution, together with the lawsuit on the systematic plan of baby theft, were the only two legal cases that witnessed any progress in the late 1990s and early 2000s in Argentina.

    Fifth, these actors *look for and generate strategic opportunities regionally and internationally* when progress could not be reached at home. In the early 1970s, the Brazilian dictatorship had brutally repressed a small guerrilla movement of students and workers, known as Araguaia. The relatives of the nearly 70 victims of disappearances had filed since the 1980s several legal claims in the country but those were always unsuccessful. In the mid-1990s, they presented a petition before the Inter-American Commission on Human Rights, which eventually referred the case to the Inter-American Court. In late 2010, the court dictated a historic sentence, arguing that Brazil's amnesty was incompatible with the American Convention on Human Rights and thereby lacked legal effect. Similar rulings have been dictated by the same court in cases relating to Peru, Chile, El Salvador and Uruguay, generating pioneering jurisprudence on the matter. These actors did not, however, stop at the regional human rights system. As described in the section on Operation Condor, Uruguayan relatives of the *desaparecidos* presented a lawsuit in 1999 in Rome, asking the prosecutor's office to investigate their murders given the lack of justice in Uruguay. Comparable foreign trials also took place in courts in France, Sweden, and Spain for victims of the Argentine and Chilean dictatorships too. These trials abroad played an important role in shaming South America's judiciaries into action.

    Finally, justice entrepreneurs *lobby governments and other relevant political actors to obtain specific public policy outcomes*, often by generating strategic alliances with key institutional actors. In late 2011, in the context of ongoing attempts to write off the Expiry Law in Uruguay, anti-impunity groups launched a public awareness campaign and sustained lobbying efforts with sympathetic allies in the executive, legislative and judicial branches (Burt et al. 2013). In particular, some legislators, including Felipe Michelini, Jorge Orrico and Luis Puig, worked side by side with activists to develop draft legislation that was eventually approved by Parliament and resulted in the derogation of the law. In a similar way, in November 2012, Argentina's Attorney General set up a Specialised Unit for Cases of Children Illegally Appropriated during State Terror. This Unit would exclusively focus on the search of the estimated 400 missing grandchildren, by conducting preliminary investigations, monitoring ongoing cases, and improving the prosecution of such crimes. The creation of this unit met a long-standing demand from the NGO Grandmothers of May Square, which has led the search for the missing babies since its creation in 1977, and pushed the establishment to find ways to accelerate and enhance the methods that would allow to identify the still unresolved cases of baby theft (Abuelas 2012).

7.6 Conclusion

The comparative analysis of the transitional justice experiences of five South American countries and efforts to criminally investigate the transnational atrocities of Operation Condor in the post-dictatorship years brought to the fore the vital role that justice entrepreneurs have played in the search for accountability across the region. The existing scholarship has offered multidimensional explanations to better understand transitional justice pathways in South America and beyond, and has importantly highlighted the complex and multifaceted dynamics surrounding such processes. I share the conclusions by scholars such as Payne et al. (2015) and Skaar et al. (2016). In this chapter, I specifically focused on the pioneering role by justice entrepreneurs in catalysing justice demands in South America. The examples used unmistakably point to how these actors have been the leading drivers of accountability processes. In Argentina, while the reopening of criminal trials for dictatorship-era crimes since 2006 took place during the government of President Nestor Kirchner, this achievement however built on long-lasting justice demands and efforts by justice entrepreneurs, including the CELS and the Grandmothers of May Square, that dated back to the early 1990s. When it comes to human rights, governments frequently tend to be reactive, rather than proactive. The same is true of Chile, where the current wave of prosecutions originated from the historic 1998 lawsuit that human rights lawyers and activists filed against Pinochet and subsequent denunciations of extrajudicial executions presented between 2009 and 2011 by the lawyers of the NGO Group of Family Members of the Politically Executed.

Even in those countries that lag behind in transitional justice, the limited progress so far achieved is undeniably the result of persistent activism and endeavours by justice entrepreneurs. The 2004 Paraguayan Truth and Justice Commission was finally established as a result of a gathering of academics and civil society activists that identified such a commission as one of three priorities in truth and memory, and had developed a blueprint for creating it by drawing upon regional experiences (Collins 2016a). Finally, justice entrepreneurs strategically employed the litigation of transnational crimes of Operation Condor as a way to push for justice when accountability seemed out of reach. In June 1999, Uruguayan and Argentine relatives of Condor victims filed a case before the Italian courts, while in November of that year, another group of Argentine, Chilean, Paraguayan, and Uruguayan women also presented a criminal lawsuit in Buenos Aires. These two examples, together with several more cases filed in Chile and Uruguay, paved the way for putting pressure on local judiciaries to eventually investigate past horrors.

No single factor fully elucidates alone diverse accountability outcomes in South America. But, indisputably, the existence, or absence, of justice entrepreneurs actively pushing for and demanding for the investigation and punishment of human rights violations helps explain the different levels of progress in transitional justice policies witnessed in the five countries considered in this chapter. These actors have relentlessly put pressure onto their respective governments to undertake all the necessary steps to try to fulfil the "Never Again," *Nunca Mas*, pledge uttered at the end of the dictatorships.

Acknowledgements This research project has received funding from the European Union's Horizon 2020 research and innovation programme under the Marie Skłodowska-Curie grant agreement No. 702004; the John Fell Oxford University Press (OUP) Research Fund, grant number 122/686; the British Academy/Leverhulme Small Research Grant, number SG142423; the University of Oxford's ESRC Impact Acceleration Account, number IAA-MT14-008; and has also been supported by Open Society Foundation's Human Rights Initiative.

References

Abella, F. 2021. Temen un enlentecimiento de la justicia tras los avances registrados en los procesamientos de crímenes de terrorismo de estado. *La Diaria*. January 2, https://ladiaria.com.uy/justicia/articulo/2021/1/temen-un-enlentecimiento-de-la-justicia-tras-los-avances-registrados-en-los-procesamientos-de-crimenes-de-terrorismo-de-estado/.

Abuelas de Plaza de Mayo. 2012. *Lanzamiento oficial de la unidad especializada para los casos de apropiación de niños durante el terrorismo de estado*. November 12, https://www.abuelas.org.ar/noticia/lanzamiento-oficial-de-la-unidad-especializada-para-los-casos-de-apropiacion-de-ninos-durante-el-terrorismo-de-estado-229.

Acuña, C.H., and C. Smulovitz. 1995. Militares en la transición argentina: del gobierno a la subordinación constitucional. In *Juicio, castigos y memorias: Derechos humanos y justicia en la política argentina*, ed. C.H. Acuña, et al., 19–99. Buenos Aires: Ediciones Nueva Visión.

Amnesty International. 1987. *Argentina: The military juntas and human rights: Report of the trial of the former junta members, 1985*. London: Amnesty International.

Barahona de Brito, A. 1997. *Human rights and democratization in Latin America: Uruguay and Chile*. Oxford: Oxford University Press.

Barahona de Brito, A. 2001. Truth, justice, memory, and democratization in the Southern Cone. In *The politics of memory: Transitional justice in democratizing societies*, ed. Paloma Aguilar, Alexandra Barahona De Brito, and Carmen Gonzalez Enriquez, 119–160. Oxford: Oxford University Press.

Burt, J.-M., G. Fried Amilivia, and F. Lessa. 2013. Civil society and the resurgent struggle against impunity in Uruguay (1986–2012). *International Journal of Transitional Justice* 7 (2): 306–327.

Collins, C. 2010. Human rights trials in Chile during and after the "Pinochet years". *International Journal of Transitional Justice* 4 (1): 67–86.

Collins, C. 2016a. Paraguay: Accountability in the shadow of Stroessner. In *Transitional justice in Latin America: The uneven road from impunity towards accountability*, ed. Elin Skaar, Jemina Garcia-Godos, and Cath Collins, 151–177. London and New York Routledge.

Collins, C. 2016b. Chile: Incremental Truth, late justice. Written with Boris Hau. In *Transitional justice in Latin America: The uneven road from impunity towards accountability*, ed. Elin Skaar, Jemina Garcia-Godos, and Cath Collins, 126–150. London and New York: Routledge.

Comissão Nacional da Verdade. 2014. Conheça e acesse o relatório final da CNV. https://www.cnv.gov.br/index.php/outros-destaques/574-conheca-e-acesse-o-relatorio-final-da-cnv.

Crenzel, E. 2008. Argentina's National Commission on the Disappearance of Persons: Contributions to Transitional Justice. *International Journal of Transitional Justice* 2(2): 173–191.

Crenzel, E. 2011. Present pasts: Memory(ies) of state terrorism in the Southern Cone of Latin America. In *The memory of state terrorism in the Southern Cone: Argentina, Chile, and Uruguay*, ed. Francesca Lessa and Vincent Druliolle, 1–13. New York: Palgrave Macmillan.

de Greiff, P. 2014. *Informe del relator especial sobre la promoción de la verdad, la justicia, la reparación y las garantías de no repetición.* Consejo de Derechos Humanos, 27th session, 28 August. A/HRC/27/56/Add.2.

Dinges, J. 2004. *The Condor years: How Pinochet and his allies brought terrorism to three continents.* New York and London: New Press.

Fried, G., and F. Lessa, eds. 2011. *Luchas contra la impunidad. Uruguay 1985–2011.* Montevideo: Trilce.

Grandin, G. 2005. The instruction of great catastrophe: Truth commissions, national history, and state formation in Argentina, Chile and Guatemala. *American Historical Review* 110 (1): 46–67.

Guembe, J.M. 2006. Economic reparations for grave human rights violations: The Argentinean experience. In *The handbook of reparations*, ed. Pablo de Greiff, 21–44. Oxford: Oxford University Press.

Hazan, P. 2017. Beyond borders: The new architecture of transitional justice? *International Journal of Transitional Justice* 11 (1): 1–8.

Jelin, E. 2003. *State Repression and the Labors of Memory.* Minneapolis, MN: University of Minnesota Press.

King, P.J. 1989. Comparative analysis of human rights violations under military rule in Argentina, Brazil, Chile, and Uruguay. *Statistical Abstract of Latin America* 27: 1042–1065.

La Repubblica. 2017. Desaparecidos, processo condor: 8 ergastoli e 19 assoluzioni. https://www.repubblica.it/cronaca/2017/01/17/news/desaparecidos_assise_8_ergastoli_e_19_assoluzioni-156247261/.

Lesa Humanidad. 2005. "A diez años del fallo "simón". Un balance sobre el estado actual del proceso de justicia por crímenes de lesa humanidad. https://www.fiscales.gob.ar/wp-content/uploads/2015/06/20150612-Informe-Procuradur%C3%ADa-de-Cr%C3%ADmenes-contra-la-Humanidad.pdf.

Lesa Humanidad. 2020. En 14 años de juicios, se dictaron 250 sentencias con 1013 personas condenadas y 164 absueltas. December 30, https://www.fiscales.gob.ar/lesa-humanidad/en-14-anos-de-juicios-se-dictaron-250-sentencias-con-1013-personas-condenadas-y-164-absueltas/09.

Lessa, F. 2012. Barriers to justice: The ley de caducidad and impunity in Uruguay. In *Amnesty in the age of human rights accountability: Comparative and international perspectives*, ed. Francesca Lessa and Leigh A. Payne, 123–151. Cambridge: Cambridge University Press.

Lessa, F. 2013. *Memory and transitional justice in Argentina and Uruguay: Against impunity.* New York: Palgrave Macmillan.

Lessa, F. 2015. Justice beyond borders: The Operation Condor trial and accountability for transnational crimes in South America. *International Journal of Transitional Justice* 9 (3): 494–506.

Lessa, F. 2020. Operation Condor: The responsibility of the middle rank, January 21. https://www.justiceinfo.net/en/justiceinfo-comment-and-debate/opinion/43584-operation-condor-responsibility-middle-rank.html.

Lira, E. 2011. Truth, reparation and justice: The past living in the present. In *Contribution of truth, justice, and reparation policies to Latin American democracies*, 81–120. San José: Inter-American Institute of Human Rights.

Lopez, F. 2016. *The feathers of Condor: Transnational state terrorism, exiles and civilian anticommunism in South America.* Newcastle: Cambridge Scholars Publishing.

Mainwaring, S. 1986. The transition to democracy in Brazil. *Journal of Interamerican Studies and World Affairs* 28 (1): 149–179.

McSherry, J.P. 2005. *Predatory states: Operation Condor and Covert War in Latin America.* Lanham, MD and Oxford: Rowman and Littlefield Publishers.

Mezarobba, G. 2016. Brazil: The Tortuous Path to Truth and Justice. In *Transitional Justice in Latin America: The Uneven Road from Impunity towards Accountability*, eds. Elin Skaar, Jemina Garcia-Godos, and Cath Collins, 103-125. London and New York Routledge.

National Security Archive. 2007. *Rendition in the Southern Cone: Operation Condor documents revealed from Paraguayan 'Archive of Terror.'* Report May 16, 1977, December 21, https://nsarchive2.gwu.edu/NSAEBB/NSAEBB239d/PDF/19770516%20Elevar%20Informe.pdf.

Observatorio de Derechos Humanos–Universidad Diego Portales. 2011. *Reacciones preliminares al informe de la comisión calificadora 'VALECH II.'* August 27, https://www.icso.cl/wp-content/uploads/2013/09/Cifras-valech_AGOSTO-2013.pdf.

Pagina12. 2004. Crímenes que no borra el paso del tiempo. August 25, https://www.pagina12.com.ar/diario/elpais/1-40161-2004-08-25.html.

Pagina12. 1999. Historia de la marcha de la resistencia. https://www.pagina12.com.ar/1999/99-12/99-12-06/pag08o.htm.

Paraguay Report. 2008. Informe final: anive haguã oiko. Sintesis y caracterizacion del regimen, Tomo I. https://www.verdadyjusticia-dp.gov.py/pdf/informe_final/Tomo%201%20-%20Parte%201.pdf.

Payne, L.A., F. Lessa, and G. Pereira. 2015. Overcoming barriers to justice in the age of human rights accountability. *Human Rights Quarterly* 37 (3): 728–754.

Pion-Berlin, D. 1988. The National Security Doctrine, military threat perception, and the "Dirty War" in Argentina. *Comparative Political Studies* 21 (3): 382–407.

Rohter, L. 2004. Judge declares Pinochet fit to face human rights charges. *New York Times*. https://www.nytimes.com/2004/12/13/international/americas/judge-declares-pinochet-fit-to-face-human-rights.html.

Skaar, E., Collins, C. and J. Garcia-Godos (eds). 2016. *Transitional Justice in Latin America: The Uneven Road from Impunity towards Accountability*. London and New York: Routledge.

Secretaría de Derechos Humanos, Gobierno de Uruguay. 2020. List of victims of enforced disappearances and list of victims of political executions. https://www.gub.uy/secretaria-derechos-humanos-pasado-reciente/victimas.

Servicio Paz y Justicia. 1992. *Uruguay Nunca Más: Human rights violations, 1972–1985*. Philadelphia, PA: Temple University Press

Smulovitz, C. 2008. In search of the snark: Accountability and justice for past human rights violations in Argentina. In *Comparing the effectiveness of the accountability mechanisms in Eastern Europe and Latin America conference*. Oxford: University of Oxford, July.

United States Institute of Peace. 2017. *Commission of inquiry: Brazil, 1979–1982*. https://www.usip.org/publications/1979/01/commission-inquiry-brazil.

Weschler, L. 1998. *A miracle, a universe: Settling accounts with torturers*. Chicago: The University of Chicago Press.

Francesca Lessa is a Departmental Lecturer in Latin American Studies and Development at the Oxford Department of International Development and the Latin American Centre, Oxford School of Global and Area Studies. She is also a Senior Member and College Advisor at St Antony's College, and an Academic Affiliate at the Bonavero Institute of Human Rights, at the University of Oxford. Previously, she was a Marie Skłodowska-Curie Research Fellow for a project on transnational human rights violations in South America and Operation Condor funded by the European Commission. She is also the Honorary President of the Observatorio Luz Ibarburu (Uruguay). Her research interests include human rights, memory, impunity, and transitional justice in South America.

Chapter 8
Mobilization and Judicial Recognition of the Right to the Truth: The Inter-American Human Rights System and Brazil

Carla Osmo

Abstract The right to the truth regarding gross human rights violations was an achievement of a transnational mobilization carried out in reaction to the violations committed by dictatorships and parties involved in armed conflicts in Latin America between the 1960s and the 1990s. This chapter shows how the judicial consecration of this right took place in individual legal actions, focusing on the Inter-American System for the Protection of Human Rights and the Brazilian case. We analyze the understandings developed by the Inter-American Commission on Human Rights and by the Inter-American Court of Human Rights in cases initiated by civil society against Latin American States. We then examine, in the Brazilian experience, how courts also recognized the existence of a right to the truth, in civil actions filed as a strategy firstly to resist human rights violations and then to challenge the limits of transitional justice in Brazil. On a "case-by-case" basis, the Brazilian judiciary accepted some of the meanings ascribed to the right to the truth by the Inter-American System and rejected others.

8.1 Introduction

The right to the truth regarding gross human rights violations has recently become one of the internationally recognized human rights. Even though there has been some debate about its status as a legally enforceable subjective right, the right to the truth has been incorporated into international instruments within the Organization of American States (OAS) and the United Nations (UN). It has also been adopted as the legal basis of judicial decisions, both internationally and nationally.

In this study, I present, develop and update results of previous investigations, especially Osmo (2014, 2016, 2019). Osmo and Vitar (2015). I would like to thank John Milton for reviewing the English language text.

C. Osmo (✉)
Federal University of São Paulo, São Paulo, Brazil
e-mail: carla.osmo@unifesp.br

The emergence of the right to the truth is closely related to the context of mass or systematic human rights violations committed by dictatorships and parties involved in armed conflicts in Latin America between the 1960s and the 1990s. As a reaction to such violations, human rights activists—mostly groups formed by politically persecuted people and family members of killed or disappeared persons, with the support of social actors such as lawyers, religious groups, local and international non-governmental organizations—developed strategies of political pressure and legal mobilization, both at national and international levels.[1]

It was this transnational activist mobilization, of Latin American origin, that propelled the unprecedented acknowledgement of the right to the truth by the Inter-American Commission on Human Rights (IACHR) and the Inter-American Court of Human Rights (IACourtHR), contributing to the evolution of international law in this area.[2] The right to the truth as established in the Inter-American System of Human Rights includes the right of families of enforced disappearance victims to know what happened to their loved ones, and, when applicable, to recover their remains; the investigation of other gross human rights violations, such as torture and extrajudicial execution; the declassification of human rights files; a social and participatory construction of narratives about the violent past; the judicial prosecution and punishment of those responsible; and the implementation of symbolic reparations such as public recognition and apologies, and the creation of memorials (see Naftali 2016; Osmo 2014).

Civil actions have been one of the legal mobilization strategies adopted against the gross human rights violations committed in Latin America and the legacies they left. These actions were carried out both in the domestic judiciary of countries such as Argentina, Chile and Brazil (Abregu 1996; Cardoso 2012: 22–27; Santos 2015b: 351), and in international systems for the protection of human rights. In most cases, they denounced individual human rights violations and requested their investigation, the declaration of responsibilities and/or the payment of financial reparations. However, they also had the broader goal of advancing legislative or political changes. They are thus examples of the type of practice called "strategic litigation", in which the aim of a legal action transcends the resolution of the individual case (such as, in a case of human rights violations, the payment of financial reparation to the victim). The cases are taken to court with the purpose of promoting advances in public interest policies (Cardoso 2012: 41–56).

During the years of Latin-American authoritarian regimes, when domestic judiciaries were not eager to accept legal actions filed against national repressive policies, petitions were sent to the Inter-American System for the Protection of Human Rights

---

[1] Cecília MacDowell Santos (2015b) defines legal mobilization as a social and legal practice that makes use of the law, inside or outside the courts, through individual or collective initiatives. This legal mobilization has a transnational character when the use of law is made beyond State borders, in institutional arenas such as the IACHR.

[2] For an analysis of the role played by the Inter-American System of Human Rights (IASHR) in the emergence of a right to the truth in human rights international law, see Martin-Chenut (2014: 188). The right to the truth was also institutionalized within the United Nations Human Rights System (see Naftali 2017; Osmo 2014).

(IASHR). But also after the democratic transition in Latin-American countries, the IASHR was mobilized as a way of pressuring States to advance their transitional justice processes, especially with respect to the investigation of enforced disappearances and to the accountability of perpetrators. On these occasions, the petitioners resorted to the international judicial arena so that, invigorated by the support they had received internationally, they could later bring the demands back to their own State, in a strategy Margaret Keck and Kathryn Sikkink have called the "boomerang effect" (Keck and Sikkink 1999; Sikkink 2011: 77).

This chapter makes a retrospective analysis of the progressive consecration of the right to the truth regarding gross human rights violations by the IASHR in cases against Latin American countries. The related judicial mobilization of the right to the truth in Brazil is then examined in the light of the meanings ascribed to the right to the truth in the Inter-American sphere. In the first part of the chapter (Sect. 8.2), we present the process through which the IACHR and the IACourtHR unprecedentedly stated the existence of a right to the truth, a human right not explicitly provided for in the American Convention on Human Rights (ACHR). We pay special attention to how the IASHR dynamically constructed the concept of this right, driven by the mobilization of the IASHR by human rights activists. Subsequently (Sect. 8.3), we analyze the mobilization of the Brazilian justice system that preceded or challenged the transitional legal policies in Brazil related to what is currently understood as the right to the truth. Finally (Sect. 8.4), we draw some conclusions regarding the relationship between the meanings that were judicially ascribed to this right in the Brazilian and Inter-American cases.[3] International documents and Brazilian domestic judicial decisions were the main sources of data employed for the investigation of the emergence of the right to the truth. Literature on transitional justice and the right to the truth, in particular works which approached these themes from the perspective of legal mobilization led by non-state actors[4], were also important for our analysis.

---

[3] In Latin America, there are other experiences of strategic use of domestic courts for the investigation and registration of repressive actions and their legacy, in countries such as Chile and Argentine (Abregu 1996; Cardoso 2012: 24–27), but their analysis is not possible in this chapter. The development of studies in which these distinct national experiences were compared would be interesting.

[4] Amongst these, the research carried out by Patricia Naftali discusses the polysemy of the right to the truth in international law as a consequence of the multiplicity of causes it embraces (Naftali 2016, 2017), and specifically assesses the mobilization for the right to the truth in Argentina (Naftali 2014). Cecília MacDowell Santos (2010, 2015a, b) discusses the role played by the legal mobilization of non-state actors in Brazilian transitional justice, without focusing, though, on case-law construction of the right to the truth.

8.2   Mobilization and Recognition of the Right to the Truth in the IASHR

8.2.1   Mobilization and Recognition of a Right to the Truth Grounded on the American Convention on Human Rights

The right to the truth began to be invoked and recognized as part of international law in reaction to the mass and systematic practice of enforced disappearance by Latin American dictatorships in the 1970s. Enforced disappearance has been defined as the detention, by a State agent, or with State support, authorization or acquiescence, and the refusal of information regarding the fate of the disappeared person.[5] Frequently, the very detention is officially denied, the person is murdered, and the body concealed. This gives rise to uncertainty regarding death, prevents the realization of funeral rituals and the closure of mourning process, and maintains the families in a state of suffering which persists indefinitely.

The first international treaty to provide for the right of the families to know the fate of their relatives was the Additional Protocol I (1977) to the Geneva Conventions (Article 32), which regulates the conduct of States engaged in armed conflicts. The Geneva Conventions, adopted in 1949, already contained rules on the registration and gathering of information on victims of armed conflicts. Anyhow, commentaries on the Additional Protocol I, based on its preparatory works, indicate that it was considered important to include a provision that drew attention to the suffering caused to the families by armed conflicts, as well as the right to access the graves, as a humanitarian necessity (Pilloud et al. 1986: 346).

But enforced disappearances had specificities in relation to the situation ruled by international humanitarian law. While the latter covers "all those situations in which the fate or whereabouts of a person are unknown",[6] enforced disappearance in Latin American dictatorships was a repression technique to spread terror and hide the evidence of the crimes perpetrated by State agents.

It was through a transnational mobilization of Latin American origin that this issue was taken to international human rights organisms, helping the concern about enforced disappearance to gain strength and repercussion in the international arena, especially after the coups in Chile (1973) and Argentina (1976). According to Patricia Naftali's research on the creation of the right to the truth in international law, the family associations that searched for disappeared persons in Latin America were at the center of this transnational mobilization that advocated for the recognition of this new human right (Naftali 2017: 54–55). Among the family associations, the

---

[5] See the International Convention for the Protection of All Persons from Enforced Disappearance, Article 2.

[6] United Nations. Office of the United Nations High Commissioner for Human Rights. Study on the right to the truth. Report of the Office of the United Nations High Commissioner for Human Rights. Doc. E/CN.4/2006/91, February 2006, note 5.

Argentine groups *Madres de la Plaza de Mayo* and *Abuelas de la Plaza de Mayo,* made up of mothers of the disappeared and grandmothers of kidnapped babies, became widely known. For the Argentine *Madres,* the search for the truth was the object of their struggle and also an essential element in the construction of their identity as a group, as seen in its first public statement, in 1977, entitled "For a Peaceful Christmas. We only demand Truth" (Naftali 2016: 3, 2017: 46).[7] Integrated into a transnational network of activism, the family groups internationalized their cause.

Although enforced disappearance was also an object of attention in the United Nations, the Inter-American System has had an innovative and influential role (Martin-Chenut 2014: 192). The IACHR had been created in 1959 with the purpose of monitoring and promoting the protection of human rights in the Americas. If initially the Commission's role was fundamentally that of promoting human rights, its powers were later strengthened, and it became one the main organs of the Organization of American States (OAS). After the adoption of the ACHR in 1969, the IACHR began to receive and process petitions about individual cases on violations of rights guaranteed in the ACHR and in other Inter-American human rights treaties, committed by States party to these treaties, with the aim of determining their international responsibility. With the establishment of the IACourtHR in 1979, the IACHR also acquired the competence to submit to the IACourtHR contentious cases of human rights violations involving States that had accepted the IACourtHR jurisdiction (Osmo and Martin-Chenut 2017). However, the political environment in Latin America at that time was still dominated by dictatorships, and the States with authoritarian regimes, like Argentina, Chile and Brazil, would only ratify the ACHR and accept the jurisdiction of the IACourtHR from the mid-1980s.[8]

Anyhow, the IACHR already had the competence to receive individual petitions alleging violations of human rights contained in the American Declaration of the Rights and Duties of Man, committed by any Member State of the OAS, even by those which had not yet ratified the ACHR. Because of this, from the end of the 1960s on, the IACHR was seen as a viable locus for complaints about the violations that were taking place in the Southern Cone. According to a survey conducted by Santos (2010: 136), between 1969 and 1973 the IACHR received at least 77 petitions against Brazil, among which all but one concerned gross human rights violations, such as arbitrary imprisonment, torture, execution and enforced disappearance. When requested to

---

[7] The *Madres*, who gave international visibility to the issue of disappeared persons, initially used the right to the truth regarding the destiny of the victims as a slogan in their protests. Later, when exhumations were carried out to identify the bodies, part of the group would object to them, demanding the reappearance alive of those who disappeared (*"aparición con vida"*), as a way to keep their cause alive and persist in the struggle for the judgment and punishment of those responsible (Bevernage and Aerts 2009; Naftali 2016: 9). Here the *Madres* stand out from other groups of family members, who fight for the search of the bodies and their identification (Teles 2005: 48).

[8] The ACHR ratification by these countries happened in 1984 (Argentina), 1990 (Chile) and 1992 (Brazil). Their acceptance of the IACourtHR's jurisdiction occurred in 1984 (Argentina), 1990 (Chile) and 1998 (Brazil).

present information about the violations, Brazil would deny them, and the IACHR—whose members were nominated by governments of the States in the region, several of which were under dictatorial regimes—in most cases either declared the petition inadmissible or decided to archive the file.[9]

Nevertheless, as Sikkink points out (2001: 64–67), throughout the 1970s a change in the composition of the IACHR took place, and human rights activists saw in this a window of opportunity to put pressure on the Commission to become an innovative organization. At that time a large number of enforced disappearance complaints were presented to the Commission (Pinto 2007: 14). In response, the IACHR started, both in its annual reports (e.g. 1979) and in its country reports, such as that of 1980 on Argentina, to urge the Latin American States to immediately clarify the enforced disappearances.[10] This duty to provide information in cases of enforced disappearance would later be recognized by the IACHR as part of a subjective right to the truth, even if this right was not expressly provided for by international treaties. In its 1985–1986 annual report, the IACHR established that "Every society has the inalienable right to know the truth about past events. [...] Moreover, the family members of the victims are entitled to information as to on what happened to their relatives".[11]

The existence of the right to the truth was also recognized when the IACHR analyzed individual petitions oh human rights violations. *Aguiar de Lapacó versus Argentina*, initiated from the mobilization of the Argentine *Madres*, is a paradigmatic case, which resulted in an amicable solution between the IACHR and the Argentine

---

[9] One exception was the case of Olavo Hansen (Case no. 1683), a union leader who was arrested, tortured and murdered in the premises of Department of Social and Political Order (*Departamento Estadual de Ordem Política e Social—DOPS*) of São Paulo in 1970. The IACHR decision in this case, included in its 1973 Annual Report, recognized the violation and recommended that the Brazilian government punish those responsible and give reparation to Hansen's family. In Case no. 1684, related to three anonymous complaints about the existence of twelve thousand political prisoners in Brazil and the practice of torture and rape, the IACHR stated, also in its 1973 Report, that difficulties were imposed on the investigation by the Brazilian government, which prevented the confirmation of the veracity or falsehood of the allegations. Nonetheless, the Commission declared that there was enough proof to allow a conclusion of the occurrence of torture, and that this violation should be investigated by the Brazilian Government. According to the Brazilian National Truth Commission's (NTC) in its final report, the Brazilian Minister of Foreign Affairs attempted to hide facts about the violations from the AICHR, and the Brazilian Government tried to prevent or at least delay the publication of the aforementioned AICHR report, with the help of the Brazilian AICHR member Carlos Alberto Dunshee de Abranches (Brazil. National Truth Commission 2014. *Relatório /Comissão Nacional da Verdade*, v. 1. Brasília: 207–211, my translation).

[10] "In the opinion of the IACHR, the fundamental question is one of ascertaining and communicating in a timely manner with the family members on the situation of the disappeared. It is necessary to establish beyond any doubt whether these persons are still alive or are dead; if they are alive, it is necessary to know where they are; if they are dead, it is necessary to know where, when and under what circumstances they lost their lives and where their remains are buried" (Organization of American States. Inter-American Commission on Human Rights. Report on the Situation of Human Rights in Argentina. Doc. OEA/Ser.L/V/II.49, doc. 19 corr.1, 11 April 1980, chap. III.F, § 11).

[11] Organization of American States. Inter-American Commission of Human Rights. Annual Report of the Inter-American Commission on Human Rights 1985–1986. Doc. OEA/Ser.L/V/II.68, doc. 8 rev. 1, September 1986, chapter V.

government.[12] The complaint brought to the IACHR by Carmen Aguiar de Lapacó – one of the *Madres de Plaza de Mayo* founders – concerned the refusal, by the Argentine judicial authorities, of a request to determine the fate her daughter, who was disappeared since 1977, based on the right to the truth and on the right to mourn.

According to Abregu (1996), Aguiar de Lapacó's legal action was one of a number of civil actions initiated after former naval officer Adolfo Scilingo confessed, in 1995, his participation in the so-called "death flights", in which political prisoners were thrown from airplanes into the ocean. At the time, The Full Stop Law and Due Obedience Law, approved in 1986 and 1987 respectively by the Argentine Congress, prevented criminal procedures from being conducted. Thus human rights organizations, deeming it important to make Scilingo's declarations have an impact on courts, initiated a series of civil actions expressly grounded in the right to the truth.

The Center for Legal and Social Studies (*Centro de Estudios Legales y Sociales*— CELS), an Argentine NGO that played a major role in the litigation in face of the crimes committed by the Argentine dictatorship, initiated the pioneer cases of Lapacó and Emilio Mignore. Based on the right to the truth, the CELS actions requested the court to use the investigation powers it holds in criminal cases to clarify what happened to the disappeared persons, and, in more general terms, to clarify what the methods used by State terrorism in Argentine were. The concept of a right to the truth had been presented before in the international arena, especially in scholarly works, but its mobilization in Argentine courts was a novelty (Abregu 1996: 18).

A debate followed on the purpose of the criminal procedure, whether its goal is exclusively to have the accused punished, or if it also includes the determination of the facts related to the crime. Argentine judicial decisions gradually recognized the right to the truth and took a stand in favor of the continuation of the investigations and the use of judicial powers with a view to determining the truth about the disappearances. But there was a reversion in this understanding in Aguiar de Lapacó's case, confirmed by the Argentine Supreme Court. According to Abregu's report, the Supreme Court ruled that "[…] the objective of a criminal procedure is to apply punishment and, thus, the victim has no right to know the truth about the committed crime – at least in the criminal justice sphere" (Abregu 1998: 118, my translation). On a later occasion, the same Supreme Court decided, in Abregu's words, that "[…] families have the right to know what happened to the victims of State terrorism via *habeas data*" (Abregu 1998: 118, my translation).

Habeas data is type of legal action designed to allow people access to information stored in government-held databases, and its procedure does not allow the use of evidence-gathering mechanisms such as a witness hearing. Hence, Carmen de Lapacó filed a petition before the IACHR, sponsored by several human rights NGOs and disappeared persons' family associations, alleging that the Argentine judicial decision violated the ACHR (Naftali 2014: 85–86). In 1999, the parties reached a friendly settlement, according to which the Argentine government "[…] accepts and

---

[12] We have already discussed this case in a paper written with Argentine law scholar Julia Vitar and published in Brazil (Osmo and Vitar 2015).

guarantees the right to the truth, which involves the exhaustion of all means to obtain information on the whereabouts of the disappeared persons".[13] The friendly settlement considered that the national federal criminal courts and correctional courts throughout Argentina should have exclusive jurisdiction in the cases aimed at determining the truth regarding the fate of the disappeared persons. This commitment made by the government of Argentina gave strength to the so called "truth trials" ("*juicios por la verdad*"), which continued even after the Supreme Court's decision in Lapacó's case (Naftali 2014: 86). These trials collected information and compiled case files that later, after the Full Stop and Due Obedience Laws were repealed, would substantiate the criminal prosecutions and punishment.[14]

Other cases, deriving from individual petitions regarding enforced disappearances in several Latin American countries, were submitted by the IACHR to the IACourtHR. In these cases the IACHR would gradually persuade the Court to adopt the right to the truth as grounds for its rulings. *Velásquez Rodríguez vs. Honduras*, the first contentious case decided by IACourtHR on its merits, concerned the disappearance of a student, after his detention by the Honduras armed forces in 1981. The IACourtHR ruled that the State is obliged to investigate the fate of enforced disappearance victims but did not yet connect this obligation to a subjective right to the truth. According to the IACourtHR, the State duty would stem from Article 1.1 of the ACHR, which contains the general obligation of States to respect and ensure the free and full exercise of the rights protected by the Convention. The Court interpreted this obligation as entailing the positive duty to "prevent, investigate and punish any violation of the rights recognized by the Convention", and, regarding enforced disappearances, the duty to investigate the fate of the victims, and if they have been killed, the location of their remains.[15]

In *Castillo Páez vs. Peru*, decided nine years later, the IACHR argued before the IACourtHR that, in cases of enforced disappearance, the State that does not conduct a serious investigation violates a "right to the truth and to information". The Commission did not refer to a specific provision of the ACHR as the legal basis for this right but remarked that it had been recognized by several international organizations.[16] The Court, in turn, stated that it is "a right that does not exist in the American Convention", recognizing, though, that it could "correspond to a concept that is being developed in doctrine and case law".[17] Anyhow, according to the IACourtHR, the same purpose sought by the invocation of the right to the truth would be achieved through the affirmation by the Court that Peru has the duty to investigate the facts that

---

[13] Organization of American States. Inter-American Commission on Human Rights. Report n. 21/00. Case 12.059. Carmen Aguiar de Lapacó. Argentina. February 2000.

[14] United Nations. Commission on Human Rights. Right to the truth. Report of the Office of the High Commissioner for Human Rights. Doc. A/HRC/5/7, June 2007, § 53.

[15] Organization of American States. Inter-American Court of Human Rights. Case of Velásquez Rodríguez v. Honduras. Merits. Judgment of July 29, 1988. Series C No. 4, § 166, 181.

[16] Organization of American States. Inter-American Court of Human Rights. Case of Castillo Páez v. Peru. Merits. Judgment of November 3, 1997. Series C No. 34, § 85.

[17] Organization of American States. Inter-American Court of Human Rights. Case of Castillo Páez v. Peru. Merits. Judgment of November 3, 1997. Series C No. 34, § 86.

produced violations of the ACHR. The IACourtHR also related the States' duty to investigate to a "right to know what happened to him [the victim] and, if appropriate, where his remains are located".[18]

It was in *Bámaca Velásquez vs. Guatemala*—also about enforced disappearance—that the IACourtHR first declared that it is possible to infer a right to the truth from the ACHR text. This time, the IACHR had argued that "it is emerging as a principle of international law under the dynamics interpretation of human rights treaties and, specifically, Articles 1(1), 8, 25 and 13 of the American Convention".[19] Naftali (2017: 180–181) points out that, in this case, the IACHR strategy before the IACourtHR was reinforced by an *amicus curiae* manifestation presented by human rights NGOs, which aimed to demonstrate the existence of a right to the truth in international law.

The Court thus agreed that the right existed, but not as an autonomous right. According to the Court's understanding, the right to the truth is subsumed in, integrated or absorbed into the rights and duties which arise from the combination of Articles 8, 25 and 1.1 of the ACHR.[20] Article 8 of the ACHR contains the so-called "right to a fair trial"—a group of rules to which court proceedings must conform—whereas Article 25 addresses the "right to judicial protection" and is related to the access to justice. From the combination of these provisions with Article 1.1, which prescribes States' obligations to respect and ensure the exercise of the rights, the IACourtHR derived a right to the truth.

Therefore, in *Velásquez Rodríguez vs. Honduras* the IACourtHR had already declared the existence of the State's duty to investigate the violations. However, it was through the subsequent combination of this obligation with the rights protected in Articles 8 and 25 that the Court affirmed the importance of effective recourses able to protect against human right violations, and construed the legal basis for a subjective right to the truth, to which the families of the disappeared are entitled (Philippe Marino 2008: 99). Therefore, the IACourtHR concluded that, under Articles 1.1, 8 and 25 of the ACHR, a right is assured for the families of enforced disappearance victims to know the truth about what happened to them, and, in case of death, about the location of their remains.

This conclusion was reiterated in subsequent cases. The Court has further stated that the deprivation of access to truth about the fate of a disappeared person constitutes cruel and degrading treatment to their family members, and thus this practice equally offends the family members' right to personal integrity, also provided for in the ACHR.[21] The guarantee of the right to the truth has also been conceived as a means of

---

[18] Organization of American States. Inter-American Court of Human Rights. Case of Castillo Páez v. Peru. Merits. Judgment of November 3, 1997. Series C No. 34, § 90.

[19] Organization of American States. Inter-American Court of Human Rights. Case of Bámaca Velásquez v. Guatemala. Merits. Judgment of November 25, 2000. Series C No. 70, § 197.

[20] Organization of American States. Inter-American Court of Human Rights. Case of Bámaca Velásquez v. Guatemala. Merits. Judgment of November 25, 2000. Series C No. 70, § 201. See also Burgorgue-Larsen and de Torres (2008: 742), and Martin-Chenut (2007: 630).

[21] Organization of American States. Inter-American Comission of Human Rights. The Right to Truth in the Americas. Doc. OEA/Ser.L/V/II.152, doc. 2, August 2014.

reparation for the families of the disappeared.[22] In some cases, in which information had been omitted or denied after requirements presented directly by the victims or their families, the IACourtHR has additionally connected the right to the truth to the freedom of information (Article 13 of the ACHR).[23] Finally, the Court's decisions shed light on the content of the duty of the State to investigate cases of enforced disappearance: it is an obligation of means and not of results but cannot be carried out simply as a formality doomed to failure; the investigation must be carried out by the State *ex officio*, regardless of the victims' initiative; it must adopt all legal means available; and it must aim at the determination of the truth and the punishment of those responsible.[24]

It was also in relation to cases of enforced disappearance that the right to the truth would for the first time be explicitly provided for in a legally binding international instrument—the International Convention for the Protection of All Persons from Enforced Disappearance, adopted at the United Nations in 2006 (Article 24.2).[25] But the IACourtHR decided that the right to the truth also concerns other gross human rights violations besides enforced disappearances, such as cases of extrajudicial executions and torture.[26] In addition, it established that the right to the truth has both an individual and a collective dimension. The individual dimension consists of the right of the victims and their family members to an investigation of their individual case. In its collective dimension, society as a whole has the right to know about the violations in order to prevent them from continuing or happening again. The collective dimension of the right to the truth requires an investigation that goes beyond the individual cases, to analyze what happened in a broad framework, encompassing contextual and structural elements, an investigation that shall be constructed in a participatory way.[27]

---

[22] Organization of American States. Inter-American Court of Human Rights. Case of Bámaca Velásquez v. Guatemala. Reparations and Costs. Judgment of February 22, 2002. Series C No. 91, § 76.

[23] Organization of American States. Inter-American Court of Human Rights. Case of Gomes Lund et al. ("Guerrilha do Araguaia") v. Brazil. Preliminary Objections, Merits, Reparations, and Costs. Judgment of November 24, 2010. Series C No. 219.

[24] Organization of American States. Inter-American Court of Human Rights. Case of Gomes Lund et al. ("Guerrilha do Araguaia") v. Brazil. Preliminary Objections, Merits, Reparations, and Costs. Judgment of November 24, 2010. Series C No. 219, § 138.

[25] The Inter-American Convention on Forced Disappearance of Persons (1994) does not have an express provision of a right to the truth although this Convention establishes that the State Parties shall supply information as to where of the persons deprived of freedom and allegedly disappeared.

[26] Organization of American States. Inter-American Court of Human Rights. Case of Vargas Areco vs. Paraguay. Judgment of September 26, 2006. Serie C No. 155 § 77, 81; Organization of American States. Inter-American Court of Human Rights. Case of Herzog and others v. Brazil. Preliminary Objections, Merits, Reparations, and Costs. Judgment of March 15, 2018. Serie C No. 353, § 328–338.

[27] Organization of American States. Inter-American Commission of Human Rights. The Right to Truth in the Americas. Doc. OEA/Ser.L/V/II.152, doc. 2, August 2014, § 15, 48.

8.2.2 The Connection Between the Right to the Truth and the Quest for Justice

The right to the truth as constructed in the Inter-American System is strongly related to what came to be called "right to justice", which basically means a right to criminal accountability. Indeed, the right to the truth was incorporated as part of the agenda of the movement known as the "fight against impunity", developed in opposition to amnesties or similar measures granted to perpetrators of gross human rights violations in Latin America during the democratic transitions between the end of the 1970s and the 1990s. The mobilizations that combatted these amnesties argued that States have international obligations regarding gross violations, which include the obligation to punish the perpetrators and the obligation to investigate and acknowledge the truth about the violations. They related impunity not only to the lack of penalties, but also to the absence of truth.

In response, the IACHR would take a clear stance against national legislation aimed at obstructing criminal proceedings against perpetrators of gross human rights violations. In Reports no. 28/92 and no. 29/92 on individual cases of human rights violations in Argentina and Uruguay respectively, published in the 1992–1993 IACHR Annual Report, the Commission already stated that the laws that hindered criminal proceedings in these two countries were incompatible with the ACHR.[28]

The IACourtHR, in turn, has ruled against amnesties and similar measures adopted in favor of perpetrators of human rights violations since the *Barrios Altos vs. Peru* case in 2001, considering that they violate Articles 1, 8 and 25 of the ACHR.[29] From these provisions of the ACHR, the IACourtHR infers the duty of the States to investigate the violations and to prosecute and punish those responsible, which corresponds to the right to justice. But the same obligation also corresponds, as seen above, to the right to the truth. In other words, in the IASHR, the right to justice and the right to the truth have the same legal basis and entail similar obligations.

According to Naftali's research on the creation of right to the truth in international law (2016: 4–5), this overlap of the right to the truth and the right to justice derives from the opposition to the creation of truth commissions as a substitute for criminal accountability. Indeed, various countries in Latin America adopted truth commissions in a period when they had laws impeding prosecutions. Naftali understands that the South African Truth and Reconciliation Commission, which acquired great visibility and offered individual amnesties to perpetrators in exchange for the full disclosure of the truth, entailed a polarization between groups of academics and militants around the necessary responses to the gross violations of human rights. The majority of family associations continued defending the annulment of amnesties, insisting

---

[28] Organization of American States. Inter-American Commission of Human Rights. Annual Report of the Inter-American Commission on Human Rights 1992–1993. Doc. OEA/Ser.L/V/II.83, doc. 14, March 1993.

[29] Organization of American States. Inter-American Court of Human Rights. Case of Barrios Altos v. Peru. Interpretation of the Judgment of the Merits. Judgment of September 3, 2001. Series C No. 83.

that the work of truth commissions was insufficient and that criminal proceedings were essential (Naftali 2017: 125–137).

In line with this demand, the IASHR organs usually encourage and value the creation of truth commissions by States so as to comply with the States' obligation to investigate systematic or mass human rights violations. For them, truth commissions contribute, among other things, to a collective reconstruction of the truth and to give voice to the victims.[30] However, the IASHR organs do not believe that there can be an effective implementation of the right to the truth without legal criminal procedures. The IACourtHR underlines that the "historical truth" presented in reports prepared by truth commissions does not replace the "judicial truth" reached in legal actions aiming to establish criminal responsibilities. The duty of the State to establish the truth will only be accomplished once those responsible for the violations have been identified, prosecuted and punished. Amnesties are considered incompatible not only to the right to justice, but also to the right to the truth.[31]

8.3   The Mobilization of the Right to the Truth and Its Acknowledgement by the Brazilian Judiciary

In Brazil the right to the truth was judicially mobilized in a convergent way to challenge the legal and political limits imposed on the process of transitional justice. Even if this right was not explicitly provided for in the Brazilian Constitution or legislation, it served as legal grounds for civil legal actions with different purposes. In order to better understand the claims that were judicially presented based on the right to the truth, it is interesting to briefly recall how the Brazilian dictatorship, which began in 1964, acted to conceal and dissimulate the crimes it committed in the repression of political dissent.

Enforced disappearance was systematically adopted in Brazil as a repression mechanism from 1971 on. Before this, the Brazilian dictatorship made use of other techniques to conceal deaths caused by torture, such as delivering the bodies to the families in sealed coffins. False versions about the circumstances of the deaths were created and disseminated, especially suicide, or that the victims had been run over, or that they had been killed in a shoot out with police officers. Even when enforced disappearance became a systematic practice, it did not always involve the conceal-ment of the body without an official notice or registration of death. Sometimes death was recognized by the State, and/or a death certificate was issued, but the families did not have access to the bodies and were not informed about the burial sites. Other times the families remained without any sort of information about what had happened to the person who had disappeared.

---

[30] Organization of American States. Inter-American Commission of Human Rights. The Right to Truth in the Americas. Doc. OEA/Ser.L/V/II.152, doc. 2, August 2014, § 176.

[31] Organization of American States. Inter-American Commission of Human Rights. The Right to Truth in the Americas. Doc. OEA/Ser.L/V/II.152, doc. 2, August 2014, § 33, 127–135.

The different techniques adopted for the dissimulation of gross human rights violations involved coordination between repression forces and other official organs and
agents, including forensic physicians, who took part in the concealment of evidence
by omitting relevant data or writing false information in the necropsy reports; cemetery administrators, who agreed to rapidly bury those killed for political reasons,
under fake names or as if their identity was not known, without the presence of
family members; and judges, who maintained communication with security organs
and sometimes knew about the death of prosecuted political activists, but did not
provide due information to the families.[32]

The use of torture upon political prisoners was a routine practice, institutionalized
and coordinated by the Armed Forces and an essential element of repression by the
military regime. The torture strategy was to disseminate fear, but at the same time
to hide its marks (Teles 2005: 29). To do so, its methods went through a process
of "sophistication", with the use of instruments capable of causing intense suffering
without leaving physically noticeable signs, and counted on the collaboration of
physicians and other health professionals. There was also great zeal in the high-level
sector of the government to avoid and refute complaints presented both nationally
and internationally concerning the torture of political prisoners.[33] One of the most
important secrets of the Brazilian dictatorship was the extermination of the Araguaia
Guerrilla by the Brazilian Armed Forces between 1972 and 1975, when about 70 militants disappeared—this would be the subject of the first decision of the IACourtHR
against Brazil regarding the dictatorship's crimes. Another emblematic case was a
clandestine grave in the cemetery of Perus, a district in the city of São Paulo, where
the remains of more than a thousand people were found in 1990, when the grave was
opened.

In 1979, an Amnesty Law was adopted which allowed the release of political
prisoners from jail and the return of exiled activists. During the previous years,
a broad social mobilization had been organized demanding amnesty in favor of the
politically persecuted, with public demonstrations in diverse locations, hunger strikes
by the political prisoners, among other strategies (Greco 2003). However, the law that
in fact was adopted did not use the same terms requested by these civil society groups.
It incorporated an ambiguous formula that was interpreted as impeding the criminal

---

[32] Pursuant to the NTC final report, "The operation to disguise the real cause of death of militants
involved, in addition to security agents, several public service sectors, with emphasis on those
of forensic medicine. Several medical reports are known to contain untruthful and contradictory
information, in which the coroners attested causes for death incompatible with the injuries in the
victims' bodies, verified by witnesses or registered in photographs taken for these very reports.
In other cases, also with the aim of dissimulating execution or death due to torture, the official
communication of death took a long time to get to the families, who also lived through the distressing
difficulty of obtaining their relative's body, frequently delivered in a sealed coffin. It was not rare for
the funerals to be watched over by policemen or military agents" (Brazil. National Truth Commission
2014. *Relatório /Comissão Nacional da Verdade*. Brasília: 443, my translation).

[33] Brazil. National Truth Commission 2014. *Relatório /Comissão Nacional da Verdade*. Brasília:
350–365.

prosecution of the State agents that had practiced gross human right violations.[34] In addition, for a long time after the democratic transition, the Brazilian government did not acknowledge the human rights violations committed during the military dictatorship, nor did it investigate the cases of enforced disappearance.

Throughout this period, only the persistent struggle of victims and families of killed and disappeared persons led to the opening up of archives and the discovery of graves in which political prisoners were buried. Groups of families, who since the 1970s had been denouncing the human rights violations of the dictatorship, continued their fight for truth and justice after the Amnesty Law, this time without broader social support. Frequently, the families alone carried out the investigations through the search for official documents and the collection of testimonies. It was their research that first gathered information about the cases of political murder and enforced disappearance, and identified torturers and doctors that collaborated with the violations (Araújo et al. 1995). The dossier they produced, gathering all the available information on cases of executions and disappearances, would be the basis for the State policies adopted later, including the work of the National Truth Commission. The family groups also urged that doctors that helped to conceal the human rights violations should be struck off the medical register, and kept pressuring for political changes (which, when adopted, always fell short of what they had revindicated).[35]

Brazil started to overcome this full omission regarding the right to the truth with the creation of two national reparation commissions, one in 1995 (Commission on Political Deaths and Disappearances of Persons) and another in 2001 (Amnesty Commission), which, notwithstanding their limited investigative power, ended up playing an important role in examining and acknowledging the violations (Torelly 2018). Differently from other Latin American countries that had truth commissions just a few years after their democratic transitions, only in 2012 would Brazil have a national truth commission to investigate the gross human rights violations committed during the dictatorship, followed by several local truth commissions that conducted parallel investigations.

Already during the Brazilian dictatorship, courts became one of the fronts of the struggle for truth carried out by the relatives of the murdered or disappeared persons, with the support of allies, such as lawyers in human rights causes. The judicial litigation continued after the democratic transition, through the initiative of the families of the victims and of former political prisoners. These actions, although

---

[34] For this reason, the Brazilian Amnesty Lay would be considered contrary to the ACHR by the IACourtHR (Organization of American States. Inter-American Court of Human Rights. Case of Gomes Lund et al. ("Guerrilha do Araguaia") v. Brazil. Preliminary Objections, Merits, Reparations, and Costs. Judgment of November 24, 2010. Series C No. 219).

[35] Commission of Families of the Political Dead and Disappeared (CFMDP) 2018. Information to the Inter-American Commission on Human Rights (IACHR) on the human rights situation in Brazil, focusing on the theme of Memory, Truth and Justice related to human rights violations in the dictatorship and its legacies. São Paulo.

formulated in individual terms, had an important political meaning and were often part of a wider social articulation (Santos 2015b: 352).[36]

The first legal actions related to the right to the truth were filed by family members of the murdered and disappeared persons, in order to obtain an official (judicial) acknowledgment of State responsibility for the violations. A pioneer legal action was initiated in 1976 by the family of the journalist Vladimir Herzog.[37] A book was published with the main documents of this legal action, whose preface, written by Raymundo Faoro, describes its background (Faoro 1978: 13). Herzog had been killed under torture in October 1975, after voluntarily attending a summons to appear before the repression authorities. In an official note, the Army announced he had committed suicide by hanging himself with a strip of cloth, after confessing his political militancy. A medical report attested that the cause of the death was suicide, and a military inquiry, initiated to investigate Herzog's death, concluded that he had hanged himself with the belt of the overalls he was wearing.

With the aim of refuting the official version for Herzog's death, his wife Clarice and sons initiated a civil action that demanded the declaration of the responsibility of Brazilian State for Herzog's arbitrary imprisonment, torture and murder. His relatives did not wish to obtain financial reparation, merely a statement attesting that Herzog did not commit suicide but was killed by State agents. However, the Brazilian legal system did not provide for a legal action for the declaration of the way the facts happened. Thus, anticipating a resistance on the part of the judge to accept a declaratory action in these terms, the lawyers in Herzog's lawsuit requested the recognition of a legal relationship between his relatives and the Brazilian State, in which the latter was the debtor of an obligation to pay damages. In other words, instead of claiming financial reparations, they demanded only the declaration that the obligation to pay damages existed. To decide in favor of the plaintiffs, the judge would have to conclude that Herzog was subjected to torture and that the State was responsible for his death (Faoro 1978: 14). In 1978—still during the dictatorship—they managed to obtain a judicial decision which not only recognized the falsehood of the suicide version and the State's responsibility for Herzog's death but also admitted, in broader terms, that the Brazilian State practiced the torture of political prisoners.[38]

---

[36] Civil society's legal actions that challenged the limits of transitional justice in Brazil were not only concerned with the right to the truth. There were legal actions with varied objects, like those seeking financial reparations. Besides this, at least one State institution—the Federal Office of the Public Prosecutor—also used litigation as a means to obtain progress in matters of transitional justice (see Santos 2015a). The central focus of this chapter, however, are the actions filed by civil society that contributed to the judicial recognition of the right to the truth.

[37] According to Santos (2015a), a previous case had been initiated in 1973 by Elizabeth Soares, the wife of Manoel Soares who had been killed in 1966, demanding reparations, but only in the year 2000 would there be a decision as to its merit.

[38] "[…] in these proceedings […] there are strong revelations that torture had been inflicted not only on Vladimir Herzog, but also on other political prisoners within the Army's facilities of DOI/CODI [*Department of Information Operations—Center for Internal Defense Operations*]" (Brazil. Federal Court of the Judiciary Section of São Paulo. Process no. 136/76. Plaintiffs: Clarice Herzog and others. Defendant: Federal Union. Judge: Márcio José de Moraes. São Paulo, October 27th 1978, my translation).

Dilma Borges Vieira and Lucia Vieira Caldas, respectively wife and daughter of Mário Alves de Sousa Vieira, proposed a legal action to obtain a judicial decision of a similar nature, but with reference to an enforced disappearance. Vieira was a journalist who had been disappeared by the Brazilian dictatorship in 1970. Ana Müller, the lawyer for the plaintiffs in this action, gave us an interview in which she said that Dilma contacted her when she learned, through other political prisoners, that her disappeared husband had been arrested, tortured and killed within the Army's facilities. However, at that moment, a civil action was not a viable alternative, as the witnesses were still in prison.

The legal action was initiated in 1979, just after the adoption of the Brazilian Amnesty Law. Similarly to Herzog's case, Vieira's relatives were not interested in financial reparation, so the action requested the mere declaration of the existence of a legal relationship of civil responsibility between the Brazilian State and the plaintiffs, without demanding the effective payment of the damages. In Müller's words, "the legal action should be merely political, its aim was that the Federal Union be declared responsible for this barbaric act" (Müller 2016: 87, my translation). In a previous preparatory action, the plaintiffs had requested the hearing of a series of testimonies. Fearful that something could happen to the witnesses, they wished to guarantee that their declarations were collected judicially, which would improve their value as proof in future legal actions.[39] The 1981 merits decision accepted the request of the plaintiffs, and declared that: "Based on the facts proven in the files of this case, we can reach the logical conclusion that Mário Alves de Sousa Vieira died of the effects of maltreatment he suffered at the facilities of the DOI-CODI [*Department of Information Operations - Center for Internal Defense Operations*]". [40]

Therefore, the cases of Vladimir Herzog and Mário Alves were initiated at a moment when there was still no space for moving a legal action with the explicit purpose of obtaining an official recognition of the crimes committed by State agents and when the right to the truth was not yet part of the juridical vocabulary. This is the reason why, even though they tried to obtain a judicial acknowledgement of the truth, they had to strategically present a request for a judicial declaration of the civil responsibility of the State to pay damages. Anyhow, they created a precedent for future legal actions, which could more clearly expose the purpose of obtaining a judicial declaration of the truth, such as the action filed by Inês Etienne Romeu in 1999.

Inês suffered arbitrary imprisonment, torture and sexual violence practiced by State agents in the context of the political repression and was the only survivor of the clandestine center of torture and extermination known as "Death House", located in

---

[39] The lawyer for the plaintiffs Ana Maria Müller said in an interview that: "[...] The judges found it very hard to understand why so many witnesses were called on in these legal actions, but the intention, as I have already mentioned, was to leave registered their testimony-declaration. For us, this was important as a preparation for a future action, because if there were any problems with that witness, we could use their testimony given in court" (Müller 2016: 86, my translation).

[40] Brazil. Federal Court of the Judiciary Section of Rio de Janeiro. Process n. 2678420. Plaintiffs: Dilma Borges Vieira and Lucia Vieira Caldas. Defendant: Federal Union. Judge: Tania de Melo Bastos Heine. Rio de Janeiro, October 1981, my translation.

the city of Petrópolis, Rio de Janeiro state. Her legal action, initiated in 1999, also sought a judicial acknowledgement of the State's responsibility for the violations she had suffered, but explicitly used the "fundamental right to know the truth" as grounds for this request. In 2003, the merits judicial decision was issued in favor of Inês to "[…] remove any existing doubt whatsoever about such legal relationship [with Brazilian State], thus restoring the truth".[41] According to the decision, the plaintiff's claim was supported by a number of rights and principles, but it was enough to refer to the dignity of the human person, protected by the Brazilian Constitution, of which the right to the truth is part. The sentence also made reference to IACourtHR's recognition of the right to the truth.

The progress achieved through these legal actions and other similar ones is clear: Brazilian courts started to accept civil legal actions as a means to obtain the declaration of the Brazilian State's responsibility for human rights violations, and admitted the existence of a subjective right to the truth. In other words, Brazilian courts recognized the right to the truth about gross human right violations as judicially enforceable.

After the judicial acceptance of the mobilization of the right to the truth to obtain a declaration of the State's institutional responsibility, the victims and the families of victims of human rights violations would seek further progress. They would mobilize the right to the truth to obtain the judicial declaration of the personal responsibility of a State agent in such a way that civil courts would do what the criminal courts were refusing to do: name those responsible.

The Teles family, whose members were tortured in Sao Paulo in 1972 by officers led by Colonel Carlos Alberto Brilhante Ustra, initiated a legal action in 2005, requesting the judicial recognition of his personal responsibility for the crime. According to a petition of the plaintiffs in this case, the action is grounded on "[…] their sacred right to the truth, which is implemented with the certification of the authorship of the outrages inflicted on them".[42] One of the action's plaintiffs, Maria Amélia Teles, explained that the action's purpose was that "Brazilian people have the right to know who kidnapped, tortured and eliminated the lives of militants who dared to fight against the dictatorship" (Teles apud Santos 2015a: 61). The legal action of Teles family was accepted by a ruling upheld by the Brazilian Superior Court of Justice (STJ). The leading vote of the STJ decision, issued in December 2014, declared that, based on the right to the truth, those who suffered from gross violations during the dictatorship can initiate a civil action to attest the identity of the perpetrators of these violations.[43] This was other important achievement of the legal

---

[41] Brazil. Federal Court of the Judiciary Section of São Paulo. Process n. 1999.61.00.027857-6. Plaintiff: Inês Etienne Romeu. Defendant: Federal Union. Judge: José Marcos Lunardelli. São Paulo, November 2002, my translation.

[42] Comparato, Fábio Konder; Sousa, Aníbal Castro de. Process no. 05.202853-5. 23rd Civil Court of the Central Forum of São Paulo. Reply of the plaintiff. São Paulo, July 2006.

[43] "[…] the right of those who experienced the saddest thing that happened during the military regime must also be recognized, through individual declaratory actions, to obtain a formal acknowledgement of the existence of the torture they experienced, in the face of those who directly or indirectly perpetrated them. […] [The creation of the National Truth Commission] did not deprive those that

mobilization of the right to the truth since it has been the only means through which the Brazilian judiciary has accepted identifying the authorship of crimes committed during the dictatorship.

Besides the judicial recognition of the responsibilities, other causes have also mobilized the right to the truth in Brazil. A civil action initiated in 1982 by the families of those disappeared in the Araguaia Guerrilla referred to the obligation of the State to clarify cases of enforced disappearance. In 1980, family members of disappeared persons, until then without any official news about their relatives, had organized a convoy to the Araguaia region, where they obtained, with difficulty, the testimonies and pieces of information that would later make up their legal action, filed in 1982. After decades receiving no satisfactory reply from the Brazilian courts, the plaintiffs would take the case to the IASHR.

Santos (2010), in an analysis of this lengthy case, observes how the object of this action has changed over time. In the beginning, the sole judicial recognition of the existence of the Guerrilla and its annihilation was important. But the action went further as a request was made, based on the Geneva Conventions, that the bodies be located, the circumstances of death be clarified, and that access to official documents on the operations be granted. A 2003 late merits decision invoked the right of the plaintiffs to the truth about the facts related to the disappearances, as well as the right of the families to recover the remains of their loved ones, ruling that the Brazilian State must identify the location of the graves and present to this court "[…] all the information about the entirety of the military operations related to the Guerrilla".[44] According to the decision, "the right to the truth surpasses the persons of the families and reaches the whole society, which wishes to prevent such barbarities from taking place again". [45] However, until today little progress has been made in this respect.

In view of the delay of the Brazilian judicial system, the plaintiffs found allies in international NGOs—the Center for Justice and International Law (CEJIL) and the Human Rights Watch/Americas—to take a complaint to the IASHR. Afterwards, the *Comissão de Familiares de Mortos e Desaparecidos Políticos (CFMDP)* [Commission of Families of the Political Dead and Disappeared]—a commission of family members—and the Torture Never More Group of Rio de Janeiro joined the case. In 2009, when the case was taken to the IACourtHR by the IACHR, the court had already ruled in previous cases that amnesty laws that impede the investigation, persecution

---

normally had the possibility to promote a legal action of the interest and the possibility of person-ally requesting, through the instrumental use of the courts, the clarification and the detailing of these aberrant episodes, with a nominal, subjective and personal declaration, encompassing what effectively occurred, to whom it happened, where, and by whose order" (Brazil. Superior Court of Justice. Special Appeal n. 1.434.498/SP. Party: Carlos Alberto Brilhante Ustra. Parties: César Augusto Teles and others. Judge-Rapporteur: Nancy Andrighi. Judge-rapporteur for the majority opinion: Paulo de Tarso Sanseverino, Brasília, Federal District, December 2014, my translation).

[44] Brazil. Federal Court of the Judiciary Section of the Federal District. Process n. 82.00.24682-5. Plaintiffs: Julia Gomes Lund and others. Defendant: Federal Union. Judge: Solange Salgado. Brasília, Federal District, June 2003, my translation.

[45] Brazil. Federal Court of the Judiciary Section of the Federal District. Process n. 82.00.24682-5. Plaintiffs: Julia Gomes Lund and others. Defendant: Federal Union. Judge: Solange Salgado. Brasília, Federal District, June 2003, my translation.

and punishment of perpetrators of gross human right violations constitute a violation of ACHR, and specifically of the right to the truth. In this context, the mobilization of the right to the truth carried out by family members of those disappeared in the Araguaia Guerrilla could include a new claim: that those responsible be investigated, prosecuted and punished, contrary to what happens in Brazil as a consequence of the prevailing interpretation of the Amnesty Law.

In a parallel initiative, in 2008 the Brazilian Bar Association initiated a legal action in the Brazilian Federal Supreme Court requesting that the Court declare the Amnesty Law invalid regarding gross human rights violations committed by State agents. According to the Bar Association, extending the amnesty to repression agents infringes fundamental precepts protected by the Brazilian Constitution. One of the constitutional principles breached by the amnesty granted for the State crimes, according to the Bar Association, is the government's duty "not to conceal the truth", which is derived, by inference, from the right to information, the democratic principle and the republican principle, all three of which are prescribed in the Constitution. The Bar Association incorporated the idea, developed in the IACourtHR case law, that a right to the truth cannot be guaranteed without criminal proceedings: "[…] between Justice and Truth there is no conceivable separation".[46] However, in 2010 the Brazilian Supreme Court decided, contrary to the IACourtHR case law, that the amnesty in favor of perpetrators of gross human rights violations could be preserved. The justices who agreed with the majority opinion did not reject the existence of a right to the truth—on the contrary, this right was expressly recognized by those who addressed the matter—, but they argued that the right to the truth would not be impaired by maintaining the amnesty.[47]

A few months later, the IACourtHR delivered its merits decision in the Araguaia Guerrilla case, ruling that, contrary to what the Brazilian Supreme Court had decided, the Amnesty Law contradicts the right to the truth, among other rights protected by the ACHR. With this decision, the IACourtHR invigorated the debate in Brazil, where the Amnesty Law would continue to be contested. It was challenged before the Supreme Court, by an appeal against the 2010 decision, and through a new action filed by PSOL, a left-wing political party. Before the federal courts, amnesty has been contested by criminal actions filed by the Brazilian Federal Office of the Public Prosecutor (see Osmo 2016: 42–46). A survey carried out in 2018 identified around

---

[46] Brazilian Bar Association. Arguição de Descumprimento de Preceito Fundamental (ADPF) n. 153. Initial Petition, 2008: 22.

[47] In this regard, Judge Celso de Mello's opinion was explicit when he stated that the right to the truth "[…] in order to be fully exercised, does not depend on the criminal accountability of the perpetrators of such facts, which means, thus, that Law n. 6683/70 does not qualify as a legal obstacle to the recuperation of the historical memory and to the knowledge of the truth" (Brazil. Federal Supreme Court. Arguição de Descumprimento de Preceito Fundamental (ADPF) n. 153/DF. Plaintiff: Brazilian Bar Association. Judge-Rapporteur: Eros Grau, Brasília, Federal District, April 2010, my translation).

forty of those criminal actions, the majority of which were rejected or suspended by the Judiciary, claiming that they had to follow the Supreme Court decision.[48]

The IACourtHR also determined in the Araguaia Guerrilla case that Brazilian State should adopt the necessary measures to determine the location where the victims were buried, and to return the bodies to the families. However, the policies carried out since then have been unsuccessful. Part of the official documents regarding the operations against the Guerrilla have never been found, and the Armed Forces—which were responsible for the extermination of the Guerrilla and have not yet recognized the human rights violations during the dictatorship—took part in the searches. In 2019, President Jair Bolsonaro's government extinguished the Araguaia Working Group, which was responsible for the searches. Before becoming president, when he was a Congressman, Bolsonaro had a poster on his office door that said, relating to the Araguaia disappearances, that only dogs look for bones.[49]

Another State supported initiative, directed to identifying the remains of victims found in the clandestine grave in the cemetery of Perus, city of São Paulo, was not discontinued by the same act of President Jair Bolsonaro's government because of a public civil action grounded on the right to the truth. The civil action on the Perus clandestine grave was initiated in 2009 by the Brazilian Federal Office of the Public Prosecutor in support of the families' demands, in order to determine the responsibilities for the problems previously verified in the identification work, and to determine to the Federal government the maintenance of a structure and funding necessary for the continuation of this work.[50] The parties reached an agreement in which the Brazilian government took on the obligation to support the forensic work to identify those who had disappeared, and to periodically report before the court on the actions taken in this respect.[51]

In the year following the IACourtHR decision on Araguaia Guerrilla case, a law was adopted that provided for the creation of the National Truth Commission (NTC), mentioning the implementation of the "right to memory and to historical truth" as one of Commission's objectives (Law 12.528/2011, Article 1). The fact that a law expressly mentioned this right helped to expand the types of requests judicially accepted. One example is the request for the rectification of death certificates containing false information on the victims' deaths. An innovative decision regarding

---

[48] Transitional Justice Studies Center (CJT /UFMG) 2018. Report of the CJT /UFMG of the monitoring of the criminal actions of individual accountability for human rights violations perpetrated in the Brazilian dictatorship. Belo Horizonte.

[49] Commission of Families of the Political Dead and Disappeared (CFMDP) 2018. Information to the Inter-American Commission on Human Rights (IACHR) on the human rights situation in Brazil, focusing on the theme of Memory, Truth and Justice related to human rights violations in the dictatorship and its legacies. São Paulo.

[50] Brazil. Federal Office of the Public Prosecutor. Public Civil Action n. 00251698520094036100. Initial petition, 2009.

[51] Centro pela Justiça e o Direito Internacional (CEJIL) et al. 2020. Information in advance of the adoption of the list of issues on Brazil. Alternative report submitted to the UN Committee on Enforced Disappearances (CED) in the context of the review of Brazil report. Rio de Janeiro; São Paulo.

this type of claim was delivered in the case initiated by Maria Ester Cristelli Drumond to request the rectification of the death certificate of her husband, João Batista Franco Drumond. This decision determined that the cause of the death originally presented in the death certificate as "Traumatic brain injury" had to be altered to "due to physical torture". Against this amendment, the Public Prosecutor's Office had argued that necropsy reports should not address which crime caused death. However, the judge decided that this was a particular case: "This case is related to the so-called Right to Memory and to the Truth, and above all, it is related to the connection of the domestic legal system to the International Protection of Human Rights".[52]

The NTC has also filed requests for the rectification of the death certificates of Vladimir Herzog (2012) and Alexandre Vannucchi Leme (2013), and achieved favorable decisions. Later, the NTC final report presented the recommendation that the competent authorities, in fulfillment of the right to the truth, swiftly proceeded towards the rectification of death certificates requested by the interested parties, in accordance with the aforementioned precedents, in which the Commission itself was the plaintiff (Recommendation n. 7). Complying with this recommendation, the Commission on Political Deaths and Disappearances of Persons created in 2017 a procedure to rectify death certificates, which was revoked in 2019 by President Jair Bolsonaro's government. After this, the Public Prosecutor's Office of the State of São Paulo, the State Public Defender's Office, and the Brazilian Bar Association made progress with initiatives aiming to meet this demand of the families.[53]

The right to the truth was also the basis for a series of judicial decisions against the conservative demands that challenged the NTC's mandate and activities. Unlike the aforementioned cases, in which the legal actions were filed with the aim of achieving progress in transitional justice policies in Brazil, these aimed at limiting the operation of one of the fronts of such policies. In any case, it is interesting to note that Brazilian courts have refused all the claims against the NTC, thus providing support for the Commission's activities, and have done so by affirming the existence of a right to the truth that it was in charge of implementing. These judicial decisions ruled that, in order to implement the right to the truth, the NTC had the power to summon those accused of crimes to testify, as well as the power to access documents containing the military officers' working records of the period under investigation (Osmo 2016: 94–99). There were also judicial decisions approving the NTC's decision to include in its final report the names of the agents identified as responsible for the violations. One of them highlighted that "[…] the historical facts that took place during the military regime, previously confidential, must be disclosed to those who lived through that period of our history and to the new generations, whether those involved agree or

---

[52] São Paulo. 2nd Public Registry Court of the Central Forum of São Paulo. Process n. 0059583-24.2011.8.26.0100. Plaintiff: Maria Ester Cristelli Drumond. Judge: Guilherme Madeira Dezem. São Paulo, April 2012.

[53] Centro pela Justiça e o Direito Internacional (CEJIL) et al. 2020. Information in advance of the adoption of the list of issues on Brazil. Alternative report submitted to the UN Committee on Enforced Disappearances (CED) in the context of the review of Brazil report. Rio de Janeiro; São Paulo.

not".[54] Therefore, Brazilian courts have expressed the understanding that the right to the truth includes the right to see revealed and publicized in an official State document the identity of the perpetrators of the violations. However, in Brazil, the IACourtHR interpretation that this must be done through criminal proceedings has not yet been accepted.

More recently, in 2018, the IACourtHR issued another decision against the Brazilian State regarding the dictatorship's human rights violations, in the Vladimir Herzog case. In this case, taken to the Inter-American System in 2009 by CEJIL, the Inter-American Foundation for the Defense of Human Rights, the Santos Dias Center of the São Paulo Archdiocese and the São Paulo Torture Never More Group, the IACourtHR once more concluded that Brazilian State has violated the right to the truth, among other human rights. According to the IACourtHR, the right to the truth has been violated because of the delay of the State to officially accept the falsehood that Herzog had committed suicide, and also because of the absence of criminal accountability and of the refusal to provide access to the pertinent archives.[55]

8.4   Final Remarks

The IASHR, called to act within a context in which the domestic judiciary in Latin American countries were closed to complaints of human rights violations, accepted the right to the truth as an international human right, through a "dynamic" or "evolutionary" interpretation of the ACHR. The framework of this right, which was initially a response to the mobilization of the families of disappeared persons, changed in order to incorporate claims of different natures, especially those related to "the fight against impunity". In the end, the IASHR established a concept of the right to the truth in which specific instruments like the truth commissions are considered auxiliary, and criminal proceedings are considered essential for its implementation.

Similarly, the Brazilian legal system did not have an explicit provision for the right to the truth when it was first mobilized in legal actions, initiated to resist human right violations or to demand advances in the transitional justice process. During a period when the Brazilian State denied that the violations took place or refused to take responsibility for them, the pioneer demands sought for an official acknowledgment that these violations actually took place, and that the Brazilian Government was responsible for them. In the case of the Araguaia Guerrilla case, the subjective right to the truth gave legal grounds for the determination that information be supplied regarding the disappearances and that the remains of the missing persons be located. Here the Brazilian judicial decision was convergent with the IASHR understanding:

---

[54] Brazil. Federal Court of the Judiciary Section of Rio Grande do Sul. Process n. 5004038-36.2015.4.04.7100/RS. Plaintiff: Paulo Chagas and others. Defendant: Federal Union. Porto Alegre, December 2016, my translation.

[55] Organization of American States. Inter-American Court of Human Rights. Case of Herzog and others v. Brazil. Preliminary Objections, Merits, Reparations, and Costs. Judgment of March 15, 2018. Serie C No. 353, § 328–338.

it accepted the idea that the right to the truth is a right of the families of disappeared persons, related to their right to mourn, but also a right of society as a whole to know the facts in order to prevent them from happening again. Later, the fact that this right was mentioned by the law that established the NTC contributed to the renovation of the type of legal mobilization accepted by Brazilian courts, such as the correction of death certificates, and also contributed to the usage of this right as the grounds for the judicial approval of the NTC powers.

Nevertheless, in Brazil there has been a greater resistance to include in the scope of the right to the truth the judicial investigation of authorship of the violations. The NTC report indicated the names of persons identified as responsible for human rights violations during the dictatorship. In the Teles family case, a judicial decision created a precedent ruling that those interested can make use of civil legal actions to obtain the judicial recognition of personal responsibilities. Yet, differently from the right to the truth established by Inter-American case law, that accepted in the Brazilian cases has not included, up to this moment, the determination of responsibilities through criminal proceedings. This issue continues to be disputed. At the same time, the struggle for justice and truth in Brazil also started to face new challenges after the 2018 election of President Jair Bolsonaro, who explicitly praises the practices of the dictatorship. Thus, it became necessary for victims, families and human rights entities, in addition to making further progress, to try to avoid setbacks, and react to the dismantling of the transitional justice policies.

References

Abregu, M. 1996. La Tutela Judicial del Derecho a la Verdad en la Argentina. *Revista IIDH*, Instituto Interamericano de Derechos Humanos 24, jul./dez.

Abregu, M. Derecho a la Verdad vs. Impunidad. 1998. *Revista IIDH*, Instituto Interamericano de Derechos Humanos 27, jan./jun.

Araújo, M.A.A. et al. 1995. Mortos e desaparecidos políticos: Resgatando a memória brasileira. Comissão de Familiares de Mortos e Desaparecidos Políticos; Instituto de Estudo de Violência do Estado—IEVE; Grupo Tortura Nunca Mais—RJ e PE. *Dossiê dos mortos e desaparecidos políticos a partir de 1964.* Recife: Companhia Editora de Pernambuco, Governo do Estado de Pernambuco.

Bevernage, B., and K. Aerts. 2009. Haunting Pasts: Time and Historicity as Constructed by the Argentine Madres de Plaza de Mayo and Radical Flemish Nationalists. *Social History* 34: 4.

Burgorgue-Larsen, L., and A.U. de. Torres. 2008. *Les Grandes Décisions de la Cour Interaméricaine des Droits de l'Homme.* Bruxelles: Bruylant.

Cardoso, E.L.C. 2012. *Litígio Estratégico e Sistema Interamericano de Direitos Humanos.* Belo Horizonte: Fórum.

Cateb, C. et al. 2020. A Comissão Especial sobre Mortos e Desaparecidos Políticos e a Comissão de Anistia no primeiro ano do governo Bolsonaro. In *Espectros da Ditadura. Da Comissão da Verdade ao bolsonarismo*, eds. Edson Teles and Renan Quinalha. São Paulo: Autonomia Literária.

Faoro, R. 1978. Prefácio. In *Caso Herzog: a sentença, íntegra do processo movido por Clarice, Ivo e André Herzog contra a União*, ed. Clarice Herzog. Rio de Janeiro: Salamandra.

Joinet, L. 2014. Os especialistas franceses na ONU e os regimes autoritários latino-americanos: Debate com Louis Joinet e Emmanuel Decaux, sob a coordenação de Mireille Delmas-Marty— Collège de France, Paris, 24 de novembro de 2011. *Revista Anistia Política e Justiça de Transição* 9 (jan./jun. 2013). Brasília: Ministério da Justiça.

Keck, M., and K. Sikkink. 1999. Transnational Advocacy Networks in International and Regional Politics. *International Social Science Journal* 51: 89–101.

Martin-Chenut, K. 2007. Amnistie, Prescription, Grâce: la Jurisprudence Interaméricaine des Droits de l'Homme en Matière de Lutte contre l'Impunité. *RSC, Chronique internationale, Droits de l'homme* 3.

Martin-Chenut, K. 2014. Direito à Verdade e Justiça de Transição: A Contribuição do Sistema Interamericano de Proteção dos Direitos Humanos. *Revista Anistia Política e Justiça de Transição / Ministério da Justiça* 9 (jan. / jun. 2013). Brasília: Ministério da Justiça.

Müller, A.M. 2016. Entrevista. In *Justiça e arquivos no Brasil: perspectivas de atores da justiça de transição*, eds. Carla Osmo and Shana Marques Prado dos Santos. Florianópolis: Tribo da Ilha; Belo Horizonte: Rede Latino-Americana de Justiça de Transição (RLAJT); Centro de Estudos sobre Justiça de Transição, Universidade Federal de Minas Gerais (CJT/UFMG).

Greco, H.A.C. 2003. *Dimensões fundacionais da luta pela anistia*. Tese de Doutorado. Departamento de História da FAFICH/ UFMG, Belo Horizonte.

Naftali, P. 2014. "Toute la vérité, rien que la vérité"? Les mobilisations du "droit à la vérité" dans les affaires *Mignone* et *Lapacó* en Argentine. *Recherches et travaux du REDS à la Fondation Maison des Sciences de l'Homme* 30.

Naftali, P. 2016. Crafting a "Right to Truth" in International Law: Converging Mobilizations, Diverging Agendas? *Champ pénal/Penal field [En ligne]* XIII. http://champpenal.revues.org/9245.

Naftali, P. 2017. *La construction du "droit à la vérité" en droit international*. Bruxelles: Éditions Bruylant.

National Truth Commission. 2014. *Relatório / Comissão Nacional da Verdade*, v. 1. Brasília.

Osmo, C. 2014. *Direito à Verdade: Origens da Conceituação e suas Condições Teóricas de Possibilidade com Base em Reflexões de Hannah Arendt*. Tese de Doutorado. Faculdade de Direito da Universidade de São Paulo, São Paulo.

Osmo, C. 2016. *Judicialização da Justiça de Transição na América Latina = Judicialización de la Justicia de Transición en América Latina* [tradução para o espanhol: Nathaly Mancilla Órdenes]. Brasília: Ministério da Justiça, Comissão de Anistia, Rede Latino-Americana de Justiça de Transição (RLAJT).

Osmo, C. 2019. Direito à verdade: parâmetros internacionais e realização no Brasil. In *Violência de Estado na América Latina*, ed. Javier Amadeo. São Paulo: Editora Unifesp.

Osmo, C. 2020. Review: La construction du "droit à la vérité" en droit international By Patricia Naftali. *Revista Direito e Práxis* 11, 1.

Osmo, C., and K. Martin-Chenut. 2017. A participação das vítimas no sistema interamericano: fundamento e significado do direito de participar. *Revista Direito e Práxis* 8: 2.

Osmo, C., and J. Vitar. 2015. A judicialização do direito à verdade sobre graves violações a direitos humanos no Brasil e na Argentina. In *Ditadura, modernização conservadora e universidade: debates sobre um projeto de país*, ed. Marcelo Mari and Priscila Rossinetti Rufioni. Editora UFG: Goiânia.

Philippe Marino, C. 2008. *Les Disparitions Forcées dans la Jurisprudence des Cours Régionales des Droits de l'Homme*. Thèse de Doctorat. Université de Rouen. Rouen.

Pilloud, C., et al. 1986. *Commentaire des Protocoles additionnels du 8 juin 1977 aux Conventions de Genève du 12 août 1949*. Genève: Comité international de la Croix-Rouge, Martinus Nijhoff Publishers.

Pinto, M. 2007. *L'Amérique Latine et le Traitement des Violations Massives des Droits de l'Homme*. Paris: Editions A. Pedone.

Santos, C.M. 2010. Memória na Justiça: A Mobilização dos Direitos Humanos e a Construção da Memória da Ditadura no Brasil. *Revista Crítica de Ciências Sociais* 88. http://rccs.revues.org/1719.

Santos, C.M. 2015a. Transitional Justice from the Margins: Legal Mobilization and Memory Politics in Brazil. In *Legacies of the State Violence and Transitional Justice in Latin America: A Janus-Faced Paradigm?* eds. Nina Schneider and Marcia Esparza. Lanham, ML: Lexington Books.

Santos, C.M. 2015b. Justiça de transição a partir das lutas sociais: o papel da mobilização do Direito. In *O direito achado na rua: Introdução crítica à justiça de transição na América Latina*, eds. José Geraldo Sousa Junior, José Geraldo et al. Brasília: UnB.

Sikkink, K. 2011. *The Justice Cascade: How Human Rights Prosecutions Are Changing World Politics*. New York: Norton & Company.

Teles, J. 2005. *Os herdeiros da memória. A luta dos familiares de mortos e desaparecidos políticos por verdade e justiça no Brasil*. Dissertação de mestrado. Faculdade de Filosofia, Letras e Ciências Humanas da USP. São Paulo.

Teles, M.A. 2019. Familiares de desaparecidos políticos em busca de justiça: uma luta sem tréguas! In *Violência de Estado na América Latina*, ed. Javier Amadeo. São Paulo: Editora Unifesp.

Torelly, M. 2018. Assessing a Late Truth Commission: Challenges and Achievements of the Brazilian National Truth Commission. *International Journal of Transitional Justice* 2018.

Carla Osmo is Professor of Law at the Federal University of São Paulo, Brazil. She received her LLM from Pontifical Catholic University of São Paulo and JSD from University of São Paulo. She has been a former researcher for the Latin American Transitional Justice Network and for the National Truth Commission. Her research interests include human rights and transitional justice

Part III
Comparative Case Studies

Chapter 9
Legitimation Narratives, Resistance, and Legal Cultures in Authoritarian and Post-authoritarian Chile: Lawyers and Judges in the (Post)-Transition

Cath Collins

Abstract This chapter draws on literature about courts, constitutionalism, and legal mobilisation in and around authoritarian regimes. It adopts both the notion of the continuing importance of constitutional 'moments', and the concept of legal mobilisation as one form of contestation and resistance, to explain and explore some of the particular meanings that law, lawyers, and legal activism acquired before, during and beyond the Chilean transition of 1990. Interpreting legal mobilisation against the backdrop of prevailing legal-cultural traditions, the chapter contends both that the authoritarian regime's constitution-making moment of 1980 should be viewed as—to date—the foundational critical juncture of Chile's past four decades; and that subsequent 'rights talk' in Chile was hamstrung for many years by its obeisance to conceptions of legality that hark back to this phase of the dictatorship. The constitution-making process triggered by a late 2020 plebiscite however offered at least the promise of transformation of these self-limiting habits, won as it was in the street rather than the courtroom or even the legislature.

This chapter draws heavily on the working paper 'Lawyers and Transition in Chile', prepared by the author for the 'Lawyers, Conflict and Transition' project carried out at Queens' University, Belfast, and electronically published in 2015; and on the hitherto unpublished conference paper 'Judicial Actors as Agents or Facilitators of Repression in Pinochet's Chile', presented by the author in Madrid in June 2015 at the conference 'The Organization of Security and Justice System Institutions in Autocracies'. The author thanks the respective organisers and convenors for permission to draw on those previous works, and conference participants and other colleagues for helpful comments and feedback. All views expressed, and any remaining errors, of course remain the responsibility of the author

C. Collins (✉)
Ulster University, Belfast, Northern Ireland
e-mail: cath.collins@mail.udp.cl

© Springer Nature Switzerland AG 2021
C. Paixão and M. Meccarelli (eds.), *Comparing Transitions to Democracy. Law and Justice in South America and Europe*, Studies in the History of Law and Justice 18, https://doi.org/10.1007/978-3-030-67502-8_9

9.1 Introduction

Recent literature on authoritarian regimes has shed considerable light on the various ways in which authoritarian powerholders attempt to resolve the twin dilemmas of social control and intra-elite coordination/ power sharing (see, inter alia, Svolik 2012). Some authors attend principally to the role in this task of parties, legislatures, periodic elections, and other political practices often superficially associated with democracies (Gandhi 2008; Levitsky and Way 2002, etc.). A strong focus on courts and the operation of law is however also visible in this literature, a useful reminder that judicialization of politics is by no means unique to liberal democracy (see for example Ginsburg and Moustafa 2008). Logically enough, these two strands of interest converge where authoritarian regimes indulge or have indulged in constitution-making, particularly where constitutional courts are part of the mix (Ginsburg and Simpser 2014; Barros 2002; Moustafa 2007).[1] In this respect, a previous conventional wisdom holding that authoritarian constitutions can be dismissed as mere window dressing, seems to be giving way to an equally conventional wisdom that they cannot (See for example Ginsburg and Simpser 2014: 5–9). While this concern is largely focused on the power of such constitutions to constrain the regime itself, the question of 'overhang' of authoritarian constitutions into post-transitional practice is perhaps prefigured, given what de Sousa Santos aptly describes as the "imprint" of old laws.[2]

Moustafa (2007) moreover argues convincingly that courts at all levels—including constitutional ones—can under certain circumstances become a "unique field of contention" within authoritarian states (2007: 20). As well as their obvious significance as a venue for the playing out of elite visions (and sometimes disputes), they may also be open to, or prised opened by, actors who clearly do not fit the intra-elite characterisation. With respect to the first of these functions, Moustafa reminds us that political economy concerns often underpin drives to establish limited legal autonomy—or, at least, predictability—even in otherwise highly personalist authoritarian regimes.[3] With regard to the second function, he describes how courts and legal mobilisation may emerge as an arena of resistance to authoritarian regimes. Political activists and others may be forced by the closing of oppositional space to seek alliance with legal activists; even when such actors themselves enjoy only precarious standing or toleration (Moustafa 2007).

These discussions—of authoritarian self-configuration, and of legal activism as an attempt to contend with authoritarianism—may speak especially to anyone with a particular interest in Chile, a case discussed by all of the aforementioned authors. In

---

[1] Although Aguilar and Rios Figueroa (2014) rightly point out that while the relationships between authoritarianism and institutions, and between authoritarianism and judicial politics, have been studied, these studies too rarely dialogue with one another.

[2] "[L]egal revocation is not social revocation" (De Sousa Santos 1987: 282). In cases such as the one that concerns us, Chile, transition moreover did not trigger either type of revocation.

[3] See, in general, ´new institutionalist´ approaches and the 'law and development' movement as characterised, and critiqued, in Moustafa op. cit. 21–25 and Chapter 7.

regard to the first issue, late C20 Chile is perhaps a prime example of authoritarian constitution-making as an exercise in political legitimation and intra-elite bargaining, responding to a particular vision of political economy. As is well known, the 1973–90 Chilean dictatorship introduced, in 1980, an authoritarian constitution enshrining a neoliberal economic model. Both enjoyed considerable subsequent longevity until, in 2020, explosive social protest triggered at least the promise of overhaul. As regards legally-framed contention and contestation, the Chilean dictatorship´s open use of extreme repression, particularly in its early years, gave rise to resistance in the form of a vocal and active human rights movement. Indeed, as Dezalay and Garth (2002) rightly remark, "human rights [concerns] and neoliberal economics" were perhaps the two principal features propelling Chile to international attention, whether approbatory or otherwise, during this period.[4] Human rights activism was moreover notably legally framed, despite the relatively unyielding attitude of a judicial branch, and indeed a legal profession, which were largely supportive of the regime (see Collins 2010b, 2013b: 67–70).

This chapter adopts both the notion of the continuing importance of constitutional 'moments', and the insight about legal mobilisation as one form of contestation and resistance, to explain and explore some of the particular meanings that law, lawyers, and legal activism acquired before, during and beyond the Chilean transition of 1990. Interpreting legal mobilisation against the backdrop of prevailing legal-cultural traditions, the chapter contends both that the authoritarian regime´s constitution-making moment of 1980 should be viewed as the foundational critical juncture of Chile's past three decades; and that subsequent 'rights talk' in Chile has been hamstrung by its obeisance to conceptions of legality that hark back to this phase of the dictatorship era. Truly critical legal traditions such as might have given birth to a more established and ideologically transversal modern rights movement, and/or to a constitutional court and political class better able to initiate, accompany or encourage effective post-transitional constitutional replacement from above, struggled to establish themselves. This is due in part to a transversally conservative discourse among social, economic and political elites that came to accept as natural not only the economic and social precepts of the 1973–1990 period (more properly, the period from 1980–1990),[5] but also the underlying depiction of 1970–1973 as an exceptional, and dangerous, departure from hallowed traditions.[6]

---

[4] Dezalay and Garth (2002: 141) and see more generally the entire chapter, pp. 141–160. See also, for the treatment of Chile's human rights emergency by international organisations and exile networks, Ensalaco 2010 or Angell 2013.

[5] Dezalay and Garth (op.cit.), like Angell (2006), Huneeus (2007) and many others, have pointed out that while Chile is often cited as the classic or a particularly extreme example of the twinning of authoritarian politics and neoliberal conversion, neoliberal precepts were fully installed only towards the end of the 1970s, as the regime cast around for an economic policy direction and more traditional contenders lost the dispute for influence. A banking collapse and generalised economic crisis in 1983–1985 was moreover dealt with in ways that departed substantially from neoliberal precepts.

[6] Thus the dictatorship—in many ways the instigator of the most profound and radical cultural transformation of Chile's republican history—claimed legitimation, and calmed fears, by conjuring

The chapter is chronologically organised. It first briefly characterises the traditions of legalism, legal practice, and statecraft for which the 1970 elected socialist government of Salvador Allende and the violent military coup of 1973 both represented, in their different ways, a rude awakening. Second, it shows how the dictatorial regime's approaches to institutionalisation and self-legitimation in general, and specifically to its deployment of coercive violence, challenged and reshaped the legal profession and the relationship of a newly-emerging class of human rights lawyers to the judiciary. Third, the chapter discusses the pros and cons of Chile's model of controlled transition, in which although openly repressive behaviour was discontinued, there was relatively little formal or substantive institutional or constitutional change. Finally, the chapter addresses the place of law and legal activism in present-day human rights and constitutional debates, including although not limited to remaining transitional justice challenges in the context of 2020's long-awaited constitutional plebiscite.[7]

9.2 The Legal Profession in Pre-dictatorship Chile: The Historical Roots of Chilean Legalism

A full history of law and legal practice in Chile, as indeed of its judicial practice, undoubtedly exceeds the scope of this chapter. Nonetheless some preliminary remarks may help to situate later developments. At the risk of oversimplification, it is reasonable to take as a starting premise that the commonplace characterisation of Chile as legalistic has some basis in fact. Thus Chile's national self-image, cultivated since formal 1810 independence from Spain, includes the belief that republican and constitutionalist traditions set it apart from many of its neighbours, and encompasses a strong commitment to the notion of law. This helps explain why lawyers and legal framings were symbolically and practically important during and after 1973–1990 authoritarian rule, as they had been before it; and also why, as Huneeus (2007) points out, the Pinochet regime, though highly personalised, was not arbitrary, preferring to reshape or rewrite the rule book rather than to openly disregard the concept of rule-boundedness.

Chile is, then, often and rightly characterised as a legalistic society which values the principles of law, or at least of predictable order. While the malleability of legal outcomes is recognised, law itself tends not to be universally regarded as an endlessly fickle, inevitably corrupted, or essentially fictitious restraint on behaviour, even on the

---

associations with stability rather than rupture. Pinochet, for example, missed no opportunity to evoke associations with figures from Chile's pantheon of national 'heroes', mostly military strongmen associated with independence or with C19 statebuilding: see Joignant (2007, 2013). However see also Loveman and Lira (1999, 2000), for strands of genuine continuity in authoritarian repression and legal toleration of it.

[7] For the purposes of what follows, 'transitional justice' challenges are defined as those arising from direct or indirect connection with the truth, justice, reparations, and guarantees of non-repetition legacies of dictatorship-era human rights violations. For Chile's 2020 constitutional moment as a 'transitional justice moment', see Collins et al. (2020) and Accatino (2020).

behaviour of the powerful. Serious elite questioning of the intrinsic legitimacy of the legal paradigm has therefore been reasonably scarce in the post-transitional period, and such belief in law is often accompanied by an equally unwavering commitment to a strong unitary state.[8] A highly centralising, law-bound state emerged soon after independence, largely constructed by Diego Portales, an influential early C19 statesman. There was little or nothing of a liberal cast in this legality: the Portalean state, decidedly republican and more than somewhat repressive, has been described as 'legal dictatorship' or 'presidential authoritarianism', prefiguring the Pinochet regime.[9]

Lawyers and the legal profession historically had the central role in national life that one might expect given such a characterisation, until relatively recent modernising trends began to reshape or even challenge law's perception of itself as the country's pre-eminent 'public profession'. Iñigo de la Maza (n.d., 2001) describes lawyers as Chile's 'statesmen par excellence' from the mid-C19. Between 1843 and 1950, 18 of 20 national presidents, most ministers, and most Senators were lawyers (de la Maza n.d.: 10). A Bar Association was formed in 1925, and affiliation to it and its code of ethics were made compulsory in 1941. Law, seen as a respectable and at the same time a forward-looking profession, was held in high regard among students from middle-class families with aspirations, considered a sure route to a future in high-level public service.

However, industrialisation and the professionalisation of statecraft began to displace lawyers from the high offices of government, sending the profession into relative decline: from statesmen, in the mid C19, to hired hands, by the mid C20. Law ceased to be a civic vocation, becoming 'a business like any other', according to de la Maza (n.d.: 15). Lawyers set up private firms or chambers, reinventing themselves as a professional service sector for emerging commercial interests (de la Maza 2001). Modernisation theory and accompanying notions about the necessary economic and social preconditions for development also played a part. By the 1960s positivistic approaches from the new social sciences—sociology, and to some extent economics—were in the ascendant as arbiters of national life, heralding a love affair with technocracy that would reach its apogee during the dictatorship. Law was 'out' and sociology was 'in'. Over the course of the same decade, legal education reforms aimed at reversing the increasing marginalisation of the profession by broadening legal training were abandoned. Would-be donors and advisors from the US gave up on their efforts to carve out a middle course between radicalisms by cajoling Chilean

---

[8] Post-transitional regionalising reforms seeking greater devolution or autonomy have gained little purchase, and there seems to be little appetite for legal pluralism. Chile is for example one of few remaining countries in the region not to enshrine any form of indigenous identity rights or self-determination rights, having made substantive and unilateral reservations to ILO 169 provisions that have elsewhere underwritten such developments. It remains to be seen whether constitution making in 2021 and 2022 will redress or reverse this neglect, although this would require a significant step change away from the militarized, confrontational and repressive attitude to indigenous mobilization in the south of the country that has prevailed since 1990 under all shades of government.

[9] Portales was one of the historical figures for whom Pinochet repeatedly professed public and fervent admiration.

legal education, and thereby legal practice, away from its determinedly fusty habits (Dezalay and Garth 2002).

The 'socialist experiment' of Salvador Allende's Popular Unity government, from 1970, accentuated the dislodging of legal traditionalists, indeed traditionalists of all sorts, from the helm of state administration. Allende himself was a medic, itself a departure from the frequent circulation of lawyers into and out of the highest office of state. Modern and modernising sciences, this time of a more Marxist hue, became the administration's trusted guides on the electoral road to socialism. Dependency theory in economics, and its counterparts and derivatives in social, industrial and even cultural policy were espoused with enthusiasm. Allende clashed repeatedly with the Supreme Court, which having been reluctant to ratify his election, went on to oppose some of his more radical transformations, often by questioning their compatibility with the 1925 Constitution.[10] The anti-privilege, pro-poor thrust of the new government's rhetoric and actions was anathema to a substantial part of the existing establishment. The legal establishment, in particular, was threatened by various developments including a project to introduce alternative 'popular courts', among other policy proposals that would in effect have put an end to the Bar Association's previous monopoly on the provision of subsidised legal aid to poor communities (Gonzalez Le Saux 2014).

Centre-right currents among Chile's judicial and legal-professional classes may have shared Popular Unity's concern for the poor, but were increasingly alienated by its revolutionary identity and methods. When Chile's traditional 'three thirds' left-centre-right political pattern finally fractured under the strain, the Christian Democrats who Allende had displaced by a narrow margin in the 1970 election sided with the right and the military. Judges, senior lawyers, businesspeople, and pillars of the (previous) established order of all kinds, supported and indeed in many cases actively promoted the coup. Their misplaced belief was that it would usher in a return to business as usual, i.e. a restoration of their former influence, and a reassertion of the rules of the game that stretched back to the 1925 Constitution and beyond.

Although the 1973 coup initially pleased many judges and other legal professionals, in the end it did nothing to reverse their generalised professional or public decline. Economists, rather than lawyers, became the new policy mandarins, particularly once the Chicago Boys school of monetarist economic thinkers came into the ascendant after 1975. Party politics, even right wing party politics, was dispensed with. While some legal expertise was needed in the exalted inner circle, not least to craft the regime's epoch-changing 1980 Constitution, a relatively small group of ultra-loyal Catholic University-affiliated *gremialistas*, headed by principal regime ideologue Jaime Guzmán, fulfilled this function. The broader legal profession continued to be relegated to a relatively narrow understanding of its role, as one more service corps within a shrinking state and an expanding market. Legal education was de-monopolised, with a raft of new private universities allowed to offer law training.

---

[10] Including the emblematic nationalisation of the copper industry, plus various types and tranches of land and other asset expropriation.

Although this increased the profession's sheer weight of numbers, it also entailed a certain de-mystification and (to some) a concomitant reduction in the profession's social prestige, rooted as it had been in class stratification and high entry barriers.[11] Law schools, like other university faculties, were subjected to censorship and direct control by the military regime, but law schools per se had never been, and did not subsequently become, hotbeds of radicalism or radical opposition. This was a role more often inhabited by the social sciences, some of which were as a result simply abolished for the duration of the dictatorship.

Lawyers' collective loyalty or at least relative meekness was hardly rewarded, however. Compulsory Bar Association affiliation was abolished, removing at a stroke the profession's central visible platform from which to take a stand on national affairs. This action was quite in keeping with the regime's strong strategic and ideological distrust of associations of all kinds, but was not at all what Association stalwarts had envisaged when imagining restoration of their former glory and privileges after the Allende period. In short, while legalism remained a force to be reckoned with, the gentleman-lawyers of yesteryear were not returned to what some at least still conceived of as their rightful place at the heart of public institutional life. Legal professionals, like other professionals, were to be employed at the pleasure of the market, rather than enjoying sinecures in high-level public administration. The content of constitutional law, and the institutional scaffolding of law's interpretation and application, was meanwhile appropriated to become the direct concern of the regime in at least two senses: firstly, as a source of intra-elite control, legitimation, and coveted legal capital, and secondly, as a stage for the playing out of 'moral opposition' framed in the language of universal rights.

9.3 Courts, Coercion and Human Rights Lawyering During the Pinochet Regime: 1973–1990

The substantial deference of the Chilean courts to the Pinochet dictatorship, which included seemingly wilful blindness to its wholesale criminality, is generally recognised. Some hold that a traditionally positivistic or formalistic approach to law on the part of Chilean judges was to blame. Hilbink (2007) however suggests that a quite particular judicial understanding of apoliticism was also in play, one which saw matters of public or constitutional law as properly for others to resolve. The possibility that many judges, like a good proportion of the population, were simply favourably disposed to, and in agreement with, military intervention is perhaps too often overlooked. Nonetheless, Barros (2002) and Huneeus (2007) inter alia have shown that over the course of the 17-year period Chile's courts were not a mere fiction or flag of convenience, given the regime's preference for ruling through, rather

---

[11] Previously only a small number of highly traditional law faculties produced the lion's share of the country's elite lawyers, a pattern which to some extent still persists.

than in spite of, law. This penchant for seeking legal as well as economic and historical legitimacy was expressed in 1980 in a new authoritarian constitution, combined with the granting of exceptionally broad powers to the constitutional tribunal (first introduced in 1970, under the Allende government).

In this way, although the content of law was from then on shaped to the regime's satisfaction at the highest level, the corresponding weight of judicial pronouncements regarding it was also potentially greater. Indeed, it was this same custommade constitutional framework that was eventually enforced to oblige Pinochet to respect the results of his own plebiscite and hand over power in 1990. In specific regard to regime-sponsored repression, the operation of the courts placed judges potentially in everyday proximity to the agencies and victims of repression.[12] Over time the courts moreover increasingly became, despite themselves, a target venue for lawyers and civil society groups seeking to construct 'rightful resistance' (O'Brien 1996). These efforts, largely fruitless in strictly formal terms, nonetheless further encouraged the regime to use 'containment techniques', including control of judicial appointments and expansion of military court jurisdiction, in an attempt to pre-empt possibly unwelcome judicial activism.[13]

This section examines the currents that shaped these dynamics as the regime evolved. It argues that during the regime's most overtly repressive period, from 1973–1978,[14] judicial acquiescence was cultivated by a deft mix of appeals to the exigencies of immediate circumstances and to tradition, combined with the siloing of the most violent manifestations of state terror into a self-regulating containment and facilitation system. That system was composed of specially-created, irregular (therefore deniable) security services, overseen, if at all, by pliable military courts. In this way, what Carlos Huneeus (2007) aptly calls "voluntary synchronisation" of the ordinary court system to the regime was encouraged and further facilitated, by relegating the least palatable manifestations of repressive violence to a 'twin track'. The creation of this parallel system within and between the justice and security sectors allowed the regime to render mass violations less visible while still enjoying the coordination and legitimation benefits accruing from not openly suspending or closing down the judicial branch.[15] The possible opportunity costs arising from having to reckon with an unwieldy, geographically extensive, and semi-autonomous court apparatus theoretically able to expose or trammel repressive or other extra-legal

---

[12] The fact that the criminal justice system was a magistrate-driven inquisitorial system, with judges rather than prosecutors or police formally directing investigations from the start, accentuates this point.

[13] Policzer (2009) discusses in detail how the regime continually monitored and rebalanced its containment strategies, alternately targeting intra-regime actors, semi-autonomous entities such as the courts, and extra-regime actors including the Catholic Church and the press. The decision as to whether to control, coerce, or persuade into acquiescence could vary over time, inter alia according to the real and perceived costs of each alternative.

[14] This is the period into which over 90% of the 3,000-plus deaths and disappearances caused by the regime were concentrated. See Collins (2010).

[15] These benefits included the opportunity to use the appearance of liberal legality as a fig leaf on the international stage, given the prevailing Cold War context.

activity were contained through a mix of appeasement, coercion, and the dualistic architecture already mentioned.[16] The ordinary courts, at the highest level, proved not at all unwilling to connive with this strategy, voluntarily renouncing their supervisory responsibilities vis a vis military courts at the first opportunity and making no subsequent move to wrest even the most flagrant incident of regime violence against civilians away from military jurisdiction.[17] Thus, pace Shapiro (1981)—but see Shapiro 2008—social control—at least, violent social control—in Chile's early authoritarian period was exercised directly by security agencies as much as or more than through the courts, particularly the civilian courts. The preferential use of ad hoc repressive agencies, reporting directly to Pinochet, moreover served to minimise or eliminate internal dissent, sharpen personalised control, and ensure loyalty by neutralising squeamishness among officer ranks of the regular armed forces about the dirtier tactics of the dirty war (see Svolik 2012).[18]

Why go to the trouble of creating special channels and institutions to first dissemble, and then largely legalise, repressive violence and the about-face in economic and social policy that ensued? Continued rule by simple diktat, or open terror, might have seemed superficially easier to engineer for a regime with unquestioned control of firepower and no serious, certainly no armed, opposition to reckon with. However, Huneeus perceptively reminds us that "Chile's long and strong legal tradition…. was a required reference point for the new rulers, since the country's […] state of law and judicial order [was] the source of enormous [national] pride" (2007: 149). An evident break with this tradition would therefore have risked alienating the considerable popular support the military's actions had enjoyed up to that point. Rule of law language, combined with rule by law behaviour, offered the optimum strategy for the circumstances. It also allowed the regime to lay claim to historical legitimacy by portraying the recently truncated Allende presidency, rather than their own clearly unconstitutional seizure of power, as extra-legal, arbitrary, and lawless. Hilbink accordingly describes the period between the coup and the new 1980 Constitution as "the rule of law show" (2007: 106), highlighting the obvious discrepancies between the rule of law justifications offered for seizing power, and the actions subsequently taken. It is worth noting, however, that even when the regime was still an improvising military junta rather than the fully fledged authoritarian refoundational

---

[16] As regards coercion, there was an early purge of magistrate and judicial employees, whose magnitude is often underestimated or simply overlooked: see Gallardo Silva (2003).

[17] One additional hidden cost of thus allowing the civilian courts to feign genuine ignorance of the full implications of repression was adverted to early on, when the regime's (civilian) justice minister warned the military junta, in the early 1970s, that allowing the Supreme Court to formally abdicate its oversight over courts martial would lead to "blame falling solely on the armed forces". Letter to the junta, cited in Huneeus (2007: 55).

[18] Thus for example Oscar Bonilla, a general killed in a helicopter crash in the early period of the regime, is widely rumoured to have been assassinated due to his principled opposition to the murderous tactics of the DINA secret police. Constitutionalist Air Force General Alberto Bachelet, father of the outgoing Chilean president Michelle Bachelet (2006–2010 and 2014–2018), died in prison as a result of torture inflicted by his own former comrades in arms, as did numerous armed forces personnel who remained loyal to the deposed government, or simply questioned the deployment of repressive violence, after 1973.

project it became, existing law was appropriated, shaped and modified rather than solely flouted or dispensed with. The issue of immediate tools for ruling was cleverly resolved by an announced return to the 1925 Constitution, combined with exploitation of all its powers and states of exception to cobble together an effective 'legal dictatorship' which did not appear—because it was not—wholly invented.

The active approval of the Supreme Court clearly made this task easier, and its rhetorical claims more convincing, and some of this approval almost certainly proceeded from the fact that the bulk of the senior judiciary, like a good proportion of the population, genuinely supported what they understood the regime's project to be. That this project openly espoused authoritarianism, and clearly entailed at least some initial level of violence, would not necessarily place it beyond the pale nor indeed outwith the nation's previous lived experience. As Loveman and Lira (1999, 2000, 2002, 2013) have shown, depictions of the Pinochet dictatorship as an exceptional departure from a peaceable, constitution-respecting republican history amount to little more than revisionist myth-making. Authoritarian government, authoritarian traits within constitutional, elected governments, and repressive policing and security force practices were, they show, recurring features of C19 and C20 Chilean statecraft. The mere perpetration of a certain quota of politically deployed violence was not, in other words, necessarily sufficient in itself to undermine any pretension to legitimacy. Moreover, as we have seen, the regime had declared, early on, that the government it had deposed—and with which the Supreme Court had repeatedly and very publicly quarrelled—had "placed itself outside the law" and "fallen into flagrant illegitimacy".[19]

The regime's early discourse moreover promised not the radical ideological (neoliberal) project eventually espoused, but a high-minded, disinterested interregnum, seeking only to halt what it regarded as the decadence of recent years. Blame for this supposed decadence, polarisation, and chaos was moreover laid at the feet not only of international Marxism but of politics in general, and civilian politicians of all stripes, in particular.[20] Symbolic bolstering of the regime's own claim to power thereby came through an apolitical or antipolitical discourse, combined with an appeal to hallowed traditions, of which apparent obeisance to law and rational order was one. Having used defence of law as part-justification for the 1973 coup, law was a useful device with which to pretend or to believe that nothing essential had changed after the coup, except for the better. The regime managed to construct and promote the view that direct military rule represented the rescuing of Chile's honoured traditions. In this version, the 1970–1973 Popular Unity government, rather than the authoritarian one installed by force in 1973, represented exceptionalism, anarchy and lawlessness.

This discourse could not fail to chime with the judiciary, the only branch of state to avoid overt usurpation of its functions by the military Junta. Since the higher judiciary, essentially conservative, believed this conservatism to be genuinely and appropriately

---

[19] Bando (Edict) No. 5, issued by the military junta in September 1973.

[20] Thus even loyal supporters were not to be trusted, or allowed, to form actual political parties again until many years hence.

apolitical, an antipolitical discourse could not but chime with their own sense that politics was the enemy of transcendent public duty and, just possibly, the antithesis of law. This conservatism was not necessarily due to any innate right-wing sympathies: indeed, as Hilbink (2007) convincingly shows and González Le Saux (2014) also implies, apoliticism was an acquired characteristic socialised into a largely solidly sociologically middle-class group.[21] Self-preserving corporate hostility to the Allende era had played a recent part, leading the Supreme Court to temporarily set aside its own longstanding tradition of deference to the executive in weighty matters of public law. That tradition of deference now reasserted itself with a vengeance, neatly circumventing any need for the regime's early promise to respect judicial autonomy 'insofar as the current situation allows' to be put to any real test.

The courts did, of course, become drawn in gradually to certain of the authoritarian control and co-ordination problems, both internal and external, that began to emerge as the new de facto regime gradually became normalised and the courts continued to go about their everyday tasks. However, the arbitration of economic and other divergent interests amongst in-groups basically allied with the regime was not a particularly highly exposed or politicizing task.[22] Pinochet, rapidly emerging as the principal regime powerholder, moreover resorted to tactics and instances other than judges and the law to concentrate power in his own hand and enforce acquiescence. Emphasis on strict military discipline and constant rotation of civilian ministers enhanced his own power within government, while the distribution of largesse obtained from the return of expropriated assets and (later) through deregulation and privatisation kept wealthy business interests largely onside, or created new and more pliable economic elites. For control, and to some extent also for coordination, there was as we have seen, the selective deployment of exemplary coercive violence, first using spurious 'wartime' legality in the form of courts martial, then moving to extreme, deniable violence unleashed by semi-clandestine security services.

The fact that such violence was, as Policzer (2009) contends, organised and goal oriented is confirmed, as he also asserts, by the fact that it was reined in during periods when its immediate objectives had been achieved and/ or its benefits were matched or outweighed by costs. He interprets the 1977 dissolution of the DINA secret police, replaced by the less deadly, although by no means harmless, Central

---

[21] The judicial profession in Chile had long been, and remains, a specific career choice with its own basic level training. To be a judge, even a senior one, is accordingly not necessarily associated with selection from the higher echelons of successful or elite legal practice, as is commonly the case in, for instance, the UK.

[22] It is no coincidence that when it became so—i.e. when the 1980 Constitution was crafted, inter alia in an effort to provide a forum for containing and resolving differences of vision and emphasis within the newly-configured civil-military elite—the pre-existing Constitutional Tribunal (TC, in Spanish) was reshaped, via changes to composition and powers, to play this role of loyal rebalancing (See, for a general study of the Tribunal Bascuñán 1993). This Tribunal has recently (since mid-2017) been drawn into the present accountability case universe, playing an ultra- conservative role. The contrast between the Chilean TC's unremittingly anti-progressive, anti-activist stance and the actions of, for example, its Colombian counterpart is striking, raising the question of whether Chile's imminent constitutional transformation may help to effect, in future, transformation along similar lines.

Nacional de Informaciones, CNI, in this vein. More broadly, this move was also part of a broader sea change which was both reactive and prospective, encompassing high politics (and economics) as well as the decision to ratchet down the intensity of repression. Its prospective aspects included paving the way for the 1980 Constitution, which gave written shape to a bold, transformative political project whose ambitious breadth and long-term scope had been foreseen by almost no-one in the early days. Its reactive elements included a specific rearguard action, the replacement of the DINA, to defuse US anger at a flagrant, and unauthorised, encroachment of Chilean coercive violence onto US soil, in the shape of the 1976 car bomb assassination of prominent Chilean exile Orlando Letelier. It is tempting, though it may be optimistic, to believe that this quite localised increment in the political costs of continued coercion—caused by sudden disapproval from a previously dependable ally—was amplified and augmented by the courageous defence of essential rights that was now being mounted in the courts. Newly-minted human rights lawyers, mostly under the protection of the Catholic Church, were attempting to use law as a brake on regime violence, or at least as a way to denounce that violence at home and abroad. Again, a full account of this quixotic and rather noble endeavour escapes the scope of this chapter, but can be found, inter alia, in Lowden (1996), Wilde (2015), and Collins (2010a, 2010b). A personal account by an emblematic human rights lawyer appeared recently as Hertz (2017), and Hertz and many other key protagonists also appear in a 2014 documentary film, Habeas Corpus.

For purposes of this chapter, the main question to ask about this undoubtedly praiseworthy endeavour of moral—or, in Moustafa's terms, ´rightful´ resistance is whether it changed law, legal practice, or legal practitioners in any measurable or lasting way. Ginsburg and Moustafa (2008) discuss the potential for networks of support or complicity to emerge, through everyday interaction, between key actors in authoritarian regimes. Their focus is largely on intra-elite dynamics within regime circles, whereby for example, as discussed above, high level regime figures might cultivate and exploit affinities with senior judges, and vice versa, with each seeking to shore up their position of power, and/or shift the political direction of the regime. However, complicity can also arise, and latent or active networks of sympathy or understanding can be forged, between and among judges and other players in the authoritarian game. Since the insulation of civilian from military judicial processes, and the compartmentalisation of oversight of repression into the latter, was never fully watertight, at least some potential for restraint or influence on repressive behaviour through access to 'regular' judges remained. Thus, defensive and denunciatory action in both systems was judged a worthwhile endeavour by many, though not all, of the newly emerging human rights organisations.[23] The networks formed by and for such action included novel alliances between the far left and the Catholic Church; and thence between radical lawyers and some of their more respectable establishment

---

[23] In the early years some refused to supply defence lawyers to the stacked and essentially meaningless 'show trials' of civilians by courts martial, arguing that to do so was to give the instances a veneer of legitimacy. Others however thought it worthwhile attempting to have sentences made more lenient or commuted, seeking and sometimes obtaining penalties such as enforced exile instead of life imprisonment or worse.

counterparts. The Christian Democrat political background of the latter left them susceptible to appeals from the Cardinal Archbishop or his subordinates to work for or assist the legal department of the Vicaría de la Solidaridad, the Church's flagship legal and social assistance organisation.[24] The same characteristic, and these lawyers' clear lack of radical sympathies or revolutionary politics also lent additional heft to their denunciations of the regime's more flagrant moral failings. These principled individuals were sadly no more than a handful,[25] and although the new human rights lawyers, both centre and left, formed their own semi-clandestine support organisations, these did not outlive the 1980s. This burgeoning human rights sensibility therefore did not amount to a more complete complicity with, or capture of, bastions of the profession such as the Bar Association.[26] Nor did the human rights movement ever fully capture public opinion: although egregious abuses certainly became a central rallying point for internationally-mobilised opposition to the regime, inside the country, regime propaganda depicting victims as few in number and terrorist by nature did much to stave off righteous indignation.

Aside from the nucleus of human rights lawyers, other legal professionals of similar respectability did nonetheless begin to come together in search of ways to channel legally framed, indeed legally focused, opposition to the regime's pretensions at consolidation. Many such efforts occurred under the shelter of academic think tanks, to escape the ban on official party politics. Thus as early as 1978, the influential 'Constitutional Studies Group', or 'Group of 24', convened jurists and other legally-literate, regime opponents to draft a democratic alternative to what later became the 1980 Constitution, the production of which was a critical juncture in the relationship between the courts, repressive agencies, economic elites, and the regime. The Group continued to meet even after the highly authoritarian Constitution was imposed. Its members were influential at and after transition,[27] and in the later years of the regime began to think seriously about justice system and judicial reform, an issue which Pinochet himself considered one of the regime's major unfulfilled modernisation agendas.[28]

In terms of judicial response to human rights framed opposition—at the supply, rather than the demand, end of the legal mobilisation dyad—one might have to

---

[24] The Vicaría was formed from an earlier ecumenical organisation, the 'Peace Committee' (Comité Pro Paz) after Pinochet ordered the latter to be dissolved. The working practices of both were similar.

[25] For more detail, including names, see Fuentes op cit.

[26] McEvoy and Rebouche (2007) point out that methodologically speaking, the attitudes of such collective professional bodies are key to understanding the behaviour of key sectors.

[27] They included Enrique Silva Cimma, who went on to be foreign minister to Patricio Aylwin, the country's first elected president after transition (1990–1994); Francisco Cumplido, made minister of justice in 1990, and Jorge Correa Sutil. Correa Sutil, then a recent law graduate, would go on to become Dean of the UDP Law School, Secretary of the Rettig Commission, undersecretary of the Interior, and judge on the Constitutional Tribunal.

[28] After 1985, members of the recently-opened law faculty of the Universidad Diego Portales, UDP, joined colleagues from a centrist (Christian Democrat)-led think tank to form the innocuously-named Corporation for University Promotion. They discussed future legal reforms, focused on the judicial branch. The group included Jorge Correa Sutil, author of an influential account of Chile's protracted judicial reform process (Correa Sutil 1999).

conclude that the lawyers of the Vicaría were left playing the long game. Despite their best efforts to hold the regime to account, no member of the security services or other regime official was ever formally convicted of a human rights related crime during the entire 17-year duration of the dictatorship. Nonetheless this does not mean that human rights defence in general, and its legal expressions in particular, were to no avail or of no account. Sentences were sometimes commuted and the definitive 'disappearance' of some detainees almost certainly prevented, when it became apparent that their detention was known about and had been noted. The information generated by even unsuccessful attempts to lodge habeas corpus writs could serve as the basis for denunciation at home and abroad, where diaspora networks were key in creating international solidarity awareness and condemnation of the regime (Angell 2013). The resulting paper trail can and has provided a wealth of usable evidence in the more accommodating accountability environment that has prevailed over the past decade or so. It has also meant that Chilean relatives and survivors have faced fewer statute of limitation obstacles than their counterparts in some other countries when attempting, in recent times, to trigger the opening or re-opening of criminal investigations into decades-old crimes.[29]

Another, and less often remarked, effect may be argued, in the shape of mutual channels of communication and influence, more often informal than official, between opposition lawyers and justice system actors at all levels. The way the Chilean criminal justice system of the time operated meant that denunciations entailed direct interaction between putative victims or relatives' lawyers and the respective judge, magistrate, or judge's clerk. Police and prosecutors played only a secondary role, and Vicaría lawyers who acted as human rights defenders throughout the lifetime of the regime cumulatively amassed many hours of access to quite senior judges with whom they had previously studied, or to whom they were linked by social ties or even previous friendships. Alejandro Gonzalez, long-time head of the Vicaría's legal team, placed considerable emphasis on the importance, for occasional positive outcomes, of these prior complicity networks. He described them as being disrupted, but usefully not always definitively broken, when respected legal professionals such as himself appeared before the courts lobbying on behalf of the disappeared.[30] Thus some judges, often although not always low down the hierarchy, could be persuaded or were indeed willing to depart from the new norm and refuse to look the other way when cases involving repression came before them. While most dutifully renounced jurisdiction to military courts, judge Carlos Cerda was famously disciplined for

---

[29] See Collins (2010a) for the contrast with El Salvador, and Lessa and Skaar (2016), or the website of the Observatorio Luz Ibarburu, for contrasts with Uruguay.

[30] González had been justice minister in the elected Christian Democrat administration (1964–1970) that had immediately preceded Allende's socialist government. He reported, inter alia, the bemusement of a former friend and Supreme Court judge who took him aside and asked how much longer he intended to 'go on about' these 'supposed' disappearances. The bemused appeal to former camaraderie was, said González, apparent throughout his tenure and worked both ways: he himself often traded on it to coax some semblance of a correct response in cases he was representing. Author's interview with Alejandro González, Santiago, 14 January 2003, parts of which are cited in Collins 2010.

refusing to do so. Other magistrates or judges, including Cristian Alfaro, Rene García Villegas, Milton Juica and Sergio Muñoz also took occasional or consistent action that was at least in keeping with rule of law principles, although never sufficient, as mentioned, to produce pre-1990 criminal convictions. Nonetheless Cerda, Juica and Muñoz all later progressed to the heights of the Supreme Court, and all held key senior judicial posts at crucial junctures in the post-1990 accountability trajectory.[31] Juica, like other senior judges, has publicly acknowledged on various occasions the pivotal role played by dictatorship-era case law in forcing the Supreme Court to modernise its approach to international law in general, and international human rights law in particular.[32]

It might perhaps be argued that the career trajectories of these particular individual judges do not per se still merit the designation of them as constituting a 'complicity network', in Ginsburg and Moustafa's sense, with human rights lawyers or the human rights cause. Nonetheless it is striking that the substantive accountability 'turnaround' of Chile since 2004[33] has been largely overseen by the same judicial system, and indeed the same (now more senior) judicial figures, that previously underwrote impunity. Since there has been no significant legislative component to this change—a 1978 Amnesty Law has not been repealed or annulled—only changes to judicial behaviour can account for it. This change is not universal within the ranks of the judiciary, and the judges most associated with it are often the same ones— including those named above—who were exposed to the issue through interaction with the Vicaría's lawyers, and through them with victims, in the 1970s and 1980s. Another cohort of judges, less senior and/or simply too young to have been in office during the worst period of repression, has come to the issue through assignment, as after 2001 a small group of appeals court level judges, varying between six and two dozen in number, has been solely or preferentially dedicated by the Supreme Court to work on resolving past dictatorship-era cases. This decision, taken after the 1998 Pinochet arrest, has concentrated case expertise in a few hands. In so doing, it has created a community of mutual endeavour and understanding between human rights case judges and an equally specialised group of specially-designated police officers, forensic experts and state-employed human rights lawyers. These professionals demonstrably tend over time to feel closer in professional and personal affinity terms

---

[31] Cerda was president of the Santiago Appeals Court during the 1998 'Pinochet cases' in Chile, and later personally investigated financial fraud and corruption charges that proved extremely harmful to the dictator's image amongst right wing politicians and sympathisers. Juica and Munoz both investigated emblematic episodes of human rights violations before and after transition, and both serve or have served on the Supreme Court criminal bench that today sees all such cases that go to the final stage of appeal. Munoz has twice served as the Supreme Court's designated coordinator for human rights-related dictatorship-era cases, most recently in 2016.

[32] Remarks made at a Universidad de Chile conference in 2016, and at a range of events held at the Instituto de Estudios Judiciales, IEJ, Santiago, Chile between 2010 and 2013 at the instigation of the Observatorio de Justicia Transicional of which this author is the Director. Reports of some events can be found online via www.derechoshumanos.udp.cl ; others were held under a version of the Chatham House rule and notes are on file with the author.

[33] The date at which the first of Chile's (now) over 1,900 ongoing and completed dictatorship-era accountability cases resulted in successful criminal conviction and imprisonment.

to each other, and to relatives and survivors, than to their own professional peers, and thus Ginsburg and Moustafa's appellation of complicity network may be apposite once again not only during but after the authoritarian phase.[34] Such networks, where they exist, self-evidently have as much potential as any structural or institutional reform to alter justice outcomes by changing legal culture and shaping preferences and understanding (see, inter alia, Couso et al. 2010).

9.4 Transition and Its Discontents

Lawyers, or at least politicians versed in law, were certainly instrumental in engineering transition itself. One lawyer and politician who played a key role in opening up the formal political system once more was Gabriel Valdés, who had been Foreign Minister in the reformist 1964–1970 Christian Democrat administration. Returning to Chile from self-imposed exile in 1982, Valdés united moderate opposition and sought dialogue with the regime. After 1983 protests, however, Pinochet returned to a hard-line position, eventually leading to a failed assassination attempt against him in 1986. Elements of the civilian right saw the urgent need to develop an exit strategy, and the so called 'National Accord for Transition to a Full Democracy', *Acuerdo Nacional*, was signed after secret inter-party meetings convened by the Church. Making no specific mention of justice sector or legal reforms, the Acuerdo did however set out a 'commitment to democratic values'; respect for the Universal Declaration of Human Rights; a fully elected legislature; possible—but vague— 'constitutional reform'; economic continuity; 'respect for private property', and a limited openness to accountability for human rights violations (Huneeus 2009). Some of these, including the latter, were never fulfilled. Others became the basis for legislative proposals by the first transitional administration.

Political parties were gradually legalized, and most—with the exception of the Communist Party—agreed to accept the transition framework that had been laid down by the outgoing regime, inter alia in the 1980 Constitution. This dictated a nationwide October 1988 plebiscite. Fifty-five percent voted against a further period of Pinochet's rule, but 43 percent voted in favour, showing continuing high levels of popular support for the political right and the military. Nonetheless Patricio Aylwin, candidate of the centre-left 17-party Concertación coalition, prevailed in the ensuing 1989 presidential election. The incoming government's freedom to act was nonetheless limited by inherited constraints. The 1980 Constitution, drawn up by the regime, set out a model of restricted democracy ('*democracia tutelada*') and cemented in the principal features of the neoliberal economic model. Appointed senators, extremely high voting thresholds for constitutional reform, and a binominal electoral system ensured an effective right-wing veto in the legislature, while Pinochet was to continue as commander-in-chief of the army until 1998.

---

[34] See, inter alia, Collins (2016, 2018 and forthcoming) for development of the argument about post-transitional accountability networking across the state-civil society divide.

Around this same time, Chileans who had just voted against the perpetuation of the authoritarian regime nonetheless gave high approval ratings to judges (and the police) as 'people who could be trusted to solve the nation's problems.'[35] This is striking, given the direct complicity of both in the outgoing dictatorship. The key may lie in Carlos Huneeus's contention, mentioned above, that the regime, though personalised, was not arbitrary. The authoritarian state had built a legally framed and rule-bound edifice whose rules were complied with even when they brought about the regime's own demise.[36] The courts offered an apparently rational (in the Weberian sense) bureaucracy which could claim to rise above, and had certainly outlasted, recent political extremes of all stripes (Corte Suprema de Chile 2003). This was perhaps an attractive lodestone for the right, the general public, and anyone longing for a still centre in the rapidly turning world of Chilean transitional politics. The Concertación played down its previous radical identity, promising to play within the rewritten, authoritarian, rules of the game. In so doing, the courts were once again implicitly handed the mantle they had never formally put down: that of disinterested arbiter of the country's supreme values, guarantor of stability in economic and political matters alike.

Formal accountability for past human rights violations was perhaps the most evident casualty of this pacted approach to transition. Two months after taking office, incoming elected president Patricio Aylwin frankly admitted that some of his manifesto promises had had to be watered down. 'Democratisation' was now rebranded as the more anodyne '[reforms to] 'administration of justice'. Where pre-election promises had spoken of 'clarify[ing] the truth and do[ing] justice over human rights violations, as an ineluctable moral prerequisite for national reconciliation', (Aylwin n.d.), Aylwin now appeared to equate the situations of political prisoners and perpetrators. He proposed pardoning political prisoners held for non-violent crimes. These proposals, along with changes to terrorism legislation and military justice, became known as the 'Leyes Cumplido' proposal, after the Justice Minister of the day. In congressional debate the package was often confused with a broader *acuerdo marco* ('general agreement') that was being sought. This agreement in effect traded off pardons for the former armed opposition against continued broad amnesty for state agents. Both proposals were decried by the left for drawing tacit moral equivalence between state terror and armed resistance. This, plus opposition from the right, proved fatal. The Leyes Cumplido emerged from legislative debate in January 1991 significantly weakened in their intended reforming effect on military courts or internal security legislation.

Nonetheless a truth and reconciliation commission (the 'Rettig Commission' was held, reporting in March 1991. Follow up on delicate topics including relations with the military was overseen by an inner circle of Aylwin's trusted political allies and

---

[35] Collins (2013b: 69). Businesspeople scored even more highly; civilian politicians, poorly. See also Huneeus and Ibarra (2013) for detailed time series work on public opinion surrounding Pinochet and his regime.

[36] The Constitution dictated the timing and terms of the 1988 plebiscite. Though Pinochet wanted to disregard the results when he lost, his subordinates and political allies refused to allow him to do so.

aides. Some figures from the Vicaría circle went on to have substantial specific influence on public policy treatment of past crimes. These include José Zalaquett, Chile's main internationally known transitional justice expert, who became associated with a highly principled, but largely conciliatory, pro-clemency position. They also included Maria Luisa Sepulveda, former Vicaría social work director, who served as a key human rights policy advisor to all successive Concertación administrations and was vice-president of the subsequent Valech Commission, a second truth commission held in 2004–2005 to recognise survivors of political imprisonment and torture. The growing gap between these policy advisors, seen as elite actors, and grassroots groups disillusioned by the continued lack of justice led to distancing and tension. Human rights lawyers from outside privileged government circles continued to feel excluded and underappreciated over the course of the 1990s. If anything, their previous contestatory identity was preserved and reaffirmed despite the new democratic moment, and for some the sense of betrayal was undoubtedly more intense given that the authorities who still failed to deliver on their expectations of justice now consisted of their own former comrades.

Innovation in transitional justice circles occurred mainly through unexpected crises or minority social demands impossible to ignore. Both circumstances combined in 1998, an *annus horribilis* for Pinochet, an unexpected headache for the government, and an equally unexpected source of revitalisation for the dwindling human rights community. The year's events conspired to put Chile back on the world map for the very issue it had been trying hard to leave behind: past human rights crimes. In January, two criminal complaints were lodged against Pinochet in Chilean courts, seeking principally to express disgust at his imminent investiture as an honorary Senator.[37] Another significant milestone of the year was attributable to cause lawyering by a member of the 'old guard' of human rights lawyers: a moderately positive verdict in September 1998 reopened a previously amnestied case.[38] The underlying logic of the ruling allowed many previously shelved cases to be reopened: it acknowledged that where ongoing crimes or crimes against humanity had been committed, amnesty and statutes of limitation could not be legitimately applied.

Meanwhile, a Spanish investigation into cross-border military repressive operations of the 1970s and 80 s - known as Operación Cóndor - had begun in 1996. Against this backdrop Pinochet was advised by military lawyers not to travel to Europe. Nonetheless, travel he did. The main outlines of what followed, including Pinochet´s detention in the United Kingdom from October 1998 to March 2000, are well known.[39] For present purposes, the main noteworthy features are various. First, the arrest galvanised domestic groups into opening or reviving proceedings of their own against Pinochet. When he returned to Chile in March 2000, the main domestic

---

[37] An honour which was due to him under the terms of his own 1980 Constitution.

[38] The long-running 'Poblete-Cordoba' case had become largely a personal crusade for ex Vicaría lawyer Sergio Concha, who had continued to work the case as a matter of conscience even after the victim's last close relative had died.

[39] See for example Brett (2009), Roht-Arriaza (2006), Davis (2003).

complaint against him had expanded to incorporate a group of ten lawyers, representing dozens of victims and relatives. The old human rights lawyer circuit was revived, while the sheer volume of new cases drew new lawyers into the issue. Relatives, survivors and left-of-centre social organisations such as trades unions vied to get in on the act by submitting their own criminal complaints, which have now produced over 1,400 active criminal cases before the courts, with 400 more resolved.[40] Second, the Concertación's intense pressure on Spain and the UK to bring Pinochet home, arguing sovereign immunity or humanitarian grounds, enraged critics on the left, increasing determination to achieve domestic prosecution. Third, the case led to a new self-consciousness among Chile's judiciary, whose every action was suddenly scrutinised: the probability of domestic justice became key to extradition arguments.

Chile's revitalised accountability scenario for past crimes has since 1998 produced new breeds and generations of cause lawyers, much as the dictatorship gave rise to the original group. These new human rights lawyers are perhaps more diverse in origin, motivation and political background than were their historical counterparts, and involve themselves in a range of emerging issue areas—most notably, gender and diversity rights, cases against police brutality, indigenous rights, and environmentalism. Some 'cause lawyers'[41] have moreover crossed over to staff a small but growing number of state-sponsored or state-run human rights institutions and bodies, a development of course unthinkable during the authoritarian era. In part, these entities represent early transitional promises only recently come to fruition: a National Human Rights Institute, Human Rights and Memory Museum, and Subsecretariat (Vice-Ministry) of Human Rights, all prefigured in the Truth Commission report, have all been installed only since 2010—the latter as recently as 2016—following protracted negotiations with reluctant right wing political parties and forces (Wilde 1999, 2013). This state rights infrastructure, while welcome, remains precarious and is often sidelined, as we will see below. 'Private' human rights lawyering is meanwhile hamstrung structurally, and perhaps to some extent also culturally, by continued adherence to a case-by-case, individual client model that inevitably dissipates the force of even successful claim-making.[42]

As far as the courts are concerned, modernising reforms introduced gradually from 1996 have produced a prosecutor-driven, adversarial criminal justice system. There

---

[40] See Collins et al., Informe Anual de Derechos Humanos en Chile, Universidad Diego Portales, editions 2010–2020 inclusive, chapter one, for cumulative qualitative and quantitative analysis of this caseload. Until 2009, all such cases were triggered privately by relatives or survivors. After 2009, the state also began to initiate investigations, although solely in respect of disappeared or executed victims.

[41] For a full development of the concept see Sarat and Scheingold (1998).

[42] There is no equivalent in Chile of the class action suit, while prevailing legal interpretative consensus is conservative in limiting the broader applicability of any particular case verdict. As far as the transitional justice case universe is concerned, a continued focus on individual violations of the right to life has not been accompanied by the same kind of broadening to collective and economic rights agendas, and to private firms and economic interests as perpetrators and accomplices, as in neighbouring Argentina and other settings. See Bohoslavsky et al. (2019) for one of few treatments of this issue.

has also been a significant albeit still limited opening to international law, and to international and regional human rights jurisprudence in particular.[43] In 2013, on the occasion of the 40th anniversary of the military coup, the Supreme Court finally publicly acknowledged its historical 'debt' in having failed to protect dictatorship-era rights (Observatorio DDHH 2013). Specialised units within the country's detective police and forensic service, formed to contribute to investigations of past human rights crimes, began to work on other relevant issue areas, and the new National Human Rights Institute began to fulfil its charter obligations in training of state personnel by, inter alia, sponsoring a joint Masters programme for prosecutors, prison officers and other justice system personnel. Under former president Michelle Bachelet (2006–2010 and 2014–2018), Chile sought to position itself on the regional and international stage as a human rights compliant state, seeking and achieving a position on the UN Human Rights Council. Bachelet, who was at the helm of UN Women between her two presidential terms, is associated internationally with support for gender rights and progressive social policy.

None of this reflects, however, widespread positive regard in the country as a whole, or its mainstream public institutions, for human rights precepts and principles. Survey work by the National Institute for Human Rights, and others, shows patchy support for human rights ideals and only a hazy grasp of the essentials of the concept.[44] As in other countries of the region hard-line law and order discourse is popular, with an exaggerated fear of petty crime going hand in hand with disdain for assertion of the rights of prisoners or detainees. Violent policing of recent student protests and the quasi-militarisation of Southern indigenous communities have attracted consistent criticism from international human rights monitors groups but only muted public concern. Even the blatant, widely televised police brutality unleashed against protesters in and after October 2019 failed to produce unanimous social or official condemnation. Human rights concerns were openly scorned by the chief of police and figures on the political right, while the state human rights institute's attempts to intervene exposed the barely disguised contempt in which it was held in police and some governmental circles.[45]

Concomitantly, there is as yet little sign of a flourishing professional human rights field, beyond the limited job openings—almost exclusively for lawyers—in the small number of aforementioned state entities. Such jobs tend moreover to be subject to political patronage and presidential turnover, and so there is little opportunity to make them the basis for a stable career. The third sector likewise offers mainly short-term

---

[43] See Hilbink (2007); Huneeus (2010); Collins (2010a, b, 2013b). Attitudes to the regional human rights system nonetheless hardened under a second (non-consecutive) right-wing administration from 2018. In April 2019, Chile joined four other conservative governments from the region in sending a letter widely interpreted as an attack on the Inter-American Commission on Human Rights. Collins et al. (2019).

[44] See INDH Annual Reports, available on the institution's website at www.indh.cl and the Public Opinion Survey of the Universidad Diego Portales, available at www.encuesta.udp.cl.

[45] See inter alia Collins et al. (2020) and other chapters of the Annual Human Rights Report in which it appears. See also reports and statistics at the website of the National Human Rights Institute, www.indh.cl.

and precarious opportunities for human rights work per se, with only a few organisations managing to thrive. Chile´s recently gained and much-prized status as a member of the OECD 'club' of relatively wealthy economies perversely perhaps plays against it in this regard: elsewhere in the region, even in relatively developed Argentina, many human rights organisations subsist on external philanthropic funding which Chile is no longer eligible to receive. Nor is there a detectable clamour among the country's law students to become human rights lawyers.[46]

The disincentives include a cultural barrier, as 'human rights' is a term with limited social acceptance, only recently overcoming an almost exclusive association with the abuses of the dictatorship. There are also structural and class barriers: Chile's higher education sector is ruinously expensive, and human rights work offers extremely limited earning prospects with which to pay off student loans. Despite all of this, as we have seen, a small but identifiable new generation of cause lawyers may be said to be emerging, whether working on past accountability cases or other fields including gender, LGBTQI+ , and/or indigenous rights. In these newer areas, particularly the more transversal and less contested ones, public interest litigation housed in university centres is also beginning to be supplemented by a certain amount of pro bono work from established commercial law firms. This may be interpreted as part of a more general dawning awareness among Chile's comfortable private sector of the moral and reputational benefits of corporate social responsibility, though as is often the case with such impulses, there is little if any underlying drive or support for more radical structural change. Further support for the contention that these developments do not really add up to a major sea change or any kind of human rights 'complicity network' within the legal profession comes when one considers that the country's principal Bar Associations—which are regionally, rather than nationally, organised—continue to return largely conservative committees.

In the political sphere, successive centre-left governments, alternating since 2010 with right wing administrations,[47] achieved some milestone rights advances, notably for example the 2017 passing of a limited but long-anticipated and highly controversial abortion law. Nonetheless, the overall human rights balance remained meagre. The incumbent right-wing administration (2018–) lived up to early promise to be even less enthusiastic about human rights than its 2010–2014 predecessor, even before the substantial regression observed from late 2019 in response first to social protests,

---

[46] This assertion is based in part on the author´s decade-long experience as a lecturer in the country's higher education sector, including the directorship of a human rights research project which is open to student participation. It also draws on broader empirical evidence such as a 2012 consultation meeting between academics and the UN Working Group on Enforced Disappearances, at which the consensus was that only five or six law schools in the country at that time offered any substantive human rights training, mostly as optional courses. There were almost no course offerings outside law schools. The country's first dedicated Masters programme in human rights was created as recently as 2014, in the Universidad Diego Portales, and there are still few such programmes nationwide.

[47] The centre-left Concertación held the presidency in unbroken succession between the beginning of transition (1990) and 2010, when the right wing candidate Sebastian Piñera was elected to replace Michelle Bachelet (2006–2010). Since then, Bachelet and Piñera have once again alternated in the presidency (2014–2018 and 2018–, respectively), with Bachelet representing a slightly modified coalition named the 'Nueva Mayoría' in her second term.

and then the Covid-19 pandemic.. As far as the 1980 Constitution was concerned, meanwhile, both mainstream political coalitions were exceedingly late to the party in understanding the pent-up demand for change that finally surfaced, in spectacular fashion, four decades later. Even the purportedly centre-left Concertación opted consistently for modest incremental reformism rather than wholesale rejection or critique.[48] Nonetheless, demand for wholesale replacement of the highly authoritarian carta magna acquired gradual purchase from 2010, before being somewhat belatedly taken up by the initially largely inchoate, and certainly acephalous, street and social movements that first materialised in October 2019.[49]

The demand, like the mass protests, proceeded from a sense that Chile's 'modelo'—the catch-all term in popular parlance for the legal, legislative, economic and social architecture inherited from the dictatorship era—is outmoded and no longer socially sustainable, favouring superficial growth and the accentuation of existing privilege, to the detriment of a common good in which it has never really been invested (Atria et al. 2003). The almost uniquely dysfunctional compulsory privatised pension scheme, a pet policy of the dictatorship, is widely hated and has been a particular target of the recent mass mobilisation. So too have the privatised health and educational provision that the 1980 Constitution enshrined and still protects. However, that which now seems so self-evident—that if the modelo is the problem, the Constitution which buttresses it must also go—appeared far from axiomatic as recently as late 2017, when Piñera was elected president for the second time. His right-wing coalition, staunch in its defence of both the 'model' and its magna carta, won a comfortable ten-point victory, less than two years before Chileans took to the streets in large numbers. Ill-fated efforts by his predecessor, Bachelet, to install some kind of constitutional process never sparked great public enthusiasm either, fizzling out after non-binding 'popular assemblies' in 2016 and not heard of again until, bizarrely, resurfacing as a draft text presented to Congress five days before the end of Bachelet's presidential term.

It may be argued, then, that the 1980 Constitution, whether loved or—as now—increasingly apparently hated, still amounts to an assertion of identity and an effort of confident (self)-legitimation that formal democratic politics after 1990 has not yet been able to match. The absence of a transformative opposition project, to replace the early glue provided by unified opposition to Pinochet, became evident early on in the Concertación's history in government. It was allowed to comprehensively impede the development of any self-confident alternative foundational narrative from the left. The civilian political right has meanwhile demonstrated an even more marked absence of creative or independent thought, with the second of its two post-1990 periods in government even more strongly marked than the first by clear authoritarian nostalgia. The dictatorship-era Constitution was continually venerated as the

---

[48] Although officialdom considered changes significant enough, by 2009, for then-president Ricardo Lagos to replace Pinochet's signature—reproduced on all official copies of the Constitution—with his own, much of the core conservative, anti-popular, and pro-market vision remained intact.

[49] For an early account, see Fuentes (2010). See also Atria (2013), Heiss (2017, 2020), Fuentes and Joignant (2017), and Garcés (2020)

keystone of continuing 'prosperity' and a necessary bulwark against the spectre of Chile's 'becoming Venezuela', an outlandish scenario regularly invoked to cultivate moral panic regarding progressive, rights-based political discourse.

It is in this sense that one might reasonably claim that 1980, as surely as 1973, proved to be a durable seismic shift in Chile's political and social self-understanding. The longer that constitution's precepts persisted, the more strongly stability, law, and the established order of things tended to become associated with them, creating the powerful and long-lasting 'overhang' alluded to in the introduction to this chapter. While October 2019, and more clearly still, October 2020, represented the beginning of the end of this legacy in its most iconic form, the prospects that this change will take a highly transformative direction, playing out as the kinds of "rights-filled" constitutionalism described by Gargarella (2012: 143–162), or the "diversity constitutionalism" discussed by Uprimny (2016) seem likely to be limited. Chile's 'October revolution', while epoch-making, will not necessarily play out as a 'rights revolution'.

9.5 Final Remarks

We have considered, in turn, how courts, law itself, and the constitutional project were mutually (re)constituted and (re)configured by contending social actors during and after Chile's 1973–1990 authoritarian 'rule by law' period, seeing how even within this period an unstable mix of coercion and legality/legitimacy narratives were used to seek consent or enforce acquiescence. In this process law and legal actors, while always active shapers of Chile's public life and recent history, proved not to be a major force for fundamental challenge to the authoritarian takeover per se. Nor have they provided the principal challenge to the imprint of that takeover in more recent post-transitional times. Law appears instead to have largely fulfilled the expectations of Marxist and critical legal theorists, acting as a preserver of existing power relations, relations which were recast incipiently—and violently—in 1973, but more lastingly in 1980. Confusing stasis with stability, and regarding the latter as self-evidently desirable, may be at the heart of this tendency, which persisted at least until 2020.

As we have seen, even vigorous and courageous defence of human rights during the worst period of dictatorship-era coercion shared this pro-status-quo, non-radical character, inspired as it often was by an avocation for supposedly timeless Chilean virtues of legalism and tradition, at least among the more 'respectable' class of human rights lawyer. Thus the complicity to which Ginsburg and Moustafa allude did arise within a small group of such lawyers, even stretching to encompass some judicial figures. The courts, then, did become an alternative space for opposition and contention, but this contention was largely around the margins of the regime's most extreme behaviours and violence. The goal and the (not inconsiderable) achievements were to contain, mitigate and increase the costs of repression, not to more dramatically impede or reverse the military takeover or the many, ambitious, socioeconomic transformations which it essayed and at which it largely succeeded. The return to democracy, while certainly not fictitious or insignificant, was a change of tone and administration rather than substance, with no real appetite on any significant part of the political spectrum for a wholesale reversal of the 1980s direction of travel. In such a context Chile's awakening to the human rights cause, while real and rapid in the early years of the coup, has subsequently amounted at best to a cautious liberal conservatism rather than radical challenge to the status quo. Its significance under a highly (neo)liberal presidency from 2018 was therefore limited to adjustments of language and emphasis, grafted onto continued pursuit of an anti-popular project whose essence, as distinct from its forms, has changed little over recent decades. The perceived efficacy of a rule-following faith in 'rights talk', like any notion that law and the courts had become an effective restraint on state violence, were moreover substantially belied by the flagrant, unrepentant, and to date unrestrained behaviour of the forces of public order in 2019 and 2020. Accordingly, far from pushing Chileans toward a more enthusiastic adoption of rights agendas in an incipient new social contract, the experience of thirty years of stasis, followed by a year of explosive demands for change, may if anything further fuel impatience with the polite forms of liberal constitutionalism.

References

Accatino, D. 2020. Justicia de transición y nueva Constitución. In *Conceptos para una nueva Constitución*, eds. Fernando Muñoz and Viviana Ponce de Léon. Santiago: DER Ediciones.

Aguilar, P., and J. Rios-Figueroa. 2014. *Judicial Institutions and the Dilemmas of Power Sharing and Control in Authoritarian Regimes*, Working Paper Series no. 271, CIDE Mexico.

Angell, A. 2006. The Pinochet Regime: An Accounting. *Open Democracy*, 12 December 2006. Last accessed 7 January 2018.

Angell, A. 2013. Chile's Coup: The Perspective of Forty Years. *Open Democracy*, 11 September 2013. Last accessed 7 January 2018.

Atria, F. 2013. *La Constitución Tramposa*. Santiago: LOM Ediciones.

Atria, F., J. Couso, J. Benavente, A. Joignant, and G. Larraín. 2003. *El Otro Modelo*. Santiago: Debate.

Aylwin Azocar Patricio. n.d. *La Transición Chilena: Discursos Escogidos Marzo 1990–1992*. Santiago: Editorial Andrés Bello.

Barros, R. 2002. *Constitutionalism and Dictatorship: Pinochet, the Junta, and the 1980 Constitution*. Cambridge: Cambridge University Press.

Bascuñan, A. 1993. Misión del Tribunal Constitucional. *Revista Chilena de Derecho* 481, 20, 2/3, (Mayo-Diciembre): 481–490.

Bohoslavsky, J.P., K. Fernández, and S. Smart. 2019. *Complicidad Económica con la Dictadura Chilena. Un país Desigual a la Fuerza*. Santiago: LOM Ediciones.

Brett S. 2009. *The Pinochet Effect: Ten Years on From London 1998*. Conference Report, Universidad Diego Portales www.derechoshumanos.udp.cl, section Observatorio Justicia Transicional.

Collins, C. 2010a. *Post-Transitional Justice: Human Rights Trials in Chile and El Salvador*. University Park: Pennsylvania State University Press.

Collins, C. 2010b. Human Rights Trials in Chile During and after the 'Pinochet Years'. *International Journal of Transitional Justice* 4 (1): 67–86.

Collins, C. 2013a. Chile a Más de Dos Décadas de Justicia de Transición. *Revista Política* 51 (2): 79–113.

Collins, C. 2013b. The Politics of Prosecutions. In *The Politics of Memory: Chile from Pinochet to Bachelet*, ed. Cath Collins, Katherine Hite, and Alfredo Joignant, 61–90. Boulder: Lynne Rienner.

Collins, C. 2014. Human Rights Policy Under the Concertación. In *Democratic Chile: The Politics and Policies of a Historic Coalition, 1990–2010*, ed. Peter Siavelis and Kirsten Sehnbruch. Boulder: Lynne Rienner Press.

Collins, C. 2015. 'Lawyers and Transition in Chile', Report for the Lawyers, Conflict and Transition Project, Queens University, Belfast/ TJI, Ulster University

Collins, C. 2016. Prologo. In *Judicialización de Justicia de Transición en América Latina*, ed. Carla Osmo. Brasília: RLAJT and Ministerio de Justicia de Brasil and UNDP.

Collins, C. 2018. Transitional Justice 'From Within': Police, Forensic and Legal Actors Searching for Chile's Disappeared. *Journal of Human Rights Practice* 10 (1): 19–39.

Collins, C. forthcoming. The Politics of Justice 'From Below': Relatives, Survivors, Human Rights Defenders and Atrocity Crime Trials in Latin America'. In *Transitional Justice Beyond Blueprints*, ed. Claire Garbett. London: Routledge.

Collins, C. et al. 2019. La Memoria en los Tiempos del Colera: Verdad, justicia, reparaciones, y garantías de no repetición por los crímenes de la dictadura chilena. In *Informe Anual DDHH en Chile 2019*. Centro de DD.HH, Universidad Diego Portales, 23–132. Santiago: Universidad Diego Portales and published in translation as Memory in Times of Cholera. https://pure.ulster.ac.uk/en/publications/memory-in-times-of-cholera-truth-justice-reparations-and-guarante or http://www.derechoshumanos.udp.cl/derechoshumanos/index.php/observatorio/Observatorio-de-Justicia-Transicional/Publicaciones/Informes-Anuales/.

Collins, C. et al. 2020. ¿Abrirán las grandes alamedas? Justicia, Memoria, y No-Repetición en tiempos constituyentes. In *Informe Anual DDHH en Chile 2020*. Centro de DD.HH, Universidad Diego Portales. Santiago: Universidad Diego Portales.

Collins, C., K. Hite, and A. Joignant (eds.). 2013. *The Politics of Memory in Chile: From Pinochet to Bachelet*. Boulder: Lynne Rienner Press.

Correa Sutil, J. 1999. Cenicienta se queda en la fiesta: el poder judicial chileno en la década de los noventa'. In *El Modelo Chileno: Democracia y desarrollo en los noventa*, ed. Paul Drake and Ivan Jaksic, 281–315. Santiago: LOM.

Corte Suprema de Justicia de Chile. 2003. Corte Suprema de Chile, Conmemoración 180 Años: 1823–2003. Santiago: Corte Suprema de Chile 2003.

Couso, J., A. Huneeus, and R. Sieder (eds.). 2010. *Cultures of Legality Judicialization and Political Activism in Latin America*. Cambridge: Cambridge University Press.

Davis, M. 2003. *The Pinochet Case: Origins, Progress and Implications*. London: Institute of Latin American Studies.

De la Maza, I. n.d. Los abogados en Chile: Desde el Estado al Mercado: Resumen de Tesis de Magister. Unpublished masters' thesis, on file with author.

De la Maza, I. 2001. Lawyers from the State to the Market. Unpublished masters' thesis submitted to the Stanford Law School, Stanford University.

de Sousa Santos, B. 1987. Law: A Map of Misreading. Toward a Post-Modern Conception of Law. *Journal of Law and Society* 14(3): 279–302.

Dezalay, Y., and B. Garth. 2002. *The Internationalization of Palace Wars: Lawyers, Economists, and the Contest to Transform Latin American States*. Chicago: University of Chicago Press.

Ensalaco, M. 2010. *Chile Under Pinochet: Recovering the Truth*. Pennsylvania: University of Pennsylvania Press.

Fuentes, C. (ed.). 2010. *En nombre del pueblo: debate sobre el cambio constitucional en Chile*. Santiago: Universidad Diego Portales and Fundación Boell.

Fuentes, C., and A. Joignant (eds.). 2017. *La Solución Constitucional: Plebiscitos, asambleas, congresos, sorteos y mecanismos híbridos*. Santiago: Catalonia.

Gallardo Silva, M. 2003. *Intima complacencia: los juristas en Chile y el golpe militar de 1973 : antecedentes y testimonios*. Santiago: El Periodista.

Gandhi, J. 2008. *Political Institutions under Dictatorship*. Cambridge: Cambridge University Press.

Gargarella, Roberto. 2012. Latin American Constitutionalism Then and Now: Promises and Questions. In *New Constitutionalisms in Latin America: Promises and Practices*, eds. Nolte and Schilling-Vacaflor, 143–162. London, NY: Routledge.

Ginsburg, T., and T. Moustafa. 2008. *Rule by Law: The Politics of Courts in Authoritarian Regimes*. Cambridge: Cambridge University Press.

Ginsburg, T., and A. Simpser. 2014. *Constitutions in Authoritarian Regimes*. New York: Cambridge University Press.

Garcés, M. 2020. *Estallido social y una nueva constitución para Chile*. Santiago: LOM.

González Le Saux, M. 2014. Forgotten Justice: Memory and the Access to Justice Program in Allende's Chile. Paper delivered at the Latin American Studies Association Congress, Chicago, USA, 2014.

Habeas Corpus. 2014. Documentary, 83 min. dir. Claudia Barril and Sebastián Moreno. Películas del Pez.

Heiss, C. 2017. Legitimacy Crisis and the Constitutional Problem in Chile: A Legacy of Authoritarianism. *Constellations* 24: 470–479.

Heiss, C. 2020. *¿Por Qué Necesitamos una Nueva Constitución?*. Santiago: Aguilar.

Hertz, C. 2017. *La Historia Fue Otra: Memorias*. Santiago: Debate.

Hilbink, L. 2008. Agents of Anti-Politics: Courts in Pinochet's Chile. In *Rule by Law: The Politics of Courts in Authoritarian Regimes*, ed. Tom Ginsburg and Tamir Moustafa, 102–131. Cambridge: Cambridge University Press.

Hilbink, L. 2007. *Judges in Democracy and Dictatorship: Lessons from Chile*. Cambridge: Cambridge University Press.

Huneeus, A. 2010. *Judging from a Guilty Conscience: The Chilean Judiciary's Human Rights Turn*. Law and Social Inquiry 35.

Huneeus, C. 2007. *The Pinochet Regime*. Boulder: Lynne Rienner Press.

Huneeus, C. 2009. Political Mass Mobilization against Authoritarian Rule: Pinochet's Chile, 1983–88. In *Civil Resistance and Power Politics*, eds. Timothy Garton Ash and Adam Roberts. Oxford: Oxford University Press

Huneeus, C., and S. Ibarra. 2013. The Memory of the Pinochet Regime in Public Opinion. In *The Politics of Memory*, eds. Cath Collins, Katherine Hite and Alfredo Joignant, 197–238. Boulder: Lynne Rienner Press.

Joignant, A. 2013. Pinochet's Funeral: Memory, History and Immortality. In *The Politics of Memory*, eds. Cath Collins, Katherine Hite and Alfredo Joignant, 165–196. Boulder: Lynne Rienner Press.

Joignant, A. 2007. *Un día distinto: Memorias festivas y batallas conmemorativas en torno al 11 de septiembre en Chile 1974–2006*. Santiago: Editorial Universitaria.

Levitsky, S., and A.L. Way. 2002. *Competitive Authoritarianism: Hybrid Regimes after the Cold War*. New York: Cambridge University Press.

Loveman, B., and E. Lira. 2013. Torture as Public Policy 1810–2011. In *The Politics of Memory*, eds. Cath Collins, Katherine Hite and Alfredo Joignant, 91–132. Boulder: Lynne Rienner Press.

Loveman, B., and E. Lira. 2002. *El Espejismo de la Reconciliación Política: Chile 1990–2002*. Santiago: LOM.

Loveman, B., and E. Lira. 2000. *Las Ardientes Cenizas del Olvido: Vía Chilena de Reconciliación Política 1932–1994*. Santiago: LOM.

Loveman, B., and E. Lira. 1999. *Las Suaves Cenizas del Olvido*. Santiago: LOM.

Lowden, P. 1996. *Moral Opposition to Authoritarian Rule in Chile 1973–1990*. Basingstoke: Macmillan.

McEvoy, Kieran, and Rebouche. 2007. Mobilizing the Profession: Lawyers, Politics and the Collective Legal Conscience. In *Judges, Transition and Human Rights*, eds. John Morison, Kieran McEvoy, and Gordon Anthony, 275–314. Oxford: Oxford University Press.

Moustafa, T. 2007. *The Struggle for Constitutional Power: Law, Politics, and Economic Development in Egypt*. New York: Cambridge University Press.

O'Brien, K. 1996. Rightful Resistance. *World Politics* 49 (1): 39–55.

Observatorio DDHH. 'Truth, Justice and Memory for Dictatorship-Era Human Rights Violations, 40 Years After Chile's Military Coup' (Centro DDHH, UDP Santiago de Chile 2013), and translated for Working Paper Series, Transitional Justice Institute, Ulster University.

Policzer, P. 2009. *The Rise and Fall of Repression in Chile*. Notre Dame: University of Notre Dame Press.

Roht-Arriaza, N. 2006. *The Pinochet Effect*. Pennsylvania: University of Pennsylvania Press.

Sarat, Austin, and Stuart Scheingold (eds.). 1998. *Cause Lawyering: Political Commitments and Professional Responsibilities*. Oxford: Oxford University Press.

Shapiro, M. 2008. Courts in Authoritarian Regimes. In *Rule by Law: The Politics of Courts in Authoritarian Regimes*, eds. Ginsburg and Moustafa, 326–336. Cambridge: Cambridge University Press.

Shapiro, M. 1981. *Courts: A Comparative and Political Analysis*. Chicago: University of Chicago Press.

Lessa, F., and E. Skaar. 2016. Uruguay: Half Way Towards Accountability. In *Transitional Justice in Latin America*, ed. Cath Collins, Elin Skaar, and Jemima García-Godos, 77–102. London: Routledge.

Svolik, M.W. 2012. *The Politics of Authoritarian Rule*. Cambridge: Cambridge University Press.

Uprimny, Rodrigo. 2016. The Recent Transformation of Constitutional Law in Latin America: Trends and Challenges. In *Law and Society in Latin America: A New Map*. ed. C. Rodríguez-Garavito, 109–138. Abingdon and New York: Routledge.

Wilde, A. 1999. Irruptions of Memory: Expressive Politics in Chile's Transition to Democracy. *Journal of Latin American Studies* 31: 473–500.

Wilde, A. 2013. A Season of Memory: Human Rights in Chile's Long Transition. In *The Politics of Memory in Chile: From Pinochet to Bachelet*, ed. Cath Collins, Katherine Hite, and Alfredo Joignant, 31–60. Boulder: Lynne Rienner Press.

Wilde, A. 2015. The Institutional Church and Pastoral Ministry: Unity and Conflict in the Defense of Human Rights in Chile. In *Religious Responses to Violence: Human Rights in Latin America Past and Present*, ed. Wilde, 159–190. Notre Dame: Notre Dame University Press.

Cath Collins is Professor of Transitional Justice at Ulster University, Northern Ireland and Director of the Transitional Justice Observatory of the Universidad Diego Portales, Santiago, Chile and is a founder member of the Latin American Transitional Justice Network. She obtained her PhD from the Institute for the Study of the Americas at the University of London.

Chapter 10
Spanish Law: Coming to Terms with the Ghosts of Francoism (1936–2017)

Alfons Aragoneses

Abstract No process of transitional justice was carried out to address the violation of rights that occurred under the Franco dictatorship. At the same time, and unlike what occurred in other countries, the emerging democratic legal regime, from the Constitution to the norms that implemented it, turned a blind eye to the legacy of the Francoism. This silence created a narrative void regarding the past that was occupied by the discourse over the Civil War and dictatorship that had been propagated by the State during the dictatorship. The normative and narrative silence in the law over the dictatorship was only broken by in 2007 at national level and later in some regions.

10.1 Introduction

Law and history do not exist separately. They dialogue and interact with each other. That they did so in the past is evident, but it is not difficult to see how they interact in our post-historical and post-ideological era (Fukuyama 1992). Law inasmuch as a legal system has memory: it makes references to the past, whether a real or mythical past (Hartog 2012; De Giorgi 2004), to legitimize itself or to lend symbolical or aesthetic support to political or legal projects. Examples of this interaction between law and history can be found in current European Law related to tragic events such as the Holocaust or Holodomor.[1] We find it in the preambles—the "law's song," to use the phrase of Marie Theres Fögen—that refer to some glorious and mythical

---

[1] European Parliament: Resolution of 23 October 2008 on the commemoration of the Holodomor, and the Ukraine artificial famine (1932–1933). *OJ C* 15 E, 78–80.

This article was written under the auspices of my stay as a visiting professor at the University of Cagliari in June and July 2017 that was financed by the Autonomous Region of Sardinia. I would like to express my deepest gratitude to Professor Giuseppina de Giudice and Fabio Botta, Professor and Dean of the Law Department, for their hospitality.

A. Aragoneses (✉)
Department of Law, University Pompeu Fabra, Barcelona, Spain
e-mail: alfons.aragoneses@upf.edu

© Springer Nature Switzerland AG 2021
C. Paixão and M. Meccarelli (eds.), *Comparing Transitions to Democracy. Law and Justice in South America and Europe*, Studies in the History of Law and Justice 18, https://doi.org/10.1007/978-3-030-67502-8_10

national past, that of the Croatian constitution being a good example. We also find such references in laws designed to preserve the memory of historic events that "prescribe or proscribe a version of the past" as Antoon de Baets define Memory Laws (De Baets 2017).

Spanish Law is no different; references to the past are easy to find. One interesting aspect of the Spanish case, however, is the number of different narratives that are employed wherever the law refers the Spanish legal system reconstructs the Civil War and Franco's dictatorship. Different memories thus not only exist in society, but also in the law, where they are found in the language of statutes, preambles, and even judicial decisions.

Because of the circumstances of the transition and early years of democracy following Franco's dictatorship, no process of transitional justice was carried out to address the violation of rights that occurred under the dictatorship. At the same time, and unlike what occurred in France, Germany, and Italy, the emerging democratic legal regime, from the Constitution to the norms that implemented it, turned a blind eye to the legacy of the Francoism.[2] This silence created a void narrative regarding the past that was occupied by the discourse over the Civil War and dictatorship that had been propagated by the State during the dictatorship (Aragoneses 2017).

This happened during the transition and continued under the democratic regime. As a result of the initial silence and consequent lack of an official version of the past, Franco's official version of the past, one that had been internalized by large sectors of society, gradually seeped into the void left by the legislators. Since the 1960s this version of the Civil War was presented as a "conflict between brothers" in which the blame and the crimes were equally shared by both sides. This version also presented the "peace" brought by Franco as the basis for the economic growth of the 1960s and imposed forgetting the past as a condition for future advancement.

The normative and narrative silence in the law over the dictatorship was only broken by the legislature on two occasions, first in 2006 and again in 2007 with the law it proposed and passed on historical memory. Although the law represents an effort to compensate the victims of the dictatorship, between 2011 and 2018 the amount allocated for that purpose in the national budget was zero. Moreover, in 2012 the Spanish Supreme Court issued a decision, which will be examined later, according to which the responsibility for identifying the cause of death of the people buried in common graves corresponded to historians, not jurists.[3]

Recently the autonomous regional parliaments of Catalonia, the Balearic Islands, and Andalusia have attempted to fill the void left by the national legislature by elaborating laws to compensate victims and provide a new official discourse regarding the past. This is the reason why there still exists an interesting contrast between the silence on the part of the national authorities that has permitted the normalization

---

[2] In referring to the set of Franco's supporters, troops, and government, I will often employ the terms Francoist and Francoism.

[3] Tribunal Supremo. Sentencia 101/2012, 27 February 2012, Caso Manos Limpias y Asociación Libertad e Identidad vs. Baltasar Garzón.

and internalization of Franco's account and the narratives at the provincial level that recount the history of the dictatorship's systematic violation of human rights.

To use the words of Bartolomé Clavero, the Spanish memory law and the regional laws on common graves and legal compensation for the victims of Franco's dictatorship seek to render justice by "countering and displacing the fiction, one still attempting to pass itself off as history, that still carries weight in our days and renders service to impunity" (Clavero 2013: 18). Spanish law, by avoiding issues of transitional justice during the 1970s, 1980s, and 1990s, and consequently neglecting to express an official discourse during this period, has helped consolidate the fiction that the dictatorship was a historical phenomenon that did not injure rights or freedoms.

In the pages that follow, I analyze how the Civil War and the repression under the dictatorship has been regulated and narrated through Spanish law. I analyze the relationship between law and history from 1936 to the present day. I examine how the Civil War was reconstructed through Franco's legislation and how the fate of the victims was avoided during the transition to democracy. I analyze the silence that passed into the law under the democratic regime and explain the significance of the "grandchildren's rebellion" and the legal reaction to it.

10.2 Historical Memory in Law Under Franco (1936–1958)

The exact number of those who died in the Civil War (1936–1939) is unknown. Paul Preston suggests that 300,000 people died at the fronts and 200,000 behind them (Preston 2012). To these must be added the thousands of assassinations that occurred after the war officially ended on April 1, 1939, and those who died of illness or hunger in prisons and concentration or labor camps.

The coup d'état led by Francisco Franco on July 18, 1936 failed to carry a good part of the national territory, but it succeeded in a few areas: Galicia, Castilla La Vieja, Navarra, and parts of Aragón and Andalusia. The Civil War did not directly affect those areas for the rebels instantly took over. There was violence, however, as many leftists, freemasons, civil servants, Republican sympathizers, and teachers in Republican schools were assassinated. As Franco's forces conquered territory in the hands of the Republican government, they eliminated people who they felt were against the "national cause" in a systematic, organized fashion, as Francisco Espinosa has demonstrated (Espinosa Maestre 2010). On the basis of speeches and official documents of the new dictatorial regime, Espinosa argues that the physical elimination of the enemy was seen as a crucial part of their project to create a new Spain. Pelai Pagès is another scholar who has examined the rebels' policy of enemy extermination (Pagès 2009).

There was also violence in the Republican rearguard, especially during the first few months following the failed coup that converted the Republic into a failed State incapable of enforcing the law and Constitution over the entirety of the territory. People were assassinated for religious, political, and even economic motives. But there was no systematic project for the elimination of the enemy. Proof can be found in the investigations initiated by the Republican authorities once the revolutionary moment had passed in 1936 to identify those responsible for such assassinations, in many cases going as far as exhuming the cadavers. The investigations of judge Bertran de Quintana, given the task of investigating the assassinations in Catalonia, are one example that has been studied recently by Oriol Dueñas and Queralt Solé (Dueñas and Solé 2012).

Franco and his supporters used the victims to support their rendition of a "National Crusade" against the "Anti-Spain" personified by the Republicans who were presented as cruel, barbarian, and not even Spanish in their propaganda (Reig Tapia 2006). For this, enormous resources were invested to honor the memory of those who "fell for God and for Spain": monuments to The Fallen, street names, plaques on churches, statues, and so on. As Franco's troops advanced, they located, exhumed, identified, and gave proper burial to the supporters they had lost. Once the war concluded, those who died fighting for the victors were exhumed and reburied, and their deaths were used to justify the dictatorial regime's repression (Ledesma 2005). The cult of those who died "for God and for Spain" was an integral element of the nationalization project carried out by the regime.

The hundreds of thousands of Republicans who died in battle or were executed by Franco's supporters remained buried in common graves—whether at the site of battles or at locations where executions took place at dawn. They were not exhumed; they were left underground in imposed oblivion. Francisco Espinosa has noted how a decree in 1936 cunningly opened a way "to legalize disappearances" (Espinosa Maestre 2015: 93). For him it is found in the decree's justification: "A natural consequence of any way is the disappearance of persons, combatants or non-combatants, victims of bombardment, fire, or other causes related to the fighting."[4] The decree explicitly mentioned the difficulty of identifying bodies and authorized the inscription as casualties of those who disappeared or died during the struggle against Marxism or outside of it upon request by family members once five years had passed since the disappearance.

The problem was that the repression and social control exercised by the victors made it very difficult for families to approach the local civil registry in order to request that those they had lost be inscribed. Francisco Espinosa relates this difficulty to the fact that the civil registries continued to receive requests for inscription on the list of war victims from relatives for sixty years all over the country (Espinosa Maestre 2015). In many cases, the civil registry merely recorded as cause of death "violent death" or "death resulting from firearm injury" without further detail. Espinosa also observed that in some cases the relatives were instructed to record the death as resulting from "natural causes" in order to avoid association with the war and thus bury the memory of the victims even deeper.

---

[4] Decree 67 establishing the rules to follow for registering the death or disappearance of individuals that occurred as a result of the current national struggle against Marxism. BOE 27, 11 November 1936, 154.

Franco's necro-politics are part of a discourse about Spain's past that served his vision for the nation. The notion of a "Crusade" played a very important role in his reconstruction of national identity. The State and the law were both vehicles for historical memory that was in many cases based on myths and falsifications, one that hid the cruelty of Franco's troops, the Falange, and the alliance with foreign powers such as Nazi Germany and fascist Italy.

This memory of the war is carried on through monuments, textbooks, and documentary films such as the obligatory newsreels that were played in cinemas that refer to the foundational moment of the dictatorship. From the outset of the dictatorship, references were made in the law to the past and the war, but there were also decrees regarding more trivial matters that made reference to the regime's founding moment.

The political and legal framework established by Franco was able to survive for almost forty years by adapting as circumstances changed. Its adaptability enabled it to survive when the Axis was defeated in 1945, when monarchist sectors protested in the 40s, and when deep changes in the Spanish economy and society occurred in the 60s. At each turn, the State renovated its discourse and law with eliminating the original fundamental elements.

The transformation of the discourse used to legitimate the State in the 1960s stands out. The regime capitalized on the 25th anniversary of the war's end to promote its new discourse, one in which the former version of the war was not replaced—the notions of *Caudillaje* (rule by political strong and charismatic leader), Catholic nationalism, and the notion of the war as foundational moment were all maintained. New discursive elements were introduced, however, that referred to "peace," stability, and economic growth. The notions of the regime's legitimate origin and the National Crusade were combined with one about the legitimacy of the regime's governance: the peace and stability thathad made it possible for Spain's economy to take off.

The references to the war did not disappear but they did undergo a significant change that was illustrated on April 1, 1964, the day of Franco's victory that was baptized the day of Spain's 25 Years of Peace. A major publicity campaign organized to commemorate the twenty-fifth anniversary of the regime's victory was the platform for the new version of history used to legitimate the regime in the 1960s and 1970s (Fernández Crehuet 2008: 3–12; Aragoneses 2009). The word "peace" (*paz*) began to appear in the names of streets, schools, and other institutions—including the hospital where Francisco Franco would pass away eleven years later. The references to the Civil War as a Crusade continued but they were now accompanied by references to the Spanish Peace that followed a "war between brothers." This discourse has successfully maintained its way to the current day. In it the blame for the war is not attributed to the mutiny of 1936 but rather to all Spaniards and the dictatorship is presented as the successor to 100 years of republicanism and civil wars.

The promotion of this version of history had begun several years earlier, during the final phases of the construction of the monument known as the Valley of the Fallen. This monument's construction, originally projected to take one year, had lasted twenty before its official inauguration on April 1, 1959. As Queral Solé explains, over the two decades of construction, there were changes of project managers, new elements were introduced that had been absent from the original plans, and, most importantly, a decision was made in 1957 by the Works Council to bring in the remains of people who had died fighting for the Republic—"reds" (Solé 2008). The Works Council of the Valley of the Fallen sought the help of the *Guardia Civil*—the national police force—for help locating common graves in several provinces from which they excavated cadavers and moved them to the monument.

Following instructions, the remains were transported in special urns that were placed inside the basilica. This required the involvement of businesses, workers, and public authorities. It took help from civil authorities, the national police, municipal governments, and associations for families of the victims of Franco's supporters. Theoretically, bodies were only to be moved with the family's permission, but the fact that many families only learned of the transfer in 2013 from a documentary film produced by Catalonia's public television channel or articles in the press is proof that this requirement was not met (Solé 2008: 73). As Solé has shown, the remains 10,001 people are known to have been transported to the Valley of the Fallen before it was inaugurated in 1959 (Solé 2008: 82). After the inauguration, however, remains continued to arrive for some time. Bringing in the remains of Republicans accomplished the operation's objective: for all those who had fallen for God and Spain to rest in peace together with all the "brothers" who had erroneously fought during the war.

Transporting Republican remains to the monument made sense in the circumstances and the new message of "peace" and "reconciliation" with which the dictatorship attempted to reach closer ties with other European countries. "Operation Fallen" thus played a role in adding legitimacy of exercise to regime's existing discourse of legitimacy of origin. It remained, however, a complete farce: neither peace nor reconciliation had been achieved; there was only a dictatorship that continued to pursue the same objectives in 1964 as it had in 1939—the defense of a particular social order, the repression of those who represented an "Anti-Spain," and a nationalization project led by The Falange and conservative Catholics.

10.3   Amnesty and Oblivion (1975–1982)

Francisco Franco died of thrombosis in the Hospital of "La Paz" in Madrid on November 20, 1975. Curiously, the founder of The Falange, José Antonio Primo de Rivera, also died on November 20, some 39 years earlier. The coincidence fueled rumors that the dictator's life had been artificially extended in order to provide the basis for the so-called "day of sadness" to connect the memories of the two historical figures.

After the funeral and burial in the Valley of the Fallen, Juan Carlos was crowned Head of State as stipulated by the dictatorship's law.[5] Shortly afterward, pressure from broad swaths of society and economic elites to join the European Economic Union would lead to the dismantlement of Franco's State (Sánchez Cuenca 2014). Spain's transition to democracy was not free of fear or violence, as was recently shown by Sophie Baby: more than 600 people died of violence between terrorist attacks from both the left and the extreme right, assassinations by paramilitary groups, and deaths at the hands of security forces (Baby 2013). The State maintained control over the transition at each instant in order to avoid disruptive lapses, as Sánchez Cuenca has shown (Sánchez Cuenca 2014). The transition ended with the promulgation of the 1978 Constitution and the electoral victory of the Spanish Socialist Worker's Party in 1982. Between the two events there was an attempted coup d'état on February 23, 1981 that, although it failed, affected the transition's conclusion as well as the way the new democratic regime looked back at the past.

Many authors have highlighted the pact of silence that kept out discussion of the victims of the Civil War and dictatorship during the transition. Francisco Espinosa speaks of a "policy of oblivion" in reference to the years between 1977 and 1982 and of a "suspension of memory" from 1982 until 1986 (Espinosa 2010). Rafael Escudero argues that democracy was obtained in exchange for a "silent path" regarding the victims (Escudero 2014). Margalida Capellà focuses on the failures to comply with the principles of justice, truth, and reparation during the Spanish transition (Capellà 2009) while Josep Maria Tamarit Sumalla speaks of a Spanish model that does not look backwards to the past and is based on a "transition without justice" (Tamarit Sumalla 2013: 61) Bartolomé Clavero, unflinchingly, speaks of "constituent amnesia" (Clavero 2014).

The amnesty law of 1977 marked and continues to characterize the relationship between Spanish law and Spain's Francoist past.[6] This law's first article grants amnesty for "all acts of political intent, whatever their result, that are typified as offenses or infractions."[7] This made possible the liberation of all political prisoners, many of whom had been punished on the basis of laws and a police and court system that violated human rights. But the second article added that also included in the amnesty were "the offenses and infractions that might have been committed by the authorities, officials, and agents of the public order that might have been the motive

---

[5] Ley de Sucesión en la Jefatura del Estado, BOE 208, 27.07.1947, pp. 4238–4239; Ley 62/1969, de 22 de julio, por la que se provee lo concerniente a la sucesión en la Jefatura del Estado", BOE 175, 23 July 1969, pp. 11607–11608.

[6] Ley 46/1977, de 15 de octubre de Amnistía, BOE 248, 17 October 1977, pp. 22765–22766.

[7] The law established different types of amnesty depending on the nature of the offense. According to the norm, amnesty was granted for "(a) All actions of political intent, whatever their result, categorized as offenses and infractions carried out prior to December 15, 1976. (b) All actions of the same nature carried out between December 15 1976 and June 15, 1977, when along with the political intent there can also be discerned the motive of reestablishing political freedoms or demands for autonomy from the peoples of Spain. (c) All actions of identical nature and intent as in the preceding paragraph carried out up until October 6, 1977, on condition that no serious violence against life or the physical integrity of persons resulted.

or occasion for the investigation and prosecution of actions covered by this Law." In other words, the amnesty also protected those who carried out the dictatorship's grave violations of human rights.

The law therefore blocked any investigation of any type of offense: the torture of detainees that took place in the 1970s, the mistreatment of protestors in the 60s, and the assassinations carried out in the 30 s and 40s. The last remaining victims of the dictatorship were granted freedom but the transition that came with it was conditioned on amnesty for the crimes of Francoism. This law blocks any attempt whatsoever to bring to trial people believed responsible for human rights violations and, in the words of Rafael Escudero, opened the path to impunity (Escudero 2014). Alejandro Baer believes that victims and legislators "opted for a tacit agreement to leave the legacy of the war and the dictatorship out of the political debate," a strategy that he called the "pact of silence" (Baer 2011: 98). I believe that it was partly due to the discourse that treated the war and dictatorship as natural occurrences given Spain's turbulent history and partly due to the fear of a violent conflict that led a good part of society to put their demands for justice on hold, just as other demands for collective rights were also temporarily withdrawn until the democratic regime was consolidated.

In parallel to the political transition playing out, the Republican victims of the Civil War began to attain timid recognition as such in the face of the law. In April 1976 a Royal Decree[8] established that the soldiers of the Republican Army had the same rights as those granted to Franco's troops by the Law for War Casualties passed in March of that year.[9] Although the benefits were originally only granted to the "nationalist casualties," in the end it was also extended to the injured Republican soldiers. In 1979 another law was passed to ensure access to healthcare and pharmaceuticals for the victims of the war on both sides and their families, although the families of those executed after receiving death sentences or those who had died as a result of "violent action on the part of the victim" were excluded.[10]

These norms are clearly insufficient and only in certain cases satisfied the rights of the victims. The norms also equated soldiers loyal to the Republic with the rebel soldiers. Yet they represent the first steps toward a policy that recognized victims' rights. This should be kept in mind given the context of the transition. These norms do not alter the assessment of the policy towards the dictatorship's treatment of the victims, which never addressed the victims' demands.

Neither the Spanish Constitution nor the new legal regime made any pronouncement regarding the dictatorship. As Antonio Baylos has observed, the drafters of the constitutional text decided not to define the dictatorship as a permanent state of

---

[8] Decreto 3025/1976 of 23 December regulating pensions for those Spaniards who suffered mutilation due to the war and could not enter in the Cuerpo de Caballeros Mutilados de Guerra por la Patria. BOE 9, 11 January 1977, 522.

[9] Ley 5/1976, of 11 March, of 'Mutilados de Guerra por la Patria'. BOE 63, 13 March 1976, 5209–5215.

[10] Ley 5/1979, of 18 September concerning pensions, medical, pharmaceutical, and social assistance for the benefit of widows and relatives of Spaniards who died in the past civil war. BOE 233, 28 September 1979, 22605–22606.

exception and, therefore, the previous regime's repressive judicial decisions formally remained in force (Baylos 2008: 188).

In the years after its approval, the recently created Constitutional Court took decisions to establish how the law of the democratic regime should read the laws of the dictatorship.

In 1982 the high Court passed judgment in a case initiated by Juan Bautista Santaella, a former member of the Republican Army who, in 1979, had solicited the recognition of his rights in accordance with the 1936 decree that regulated them. The Constitutional Court decided that the Francoist 1936 law remained valid and that at the time Franco was dominant it was the valid law and that, therefore, the law of the Republic could not be considered as valid or in force.[11] The Court observed that this was "the hard reality of history" that could not be forgotten.

Indirectly, then, the highest interpreter of the recently approved Constitution recognized the full legality of the law of the dictatorship, despite its illegitimate origin, and moved the Republican legal system outside the bounds of the democratic regime's law.

In 1983 the Constitutional Court faced a similar case. An association of aviators of the Second Republic demanded their right to enjoy the same rights as those granted by the dictatorship to their aviators. In this case, the Court decided that it should apply norms that only recognized the rights of the nationalist aviators and that it did not have the competence to correct the omission the legislators committed while regulating the rights of officials of the Republic.[12]

These two decisions do not only put in question the validity of an illegitimate legal system, but also, in addition, they helped, according to Antonio Baylos, normalize the dictatorial past within the new democratic regime (Baylos 2008: 188). Although the magistrates of the time were aware of the debates over the validity of the illegitimate law, they did not consider that the issue should be considered in the Spanish case. So it was decided that no pronouncement on the nation's dictatorial past should be made in the law of the democratic regime, which created a narrative void that was occupied by the old version elaborated in 1964, the version about the war between brothers and the "peace" Franco brought, a version that treated the war, the dictatorship, and the thousands of people that were victims of it, as natural occurrences.

10.4 Democratic Consolidation: Legal Silence (1982–1999)

The democratic transition, as I have noted, was deeply marked by the amnesty for the dictatorship's crimes and by the pact of silence regarding the past. As the transition advanced, the fear that violence might break out explains why the pact of silence was reached and the demands for justice put off until democratic institutions

---

[11] Decision of the Constitutional Tribunal 28/1982 of 26 May, BOE 137, 9 June 1983, 19–21.

[12] Decision of the Constitutional Tribunal 63/1983 of 20 July, BOE 189, 9 August 1983, 21657–21659.

could be consolidated. But in 1984 the State turned its back definitively on the past. The Socialist Party's victory in 1982 supposedly represented the consolidation of democracy but it brought with it the closing of any path towards justice, truth, and reparation. This is surely related to the attempted coup of February 23, 1981.

There were private initiatives to exhume and rebury with dignity bodies from common graves and to identify others and recuperate the memory of the victims. Their number is unknown and the support from government administrations has been practically null. There was no initiative by the government or Parliament, although they have approved some norms for the granting of pensions to former Republican soldiers. A veil of silence was brought down. Spain was able to join the European Economic Community, experienced significant economic growth, and the successive administrations developed laws for the exercise of individual freedoms that the Constitution had established.

There were only two norms that recognized victims' rights. A 1984 law explicitly recognized the rights of members of the Republican police and armed forces.[13] In 1990 a disposition of the General State Budget Law included economic compensation for a limited number of former political prisoners: those who had spent more than three years in prison and who at the moment of the law's passing were at least 65 years of age.[14]

I have only found one case in which victims of the dictatorship successfully brought a case to court in this period—the *Ruano* case. Enrique Ruano was a student in Madrid who died in police custody in 1969. The government presented his death as resulting from a suicide attempt. In 1995, his relatives filed a complaint against the officers in whose custody Mr. Ruano died. The defendants pleaded innocence and demanded application of the amnesty law. Their motion was accepted on condition that the policemen acknowledge that the crime had been committed for political reasons. The defendants would not accept this condition but were still acquitted for lack of evidence.[15] The decision from the Provincial Court of Madrid nonetheless opened a path by which the amnesty law could be used to determine whether assassinations carried about by Francoists were political in nature. Unfortunately, this path was never explored further in any other case.

The State's silence over its past did not provoke much protest from Spanish society. Spain's entry into the European Economic Union in 1986, economic growth, and the recently obtained freedoms all contributed to a cultural shift in which the unresolved questions about the past were secondary. The new cultural moment was masterfully portrayed in the novel *La Buena letra* ("nice handwriting"), by Rafael Chirbes, that tells the story of a Republican family who gradually abandon their ideals and memories as their economic prospects brighten (Chirbes 2007). This new reality can also be seen in many of the films of Pedro Almodóvar, in which we see a modern, open Spain, removed from and indifferent to the past (Delgado 2014: 33).

---

[13] Ley 37/1984, of 22 October, recognizing the rights and services to those who were members of the Armed Forces, Public Order Forces of the Republic. BOE 262, 1 November 1984, 24433.

[14] Ley 4/1990, of 29 June, of General State Budget for 1990. BOE 156, 30 June 1990, 18669–18710.

[15] Audiencia Provincial de Madrid, Auto, 19 December 1995.

The passivity of the Spanish legislators and judges in the face of the country's dictatorial past contrasts sharply with the reaction of the Spanish legal system to human rights violations that took place in other parts of the world. Judges from the National Court initiated criminal proceedings against former officials in Chile and Argentina invoking universal jurisdiction. While these cases were very distant geographically speaking, the behavior of the Spanish judges might have helped change the perception at the turn of the century in Spain regarding its own past crimes.

10.5 "The Grandchildren's Revolt" (2000–2016)

The novel *Blutorangen* by Verena Boos is a marvelous portrayal of the change in the cultural memory of Spain that took place towards the end of the twentieth century (Boos 2015). Boos's narrative follows the daughter of a soldier in the Blue Division that fought alongside German forces in the Soviet Union during WWII. She goes to study in Munich on the Erasmus program. There she meets and becomes friends with descendants of Republican soldiers. The encounter reveals her country and her family's history to her, forcing her to question the silences that characterize both, a process that leads to involvement in the historical memory movement.

Maite, the protagonist, represents paradigmatically what Margalida Capellà coined "the grandchildren's revolt" that began in 1999 when a transgenerational movement, but one with a preponderant number of grandchildren of Civil War victims, mobilized for truth and justice. It was in 1999 that the journalist Emilio Silva traveled to Priaranza de Bierzo in the province of Léon to dig up—literally—the common grave where his grandfather was buried after being executed by nationalists in 1936. With the help of friends and relatives he managed to exhume the bodies of his grandfather and twelve others who had been executed. The remains were identified using DNA samples and the help of forensic scientists from Chile and the Balkans with experience in exhumation.[16]

An article in the New York Times brought the story to the world's attention, stirring many people to travel to Léon to see firsthand the operation and even to help with the exhumation. The visibility that the work attained and the creation in the year 2000 of the Association for the Recuperation of Historical Memory (*Asociación para la Recuperación de la Memoria Histórica*, hereinafter the ARMH) by Emilio Silva and others marked the beginning of a new phase in the relationship between Spanish politics, society, and the victims of the Civil War. It was the beginning of "the grandchildren's revolt." The way the victims, the dictatorship, and even the Valley of the Fallen were seen all began to change.

This transversal, intergenerational movement—one in which elderly witnesses of the dictatorship's repression and youth who challenged the official memory of their country's history played leading roles—was comprised of separate organizations

---

[16] For more on the exhumations and their international impact, see: Tremlett (2008).

that were founded and spread throughout the national territory. Their demands and objectives were fundamentally the following: justice for the victims, knowing the truth about their final resting place and the circumstances leading to their deaths, and economic, symbolic, or political reparation. These three objectives were manifested in demands to excavate common graves and perform proper burials, to annul the legal standing of military commissions that had been used to legalize the deaths of Republicans, and an end to the culture of impunity that was evident not only from the lack of any criminal prosecution of Francoists, but also in the indifferent assimilation—when not active defense—of the dictatorship's lasting presence in political organizations, in street names, even in some cities' public monuments and the Valley of the Fallen itself, "one of the most outlandish monuments of Spanish National Catholicism" in the words of Francisco Ferrándiz, an expert in common graves (Ferrándiz 2011: 481).

The exhumation of common graves may have been initiated privately by descendants of the victims but it became a phenomenon in the media that carried a heavy emotional charge. We should not forget that in many cases the descendants of the victims were seeing the remains of their loved ones for the first time. They felt the necessity to give a proper burial to the remains in order to close the cycle of mourning. The emotionality and the meaning of the exhumations for the younger generations generated a new political culture, as Ferrándiz observed, that was not necessarily tied to a particular ideology or political party (Ferrándiz 2016: 248). Despite the political or ideological profile of certain associations such as the Memory Forum (*Foro de la Memoria*), the ARMH evolved into a transversal movement unaligned with any party that advocated, notwithstanding, a new political cultural and new historical memory.

The impulsion of a new political culture by the exhumations forced the public institutions and also the legal order itself to address the popular reaction to the 'discovery' of one hundred thousand cadavers that until then lacked any political dimension. At the same common graves were being exhumed in locations across Spain,[17] a few associations were filing motions before the Supreme Court to annul the decisions of courts and military commissions that had distorted the law in order to maintain the legality of assassinating the regime's opponents.[18] Complaints were also lodged requesting that honor be restored to those who had fought against the nationalists during the Civil War and against the Nazis in World War II.

The social pressure forced legislators, government officials, and courts to issue some response. The response was timid at first, at least until the legislative elections of 2004, after which they became bolder. In November 2002, the lower house of Parliament approved a resolution—not a law—affirming the moral recognition of all men and women who suffered repression in the Civil War and under Franco.[19]

---

[17] "Spaniards at Last Confront the Ghost of Franco", New York Times, 11 November 2002.

[18] "Familiars d'afusellats durant el franquisme demanen al Suprem la revisió dels seuscasos", CCMA, 09 November 2006.

[19] Proposition without the force of law on the moral recognition of all men and Women who suffered repression under the Francoist regime for defending freedom and professing democratic convictions, BOCG-Congreso de los diputados 448, 29. November 2002, 12–15.

The resolution approved not only called for moral recognition but also reparations. Another interesting aspect of the resolution is how it spends more time praising the transition and its "spirit of harmony and reconciliation" than describing the suffering of the victims or condemning the 1936 coup. In fact, the resolution goes so far as to declare "the practically unanimous vote of the legislature for the Amnesty Law of 1977 was a historical event, for it put an end to the conflict opposing the two Spains, that will be buried there forever."[20] This phrase conveys enormous value to the amnesty law inasmuch as it is seen as ending the long history of civil wars, military coups, dictatorships—basically political regimes or systems based on the violent imposition of an ideology or form of government.[21]

We see, then, how the first responses to the movement for historical memory from the legal and political spheres reflected a culture that viewed the transition as a sort of foundational myth without taking into account the lack of justice for the dictatorship's victims. Yet the demands from social groups continued, and the legislators gradually adapted their discourse to them.

Through a decree passed in the year 2000, the Catalan government recognized the right of those imprisoned under Franco to compensation.[22] These rights were broadened in 2002. In 2003, an institution was created (*Direcció General de Memòria Democràtica*) that financed research and victim recognition projects as well as a network of memorials located in Catalonia.[23] It was also during these years that the first legal commemorations of the Holocaust appeared.

Article 54 of a Catalan Statute (Regional Constitution) passed in 2006 obliged the Catalan government to work to further and maintain the knowledge and memory of pro-democratic forces in Catalonia as a collective heritage. In 2007 the government thus created *Memorial Democràtic* whose mission was the elaboration of public policies on historical memory to recuperate, commemorate, and propagate the memory of democracy's advocates.[24]

Following the 2004 elections, the Spanish government and Parliament also addressed the matter. In 2005, President José Luís Rodríguez Zapatero paid an official visit to the concentration camp at Mauthausen where more than 7000 Spanish were deported. A statute was passed to officially designate 2006 the year of historical memory.[25] That is also the year that elaboration began for a law that would respond to the demands of victims and associations.

---

[20] Ibid., 13.

[21] Ibid.

[22] Decret 330/2002 de 3 de desembre pel qual es regulen les compensacions econòmiques de les persones menors de 65 anys el 31 de desembre de 2000 que van patir privació de llibertat i que es troben incloses en els supòsits previstos a la Llei 46/1977, de 15 d'octubre, d'amnistia, DOGC 3777, 9 December 2002.

[23] Llei 13/2007 del 31 d'octubre del Memorial Democràtic, DOGC 5006, 12 November 2007, 45172–45180.

[24] Llei 52/2007 of the Democratic Memorial, DOGC 5006, 12 November 2007, 45172–45179.

[25] Ley 24/2006, de 7 de julio, sobre declaración del año 2006 como Año de la Memoria Histórica, BOE 162, 08 July 2006, p. 25573.

The debates over the law, which took place in a climate of palpable tension, were particularly intense. Conservative politicians and figures in the media after having been removed from power in the 2004 elections, accused the ruling PSOE of "breaking the spirit of the Transition," the authentic foundational myth of Spanish democracy.[26] One metaphor that was very common held that the "wounds from the War" should not be reopened.[27]

Lastly the Parliament approved Law 52/2007 that recognized broader rights and established mechanisms to aid those who suffered persecution or violence during the Civil War or dictatorship.[28] The law is commonly known as the "Law of Historical Memory." Strictly speaking and following the definition by Antoon De Baets, it is not a memory law because it does not prescribe or proscribe a determined reconstruction of the past (De Baets 2017: 38). The law increased pensions, regulated the presence of symbols in public spaces, and determined the appropriate compensation for prison sentences served for being Republican.

There is condemnation of the coup and dictatorship in the law's preamble, but only indirectly. The authors refer to "the content of the report of the Council of Europe Parliamentary Assembly signed in Paris on the 17th of March, 2006" that condemned the broad and serious human rights violations committed by Franco's regime between 1939 and 1975.[29] Such an indirect approach was certainly adopted because of the political tension in the background of the law's passing, and this tension would also explain the references to the spirit of the transition came along with the recognition of victims' suffering.

In a first place the resolution issues a declaration regarding the repressive criminal sentences of the Franco regime. The law does not annul these judgments but Article 2.1 affirms that they were "unjust and illegitimate." Article 3 declares that the organs that issued the judgments were also illegitimate. As Escudero observes, the law leaves the door open for nullification but does not itself nullify them, and thus fails to place them outside the legal ordering. The burden is placed on the victims who are still living or their families to file a lawsuit in court for their definitive annulment. In addition, according to the law, the victims of repressive sentences or their relatives may solicit a "reparation declaration of personal recognition."

Articles 11 and 14 of the bill regulate the treatment of the common graves that resulted from Franco's repression. Article 11 establishes the duty of administrations to aid "the direct descendants of the victims" in "the activities of investigation, location, and identification" of missing persons. Articles 12 and 14 prescribe the type of facilitation at the legal-administrative level to be provided for the excavations and obtaining the right to access the properties in question.

---

[26] 'El PP rechaza la ley de memoria y dice que rompe el pacto de concordia sobre el pasado', El País, 06 December 2007.

[27] 'Rajoy: Abrir heridas del pasado no conduce a nada'. El País, 06 October 2008.

[28] Ley 52/2007, de 26 de diciembre, por la que se reconocen y amplían derechos y se establecen medidas en favor de quienes padecieron persecución o violencia durante la guerra civil y la dictadura, BOE 310, 27 December 2007, pp. 53410–53416.

[29] Parliamentary Assembly. Council of Europe.Report of the Committee on Political Affairs and Democracy. Report. Document 10737. Rapporteur: Mr. Brincat.

The regulation did not satisfy the associations or certain sectors among jurists who believed that Spain, by delegating the exhumation of cadavers to the victims' relatives, was "outsourcing human rights" (Ferrándiz 2016) in a failure to comply with its commitments under international law. According to Margalida Capellà, investigating, locating, and determining the causes of death and the guilty parties in the case of common graves are all prerogatives of the State. Capellà emphasizes the important emotional burden born by the families obliged to organize and carry out the exhumations themselves (Capellà 2009).

Article 16 prohibits all acts of political character or glorification of the Civil War or dictatorship at the Valley of the Fallen monument. This stipulation put an end to the pilgrimages to the monument by groups nostalgic for the past dictatorship who regularly gathered at the monument every November 20 to commemorate the deaths of Franco and Primo de Rivera. The law does not, however, determine the space's ultimate purpose; it only says that it will be regulated and managed according to the norms for places of worship and cemeteries.

10.6 The Implementation of the Memory Law (2008–2016)

As it progressed, the memory law became less and less attractive to the associations, activists, and jurists who had pushed for it. Notwithstanding, it also provided an incentive for people to file claims, undertake the exhumation of common graves, and opened space for governments at the local and autonomous province level to develop their own laws for eliminating Francoist symbols from the spaces over which they held jurisdiction.

In 2006, some of the victims' associations filed a complaint before the National Court—the organ that had investigated the crimes of Chilean and Argentine dictators—against individuals responsible for repression under Franco. The judge Baltasar Garzón took up the case and issued the famous "Resolution of October 8, 2008" (*Auto del 8 de octubre del 2008*) that initiated a legal investigation into the presumed crimes against humanity committed by the rebel troops starting July 18, 1936. An order was issued to identify those who might have been guilty, among them Francisco Franco and his generals. This sparked opposition from certain political sectors and even from prosecutors, who in another resolution argued that those crimes had been covered by the 1977 amnesty law.[30] While this judicial battle was still underway, another judge, Santiago Pedraz, ordered the exhumation of several victims whose remains were located in the Valley of the Fallen at the behest of family members who had filed motions with the help of the ARMH.

In December 2008, Judge Garzón dropped the investigation citing the questions over the National Court's jurisdiction, which did not have the competence to judge crimes against humanity committed inside national borders and passed the case to

[30] Recurso a las diligencias previas 399/2006 del Juzgado Central de Instrucción n° 5 (sumario 53/08).

regional courts. His renunciation had the effect of ending the exhumations ordered by Judge Santiago Pedraz but did lead to some other lawsuits that are either dormant today or have been archived.

In response to the case opened by Garzón, associations on the extreme right filed a complaint before the Supreme Court for the presumed offense of perversion of justice as described in Article 404 of the Criminal Code that sanctions civil servants or authorities who issue decisions with the knowledge that they are illegal. One of the arguments of these associations was that the crimes Judge Garzón was investigating had been proscribed by the 1977 amnesty law, and thus took up the arguments of dissenting prosecutors of the National Court despite the fact that many other jurists felt the amnesty law did not cover the crimes in question.

The Supreme Court's decision, 101/2012, handed down on February 27, 2012, is interesting because it marks a turning point in the investigations of crimes committed by Franco's regime. The Court ruled that no perversion of justice had been committed by opening the investigation of crimes committed by under Franco's regime but that doing so had reflected "an erroneous interpretation of legality." The collegial organ praised the "model transition" that had made passing the amnesty law possible, a law that blacked any judicial investigation of the crimes from the period. The high court continued by saying "the search for truth is a pretention as legitimate as it is necessary. It is a task that corresponds to the State through other organisms and should involve the participation of all the disciplines and professions, especially historians. But it does not correspond to judges."[31]

The decision represented an important step in the process of giving new meaning to the common graves and pursuing justice for the victims' families. It basically closed down the path to prosecution through the criminal law for families' seeking the legal system's help to discover the true causes of their relatives' deaths. In Escudero's opinion, the Supreme Court's decision contradicts the international law doctrine on forced disappearances that establishes the State's duty to investigate disappearances even when punishing those responsible is not possible (Escudero 2014: 124).

In 2012, the Supreme Court thus closed, at least temporarily, the path to justice through criminal law. Yet the cadavers obstinately continued to attract the attention of relatives, social movements, and communication media. The exhumations went on as well as the media coverage of them in the local and foreign press. A special envoy from the UN who visited Spain in 2014 also denounced the human rights abuses suffered by the victims' families.[32]

Particularly interesting are some other lawsuits that despite a lesser degree of impact in the media relate directly to the theme of the common graves dating from the Franco regime. In May 2016 a judge opened a path to exhuming cadavers from the Valley of the Fallen.[33] In July of the same year, the ARMH notified the national

---

[31] Sentencia del Tribunal Supremo 101/2012 de 27 de febrero.

[32] Report of the Special Rapporteur on the promotion of Truth, Justice, reparation and guarantees of non-recurrence, Pablo de Greiff. *Mission to Spain*. New York 2014.

[33] "Un juez abre la puerta a exhumar los cadáveres en el Valle de los Caídos", El Mundo, 09 May 2016.

police force that it had found two common graves in the vicinity of Léon.[34] These actions illustrate the new strategy adopted by the historical memory movement to provoke the intervention of Courts of justice in the exhumations. In addition to the positive social effect this has had on the families, the shift seeks to provoke an official reaction to the crimes.

The Spanish Parliament that took office following the 2011 general elections did not repeal the historical memory law but it did eliminate the clause stipulating a budgetary allocation for its implementation, which left important parts of the law without effect. Moreover, reforms in the laws regulating education that were pushed through by the government reduced the amount of attention given to the Civil War and increased the attention that teachers were to devote to the Second World War.[35]

This new policy with regards the country's past was developed in parallel to the dismantling of the historical memory law. For three consecutive years, the budget for the exhumations was reduced to zero.[36] Something similar had occurred in Catalonia, hitherto a pioneering force in public policy on historical memory, following their 2010 elections, Catalan government and parliament drastically reduced, although they did not eliminate, the budget for democratic memory, and also shifted towards treating equally the victims on both sides of the conflict.[37]

10.7 The Current Moment: Dominant and Subaltern Memory

At present, it is possible to speak of a dichotomy between the discourse on the past that has been developed in Spanish law and that developed by basically three autonomous communities, Catalonia, the Balearic Islands, and Andalusia. On one side, several state laws have been passed that contain historical references, but their object is the Holocaust or the Second World War. On the other side, the parliaments of the three autonomous communities cited have deepened their recognition of the rights of victims of the Franco regime through legislation that are part of a historical interpretation that negatively views the dictatorship.

---

[34] "La ARMH denuncia ante la Guardia Civil hallazgo de dos fosas en León", La Vanguardia, 21 July 2016.

[35] Ley Orgánica 8/2013, de 9 de diciembre para la mejora de la calidad de la educación (LOMCE), BOE 295, 10 December 2013 pp. 97858–97921; Real Decreto 1105/2014, de 26 de diciembre estableciendo el contenido básico de la educación secundaria, BOE 3, 03 January 2015, pp. 169–546; Real Decreto 126/2014, estableciendo los contenidos básicos de la educación primaria, BOE 52, 01 March 2014, pp. 19349–19420.

[36] The full answer can be found on the Spanish Government website: www.lamoncloa.gob.es (Last accessed 1 November 2017).

[37] Accordingly, in 2015 a resolution was passed that treated victims of violence in the Republican rearguard and those of Francoism on the same level without distinguishing the differing circumstances between the two. 'El Memorial dóna veu als monistrolencs que van patir la guerra civil'. Regió7, 7 May 2015.

The interest of legislators in the Holocaust derives from what Daniel Levy and Natan Sznaider have called the "global culture of memory" in which the Holocaust serves as a cornerstone (Sznaider and Levy 2002). Both authors have observed recent contributions from institutions in many countries in the construction of a cosmopolitan memory that is independent of the country's relationship to the historical episode. The tendency to include the Holocaust in official discourses on the past can be seen in Spain starting in 2005,[38] although it has gathered more force in the past few years.

In 2014, the Organic Law for Improving Educational Quality called for including the "Jewish Holocaust" in primary and secondary school curricula.[39] The Royal Decrees that implemented the law and established the pedagogical content at the secondary[40] and primary[41] levels introduced the Holocaust as an obligatory subject in all schools. Strangely, that same norm did not consider that the deportation of Spanish prisoners to Nazi concentration camps warranted attention, as it did not pertain directly to the Shoah, because the number of deportees was relatively low (9500 according to the database constructed by Catalonia's Democratic Memorial[42]), and because it was not deemed to have very much pedagogical potential. Regardless, the law demonstrates the interest of the legislators in linking the collective memory of the Holocaust to the Spanish state and society.

Then, in 2015, another law was passed making it possible for Sephardic Jews with ties to Spain to obtain Spanish nationality.[43] This law also represents an attempt to connect Spanish law with the memory of the Holocaust. In its preamble, reference is made to the "brutal sacrifice of thousands of Sephardic Jews" as an "imperishable bond that connects Spain to the memory of the Holocaust."[44] It is therefore a law that incorporates a version of the past excluding any consideration of the relationship of Franco's dictatorship with Nazism and the Holocaust, a relationship that was ambivalent at the very least (Aragoneses 2016).

Something similar occurred when the Spanish Parliament implemented a directive of the Council of Europe from November 28, 2010 that covered punishment for denying the Holocaust.[45] The reform introduced a new Article into the Criminal Code, Article 501.1.c, which sanctions those who "publicly deny, seriously trivialize, or

---

[38] See Baer, 'The Voids of Sefarad'.

[39] Ley Orgánica 8/2013, of 9 December, to Improve Quality of Education (LOMCE). BOE 295, 10 December 2013, 97858–97921.

[40] Real Decreto 1105/2014, of 26 December establishing the basic content of Secondary Education. BOE 3, 3 January 2015, 169–546.

[41] Real Decreto 126/2014, establishing the basic content of Primary Education. BOE 52, 1 March 2014, 19349–19420.

[42] For more info see www.memoria.gencat.cat (Last accessed 1 November 2017).

[43] Ley 12/2015 of 24 June granting Spanish citizenship to Sephardim originally from Spain. BOE 151, 25 June 2015, 52557–52574.

[44] Ibid., 52558.

[45] Ley Orgánica 1/2015, of 30 March modifying the Ley Orgánica 10/1995 of 23 November of the Criminal Code, BOE 77, 31 March 2015, 27061–27176. See chapter by Luigi Cajani in the present volume.

glorify crimes of genocide, against humanity, or towards persons and goods protected in circumstances of armed conflict."[46]

All of these norms follow the general tendency in that they generate or reinforce a certain version of past events. In the Spanish case, what is surprising is that these references in the law to the past do not also refer to the Civil War, Francoist repression, or even the deportation of Spanish citizens to Nazi camps. The progression of memory law at the national level contrasts with the development at the level of the autonomous parliaments that, in the face of the inaction at the national level, sought own their own to address the crimes of the dictatorship and rights of its victims.

The first of these laws dates from 2009, thus well before the latest developments at the national level. That year the Catalan parliament approved Law 10/2009 of June 30 "on the location and identification of the persons who disappeared during the Civil War and Franco dictatorship, and rendering dignity to the common graves."[47] The law was designed to establish assistance to the families of victims and victims' associations in locating and exhuming the remains in the common graves in Catalonia from the Franco period. The law grants competence to the Catalan government for overseeing the process of locating and digging up the graves, regulates the circumstances in which third parties may undertake such operations, and determines the assistance to be provided to the associations or families that carry out exhumations. It also establishes the process for informing the appropriate judicial authority when human remains are found during exhumation (Article 7.6). The Catalan legislation represented a significant step forward but its application has been subject to budgetary restrictions. Hence, it was only after a long period during which the government did not carry out any exhumations that in 2016 an ambitious "plan for the location and exhumation of graves" was presented.[48]

Another important law at the autonomous community level was that of the Balearic Islands parliament, Law 10/2016 of June 13 "for the recuperation of persons who disappeared during the Civil War and under the Franco regime."[49] This law, which was unanimously passed, is interesting because its Article 10 qualifies forced disappearances as crimes against humanity and requires that the judiciary be informed of the possible whereabouts. This rule distinguishes itself from the Spanish memory laws and the Catalan ordinance on common graves by qualifying some of the crimes committed by the Francoist regime as crimes against humanity and by calling for judicial intervention in those cases.

---

[46] While a 1995 reform of the criminal code had previously specified Holocaust denial as a crime, a 2007 decision of the Constitutional Court declared this article void for violating fundamental rights: (Rubí Puig and Salvador Coderch 2008).

[47] Llei 10/2009 de localització I identificació de persones desaparegudes Durant la Guerra civil I el franquisme, DOGC (Diari oficial de la Generalitat de Catalunya) 5417, 09 July 2009, pp. 55065–55071.

[48] Information about this plan can be found at the webpage: www.fossesirepressio.cat (Last visited July 12, 2017).

[49] Llei 10/2016, sobre recuperació de persones desaparegudes Durant la Guerra civil i el franquisme, BOIB (Butlletí Oficial de les Illes Balears) 76, 16 June 2016, pp. 18241–18247.

In March 2017, the Andalusian parliament approved, after much deliberation, Law 2/2017 of March 28, on Historical and Democratic Memory in Andalusia.[50] After an extensive preamble that details the experience of Andalusia during the Second Republic, under Franco, and through the transition to democracy, Article 3 of the law recognizes the right to the truth, the right to knowledge of the history of the Andalusian people's struggle for liberty, to investigations of the persecution that the Andalusians suffered, and to reparation.

It establishes the responsibility of the government of Andalusia in locating, exhuming, and identifying victims (Article 5), and in recording all the data from and maps of the common graves. Formulas are given for victim reparation (Articles 15 and on) and for proper documentation and access to it (Articles 25 to 27). Unlike the Catalan and Balearic laws, the Andalusian law does not stipulate judicial involvement in the exhumation of the graves.

Finally, in July 2017, the Catalan parliament approved another law which, like the Balearic law, was passed unanimously. The "Law for the legal reparation of the victims of Francoism" represented a change in the approach to this issue in that it took up the matter of the nullity of the decisions issued by repressive organs under Franco.[51] The law, which grew out of an initiative from one of the historical memory associations, declared the judicial decisions of the military courts in Catalonia between 1938 and 1978 void. It affirms that their illegality is "in accordance with the overall legal ordering, which includes norms from international law as well as internal law" on the basis of which the offenses violate the law and "the most elementary requirements of the law for fair judgment." From their illegality, "the nullity, be it original or occasional, of all the sentences and resolutions issued from court cases or war commissions based on political arguments in Catalonia by the Francoist regime." This extensive citation of the bill's only article shows its reach and potential for the legal deconstruction of the dictatorship and the satisfaction of victims' rights.

The law affirms, on the basis of rights already in force, the illegality of the repressive organs of the dictatorship. The law in force is not cited but we can imagine that it includes norms from international law and the historical memory law that declared those organs to be illegitimate. The nullity, original or eventual but not specific, of the judgments in question derives from their illegality. The reason why the law is able to affirm something as 'already in force' in 2017 but not in 2008 following the passing of the historical memory law can be explained by the transformation in the culture of memory that made possible the unanimous promulgation of the Catalan law that expressly established the nullity of the decisions that had been declared unjust by the 2007 law. This law is only valid in Catalonia but it is possible for other autonomous communities and even the Spanish Parliament to pass similar legislation.

---

[50] Ley 2/2017, de 28 de marzo, de Memoria Histórica y Democrática de Andalucía, BOJA 63, 03 April 2017, 11–41. En internet: http://www.juntadeandalucia.es/boja/2017/63/1 (12 July 2017).

[51] Llei 11(2017) de 4 de julio de reparació jurídica de les víctimes del franquisme.

10.8   Conclusions

If, as argues Christian Giordano (Giordano 1996), the actualization of the past represents one way institutions and political projects are legitimated, it seems clear that an
official version of the recent past in Spain, one based on broad consensus, is missing.
State law wavers between remembering the Holocaust and ignoring the victims
of Francoism. At the same time, society and some institutions at the autonomous
community level have been generating alternative renditions that broaden recognition
of the victims and configure collective memory as a social value.

   If a sort of palimpsest of legal cultures was produced under Franco, some aspects
of which survived the transition to democracy, perhaps we should now speak of a
palimpsest of cultures of memory, for it does not appear that the State will, in the
short term, incorporate a version of the past that resembles the versions adopted in
Catalonia, the Balearic Islands, or Andalusia. It remains to be seen whether it is
possible for such a plurality of historical interpretations, some contradictory, will
impede or generate consensus and legitimacy around the law.

References

Aragoneses, A. 2009. El derecho bajo el franquismo. Transformaciones del sistema jurídico español
    (1936–1978). In *Represión política, justicia y reparación: La memoria histórica en perspectiva
    jurídica (1936–2008)*, ed. Margalida Capellà and Ginard David, 123–139. Palma: Documenta
    Balear, S.A.
Aragoneses, A. 2016. Convivencia and filosefardismo in Spanish Nation-building, Max Planck
    Institute for European Legal History Research Paper Series No. 2016–05. Available at https://
    papers.ssrn.com/sol3/papers.cfm?abstract_id=2798054. Last accessed 1 November 2017.
Aragoneses, A. 2017. Legal silences and the remembrance of Francoism in Spain. In *Law and
    Memory. Towards Legal Governance of History*, ed. Uladzislau Belavusau and Aleksandra
    Gliszczynska-Garabias, 175–194. Cambridge: Cambridge University Press.
Baby, S. 2013. *Le mythe de la transition pacifique. Violence et politique en Espagne (1975–1982)*.
    Paris: Casa de Velazquez.
Baer, A. 2011. The Voids of Sefarad: The Memory of the Holocaust in Spain. *Journal of Spanish
    Cultural Studies* 12: 95–120.
Baylos, A. 2008. Derechos económicos e indemnizaciones derivados de la memoria histórica. In
    Derecho y memoria histórica, ed. José Antonio Martín Pallín and Rafael Escudero, 185–208.
    Madrid: Trotta.
Boos, V. 2015. *Blutorangen*. Berlin: Aufbau.
Cajani, L. 2017. Legislating History: The European Union and Denial of International Crimes.
    In *Law and Memory. Towards Legal Governance of History*, ed. Uladzislau Belavusau, and
    Aleksandra Gliszczynska-Garabias, 109–128. Cambridge: Cambridge University Press.
Capellà, M. 2009. Represión política y derecho internacional: una perspectiva comparada (1936–
    2006). In *Represión política, justicia y reparación*, ed. Margalida Capellà and David Ginard,
    161–254. Palma: Documenta Balear, S.A.
Chirbes, R. 2007. *La Buena letra*. Barcelona: Anagrama.
Clavero, B. 2013. *El árbol y la raíz*. Barcelona: Editorial Critica.
Clavero, B. 2014. *España 1978: La amnesia constituyente*. Madrid: Marcial Pons.

De Baets, A. 2017. The United Nations Human Rights Committee's View of the Past. In *Law and Memory. Towards Legal Governance of History*, eds. Uladzislau Belavusau and Aleksandra Gliszczynska-Garabias, 29–47. Cambridge: Cambridge University Press.

De Giorgi, R. 2004. Rom als Gedächtnis der Evolution. In *Rechtsgeschichte: Zeitschrift des Max-Planck-Instituts für Europäische Rechtsgeschichte* Rg. 4, 142–161, 143. Online at http://dx.doi.org/10.12946/rg04/142-161. Last accessed 1 November 2017.

Delgado, L. E. 2014. *La nación Singular: Fantasías de la normalidad democrática española (1996–2011)*. Madrid: Siglo XXI.

Dueñas, O. and Solé, Q. 2012. *El jutge dels cementiris clandestins. Josep M. Bertran de Quintana, 1884–1960*. Barcelona: Gregal.

Escudero, R. 2014. Road to Impunity: The Absence of Transitional Justice Programs in Spain. *Human Rights Quarterly* 36: 123–146.

Espinosa Maestre, F. 2010. *Violencia Roja y Azul. 1936–1950*. Barcelona: Crítica.

Espinosa Maestre, F. 2015. *Lucha de historias, lucha de memorias*. Sevilla: SL Aconcagua Libros.

Fernández-Crehuet, F. 2008. Recht und Fiktion im Franco Regime. In *Franquismus und Salazarismus: Legitimation durch Diktatur*, eds. Federico Fernández-Crehuet and António Manuel Hespanha, 3–12. Frankfurt am Main: Vittorio Klostermann.

Ferrándiz, F. 2011. Guerras sin fin: guía para descifrar el Valle de los Caídos en la España contemporánea. *Política y Sociedad* 48 (2011): 481–500.

Ferrándiz, F. 2016. From Tear to Pixel. Political Correctness and Emotions in the Exhumation of Mass Graves of the Civil War. In *Engaging the Emotions in Spanish Culture and History*, ed. L. E. Delgado et al., 242–261. Nashville: Vanderbilt University Press.

Fukuyama, F. 1992. *The End of History and the Last MAN*. London: Free Press.

Giordano, C. 1996. The past in the present. Actualized history in the social construction of reality. *Focaal*, 26–27: 97–107.

Hartog, F. 2012. *Régimes d'historicité*. Paris: Présentisme et expériences du temps.

Ledesma, J.L. 2005. La "Causa General": Fuente sobre la violencia, la Guerra Civil (y el franquismo). *Spagna Contemporanea* 28: 203–220.

Pagès, P. 2009. La represión franquista durante la guerra civil. In *Represión política, justicia y reparación. La memoria histórica en perspectiva jurídica (1936–2008)*, ed. Margalida Capellà, and David Ginard, 19–42. Palma: Documenta Balear, S.A.

Preston, Paul. 2012. *The Spanish Holocaust*. London: Harper Press.

Reig Tapia, Antonio. 2006. *La Cruzada de 1936. Mito y memoria*. Madrid: Marcial Pons.

Rubí Puig, A., and Salvador Coderch, P. 2008. Genocide Denial and Freedom of Speech Comments on the Spanish Constitutional Court's Judgment 235/2007, November 7th. *INDRET* 4. Available at: www.indret.com/pdf/591_en.pdf. Last accessed 1 November 2017.

Sánchez Cuenca, I. 2014. *Atado y mal atado. El suicidio institucional del franquismo y el surgimiento de la democracia*. Madrid: Alianza Editorial.

Solé, Q. 2008. El Valle de los Caídos o la petrificació del franquisme. *Revista de Catalunya* 304: 82–88.

Sznaider, N., and D. Levy. 2002. Memory Unbound: The Holocaust and the Formation of Cosmopolitan Memory. *European Journal of Social Theory* 5: 87–106.

Tamarit Sumalla, J.M. 2013. *Historical Memory and Criminal Justice in Spain. A Case of Late Transitional Justice*. Cambridge and Antwerp-Portland: Intersentia.

Tremlett, G. 2008. *Travels Through a Country's Hidden Past*. London: Walker & Company.

Alfons Aragoneses is Professor of Legal History at the University Pompeu Fabra (Barcelona) and affiliate researcher at the Max Planck Institute for European Legal History (Frankfurt am Main). He obtained his PhD at the University of Girona. He has made research on Francoist Law, transitions and memory laws and also on Private Law. He has recently participated in the elaboration of the law on reparation of Francoist's victims by the Catalan parliament.

Chapter 11
The Failed Reconciliation: The Role of the Judiciary in Post-fascist Italy and the Togliatti Amnesty

Antonella Meniconi

Abstract The 1946 could be seen as a watershed for the Italian transition. In that year the Amnesty issued by the communist Minister of Justice, and secretary of the Italian Communist Party, Palmiro Togliatti, represented a crucial passage towards a new pacific order. Not just because it took place few weeks after the proclamation of the Italian Republic, with the victory of the referendum of 2 June, but also for its general significance: to come to terms with the recent past for a country just sorted out from the war and the fascist regime. The paper focus on: (1) the failure of the purge phenomenon, especially concerning higher ranks of the judiciary involved with the dictatorship (Court of cassation, Appeal courts, Ministry of justice), which were implicated in the purge processes as judges and as defendants; (2) the transitional justice, implemented in 1944–1946 by the High Court of justice for Sanctions against Fascism and the Special Courts of Assize, that were special tribunals, but under the control of professional judges; (3) the wide application of amnesty to fascist collaborators and hierarchs. Finally, it will be stressed that transitional justice was an important but controversial moment on the road back to democratic life and the primacy of law in Italy.

> The whole of Italy rushed from one end of the country to the other in cattle cars and little trucks, in a continuous voyage that was a discovery, an adventure, a revelation to everyone. People who had never moved in their whole lives were traveling, and a completely new land, a different Italy, opened before their eyes.
>
> (Levi 1951, 278)

A. Meniconi (✉)
Department of Literature and Modern Cultures, University of Rome, La Sapienza, Italy
e-mail: antonella.meniconi@uniroma1.it

© Springer Nature Switzerland AG 2021
C. Paixão and M. Meccarelli (eds.), *Comparing Transitions to Democracy. Law and Justice in South America and Europe*, Studies in the History of Law and Justice 18,
https://doi.org/10.1007/978-3-030-67502-8_11

11.1   Introduction

A "different" Italy, a "completely new country" is what, in 1945, appeared to the intellectual and politician Carlo Levi, author of *L'orologio* (translated as *The Watch* in 1951), the novel that best depicts the transition in Italy from Fascism to democracy. It is a vivid and poetic account of those difficult but fascinating years and it focuses on the end of 1945, the crucial moment of transition for Italian history when the illusions generated by the Resistance had to reckon with the inertia of continuity and pre-existing interests. It was, in fact, in the first days of December 1945, that the government of Ferruccio Parri,[1] expression of the Committees of National Liberation (CNL) and of a very clear desire for institutional and moral regeneration, fell, and with it—it was said—stopped the "wind from the North" (the area where the partisan struggle had been stronger in 1943–1945). Subsequently, on 10 December, a new government was formed led by Alcide De Gasperi, leader of the Christian Democrats (*Democrazia Cristiana*, a Catholic-inspired centrist party that went on to become the dominant party for almost half a century), in which the anti-Fascist parties still participated, in particular, Palmiro Togliatti, secretary of the Communist Party (*Partito comunista italiano*) who held the position of Minister of Justice. It was, above all, a troubled period from the point of view of the material needs of the population emerging from the war. The tendency of the new government was to mitigate a general initial anti-Fascist intransigence, given that the future institutional structure was being defined in a difficult dialectic with the monarchy and the Allies. It sought "pacification" to "make the fragile plant of democracy take root" (Woller 1997: 13). A "new" country, perhaps, but not entirely "different", then (to quote again Levi).

It is significant that historiography focuses on the theme of transition almost at regular intervals, in moments of crisis or in acute phases of change when the gaze turns to the past, to what could have been and has not been. This is especially true in the Italian situation. For example, in the period of protest in the 1960s and 1970s, criticism of the failure to purge Fascists from the new Italian state and the persistence of the Fascist order in the young Republic certainly had an impact on the beginning of research when Claudio Pavone, Guido Quazza and Guido Neppi Modona began to raise the issue of the continuity of Fascist institutions and public officials (Neppi Modona 1973, 1984; Pavone 1991, 1995). Analysis was resumed in the 1990s when the political system drawn up by the post-war parties went into crisis, and the concept of transition began to be elaborated, in part thanks to new archival sources and new studies on memory and oblivion. Finally, from 2000, once again in conjunction with the almost definitive disintegration of the forces that had contributed to the creation of modern Italy and new archival discoveries, there have been important studies on transitional justice, considered a significant category also at the European and world level (Teitel 2000; Franzinelli 2002; Giustolisi 2004; Focardi and Nubola 2015; Bolzon and Verardo 2018; Nubola et al. 2019, Marini 2019, among others). The unanswered questions that have been raised and the current lines of research

---

[1] Prime Minister from 21 June to 10 December 1945.

indicate the willingness to understand the critical issues and problems of the present by analysing—as often happens—the missing or misguided decisions of the past.

In this context, 1946 can certainly be regarded as a real watershed for Italian transition from Fascism to democracy. It was, in fact, this year that saw the amnesty determined by De Gasperi's government and realised by Togliatti (and came to be known as the Togliatti Amnesty), and it represented a crucial change towards a new desired order of reconciliation, not only because it was declared a few weeks after the proclamation of the Italian Republic (which followed the referendum held on 2 June between monarchy and republic), but also because of the role it played in bringing closure to the past in a country emerging from war and the Fascist regime. Past and future were inextricably linked in 1946, since it was also the year that saw the work of a new constitutional design in the new Constituent Assembly, also elected on 2 June.

The Togliatti Amnesty can be considered an attempt to reconcile the country after the civil war. It primarily addressed the crimes committed by representatives of the puppet government set up in September 1943 in the German-controlled north called the Italian Social Republic (RSI) and known as the Salò Republic, as well as collaborationists, and partisans, but it also caused a general change in the political, social and cultural climate which led to the perception that the resistance period had really ended, so much so that many wanted to consider the 20-year period of the Fascist regime an obscure historical parenthesis (as Benedetto Croce, a leading Italian intellectual wrote in the aftermath of Fascism).

To judge each case, while also taking into account the overall picture, was the Italian judiciary, which found itself in a somewhat ambiguous situation. Only minimally purged of its own members who had been most closely tied to the Fascist regime, the judiciary body had to deal with confusing and contradictory regulations that were thrown together over time as well as with politicians who were divided among themselves about the direction that the so-called "defascistisation" (a term that was borrowed not incidentally by the Allies) should take. It was no surprise that under those conditions, transitional justice was administered in an oscillating and, ultimately, disastrous manner.

This chapter will address the role of the judiciary in the transition period both from the "internal" point of view, concentrating on the purge, as well as the most important question of the "external" point of view, highlighting the concrete judiciary implementation of amnesty regulations and sanctions, and finally will offer a conclusion.

11.2 The "Impossible" Purge of the Judiciary

From 8 September 1943 (when Badoglio forced by the Allies announced the armistice throwing Italy into a state of confusion and German occupation), the judiciary quickly found itself subject to the anti-Fascist purge, from which it was clearly not excluded.

From the first provisions it was stated explicitly that the judges could not be guaranteed tenured positions as had been specified in the *Statuto Albertino* of 1848 (the constitution of the time).[2] It was not by chance that the slogan "*Ancora e sempre: Epurare la magistratura*" ("Once again and always: to purge the judiciary") appeared in one of the numerous publications that came out following the fall of the Fascist regime.[3] Other articles denounced the failure to renew the institutions of the Ministry of Justice, with the continuity of officials that had been involved in, among other things, the so-called Race Court (*Tribunale della razza* instituted by the fascist racial laws of 1938–1939) such as Gaetano Azzariti (head of the legislative office) and Antonio Manca (head of personnel).[4] Then again, the anti-Fascist front was not unified even on this issue, judging by the column in *Il popolo clandestino* (the newspaper of the Christian Democrats) in 1944 that affirmed that "most of the judges had fought from the beginning of the dictatorship, in the field of anti-Fascism".[5]

The purge of the most compromised judges was not decisive and history has by now shown that it was limited to few cases. Only about 400 judges, out of a total of more than 1000 cases that were examined, were subjected to a process of purging, which is equal to about 10% of the entire judiciary corps. Of these, only a few dozen were actually expelled from the judiciary corps, while others preferred going into early retirement, although some of these returned to the judiciary in later years (Saraceno 1999: 521; Cardia 2014).

More generally, after the first "ascending" phase of the anti-Fascist purge (begun in December 1943, and then again from the summer of 1944 and the first half of 1945) that saw thousands of civil servants on trial, the new De Gasperi government toned down the efforts for a more radical purge of the state apparatus, starting the "descending" or retreat phase with the liquidation of the High Commission for Sanctions against Fascism (the *Alto commissariato delle sanzioni contro il fascismo*) in February 1946.[6] To be sure, in November 1945 about one hundred of the most compromised officials had been removed from the government due to "interest of service" (Domenico 1996; Canosa 1999).[7] In regards to the judiciary body, there were protests and condemnations of the "attack on the independence of the judiciary" by the National Association of Judges (*Associazione nazionale magistrati*, the ANM) as soon as it had re-formed, while silence and reticence about the past, which had led to exemptions from work, were what was generally and tacitly adopted. (Scarpari 2008: 115).

---

[2] Art. 11 r.d.l. no. 29/b of December 28 1943 (modified by r.d.l. no. 101 of April 12 1944).

[3] "L'intransigente. Settimanale politico", 12 maggio 1945.

[4] E. Colozza, *Dal Tribunale Speciale a quello della Razza*, in *L'Italia del lavoro*, 2 luglio 1945, in Fondazione Istituto Gramsci, *Fondo Palmiro Togliatti*, Serie 2: Scrivania di casa, Sottoserie 1: "Settore 3": attività istituzionale e di partito, b. 10.

[5] *Rinnovare l'amministrazione della giustizia*, a firma IUDEX, in *Il popolo*, ed. romana, 23 gennaio 1944, cit. in Pavone (1995: 130).

[6] D.Lgt. no. 22 of February 8 1946.

[7] D.l.Lgt. no. 716 of November 9 1945; see also d.Lgt. no. 702 of November 9 1945.

The "softer" phase culminated with the Togliatti Amnesty of 1946, which, although did not directly concern public officials, irreparably marked the end of the purge (Melis 2003: 17; Meniconi 2017). Among the causes of its failure are: the overall inefficiency of the structures set up for the purge, an insufficient number of investigating offices, the succession of confused regulations, and the nature of judging in a purge in which—as underlined by Massimo Severo Giannini—it was difficult to prove that "the generic Fascist sentiments of the majority of the public officials could be translated in one of the criminal behaviours identified by the legislator" (Giannini 2008: 285).

For the most part, firmly at the helm of the judiciary remained the veteran officials who had been most strongly influenced by their close relationship with the Fascist regime. Despite various attempts by the political forces most closely tied to the Resistance, in the De Gasperi government prevailed the desire not to break with the establishment, even at the cost—as Togliatti underscored in the Council of Ministers—of "having non-democratic people in the higher ranks of the judiciary".[8] The majority of new politicians, even those on the left, believed that a radical reform of the upper ranks of the judiciary was impossible given the conditions in the country, because even in the middle ranks (whose personnel was younger and had been educated and trained during the Fascist period) the modality, style and behaviour typical of the authoritarian regime had taken root. They chose instead to trust the authorities who had proven experience and skill even though they were not of an equally democratic leaning.

In a highly hierarchical career, the judiciary corps had gone through the Fascist period in most cases (apart from a few notable exceptions) displaying a mix of conformism and a pronounced focus on juridical technicalities. These features had allowed the judiciary to accept and apply the most repressive laws of the dictatorship (for example the anti-Jewish laws of 1938 to which only very few judges raised even the slightest opposition). Moreover, almost all judges were card-carrying members of the Fascist party (Meniconi 2012: 143–243). Indeed, the judiciary body had never argued with the regime about its authoritarian foundation, instead it provided the Fascist state its technical-judicial expertise.

Busy with defending themselves from the accusations that were made against them, the upper echelons of the judiciary naturally refused to confront their own and Italy's Fascist past (Neppi Modona 1997: 97; Soddu 2001). They justified their choices (in their judgements and the language they used without shame in hundreds of public occasions) by necessity and declared themselves uncompromised by politics, which although had often been the case had not stopped the daily functioning of the judiciary working along the lines of the regime without ever upsetting its equilibrium. In actual fact, as was affirmed in one the few decisions of exemption from service made by the ministerial purge commission—"it was not possible to differentiate the technical participation/input from the political one, at least at the

---

[8] Archivio centrale dello Stato, *Verbali del Consiglio dei ministri, luglio 1943–maggio 1948*, edizione critica, a cura di A.G. Ricci, *Governo De Gasperi 10 dicembre 1945–13 luglio 1946*, VI, 1, 178 (18 January 1946).

highest level, even though (he) had collaborated with the construction of the 'works of the regime' in exchange for undeserved promotions or other gains" (Meniconi 2015a).[9] Paradoxically, the same people having survived the regime and avoided the purge would now lead the transition period of the judiciary of the new republic.

Nor was there a renewal of the judiciary system, which remained as Minister Grandi had wanted in 1941 apart from some important "surgical" modifications. Togliatti's law on guarantees in 1946 eliminated all or almost all the most repressive regulations from the preceding law, but maintained unaltered the rules regarding careers, promotions, and the modality of selection of officials, all of which were salient questions for the judicial profession.[10] Moreover, two other elements of continuity with the existing law remained: the rigidity of the hierarchical structure which was reconfirmed by the supervisors' powers of monitoring their subordinates, and the power of disciplinary action that remained in the hands of the Minister (who was now supported by the Public Prosecutor of the Court of Cassation), while arbitration was entrusted to the Disciplinary Court (called for in the previous decrees) and to the disciplinary tribunals (which were now created). The "external" independence of the judiciary and the public officials from the executive power was recognised but the internal organisation of the judiciary remained the same (Neppi Modona 1986: 294).

Another significant fact is that the judges were included, thanks to their positions, in the purge commissions of various administrations (as had been required by specific regulations) thus creating for them a sort of an ambiguous double role (summarised by the rhetorical question "who is purging whom") while conferring on them an irrefutable centrality (Neppi Modona 1997: 84–85; Focardi 2005: 63). The point is that after all was said and done, in an administrative structure of several hundreds of thousands of people only 10,000–20,000 employees were purged, too few as well as not in the right way (Melis 2020: 410–419). The situation was summed up by Gaetano Salvemini's ardent words written on 13 February 1945 to his anti-Fascist friend Ernesto Rossi:

> The situation in Italy is such that you can't see how the basis of a democratic rebirth can be laid. The army, the bureaucracy, the judiciary is all in a state of putrefaction. How can you "purge" if the majority of purgers need to be purged? (Rossi and Salvemini 2004: 56)

These are recurring sentiments in these months together with a certain dejection that was spread among those who knew the reality of Italian institutions, their viscosity and their tendency to resist change. From the pages of *Il Ponte* in November of 1945 even the jurist and lawyer Arturo Carlo Jemolo asked himself, somewhat rhetorically, if another choice would have been possible, and since the answer was no, there was then no new governing class ready in that moment and capable of taking charge of the vital nerve centre of the state (administrative and judicial corps, armed forces and universities) without "risking destroying the bone structure" of the county already ruined by the war (Jemolo 1945: 284).

---

[9] Archivio centrale dello Stato, *Ministero della giustizia., Direzione generale dell'organizzazione giudiziaria, Epurazione*, busta 5, fasc. 39.

[10] Rdl no. 511 of May 31 1946.

On the other hand, one must not omit to mention that in the months between the winter of 1943–1944 and 25 April 1945 the fight against the Nazi-Fascist forces saw an active and courageous involvement of many judges, both individually and as a collective. In northern and central Italy many organised resistance groups were formed such as the one in Piedmont (led by Giorgio Agosti, Alessandro and Carlo Galante Garrone) and in Veneto (led by Giovanni Colli). In the vivid account by Domenico Riccardo Peretti Griva (the key figure in northern Italy) emerge exemplary figures of judges who built the web of the Resistance in the judiciary concentrated above all in Turin where judges from all of northern Italy congregated (Peretti Griva 1956: 29 ss.). Many of them were killed in retaliation by the Nazi-Fascist forces, such as judge Mario Fioretti in Rome (Consiglio superiore della magistratura 1976).

Peretti Griva would go on to participate in the anti-Fascist purge as a High Commissioner (*Alto commissario dell'epurazione*) from July to December 1945, and then, disappointed from this experience, he returned to Turin to hold the position of the first president of the Court of Appeal until 1952 when he was sent into retirement (Meniconi 2017: 73–85).

In Rome, based on party representation, a National Liberation Committee (CLN) inside the judiciary was formed, almost as a projection of the judiciary as an "autonomous body" in the same CLN. Its members included: Michele Fragali (future constitutional judge from 1960 to 1969), Paolo Silvio Migliori, Nicola Picella (soon to be secretary of the Presidency of the Republic), Salvatore Zingale, Romolo Gabrieli (in 1944 prosecutor in the trial against the members of the Fascist Court for the Defence of the State, *Tribunale speciale per la difesa dello Stato*), Italo D'Abbiero and Andrea Lugo (who became a state councilor in 1947, Melis 2006). Moreover, there was widespread refusal to swear allegiance to the Salò Republic, and it was because of this that the Minister Piero Pisenti was forced to drop his demands, after having repeatedly called for it in various places. (Meniconi 2012: 241–243; De Nardi 2016).

11.3 A Special Justice?

From the beginning, in 1944, questions about the exceptionality of the laws and trials against high-ranking Fascists were at the centre of the political as well as the doctrinal debate. An example of this was the difficult enactment of the document that was fundamental for the sanctions against Fascism, the quickly and ironically dubbed Magna Charta of "defascistisation", that is the *luogotenenziale* decree no. 159 of July 29 1944 that, among other things, was aimed at bringing the Fascist leaders to trial and instituting the ACGSF in Rome (Woller 1997).

It must be kept in mind that the whole system of sanctions against Fascism, in reality, would be imposed by the Allies who were in military control of Italy, and, as has been authoritatively claimed in the years immediately following this period, would have been the demonstration of "an overall historical incomprehension in general" and of "the Italian things in particular". According to this perspective, the

Allies were in the grip of an "abstract stuffy bourgeois Protestant mentality" that did not take into account that it would be very demanding and difficult to bring about the "disinfestation" of Italy in order to arrive at a "democratically clean" body (Bracci 1947: 1096).

In any case, according to the documents and accounts from the time, already starting from the meeting held on 31 March 1944, the text of the Magna Charta was in fact the result of a complex operation of mediation and work on various drafts by the three ministers (Ettore Casati, Vincenzo Arangio Ruiz and Umberto Tupini) that took place between Brindisi and Salerno (Badoglio governments)[11] and Rome (first Bonomi government).[12] It was indeed a complex period for the functioning of institutions in Italy; following the fall of Fascism and the removal of Mussolini (25 July 1943), the Italian government left Rome the same day as the announcement of the armistice with the Allies (8 September 1943) and until the liberation of Rome (4 June 1944) it had established itself in various areas of liberated and war-torn Italy following the advance of the Allies (first Brindisi, then Salerno, until at last Rome).

Coming back to the 1944 Magna Charta decree, there were, obviously, other important factors: the aforementioned determining influence of the Allies (who were not satisfied with previous decrees) and the presence of jurists such as Enrico Altavilla, Ugo Forti and, from a distance, Enrico De Nicola. In particular, the former Minister of Justice in the first Badoglio government and first president of the Court of Cassation, Casati (Meniconi 2012) clashed with the new executive branch (second Badoglio government) in which the six parties of the CLN were now represented. In April 1944 Casati accused Badoglio and his "moderate" ministers of "being animated by a somewhat Fascist-leaning spirit" for their divergences on the document that he had drafted. Casati, the elderly president, wrote to Badoglio on 25 April 1944:

> I believe that if the new government, which assembles all the political parties and social classes, does not have the will or ability to prepare the judicial instrument in a timely manner in order that the purge takes place as Justice requires, the arduous task will be taken on by the Communist Party and it will be carried out in such a way as not to purge Fascism, but rather to suppress the middle class, held responsible for its advent and for its actions.[13]

In the end, as the result of the work of Casati, the *luogotenenziale* decree no. 134 of May 26 1944 (*Punizione dei delitti e degli illeciti del fascismo*) was issued, but, although not openly so, was considered too punitive towards the recent past of those who were governing at the time (Marshall Badoglio had been, in primis, Army Chief of Staff until December 1940).

In June 1944, the new minister, the jurist Arangio Ruiz, after further examination, managed to bring to an end "that hybrid project", whose application was defined, in fact, as "contorted and partial".[14]

---

[11] The first Badoglio government stayed in office from 25 July 1943 to 22 April 1944, the second from 22 April to 18 June 1944.

[12] From 18 June to 2 December 1944.

[13] Archivio centrale dello Stato, *Ministero di grazia e giustizia*, Gabinetto, b. 7.

[14] "Il Massimario penale", 1947, A. II, nn. 6–7, coll. 171–172.

The new decree, however, did not actually see the light of day until July 1944 (under the aegis of a "political" minister, the Christian Democrat lawyer Tupini). Like all legislation of the period, it was quite badly written with "lamentable formulas" (Calamandrei 1945: 285), in which multiple normative references to apply or to keep in mind become intertwined (for example the penal code from 1889 no longer in vigor, the wartime military penal code and the 1930 criminal procedure code for summary rite). It subsequently required numerous addendums and updates, as many as 40 decrees in a year (Giannetto 2003: 62). Perhaps this was unavoidable given the confusion of the period, but certainly it did not facilitate the exercise of jurisdiction.

In August of the same year in a manifesto published in *Domenica* (one of many of the newspapers that came out following the fall of Fascism) 18 Italian legal experts "of different political belief" had warned against abandoning "the great foundations of modern penal rights" in the sanctions against Fascism. Initiated by Jemolo, it was endorsed by, among others including Massimo Severo Giannini, Rosario Nicolò, Edoardo Ruffini and Guido Astuti (Giannetto 2003: 64; Colao 2015: 176). Moreover, an incessant debate accompanied each of the "too many" norms that were thrown together in the transitional period (see Meccarelli's chapter in this volume).

Despite the criticisms the government decided to go ahead with the implementation of the decree. The will of the more moderate forces and Allies prevailed not to make a "trial against Fascism, the monarchy and the conservative middle class" (as demanded by the socialists in particular), but rather to set up a normative, institutional, and uniform solution of the four branches of defascistisation ("Fascist crimes", "purging of the administration", confiscation of the "profits of the regime", and the liquidation of these profits) (Giannetto 2003: 61). In the Magna Charta it was decided to give the judiciary an essential role in all four of these branches.

The High Court of justice for Sanctions against Fascism (ACGSF) was created in July 1944 when it was still believed that this special justice could be restricted to a few people responsible politically and materially for the "catastrophe" of the Second World War and the civil war, while ordinary justice would be applied to the rest. The decisions to hold the court in Rome that had just been liberated and the fact that the judgements had no right of appeal at the Court of Cassation (a similar institution with the same name, *Haute Cour de justice* and functions was also created in France) were of symbolic and legal significance respectively.[15] The ACGSF, which begun working on 20 September, was comprised of "a president and eight members nominated by the Council of Ministers from high judges currently working or in retirement and from some other figures of irreproachable rectitude", while the High Commissioner for Sanctions against Fascism performed the functions of a public prosecutor.[16]

The decision to publicise the hearings and to put the crimes "on show" meant that the ACGSF was "quickly transformed into a staging of impunity". The anti-Fascist forces were not able to effectively manage the trials in front of a high court since they were facing internal struggles between old and new forces, with the latter ultimately prevailing and even managing to have appointed as president Lorenzo

---

[15] D.l.Lgt. no. 198 of September 13 1944.
[16] D.l.Lgt. no. 159 of July 27 1944.

Maroni, previously a councilor of the Court of Cassation and not exactly above suspicion with a Fascist past as late as 1943. Indeed, during a hearing he was rebuked by a defendant for "having worn the black shirt under the toga for the 20-year Fascist period" (Dondi 2004: 44).

Ultimately, in this court only the second tier Fascists would be put on trial. Moreover, some "excellent" escapes by defendants undermined the public trust in the AGCSF and, more in general, in the judiciary, held incapable of actually carrying out justice. In this context, there were some cases that caused a furor, like of the general Mario Roatta (once Chief of Staff of the Italian Army and head of the Fascist Regime's secret service, OVRA). He was on trial for the homicide of the Rosselli brothers, anti-Fascists killed in 1937 in France by emissaries of OVRA. Roatta escaped from prison between 4 and 5 March 1945 with the help and almost certain collusion of some officials of the government (while his accomplice Filippo Anfuso was already in hiding) causing "fierce" protests in front of the Quirinal (the seat of the Presidency of the Council of Ministers) and the Viminal (the headquarters of the Ministry of the Interior). Beyond specific incidents, a diffidence towards "legal" justice quickly grew in the anti-Fascist population, and it was probably this that led to the partisans eliminating Mussolini (28 April 1945) and the last Fascist leaders that should have stood trial in the ACGSF. Moreover, in 1945 a considerable number of the defendants and Fascist leaders before the Court were on the run (such as Giuseppe Bottai and Dino Grandi). In the same year the decision to abolish the judicial body derived from an almost unanimous judgement of its ineffectiveness (Dondi 2004: 32–33).[17]

Be that as it may, in November 1945, when the ACGSF concluded its work, its president Maroni presented its results in a report to Italian President Parri: out of 31 defendants judged in public hearings 27 were convicted (of which 14 received the death penalty and 4 were acquitted), and out of the 68 defendants judged in the council chamber 4 were convicted and 64 absolved (of which 23 died from natural causes). Therefore, there was a total of 31 convictions and 69 acquittals (from a total of 99 defendants in 16 trials that were held according to the rules of summary procedure), but the high number of fugitives reduced the punishments that were actually delivered. According to Maroni, given the complexity of the "questions of juridical, political and military nature" that the court had to face, the proceedings were carried out "in the highest orderly fashion and without significant incidents, despite the gravity of the charges, the animation of the arguments and their reverberation in public opinion" (Maroni 1947: 297). However, the cutting appraisal of the young Giannini on the operations of the ACGSF is more compelling: "they made a cruiser ship in order to fish sardines and tuna" (Giannetto 2003: 79).

Not even the affirmation "without significant incidents" appears a fair judgement in light of what happened during the first trial that was carried out at the ACGSF, that of the ex police commissioner Pietro Caruso for the massacre at the Fosse Ardeatine in Rome (which took place on the 24 March 1944). On 18 September 1944 after the rather tempestuous hearing held at the Court of Cassation in Piazza Cavour (badly

---

[17] D.l.Lgt. no. 625 of October 5 1945.

organised for managing an event of such importance for the city), the director of the Regina Coeli prison Donato Carretta was seized, beaten and lynched by the crowd (Algardi 1958: 82). It was no accident that the subsequent hearings of the trial, which concluded with the death sentence and then execution of Caruso, were carried out under stricter controls in a room in Palazzo Corsini (currently the location of the Accademia dei Lincei).

Previously in northern Italy with the civil war still raging, Peretti Griva (nominated clandestinely as head of the Piedmont judiciary of the CLN), in a memorandum of 15 August 1944 to the heads of the offices in secret communication with him, had already exhorted them about the necessity that "the people should already feel from the very beginning that justice exists, that members of the judiciary order are still present and in place, and that the work of claiming responsibility for innocent victims and punishment of the guilty parties is already taking place". He went on to say that the work of resisting judges should be centred on "the composition and the functioning of judicial bodies destined to apply penal sanctions for crimes of collaborationism". For the formation of these courts Peretti Griva had advanced a proposal of having Assize Courts (*Corti di assise ordinarie*) with anti-Fascist jurors from the community and non-appealable sentencing in an attempt to mitigate the "principle of legality and the continuity of the legal order" with certain realism. He advocated for maintaining the principle of procedural guarantees while opposing *ex post facto* penal laws, and considered possible the punishment of "traitors of the nation under the Fascist penal code".[18] In this vision, which was both resolute and strongly based on the defence of civil liberties, Peretti Griva clashed with the Piedmont CLN that was distinctly calling for a "political justice" and for "the people's courts" that operated in some parts of the country after they were liberated from Nazi occupation in a "very long 25 April" (the day recognised as Liberation Day in Italy) (Rovatti 2015: 16; Filippetta 2018: 143). Thanks to the esteem that Peretti Griva enjoyed in the partisan ranks a compromise was reached on 6 April 1945 with the insertion of two modifications to the CLN project: the nomination of the first president of the Court of Appeal by the presidents of the ordinary Assize Courts and the clarification that there could be no more than two women jurors in these courts (Peretti Griva was against having women jurors) (Neppi Modona 2017: 65).

In order also to block this project the government led by De Gasperi hastily issued a *luogotenenziale* decree (no. 142), on 22 April 1945 that had been in gestation for a long time and was influenced by the contemporary French model of the *Courts de Justice* (Galimi 2014: 205). The measure instituted the Special Courts of Assize (*Corti di assise straordinarie* or CAS) presided over by a judge, with the seniority of a Court of Appeal judge (fifth grade) or higher, and formed by four jurors extracted randomly by 100 people nominated by the CLN and subsequently reduced to 50 following a selection by the president of the court, and with the presence of a public prosecutor who was a part of the magistrature and nominated by the Public Prosecutor's office of the Court of Appeal or of a lawyer of "irreproachable" anti-Fascist faith nominated by the CLN (Neppi Modona 1984; Rovatti 2015: 21; Nubola 2017). In this new legal

---

[18] Peretti Griva, D.R. 1956. *Esperienze di un magistrato.* Torino: Einaudi, 35 ss.

framework the importance of the ordinary judges increased and was progressively reinforced by the introduction of the possibility of making an appeal (not foreseen by the Peretti Griva and the CLN projects) before a special temporary Section of the Court of Cassation instituted in Milan. This helped to bring the trials back into the fold of a justice that, if not quite ordinary, was at least not special or solely political.

Clearly, the decree also entrusted the "technical" duty of writing the verdicts to the judges of the CAS. It happened, then, that sometimes, using their juridical and professional expertise, the judges opposed the expressed will of the popular jury. Moreover, as denounced in 1947 by Giuliano Vassalli, at times it happened that not only did formal errors go uncorrected, but judgements were written in a way so that they would be annulled by the Court of Cassation (the so-called "suicidal sentences", a phenomenon that already existed in the past) (Vassalli 1947; Dondi 2004).

Nevertheless, the role of the CAS must not be underestimated. Between May and June of 1945 there were between 50 to 100 provinces in northern Italy where these courts were established, and until December 1947 (the end date of the last legal actions) the number of trials for "collaborationism with the German invaders" are estimated between 15,000 and 20.000. More precisely, from November 1945 (when the numbers correspond to the total) there were legal actions (both exhausted and pending) that concerned 21,454 defendants, of which 5,928 were convicted for collaborationism. For the death sentences, estimates oscillate between the figure of 259 made in 1952 by the Ministry of Justice and, according to more recent studies, between 500 and 550, while convictions that were actually carried out were 91 (Woller 1997: 434; Dondi 2004: 48).

Hundreds of defendants were brought to justice in a situation of conceivable material and operative difficulties tied to the functioning of the judiciary system in areas just liberated and to the risks of hurried investigations or the unfounded archiving of claims (Nubola 2017). It would seem that serving as president or public prosecutor in the CAS was not necessarily a sought-out role nor did it have positive consequences for one's subsequent career given the certain silence (both in the judgement of superiors or in other documents) about this experience that emerges from the judges' personal files. From the most recent historical studies it has emerged that leading and taking part in the CAS was a group of judges that was generally compromised very little by their relationship to the Fascist regime, but at the same time was similarly removed from the Resistance, apart from a few exceptions such as in Piedmont where they made up a small portion of the judicial body (10–12% of about 4000 judges) (Focardi 2019: 72).

Compared with the people's or partisan courts—institutions that functioned for a limited period—the CAS undoubtedly represent the first legal and institutional response to the crimes committed by Fascists during the war, differentiating themselves starkly from political justice, and, explicitly, from the Fascist Court for the Defence of the State (Dondi 2004: 33–39; Rovatti 2015: 33). The CAS were not therefore concerned with "special" justice even in the technical sense of the word, but rather were "special (bodies) of ordinary justice: specialised but not special judges", as the Court of Cassation would later confirm (Franzinelli 2006: 19).

What is more, this was taking place (as we saw with the case in Rome), in a climate that was still inflamed by the conflict and in areas of civil war; the violence that was a normal part of daily life inevitably reverberated in the courtrooms where the tragic nature of the events of the recent past were relived in an almost cathartic way through the accounts of the victims and witnesses. A climate steeped in violence and pain accompanied the debates and, at times, resulted in lynchings. Indeed, during these months in all of Italy the "map of lynchings (or attempted lynchings)" corresponds "generally to the areas of pain" of the Nazi-Fascist occupation; their occurrences refer dramatically to where the Nazi-Fascist massacres had taken place (Crainz 1995; Storchi 2008). In Italy (not only as it was a European phenomenon) 1945 and 1946 would be marked by the resorting to summary justice with killings of Fascists or people held responsible for crimes against the people or against partisans who had escaped "legal" justice" (Nubola 2017: 33 ss.).

The decision to institute the CAS (and before that the ACGSF), although technically imperfect from a normative point of view, can be explained by Togliatti's crude but significant words referring to the lynching of Carretta that had just happened: "The people's rage must be taken as it is, we shouldn't provoke it, rather, working quickly and with energy and justice, we should stop it from exploding. This is what we need to do."[19]

The variety of laws to apply, of behaviour that was adopted, of different courts present in the territory (from the courts of the Allies, to the military ones in central and southern Italy, including the Courts of Assize) makes it difficult to refer to a singular model of CAS or to an administration of homogenous justice throughout Italy (Focardi 2018: 91). One can, nonetheless, identify a tendency of how these courts acted, a tendency confirmed also by recent studies that concentrate on this form of transitional justice conducting a census of and cataloguing the judgements issued.[20] There was certainly an initial phase when the verdicts largely corresponded to the popular "will", to which the judges complied because they shared the restorative intent of healing (and not only of punishing) or due to pressure that the public exerted during the trials, with the risk of injustice. Moreover, it has been argued that "national history lessons" took place in the courtrooms (Woller 1997: 421), with the hearings, in some cases, transmitted by speakers to cram-packed piazzas. Nevertheless, it is evident that trusting trials to courts scattered throughout all the provinces in Italy did not allow for a clear and unequivocal recognition of guilt by the state in regard to crimes committed during the 20-year Fascist period and the Second World War, like in the Nuremberg trials of the Nazi leaders (Rovatti 2015). However, it has recently been shown that in many cases the judgements given, through the evaluations of the defendants and of those about this historical period, the argumentations and the language used by the judges in the rulings, did in fact express a "political"

---

[19] Togliatti, P. 1969. *Avanti verso la democrazia! Discorso al congresso della Federazione romana del Pci 24 settembre 1944*. In *La politica di Salerno aprile-giugno 1944–*, P. Togliatti, 96. Roma: Editori Riuniti.

[20] http://www.straginazifasciste.it/cas/.

condemnation of the Salò Republic beyond the expressed outcomes of conviction or acquittal (D'Alessandro 2019: 56).

A second phase began soon after as the Italian state's justice system gradually became reinstated in the liberated territories (although the process would not be complete in northern Italy until 1 January 1946). Especially during the revision of sentences, the judges had a tendency to rather quickly lean towards a moderate application of the new laws, requiring conditions for incrimination quite difficult to demonstrate (such as the casual connection between individual behaviour and the maintenance the regime's power) (Battaglia 1962: 79). This took place despite the circulars of the various ministers of Justice (Tupini and Togliatti) ordering the application of the legislation against Fascism "with velocity and rigour". In a message to the judicial body on 30 June 1945 the newly-appointed Minister of Justice and communist Togliatti hastened to entrust the Italian judiciary with the task of "creating public trust in the country" and of "making an enormous step forward on the road of rehabilitation and a return to a democratic order".[21] Moreover, at that time (30 June 1945, for example) meetings were held in Milan between the authorities of the Allies, the presidents of the Courts of Appeals of northern Italy and the representatives of the Ministry to establish the most uniform and effective direction possible for the individual CAS. From the archival documents it is clear that there was intense ministerial activity carried out in order to guarantee the minimal conditions for the functioning of the exceptional judicial bodies, even in the delicate phase of transition from the CAS to the special sections of the Courts of Assize in October 1945 (24 in Italy and they remained active until 31 December 1947) (Neppi Modona 1986: 299).[22] The breadth of the work of these courts can also be shown by the fact that from 1 January 1946 to 31 July 1947 out of 37,800 charges filed 37,335 investigations were carried out and 8,800 of which were brought to trial (Bracci 1947: 1106).

The Special Provisional Section of the Court of Cassation of Milan began working on 13 June 1945 and concluded on 12 November of the same year after having delivered 426 sentences. It comprised, among others, judges who had been expelled in 1926 from the judiciary body by the Fascist regime such as Vincenzo Chieppa and Giuseppe Badia (who had just been reinstated) and who were noticeably anti-Fascist, such as Mario Dalla Mura (Meniconi 2012: 173). In the appeals submitted to this body many judgements of the CAS were annulled when the "emotional climate (both due to popular pressure or the closeness of the subjects who were judged) had precluded the guarantees of a defence and had determined capital punishment", or the trials were moved to different courts from where the original ones had taken place (Franzinelli 2006: 30). When the Section of Milan ceased to function the pending trials were transferred to the Court of Cassation in Rome,[23] and were assigned to the Second Penal Section presided over by Vincenzo De Ficchy, a veteran judge who

---

[21] *Togliatti saluta la Magistratura italiana e invoca il ritorno ad un ordine democratico*, in "l'Unità democratica", 1° luglio 1945, 1.

[22] Archivio centrale dello Stato, Ministero di grazia e giustizia, Gabinetto, busta 9.

[23] D.l.Lgt. no. 625 of October 5 1945.

was already, albeit with scarce enthusiasm and effectiveness, head of the commission for the purge of the Ministry of the Interior (Franzinelli 2006: 57–61).

In Togliatti's opinion expressed in the Constituent Assembly, the Section of Milan had "brilliantly" fulfilled its task, while in Rome it became clear that "the spirit of the judiciary was no longer in touch with the spirit of the people, and so judgements had arisen that required revision".[24] Conversely, the ANM gave a positive evaluation of the transferal of the trials against collaborators to Rome; as one judge who had been a part of the so-called Race Court stated, there would finally be "a peaceful environment" where the judges "were intent on carrying out justice that was above the passions and biased resentments".[25] Very quickly the direction of the Second Section of the Court of Cassation changed and began to annul the CAS's sentences with inventive motivations, ending in exonerations even for judges of the Fascist Court for the Defence of the State (Vassalli 1945; Scarpari 2008: 116; D'Alessandro 2020).

In some cases, there was also an actual "counter-narrative of the past" (Woller 1997), so much so that the Second Section of the Court of Cassation in April 1947, confirming the acquittal determined by the Special Section of the Court of Assize of Bergamo in July 1946, went so far as to describe the Minister of the Salò Republic Piero Pisenti, who had unquestionably collaborated with the Nazis, "neither a Fascist nor an anti-Fascist, rather a simple patriot". In this emblematic trial (but also in others) the will of the judiciary played a role in absolving themselves together with their Minister, celebrating a painless transition from Fascism to democracy (Meniconi 2006: 310–312; Scarpari 2015: 167; Grilli 2019).

Another signal of this tendency of increasing leniency towards the defendants can be seen in, among other things, the recognition by the United Sections of the Court (*Sezioni Unite della Corte di Cassazione*) of the possibility of appealing against the ACGSF's sentences,[26] something that was not contemplated by the law (the right to make an appeal would be introduced only later by a decree in May 1947) (Barile 1947: 1072–1073).[27] This appears even stranger (and more serious) if we consider that in this case the mutation of the Court's direction concerned the sentence by the ACGSF for the homicide of the Rosselli brothers for Anfuso and others, in violation of the principle of *res giudicata* and, ultimately, led to a new "ordinary" trial in Perugia that absolved the defendants (Battaglia 1955: 355; Canosa 1974: 160).

The argument is obviously a complex one given that the court's direction was not always uniform, instead it varied according to the cases that were presented. Reading the sentences and commentary of the era in judicial and non-judicial publications, it is nonetheless striking the political and general significance of the law in the difficult

---

[24] Assemblea costituente, Atti, seduta del 27 novembre 1947, p. 2581.

[25] Petraccone Giovanni, *Difesa della Cassazione unica*, in *La Magistratura*, n. 5–6, maggio-giugno 1946.

[26] Corte di Cassazione, Sezioni unite penali, sentenza 22 giugno 1946, in 1944–1946. *Il Foro Italiano*, II, 129–132.

[27] D.l.Cps. no. 494 of May 17 1947.

period that Italy was facing, as well as the onerous task that the judiciary had assumed in the transition to democracy.

We can say that the "imperfect" machine of the sanctions against Fascism was put through the wringer by the judiciary and it did not emerge from this in such great shape.

11.4 The Togliatti Amnesty

The Togliatti Amnesty,[28] from the moment it was issued on 22 June 1946, became the object of conflicting opinions; according to some it was a "sponge strike" that would unfairly cancel the responsibility of the Fascists even at the highest levels, while according to others it was an inevitable result of pacification desired by the all the political forces following the proclamation of a new, young republic (Franzinelli 2006; Caroli 2020).

Already in 1986 when talking about the genesis of the decree, Neppi Modona revealed how, in the idea of the communist leader Togliatti, it was very clear that Fascist crimes carried out by "people who held elevated roles of civil or political leadership or military command" should be necessarily excluded from the amnesty, as well as the cases of "massacres, particularly heinous torture, homicide or plundering", that is if the latter had been carried out "for an objective of profit". But it was the very danger of ambiguous definitions in the wording of the amnesty that was underestimated by the communist minister, who acted out of fear of limiting the vast benefits foreseen for the ex-partisans. What is more, at least in so far as it concerned the adverb "particularly" (referring to torture) added to the text of the amnesty in the Council of Ministers by the most moderate forces present, Togliatti had been warned of the interpretative risks by the young judges of his private secretary and also by the Minister from the Party of Action (*Partito d'Azione*) and future constitutional judge, Mario Bracci (even the socialist ministers expressed some concern) (Bracci 1947: 1102; Lajolo 1981: 52; Neppi Modona 1986: 308; Caprara 1997; Agosti 2003: 311). Ultimately, however, these "details" would prove critical for the concrete application of clemency.

Just in the very first days of its application (25–28 June 1946), the Court of Assize of Rome released 89 Fascists accused of collaborationism or of "relevant acts" (for the establishment and maintenance of the power of the Fascist regime, article 3 of decree no. 159 of 1944) (Franzinelli 2006: 49). In early July, overwhelmed by alarming news coming from the Communist Party about the "release of Fascist criminals", Togliatti issued a "telegraphic" and curt circular addressed to the heads of the Courts of Appeal specifying that amnesty was to be applied "according the legislative spirit that required the continuation of punitive actions" (as specified in the explanatory report), and he "ordered" that in the case of doubt that they tend

---

[28] D. pres. 22 giugno 1946, n. 4.

towards "presumption of collaborationism" contemplated by the decree no. 142 of April 22 1945 (Neppi Modona 1997: 103).

However, this was all to no avail and despite the fact that the law gave explicit orders to the contrary, the application of the amnesty of 1946 was extended so far as to exempt even the leaders of the Salò Republic (Battaglia 1955: 339). The decree was instead applied to those held responsible of "relevant acts" not considered officials of significance of the Salò Republic, such as directors of large political newspapers, undersecretaries and ministers, and presidents of extraordinary tribunals who had played a concrete role in repressing Resistance activities beyond the rules of the military wartime penal code, often with summary trials (Algardi 1958: 19). It is worth remembering that it was exactly incrimination for "relevant acts" that was not well looked upon by many jurists for their retroactive nature (Battaglia 1955: 339).

In one of the first post-amnesty sentences, on 13 July 1946, the Second Section of the court presided over by De Ficchy (who was also the rapporteur) laid out its own doctrine of applying the decree to Vito Mussolini, the dictator's nephew who had been director of the *Popolo d'Italia* for a long time and who had been convicted for "relevant acts" by the CAS in Milan. In the decision, it was claimed that since one could not carry out "relevant acts" without having a leading role, the amnesty should not be applied to anyone, and since this was not possible, amnesty should be applied to everyone and therefore also the defendant in question (Battaglia 1955: 339). But, one could ask, did the intention of the legislator, evidently in contrast with its interpretation, not count at all? (Canosa 1974: 141).

The Supreme Court played a decisive role in these months, directing justice towards an almost general "forgiveness" and opening the way towards a "compassionate" justice even in the application of sanctions against Fascism, for which men with serious liability were acquitted by claiming they had played a "double game", that is of keeping hidden their own "interior" hostility towards Nazism while "collaborating with the German invader" (Algardi 1958: 21–22; Galante Garrone 1947; Vassalli 1948).

Once again, the approach of the Second Section, perhaps justified initially in order to temper the severe judgements pronounced in the period immediately following the institution of the CAS, came over time (and rather quickly at that) to take a very decisive turn to always favour the defendants. This occurred—as many observers highlighted straight away—in the cases of amnesty for the defendants in hiding, confiscation of property, in the appealable nature of the sentence (as we have seen) and the disputed definition of the notion of "particularly" heinous torture (almost always not recognised as such that would demand exclusion from the amnesty) (Battaglia 1955: 347).

The "broad-sweeping" approach of the Supreme court had a dual effect not only of annulling a considerable portion of the punishments already handed out but also of approving the inappropriateness of proceeding in many lawsuits still to be brought before the courts, with the consequence of immediate release for a large number of defendants held serving a sentence or awaiting trial. Moreover, the application of the amnesty entailed the concession of reductions of sentences that, thanks to their accumulation, led quickly to release or, even then, the possibility of asking for a pardon or a conditional release (having served two thirds of their sentence) (Nubola 2017: 46–47).

In essence, two tendencies can be identified from the jurisprudence of the judiciary under the influential control of the Second Section: the wide application of the decree of clemency to the Fascist leaders and collaborators and, by contrast, the low application for members of the Resistance called before the civil judges even to answer charges about acts done during the armed conflict (Bianco 1947: 1033).

It must be added that the Supreme Court had received wide discretionary powers about who to apply the amnesty to by those who had written (in an imprecise manner) this piece of legislation.

Some, such as the anti-Fascist jurist Piero Calamandrei, in explaining at least in part the legal orientation that he read "with bitterness and regret", identified the "superlative technical incompetence" of the "legislators emerging from the clandestine struggle" (Calamandrei 1947: 967). Togliatti rejected this accusation and indicating various times the limits of the decree of clemency pointed to, instead, the conservative judiciary and its reactionary roots (Togliatti 2014: 1342; Franzinelli 2006: 330–335). Besides the controversy caused also by political motives (the Constituent Assembly was in full swing and in May 1947 the parties of the left were excluded from the government), more generally there emerged the incapacity of the new ruling class to deal with the complexity of legislating and administrating in a post-war period in which the united anti-Fascist thrust was dying out.

The bitter criticisms widespread throughout the country (expressed in hundreds of private and public letters and in protests) about the judges' conduct had an immediate echo in the Constituent Assembly. There, on 22 July 1946, the communist Minister of Justice Fausto Gullo (who had taken over from Togliatti in the second De Gasperi government) responded to a specific question from the socialist (and future President of the Italian Republic) Sandro Pertini (who, together with Parri, was against the amnesty) in the most classic style of his liberal predecessors. Gullo affirmed that he had already sent a ministerial circular asking the public prosecutors to proceed in applying the amnesty to partisans in a greater manner that what they had so far been doing, and to monitor the situation so that it was not applied too much to exonerate crimes committed by Fascists. Pertini had then objected that there was only one instrument that could be used in the place of the old arsenal of circulars to guide the actions of the judiciary in a democratic regime, and that was an interpretative regulation of legislative nature (approved by the government that had this faculty) which the judiciary would be forced to abide by.[29]

For that matter, even in public occasions such as the inauguration of the 1947 judicial year at the Court of Cassation, the high judges exhibited their distance—in the words of the public prosecutor Massimo Pilotti—from the Republic, almost going as far as to deny the beginning of a moral and institutional transformation (Meniconi 2015b).

On 31 July 1946 the number of people granted amnesty were 219,481 of which 10,040 were "political" (153 partisans, 7106 Fascists, 802 miscellaneous) (Bracci

---

[29] Atti Assemblea Costituente, *Discussioni*, seduta del 22 luglio 1946, 207 ss.

1947: 1103–1104). They were not many but were destined to increase. Moreover, starting from the summer of 1946 and even more in 1947 and successive years, the release of culprits generated further violence and pain in the populations in the places of the tragic incidents that had rendered them protagonists. In this way the goal of pacification after the civil war seemed harder rather than easier to reach, as the Togliatti Amnesty and the measures that followed had intended to do (Franzinelli 2006).

After 1946, the debate continued in a heated manner especially during the application of amnesty to figures who were "distressingly" famous. The ones that caused the most uproar were, among others, the clemency extended to members of the groups of torturers such as the famous Koch group, and, in 1949, the amnesty for Junio Valerio Borghese, leader of the infamous Decima Mas or Tenth Torpedo-Boat Squadron (one of the "independent" military divisions of the Salò Republic dedicated to repressing partisans) sentenced to two life sentences for various massacres but released by the "benevolent" Court of Assize of Rome (this prince would later go on to lead a failed coup d'etat in 1970). All of this was entangled, naturally, in the more general political dispute that was taking place in the piazzas and in Parliament between the government, by now with a Christian Democrat majority, and the left parties, as was evident in the scathing debates about the responsibility of the amnesty that took place in February 1949 following the Borghese trial between Togliatti and Mario Scelba, the powerful Christian Democrat Minister of the Interior (Algardi 1958: 183; Franzinelli 2006: 330–335).

In the meantime (and for the 1950s), many public prosecutors of the Republic exhumed trials that had been archived in 1945 and 1946 and revoked sentences that had acquitted partisans (among others, those who had carried out the attack against the Nazis in Via Rasella in Roma which had led to the Nazi reprisal and the massacre at the Fosse Ardeatine) (Bocca 1973: 459; Nubola 2017: 28). Already at the time, the direction of the public prosecutors had worried Minister Togliatti who had sent various circulars to the highest ranking judges and had arranged for an ad hoc amnesty in order to stop the anti-partisan judicial repression (Neppi Modona 1986: 299).[30] But despite this, the "trial against the Resistance", which would mark the post-war period in Italy, had inexorably begun. (Neppi Modona 1984: 28).[31]

11.5 Conclusion

In 1952, the report compiled by the Minister of Justice (the Christian Democrat Adone Zoli) showed that after numerous further measures of clemency (even individual), the number of people already being held and convicted for collaborationism was 266 (and the number of those convicted while in hiding was 334), which was just 4.4% of the total of convictions (5,928).

---

[30] Archivio centrale dello Stato, Ministero di grazia e giustizia, Gabinetto, busta 9.

[31] Archivio centrale dello Stato, Ministero di grazia e giustizia, Gabinetto, busta 44.

These are the numbers that have convinced Italian and other historians to claim a "failure" of the transitional justice, in other words the failure of reckoning with the Fascist past that would then damage the future of the buiding Republic (Baldissara and Pezzino 2005; Battini 2003; Focardi 2008). In truth, it appears in some paradoxical way, that in the historical field, the minority view prevails, which, largely ignored by the most influential (and most popular) forces on the political stage, claimed already at the time the predictable failure of those laws in their practical implementation, even for how they were configured. In this regard, Peretti Griva's negative evaluation of the carrying out of the purge is significant. He said: "the spirit of pacification should not go beyond certain limits at the risk of determining a completely opposite effect to the very spirit, and to fail, before history, in the educational task of justice" (Peretti Griva 1947: 1080). One could argue that historical judgement has brought about a sort of moral victory for these appeals.

However, at a distance of more than 70 years, questions arise about if the transitional justice was indeed a failure, if the "legal justice" was so ineffective and if the unsuccessful reconciliation of the country (that would last for a long time) was due to the choices made by the Italian ruling class between 1943 and 1946.

In Italy—it is claimed—there was a diachronic combination of models: from one (implemented with the decree no. 159 in 1944) that was essentially of a penal nature with little room for forgiveness and reconciliation, it changed, first through jurisprudential interpretation and then with legislative intervention, to one that attenuated the punitive drive and instead focused on social and civil pacification (Fornasari and Wenin 2015: 52–53; Portinaro 2013).

The change of national and above all international political outlooks at the end of the Second World War certainly played a role in this, likewise the behaviour of the Italian judiciary, to whom it has, perhaps inevitably, been assigned the judgement of the responsibility of the Fascist regime, of the involvement in the war and of crimes committed by the Salò Republic. It was decided from the beginning to not come to terms with the past using summary or political justice, even if, for some time, there were those who felt it would have been better not to transfer "the greatest political responsibility of Fascism on the level of penal culpability" (Elster 2008). Based on this view it was claimed that the result of the original choice had been to obtain "an uncertain legality and a falsified justice" with the end of "the transformation of the state" (Battaglia 1955: 339). On the contrary, Calamandrei remarked on the spur of the moment how, in any case, the sanctions "machine" avoided violating the "essential, indispensable principle of civil coexistence that forbids individuals taking justice into their own hands" (Calamandrei 1945: 285).

It is also true that the pace of justice adapted itself to the political changes that happened in the period of transition. The government went from one that comprised anti-Fascist parties to an executive branch dominated by the more moderate focus (the Christian Democrats in particular) with the exclusion of the left wing parties already from May 1947 (then subsequently confirmed by the election results in 1948). This change certainly played a critical role in the failure of the transitional justice system and in the failure to change the state's essential structures. Moreover, Italian judges had always been sensitive to political power, with antennae capable of perceiving the slightest change and consequently would adapt themselves quickly to the new environment. In this manner, the laws against Fascism were applied by the judges with the highest rigour when the political force of anti-Fascism was at its height, to then be "interpreted in the opposite way", that is with "the greatest indulgence as soon as it was on its way down" (Battaglia 1955: 351). Furthermore, it is true—as Mario Bracci wrote in 1947—that this tendency seemed to be an "ill-concealed antipathy" towards a "new" world that was emerging perhaps in a "haphazard manner" but that sought to rise the country from its ashes. Above all, the high courts appeared to almost practice a sort of "isolation" from the turbulent reality inside its walls, protected by law and tradition against a presumed revolution (Bracci 1947: 1107). It could well be argued in 1955 that the politics of sanctions against Fascism had been a failure, which became discombobulated amongst amnesties, revisions, revocations, "suicidal sentences", even the violation of the *res giudicata*, and that the responsibility lies instead in the errors of the legislators and in the resistance of the judiciary body (Battaglia 1955: 356).

Nonetheless, if we examine now the justice of the time with the distance of the years that have passed, we cannot but make a reflection, which certainly does not question the judgement of some of the contemporaries cited.

Despite everything, transitional justice was an important moment on the road back to democratic life and the primacy of law in Italy. Administered largely by Italian judges, with the right weight of the popular jury reintroduced after Fascism, practiced in a public way, with the emotional, political and civil participation of the population, jurisdiction in those difficult years appears to us to be delicate, fragile, also if brought thousands of defendants to justice in thousands of trials. However, it should be considered that the power delegated by political class to judiciary was in every aspect excessive and ultimately delayed the real transition to democracy.

References

Agosti, A. 2003. *Togliatti. Un uomo di frontiera.* Torino: Utet.

Baldissara, L., and P. Pezzino (eds.). 2005. *Giudicare e punire. I processi per crimini di guerra tra diritto e politica.* Napoli: L'Ancora del Mediterraneo.

Battaglia, A. 1955. Giustizia e politica nella giurisprudenza. In *Dieci anni dopo 1945–1955, Saggi sulla vita democratica italiana,* A. Battaglia et. al., 317–407. Bari: Laterza.

Battaglia, A. 1962. *I giudici e la politica.* Bari: Laterza.

Battini, M. 2003. *Peccati di memoria. La mancata Norimberga italiana.* Roma-Bari: Laterza.

Bocca, G. 1973. *Palmiro Togliatti.* Roma-Bari: Laterza.

Bolzon, I., and F. Verardo (eds.). 2018. *Cercare giustizia. L'azione giudiziaria in transizione.* Trieste: Istituto regionale per la storia della Resistenza.

Canosa, R. 1974. *La magistratura dal 1945 a oggi.* Bologna: Il Mulino.

Canosa, R. 1999. *Storia dell'epurazione in Italia. Le sanzioni contro il fascismo 1943–1945.* Milano: Baldini & Castoldi.

Caprara, M. 1997. *Quando le Botteghe erano oscure. 1944–1969, uomini e storie del comunismo italiano.* Milano: Il Saggiatore.

Cardia, M. 2014. L'epurazione dei magistrati del Consiglio Superiore della Magistratura alla caduta del fascismo. In *Autonomia, forme di governo e democrazia nell'età moderna e contemporanea. Scritti in onore di Ettore Rotelli*, ed. Piero Aimo, Elisabetta Colombo, and Fabio Rugge, 65–78. Soveria Mannelli: Rubbettino.

Caroli, P. 2020. *Il potere di non punire. Uno studio sull'amnistia Togliatti*. Napoli: Edizioni Scientifiche Italiane.

Colao, F. 2015. I processi a Rodolfo Graziani. Un modello italiano di giustizia di transizione dalla Liberazione all'anno Santo. In *Nei tribunali. Pratiche e protagonisti della giustizia di transizione nell'Italia repubblicana*, ed. Giovanni Focardi and Cecilia Nubola, 169–220. Bologna: il Mulino.

Consiglio superiore della magistratura. 1976. *La magistratura nella lotta di liberazione: i caduti*. Roma: Consiglio superiore della magistratura.

Crainz, G. 1995. Il dolore e la collera: quella lontana Italia del 1945. *Meridiana* 22–23: 249–273.

D'Alessandro, L.P. 2019. Per uno studio delle sentenze della Corte d'assise straordinaria di Milano. Il giudizio sulla Repubblica sociale italiana e sulla sua classe dirigente. In *Giustizia straordinaria tra fascismo e democrazia. I processi presso le Corti d'assise e nei tribunali militari*, ed. Cecilia Nubola, Paolo Pezzino, and Toni Rovatti, 31–56. Bologna: il Mulino.

D'Alessandro, L.P. 2020. *Giustizia fascista. Storia del Tribunale speciale (1926–1943)*. Bologna: il Mulino.

De Nardi, S. 2016. La 'resistenza' della (e nella) magistratura ordinaria all'imposizione di giurare fedeltà alla Repubblica sociale italiana. In *Resistenza e diritto pubblico, Resistenza e diritto pubblico*, ed. Fulvio Cortese, 47–89. Firenze: University Press.

Domenico, R.P. 1996. *Processo ai fascisti. 1943–1948: storia di un'epurazione che non c'è stata*. Milano: Rizzoli.

Dondi, M. 2004. *La lunga liberazione. Giustizia e violenza nel dopoguerra italiano*. Roma: Editori Riuniti.

Elster, J. 2008. *Chiudere i conti. La giustizia nelle transizioni politiche*. Bologna: il Mulino.

Filippetta, G. 2018. *L'estate che imparammo a sparare. Storia partigiana della Costituzione*. Milano: Feltrinelli.

Focardi, F. 2008. *Criminali di guerra in libertà. Un accordo segreto tra Italia e Germania federale, 1949–1955*. Roma: Carocci.

Focardi, G. 2005. Le sfumature del nero: sulla defascistizzazione dei magistrati. *Passato e presente* 64: 61–87.

Focardi, G., and Nubola, C. (eds.). 2015. *Nei Tribunali. Pratiche e protagonisti della giustizia di transizione nell'Italia repubblicana*. Bologna: il Mulino.

Focardi, G. 2018. Le Corti d'assise straordinarie: nuove prospettive di ricerca. Nota introduttiva. In *Cercare giustizia. L'azione giudiziaria in transizione*, ed. Irene Bolzon, and Fabio Verardo, 89–93. Trieste: Istituto regionale per la storia della Resistenza.

Focardi, G. 2019. Sotto la toga con la camicia nera? Presidenti ordinari per una giustizia straordinaria. In *Giustizia straordinaria tra fascismo e democrazia. I processi presso le Corti d'assise e nei tribunali militari*, ed. Cecilia Nubola, Paolo Pezzino, and Toni Rovatti, 71–96 Bologna: il Mulino.

Fornasari, G., and Wenin, R. 2015. La giustizia di transizione. In *La persecuzione dei crimini internazionali. Una riflessione sui diversi meccanismi di risposta*, ed. Roberto Wenin, Gabriele Fornasari, and Emanuela Fronza, 47–64. Università di Trento, Facoltà di Giurisprudenza, Collana dei Quaderni della Facoltà di Giurisprudenza 15.

Franzinelli, M. 2002. *Le stragi nascoste. L'armadio della vergogna: impunità e rimozione dei crimini di guerra nazifascisti 1943–2001*. Milano: Mondadori.

Franzinelli, M. 2006. *L'Amnistia Togliatti: 1946. Colpo di spugna sui crimini fascisti*. Milano: Feltrinelli.

Galimi, V. 2014. Circulation of models of Epuration after the Second World War: from France to Italy. In *Dealing with Wars and Dictatorships. Legal Concepts and Categories in Action*, ed. Liora Israel and Guillaume Mouralis, 197–208. Berlin: Springer.

Giannetto, M. 2003. Defascistizzazione: legislazione e prassi della liquidazione del sistema fascista e dei suoi responsabili (1943–1945). *Ventunesimo Secolo* 2 (4): 53–90.

Giannini, M. S. 2008. L'epurazione del secondo dopoguerra. *Scritti giuridici*, X, 283 ss. Milano: Giuffrè.

Giustolisi, F. 2004. *L'armadio della vergogna*. Roma: Nutrimenti.

Grilli, A. 2019. *Una legalità impossibile. RSI, giustizia e guerra civile (1943–1945)*. Roma: Carocci.

La Rovere, L. 2008. *L' eredità del fascismo. Gli intellettuali, i giovani e la transizione al postfascismo, 1943–1948*. Torino: Bollati Boringhieri.

Lajolo, D. 1981. *Ventiquattro anni. Storia spregiudicata di un uomo fortunato*. Milano: Rizzoli.

Marini, A. 2019. *Dopo Mussolini. I processi ai fascisti e ai collaborazionisti (1944–1945)*. Roma: Viella.

Melis, G. 2020. *Storia dell'amministrazione italiana*. Bologna: il Mulino.

Melis, G. 2003. Note sull'epurazione dei ministeri, 1944–1946. Ventunesimo secolo. *Rivista di studi sulle transizioni* 2(4): 17–52.

Melis, G. (ed.). 2006. *Il Consiglio di Stato nella storia d'Italia. Le biografie dei magistrati (1861–1948)*. Milano: Giuffrè.

Meniconi, A. 2006. *La "maschia avvocatura". Istituzioni e professione forense in epoca fascista (1922–1943)*. Bologna: il Mulino.

Meniconi, A. 2012. *Storia della magistratura italiana*. Bologna: il Mulino.

Meniconi, A. 2015a. La magistratura e la politica della giustizia durante il fascismo attraverso le strutture del ministero della Giustizia. In *Il diritto del duce. Giustizia e repressione nell'Italia fascista*, ed. Luigi Lacché, 79–95. Roma: Donzelli.

Meniconi, A. 2015b. Pilotti, Massimo. In *Dizionario biografico degli Italiani*, 83. Roma: Istituto dell'Enciclopedia Italiana.

Meniconi, A. 2017. La breve esperienza come commissario per l'epurazione. In *Una spina dorsale. Domenico Riccardo Peretti Griva: magistrato, antifascista, fotografo*, ed. Francesco Campobello, 73–85. Torino: Edizioni SEB27.

Neppi Modona, G. 1973. La magistratura e il fascismo. In *Fascismo e società italiana*, ed. Guido Quazza, 127–181. Torino: Einaudi.

Neppi Modona, G. 1984. Il problema della continuità dell'amministrazione della giustizia dopo la caduta del fascismo. In *Giustizia penale e guerra di liberazione*, ed. Luigi Bernardi, Guido Neppi Modona, and Silvana Testori, 11–40. Milano: Franco Angeli.

Neppi Modona, G. 1986. Togliatti guardasigilli. In *Togliatti e la fondazione dello Stato democratico*, ed. Aldo Agosti, 284–321. Milano: Franco Angeli.

Neppi Modona, G. 1997. La Magistratura dalla Liberazione agli anni Cinquanta. Il difficile cammino verso l'indipendenza. In *Storia dell'Italia repubblicana*, ed. Francesco Barbagallo, 83–137. Torino: Einaudi 3, 2.

Neppi Modona, G. 2017. Il magistrato "cospirante" negli anni della Resistenza. In *Una spina dorsale. Domenico Riccardo Peretti Griva: magistrato, antifascista, fotografo*, ed. Francesco Campobello, 55–71. Torino: Edizioni SEB27.

Nubola, C., Pezzino, P., and Rovatti, T. (ed.). 2019. *Giustizia straordinaria tra fascismo e democrazia. I processi presso le Corti d'assise e nei tribunali militari*. Bologna: Il Mulino.

Nubola, C. 2017. Governare la transizione attraverso la giustizia. In *L'età costituente. Italia 1945–1948*, ed. Giovanni Bernardini, Maurizio Cau, Gabriele D'Ottavio, and Cecilia Nubola, 28–51. Bologna: il Mulino.

Pavone, C. 1991. *Una guerra civile. Saggio storico sulla moralità della Resistenza*. Torino: Einaudi.

Pavone, C. 1995 (1973). *Alle origini della Repubblica. Scritti su fascismo, antifascismo e continuità dello Stato*. Torino: Bollati Boringhieri.

Portinaro, P.P. 2013. Il problema della giustizia politica. A partire da Otto Kirchheimer. *Materiali per una storia della cultura giuridica. Rivista fondata da Giovanni Tarello* 1: 225–242.

Rovatti, T. 2015. Tra giustizia legale e giustizia sommaria: forme di punizione del nemico nell'Italia del dopoguerra. In *Nei Tribunali. Pratiche e protagonisti della giustizia di transizione nell'Italia repubblicana*, ed. Giovanni Focardi and Cecilia Nubola, 15–49. Bologna: il Mulino.

Saraceno, P. 1999. I magistrati italiani tra fascismo e Repubblica. Brevi considerazioni su un'epurazione necessaria ma impossibile. *Clio* XXXV (1): 65–109.

Scarpari, G. 2008. Obiettivo. I magistrati, il fascismo, la guerra. *Questione giustizia* 2: 71–118.

Scarpari, G. 2015. Processo a un ministro della Giustizia. In *Nei Tribunali. Pratiche e protagonisti della giustizia di transizione nell'Italia repubblicana*, ed. Giovanni Focardi and Cecilia Nubola, 151–168. Bologna: il Mulino.

Soddu, P. 2001. La transizione dal fascismo alla democrazia nella «memoria» della magistratura italiana. In *La grande cesura. La società europea tra memoria della guerra e della Resistenza e ricostruzione*, ed. Giovanni Miccoli, Guido Neppi Modona, and Paolo Pombeni, 309–326. Bologna: il Mulino.

Storchi, M. 2008. *Il sangue dei vincitori. Saggio sui crimini fascisti e i processi del dopoguerra (1945–1946)*. Reggio Emilia: Aliberti.

Teitel, R.G. 2000. *Transitional Justice*. Oxford: Oxford University Press.

Woller, H. 1997. *I conti con il fascismo. L'epurazione in Italia 1943–1948*. Bologna: il Mulino.

Sources

Algardi, Z. 1958. *Processi ai fascisti*. Firenze: Parenti.

Archivio centrale dello Stato, Presidenza del Consiglio dei ministri, Segreteria particolare del presidente del Consiglio Alcide De Gasperi 1945–1953, busta 2, fasc. 11, "Collaborazionismo".

Archivio centrale dello Stato, Ministero di grazia e giustizia, Gabinetto, buste 6, 7, 8, 9, 44.

Archivio centrale dello Stato, Ministero della giustizia, Direzione generale dell'organizzazione giudiziaria, Epurazione, busta 5, fasc. 39.

Archivio centrale dello Stato. 1996. Verbali del Consiglio dei ministri, luglio 1943–maggio 1948, eds. Ricci, Aldo Giovanni, Governo De Gasperi 10 dicembre 1945–13 luglio 1946, VI, 1, Roma, Presidenza del Consiglio dei ministri, Dipartimento per l'informazione e l'editoria.

Atlante delle stragi naziste e fasciste in Italia, http://www.straginazifasciste.it/cas/.

Atti Assemblea Costituente, Discussioni, seduta del 22 luglio 1946.

Barile, P. 1947. La magistratura si ribella alle leggi? *Il Ponte III* 11–12: 1067–1074.

Bianchi D'Espinosa, L. Il «caso Pilotti». *Il Ponte* III 11–12:1108–1111.

Bianco Dante Livio. 1947. Partigiani e C.L.N. davanti ai tribunali civili. *Il Ponte III* 11–12: 1033–1040.

Bracci, M. 1947. Come nacque l'amnistia. *Il Ponte* III 11–12: 1090–1107.

Calamandrei, P. 1945. Postilla a Carlo Arturo Jemolo Le sanzioni contro il fascismo e la legalità. *Il Ponte I* 4: 285–286.

Calamandrei, P. 1947. Restaurazione clandestina. *Il Ponte* III 11–12: 959–968.

Galante Garrone, C. 1947. Guerra di liberazione (dalle galere). *Il Ponte III* 11–12: 1041–1066.

Jemolo, A.C. 1945. Le sanzioni contro il fascismo e la legalità. *Il Ponte I* 4: 277–285.

Jemolo, A.C. 1946. La magistratura: constatazioni e proposte. In *Per l'ordine giudiziario—Quaderni di Temi*, L. Ammatuna, P. Calamandrei, A. Candian, F. Carnelutti, E. Danzi, G. Gorla, M. Longo, A.C. Jemolo, R.D. Peretti Griva, M. Pilotti, F. Polistina, G.A. Raffaelli, E. Redenti, 29–36. Milano: Giuffrè.

Il Massimario penale. 1947 II 6–7: 171–172.

"L'intransigente". Settimanale politico, 12 maggio 1945.

La nuova legge sull'ordinamento giudiziario. Relazione del Guardasigilli al Duce 1° marzo 1940. 1940. Roma.

Levi, C. 1989 (I ed. 1950). *L'orologio*. Torino: Einaudi (South Royalton VT, Steerforth Press, 1951).

Liuzzi, F. 1945. Bilancio dell'Alta Corte. *Rivista penale* LXX: 345–352.

Maroni, L. 1947. Relazione sul lavoro giudiziario dell'Alta Corte di giustizia presentata dal Presidente dell'Alta Corte alla Presidenza e al Ministro di grazia e giustizia. *Rivista penale*, LXXI: 294–298.

Riccardo, Peretti Griva Domenico. 1947. Il fallimento dell'epurazione. *Il Ponte III* 11–12: 1075–1081.

Riccardo, Peretti Griva Domenico. 1956. *Esperienze di un magistrato*. Torino: Einaudi.

Petraccone, G. 1946. Difesa della Cassazione unica. *La Magistratura* 5–6, maggio-giugno.

Rossi, E., and G. Salvemini. 2004. Dall'esilio alla Repubblica. In *Lettere 1944–1957*, ed. Mimmo Franzinelli. Torino: Bollati Boringhieri.

Sezioni unite penali. 1944–1946. Sentenza 22 giugno 1946, Pres. De Ficchy P., Est. Giocoli, P.M. Battaglini (concl. conf.); ricc. Anfuso, Navale, Angioi (Avv. D'Amico, Jacobelli). *Il Foro Italiano* 69 parte II: 129–132.

Togliatti saluta la Magistratura italiana e invoca il ritorno ad un ordine democratico, *l'Unità democratica*, 1° luglio 1945: 1.

Togliatti, P. 2014. È possibile un giudizio equanime sull'opera di Alcide De Gasperi?, (Rinascita 1955.1956). In *Palmiro Togliatti. La politica nel pensiero e nell'az*ione, eds. Michele Ciliberto and Giuseppe Vacca, 1312–1389. Milano: Bompiani.

Vassalli, G. 1945. La collaborazione col tedesco invasore nella giurisprudenza della Sezione speciale della Cassazione. *La Giustizia penale* I parte II:1–15.

Vassalli, G. 1947. Ancora sentenze suicide. *La Giustizia penale* parte III: 345.

Vassalli, G. 1948. La collaborazione col tedesco invasore nella giurisprudenza della Sezione speciale della Cassazione. *La Giustizia penale* LIII parte II: 128–132.

Antonella Meniconi is Professor of History of Political Institutions at University of Rome La Sapienza (Italy). Ph.d at University of Pavia. She partecipated to "Ius Publicum Europaeum", promoted by the Max-Planck-Institut für Recht ausländisches öffentliches (Heidelberg) and was visiting researcher at the John D. Calandra Italian American Institute (City University of New York). She is deputy editor of the review on the history of institutions "Le Carte e la Storia". Her main research interests are history of Italian advocacy and judiciary, transitional justice from Fascism to the Republic, biographies of some important jurists and the relationship between Italian anti-jewish laws and the world of law.

Chapter 12
Punishing the Wrongdoers During the Portuguese Transition to Democracy: A Comparative Historical Analysis

Filipa Raimundo

Abstract What leads democracies to make the leaders and collaborators of the authoritarian regimes that precede them accountable? In this chapter, we offer a contribution to the study of transitional justice by developing a case study analysis of the transitional justice process that took place in Portugal during the second half of the 1970s. In Portugal, a number of retributive measures were implemented in the years that followed the transition 'by rupture', including trials and a vetting process. From 1974 to 2017, more than 100 laws and decree-laws on transitional justice were issued, predominantly covering retributive justice and reconciliation. Using comparative historical analysis, we show it was the combination of a profound rupture with the past, the predominant role of political actors that based their action on an alleged revolutionary legitimacy in the early stages of the transition, the limited role played by the judiciary in the transitional justice process, and the strong left-wing bias during the 18 months of the transition that produced the outcome.

12.1 Introduction

What leads democracies to make the leaders and collaborators of the authoritarian regimes that precede them accountable? This question has been alive for two decades in the democratization and in the transitional justice literature. Initially, qualitative scholars developed theories in which they either highlighted the role of regime factors—including the degree of repression (Pion-Berlin 1994), the level of dissent allowed by the previous regime (Moran 1994), the duration of the regime (De Brito et al. 2001), the proximity of the episode of higher repression (Elster 2004)—or the role of elites—the mode of transition (Huntington 1991) or the strength of old forces (Welsh 1996). Later, comparative scholars found little evidence of the former. For instance, while some studies suggested that the shorter the duration of the regime, the higher the likelihood that it would implement transitional justice, others have shown

F. Raimundo (✉)
ISCTE-Lisbon University Institute, Lisbon, Portugal
e-mail: Filipa.alves.raimundo@iscte-iul.pt

© Springer Nature Switzerland AG 2021
C. Paixão and M. Meccarelli (eds.), *Comparing Transitions to Democracy. Law and Justice in South America and Europe*, Studies in the History of Law and Justice 18, https://doi.org/10.1007/978-3-030-67502-8_12

that "in countries that adopted trials, lustration policies, or reparations, the author-itarian regime had endured more than twice as long [as in countries that adopted amnesties] (25 to 31 years)" (Olsen et al. 2010: 53–54). Conversely, some of the hypotheses regarding the role of elites were confirmed through statistical analysis: "trials occurred almost twice often after regime defeat or collapse as after negotiated transitions" (idem: 54; Kim 2012).

One question that remains largely unanswered has to do with the determinants of retributive transitional justice. Olsen, Payne and Reiter find, that "clean breaks seem to bring high levels of all types of mechanisms, suggesting that such transitions inspire and facilitate the process but perhaps have less influence on the type of mechanism adopted than many transitional justice scholars suppose" (idem: 54). Hence, although they confirm that the mode of transition influences the implementation of transitional justice, this factor alone does not help explain the type of mechanisms adopted.[1]

In this chapter, we develop a case study analysis of Portugal's transitional justice process, where a number of retributive measures were implemented in the years that followed the transition 'by rupture' (Linz and Stepan 1996). From 1974 to 2017, more than 100 transitional justice laws were issued, predominantly on retri-bution and reconciliation (Raimundo and Morais 2018). In addition, a number of ad hoc and extra-legal proceedings were adopted to deal with the legacies of the authoritarian regime. We can group them into three dimensions: first, those linked to the criminalization and prosecution of individuals involved in political repression (trials); second, those related to the process of vetting regime collaborators from public service and even from private sectors (vetting); and third, those aiming at the suspension of political rights of individuals who held public office from 1926 to 1974 (lustration). As a result, 2667 individuals were tried in military courts (Raimundo 2015), more than 12,000 were dismissed from their jobs (Pinto 2006), and those who held at least one among 71 positions in regime institutions saw their polit-ical rights being restricted (Morais 2020). From a comparative perspective, these numbers place Portugal amongst the most comprehensive accountability and justice processes in the third wave of democratizations (Sikkink 2011), comparable to those in Greece (Sotiropoulos 2011), the Czech Republic (David 2011), and East Germany (McAdams 1997), which also represent transitions to democracy 'by rupture' or 'collapse'. In many ways, the transitional justice processes that were implemented in those countries resemble those of the second wave of democratizations, which also involved vetting processes and domestic trials (Elster 2004).

We show that, in the Portuguese case, it was the combination of a profound rupture with the past, the predominant role of political actors that based their action on an alleged revolutionary legitimacy in the early stages of the transition, the limited role played by the judiciary in the transitional justice process, and the strong left-wing

---

[1] In Olsen et al. (2010), the authors coded each year in which a TJMs was in existence in each country—which enabled them to generate panel data—and classified each TJMs using only five categories (trials, truth commissions, amnesties, reparations, and lustration). Consequently, they treated TJMs as homogeneous variables, despite the authors' acknowledgement that 'the scope of these mechanisms varies dramatically across cases'.

bias during the 18 months of the transition that produced this outcome. Let us define each factor.

First, a 'rupture with the past' occurs only in certain democratization processes—i.e., cases that have been classified as 'by rupture' or 'by collapse' to use Linz and Stepan's (1996) typology. During negotiated transitions there is usually a pact involving some sort of amnesty or pardon that prevents retributive transitional justice from being implemented (Mallinder 2007). Pursuing punitive measures when the democratic elite is still negotiating the transition to democracy is likely to destabilize the process. Yet these pacts may or may not be broken later on, depending on a number of estimations that elites make on the basis of strategic pre-emption (Nalepa 2010), particularly when those who are willing to put the past back onto the agenda acquire or are on the verge of acquiring institutional capacity to break them (Raimundo 2012). In Poland, the new President "pledged to draw a 'thick line' under the communist past and to forgive (if not necessarily forget) in the name of reconciliation and transformation", and this can be explained by the level of elite continuity (Sczcerbiak 2002: 556). A few years later, post-communist elites adopted self-hurting laws, without properly engaging in a rupture with their own past, essentially to avoid being hurt by stricter legislation, essentially due to increasing levels of polarisation (Nalepa 2010).

The mere fact that there is a rupture with the past does not guarantee the level of punishment as we have seen in Portugal. For instance, in South Africa, "the process of reconciliation, nation-building and abolition of the colour line has engaged a definitive rupture with the past" (Fassin 2008: 312), yet South Africa opted for a kind of religious healing process through the creation of the Truth and Reconciliation Commission, in which wrongdoers could claim for amnesty in exchange of testimonies in public hearings, therefore avoiding punishment (Gibson 2002).

Second, "revolutionary legitimacy" was not particularly present in democratization processes of the third wave, because most transitions occurred through negotiation or collapse (Linz and Stepan 1996). The type of extra-legal measures observed in Portugal are more characteristic of the second wave, which were particularly active in administering domestic transitional justice measures: in Germany, courts prosecuted around 60,000 individuals between 1947 and 1990; France experienced the famous *epuracion sauvage* (wild purge of collaborators); in Austria, around 500,000 individuals were affected by the de-Nazification (Elster 2004). But revolutionary legitimacy is in itself not sufficient if the actors that act upon such alleged legitimacy do not hold sufficient political power. In Tunisia "supporters of the martyrs for the revolution staged protests that addressed the stagnating process of transitional justice and the lack of reform in the police and justice sectors", yet "because the activists had little direct access to decision makers and decision-making processes, their repertoire has been restricted to contentious action, while the allied Group of the 25 Lawyers has successfully pushed for reform of transitional justice laws" (Antonakis-Nashif 2016: 140).

Third, if the judiciary plays a central role in the transitional justice process, punishment may be difficult to implement, particularly if the judicial institution has not been purged. This happens because in many cases the degree of judicialization of repression during the regime leads to institutional complicity regarding the use of state violence against the regime opposition and/or ethic or religious groups (Pereira 2005; Aguilar 2013; Pinto and Raimundo 2016). For instance in Spain "such a system was hardly likely to approve of measures that might raise doubts about its honourable conduct during and after the dictatorship, since many judges were known to have tolerated the brutality of the police and the far-right violence that occurred during the transition" (Aguilar 2013: 259). In similar vein, in Chile, despite the fact that "courts were capable of investigating human rights abuses and convicting perpetrators (…) judges remained unwilling to challenge the legitimacy of the legal edifice that protected most authoritarian regime officials from prosecution" (Hiblink 2007: 198). This being said, it is also true that in many cases, particularly in belated transitional justice, it is the change in paradigms within the judiciary that enables the prosecution and punishment of repressive agents (Collins 2010). Hence, in itself, the limited involvement of the judicial system does not explain a harsher punitive process.

Finally, if the political spectrum is biased towards the left (in case of right-wing dictatorships) or the right (in case of communist regimes) this works in favour of punishment, even if it does not guarantee it. The left/right wing bias can be better observed in cases that went through a process of delegitimation of the previous regime, usually typical of transitions by rupture or collapse. These are the cases in which the political elite engages in 'inverse legitimation': that is, they tried to 'validate the new regime and even garner support for it by pointing to the real or exaggerated faults of the previous regime' (Valenzuela 1992). In East Germany, where the communist regime collapsed, "none of the major political actors making up the post-unification German party system, not even the PDS, could afford to oppose criminal prosecution as an instrument of dealing with the personnel of the old regime. Any such opposition would have been scandalized by political competitors as a proof of inappropriate permissiveness and leniency" (Offe and Poppe 2006: 262). This is very distinctive from strategies adopted in cases of gradual transition to democracy, which can involve, for instance, a strategy of 'backward legitimation', to use di Palma's expression: that is, they do not condemn the previous regime but rather search for distant sources of legitimation (Di Palma 1980), therefore allowing the old elite to more easily adapt to the new setting.

In this chapter, we show that the combination of these four factors provides a powerful explanation for why Portugal favoured retribution in its transitional justice process. The chapter relies on four types of empirical data, including: data on all legislation issued between 1974 and 2017; interview data with key actors collected on different occasions between 2007 and 2017; parliamentary party discourses; and party manifestos of the main political parties for the period 1974–1976.

The chapter is organized as follows. The next sections will summarize the main features of the Portuguese democratization process and is divided into four sub-points representing the factors identified in the model: rupture with the past, revolutionary legitimacy, limited judicial role, and left-wing bias. The article concludes with some considerations regarding the relationship between the four conditions.

12.2 The Portuguese Democratization and Transitional Justice Processes

The Portuguese transition to democracy began on April 25, 1974, when some middle rank military brought down the authoritarian regime through a bloodless *coup*. This was the beginning of a transition 'by rupture' in which regime institutions were immediately replaced by provisional power structures and the old elite was forced to step aside, maintaining very limited political power. The *coup* created a window of opportunity to break with the past and gave way to competing views on how to deal with the elite and the institutions of the *Estado Novo*, the authoritarian regime that ruled from 1930 to 1974 (Pinto 2006; Cerezales 2003).

During the course of the democratization process, several transitional justice mechanisms were created that represented two distinctive approaches to dealing with the past: one based on an alleged revolutionary legitimacy and another based on democratic legitimacy. The former prevailed during the first 18 months, while the latter only became dominant after the end of 1975, when a failed coup attempt put an end to the period of intense political radicalization and substantially reduced the left-wing bias, giving way to the consolidation of democracy.

The first retributive measure to have been adopted was the trial of the officials and informers of the political police, the main repressive institution (PIDE/DGS). Although some radical left-wing factions did demand the summary execution of those responsible for repression under the regime, the prevailing view was that they should be tried. After several months of preventive detention, a retroactive law was approved that criminalized all those who had worked or collaborated with the political police until April 1974.[2] Under revolutionary legitimacy, they were tried in military courts not for any specific acts but for belonging to an organization of "social and political terrorism", based on their position in the hierarchy, from Minister of Interior to informer.[3] Ranks were technical and did not take into account the length of collaboration and type of activity. Sentences went from two to twelve years of imprisonment (Raimundo 2015).

The second measure to have been implemented was the vetting of all alleged collaborators of the previous regime from civil service positions. For that purpose, several vetting commissions were created within the various ministries and several pieces of legislation were issued to ensure that all state sectors were duly screened. The vetting process could implicate dismissal, compulsory retirement, and suspension of duties or similar measures, depending on the case. Initially, in 1974, individuals could be purged for one of three reasons: undemocratic behaviour, inability to adapt to the new democratic context and incompetence.[4] When the level of political radicalization increased, in the beginning of 1975, new legislation explicitly

---

[2] Law 8/75, 25 July (DR Series I, n.170, 25.07.1975, pp. 1030).

[3] The exception was the case of the assassination of the Presidential candidate, Humberto Delgado.

[4] Decree Law 277/74, 25 June (DG Series I, n. 146, 25.06.1974, 743–744).

defined the former regime as fascist, and determined that purges could be based on the behaviour of the person before April 1974[5] (Pinto 2006).

Finally, the third measure was the exclusion of individuals who had collaborated with the previous regime from the electoral process of April 1975, the first democratic elections.[6] The electoral commission first debated this measure, which was approved by the provisional government in November 1974. The law determined that the individuals who held certain political positions or were involved in para-state institutions between 1926 and 1974 could not participate in the founding elections, with the exception of those who had been nominated to integrate the provisional power structures after April 1974 and those who, despite their involvement in the institutions and organizations of the regime, had acted in a way that attested their undisputable rejection of the regime. The list of those who could not be elected included former: mayors, members of the single party, members of the paramilitary militia and the political police, members of women and youth para-state organizations, and members of the censorship commission. There was, however, some level of leniency, as the list of those who could not be elected was significantly more restricted that the list of those who could not vote. Note that, for instance, former members of government could not vote but were not included in the list of those who could not be elected. The list did include members of the single party, but under Salazar and Caetano's dictatorship members of government did not have to be affiliated in the single party.

In the rest of the section we will explain each of the factors that contributed to this outcome. We first present evidence of their presence, based on specific events or trends, then explore the relationship between the cause and the effect in each case and, finally, we elaborate on the consequences of counterfactual events, that is, of what would have changed had the factor not been present. As Capoccia and Ziblatt argue, "historically informed and theoretically driven counterfactual reflection on the possible consequences of the nonselected options of institutional reform is essential to 'bring back to history' the full range of difficulties and contradictions that characterize democratization" (2010: 943–944).

12.2.1 Rupture with the Past

The level of rupture with the past that occurred in Portugal following the *coup* can be observed at the institutional and protest level. At the institutional level, there was a complete replacement of the existing political structures. The military junta that took office on the day of the *coup* of April 25 1974, the National Salvation Junta (JSN), proceeded with the immediate dissolution of the main political institutions, including the government, the parliament, and the corporatist chamber, as well as the para-state institutions such as the single party, the political police, the political courts, youth

[5] Decree Law 123/75, 11 March (DG Series I, n. 59, 11.03.1975, pp. 375–378).

[6] Decree Law 621-B/74, 15 November (DR Series I, n.266-3°Supl, 15.11.1974, pp. 1388).

organizations, and the state-run unions. In their place, the JSN created provisional (and in some cases overlapping) civilian-military institutions, which ensured the involvement of the military in the decision-making process. Table 12.1 illustrates this process of institutional dissolution/dismissal and replacement.

In order to better illustrate the presence of the military in the political institutions, Table 12.2 provides a systematic description of the institutions in which the military were present as well their functions. Initially, the military junta assumed most of the legislative power, assigning legislative capacity to a Council composed of the Chiefs of Staff of the Armed Forces (CCEMFA) only in matters relating to internal affairs and the structure and organization of the armed forces. In March 1975, the

Table 12.1 Rupture with the past at the institutional and para-state level (April–May 1974)

Old institution	Decision and legal framework	New institution (1974–1976)
President of the Republic _ directly elected (until 1959)[a]	Dismissed_ Law 1/74, April 25	The President of the Republic is the head of the Military Junta (April 1974–July 1976)
Government	Dismissed_ Law 1/74, April 25	Provisional Governments, civilian and military portfolios (May 1974–July 1976)
Parliament _ directly elected	Dissolved_ Law 2/74, May 14	None (April 1974–April 1975); Constituent Assembly without legislative powers (April 1975–April 1976)
Corporatist Chamber _ appointed by the Corporatist Institutions	Dissolved_ Law 2/74, May 14	None (ceases to exist)
Civil Governors _ appointed by the Ministry of Internal Affairs	Dismissed_ DL 170/74, April 25	Civil Governors Secretaries (until new nominations by the Ministry of Internal Affairs in 1974)
Single Party	Dissolved_ DL 172/74, April 25	Legalization of all parties (illegalization of those not in line with the MFA program)
Portuguese Legion	Dissolved_ DL 171/74, April 25	None (ceases to exist)
Political Police	Dissolved_ DL 171/74, April 25	None (ceases to exist, except in the colonies approximately until the conclusion of the decolonization process)
Political Courts	Dissolved_ Law 3/74, May 14	None

Source Own elaboration, adapted from Pinto (2006: 180)

[a]Note that under the authoritarian regime, elections were regular but not free or fair, despite some level of competition and limited pluralism. Universal suffrage did not exist and in one occasion the (Presidential) candidate, Humberto Delgado, was assassinated by the political police after losing the elections

Table 12.2 Political institutions in the Portuguese transition to democracy

Political institutions in which the military were present	Functions/Composition	Dissolution/Reform
President of the Republic (PR)	Chosen by the JSN/CR Presided over the JSN and the Council of State (appointed 1/3 of its members) Had the power to dismiss members of government; Called and presided over the Council of Ministers whenever necessary (only until August 1974) Was the head of the Armed Forces	April 1976 (first civilian President elected in 1986)
National Salvation Junta (JSN)	Supervised the work of the MFA Supervised the Constitutionally of rules Had a delegate in every ministry to report on urgent matters requiring a quick solution Could dismiss civil servants and dissolve state organs connected to the former regime (after 02/1975) Had the power to suppress political parties whose activity was contrary to the MFA Program (after 03/1975)	March 1975 (replaced by the CR)
Council of the State	Performed the duties of a Constitutional Court Was composed by the JSN, the Coordination Commission of the MFA and 7 citizens appointed by the PR (16 military, 7 civilians) Its support was required to pass new legislation	March 1975; the military were transferred to the CR, civilians were dismissed

(continued)

JSN was dissolved and replaced by a more left-wing institution called Council of the Revolution (CR), which not only inherited the Junta's legislative powers (and those of the CCEMFA) but also took the role of a second chamber, supervising the constitutionality of ordinary laws (Magalhães 1995; Rezola 2007). In addition, from April 1975 to April 1976, all political parties with seats at the Constituent Assembly (which had no legislative powers) were subject to special pacts with the military,

Table 12.2 (continued)

Political institutions in which the military were present	Functions/Composition	Dissolution/Reform
Council of the Revolution (CR)	Replaced the JSN and the Council of the State; Performed the role of a supplementary chamber in the regular legislative process and exercised 'abstract *a priori* review of legislation' Fulfilled the role of the Council of the PR and safeguarded democratic institutions, respect for the Constitution, and for the spirit of the Revolution Political and legislative organ on military issues	Dissolved in 1982, following the approval of the *National Defence and Armed Forces Law*
Provisional Governments	Changes in their composition could only take place by the initiative of the President, who first had to listen to the PM and the CR (after 04/1975) Percentage of military ministers: 1st Provisional Government: 6.6%; 2nd PG: 47%; 3rd PG: 52.9%; 4th PG: 52.9%; 5th PG: 36.8%; 6th PG: 50%	June 1976 (when the first Constitutional government was formed)
Constitutional Assembly	No legislative powers Subject to the Pact MFA/Parties which established a military commission to supervise the work of the MPs	From April 1975 to 1976

Source Own elaboration

known as the 'MFA/Parties pacts', which essentially sought to reduce the role of the civilian elite and ensure the CR's powers (Rezola 2007).[7]

Democratic civil-military relations were (partially) re-established in April 1976, after the approval of the new Constitution and the direct election of the President of the Republic and of the first constitutional government. Yet the military maintained important prerogatives until 1982, as shown in Table 12.2. These privileges included exclusive legislative power on matters relating to the armed forces at the domestic level (organization, operation, and discipline) and internationally (ratification of international agreements by decree-law), as well as the role of reviewing the

---

[7] There were two pacts made between the Armed Forces Movement and the political parties known as MFA/parties pacts: the first before the first elections, in April 1975; the second right before the formation of the Council of the Revolution, in February 1976. These pacts 'constitutionalized' the military's tutelary powers until 1982 (Magalhães et al. 2006).

constitutionality of laws, including the possibility of declaring parliamentary decrees unconstitutional, if they did not serve the revolution. In 1982, the first constitutional revision led to the dissolution of the CR and to the creation of the Constitutional Court, the new body responsible for reviewing the constitutionality of laws. It was from that moment that the parliament became the sole holder of legislative power, thus putting an end to the simultaneous democratic transition and consolidation (Linz and Stepan 1996). Hence, even if civilian control over the armed forces was partially restored in 1976, strictly speaking the military only withdrew to the barracks in 1982.

The complete dissolution of the political institutions of the authoritarian regime and their replacement with provisional civilian-military institutions had an important effect on transitional justice, as shown by the fact that the political-military institutions issued more than 40% of all transitional justice legislation (Raimundo 2017). This includes also the vetting process within the armed forces, but also the trials of the political police. The provisional governments were the second most active in issuing transitional justice legislation, which shows how this was a topic that was dealt with essentially during the first two years of the transition.

At the protest level, the rupture with the past can be observed in a number of symbolic actions targeting para-state institutions and other elements of the regime. Places such as the headquarters of the political police in the cities of Lisbon and Oporto, the paramilitary militia, the censorship, among others, were important cites of protest during the first days of the revolution. In addition, a number of symbols of the regime were removed or destroyed. For example, the public statue of Salazar located in his hometown was bombed twice in 1975 (initially only partially, it was irreversibly damaged three years later). Although there were few symbols in public spaces, they were not forgotten by extreme-left groups eager to erase the past. The streets and squares named "28 May"—the day of the military coup that established a military dictatorship in 1926—were quickly renamed "25 April" or "Armed Forces". In addition, one of the most emblematic gestures taken soon after the beginning of the 'Carnation Revolution' was the renaming of the bridge over the river Tagus in Lisbon—built by order of Salazar and named after him—which was quickly renamed the 25 April Bridge (*Ponte 25 de Abril*). All this shows the general feeling of 'catharsis' and the widespread denunciation of everything connected with the previous regime. In terms of political attitudes, a public opinion survey conducted less than one year after the coup revealed that only 1% of individuals declared themselves as 'fascists' and only 2% as conservatives (Marchi 2012). These percentages are likely to also express the left-wing bias that we will explore later on but are still sufficiently low to serve as a proxy regarding the popular acceptance of the *coup* and the decision to put an end to the regime.

Without such level of rupture with the past, the adoption of retributive measures would have been significantly more difficult for one main reason: had the political institutions not been immediately dissolved, the former elite would have been included in the decision-making process and would likely have attempted to block or change the approach.

12.2.2 *Revolutionary Legitimacy*

Due to the nature of the transition, those acting on the basis of an alleged revolutionary legitimacy were able to impose their agenda during the first 18 months following the coup, corresponding to the decisive months for the implementation of the main retributive measures during the Portuguese transition to democracy.

Immediately after the *coup,* supporters of revolutionary legitimacy argued for the immediate removal of those responsible for the crimes committed during the previous regime as well as their collaborators, either as a way to achieve justice or to ensure a successful democratization and decolonization process. According to this view, retroactive and extra-legal means should be employed to punish those who had collaborated with the Salazar/Caetano regime. The main supporters of this approach at the Constituent Assembly were the orthodox Communist Party (PCP) and the radical leftist (Maoist) Popular Democratic Union (UDP). Both their Constitutional drafts included articles anchored in revolutionary legitimacy. In the Communists' proposal, it was said that "the law is not retroactive, with the exception of the legislation to prosecute fascist leaders and leaders of the former PIDE/DGS and of other repressive organizations or leaders in counterrevolutionary activities" (quoted in Raimundo 2015). The Radical left's proposal also contained similar ideas: "The Portuguese Republic will severely repress all fascist and reactionary activities, as well as those who oppose the democracy of the masses. The fascists, reactionaries and enemies of all people will be judged in popular revolutionary courts, according to revolutionary legislation to be specially issued" (quoted in Raimundo 2015: 1065).

Without revolutionary legitimacy the retributive process would have been significantly more difficult to accomplish for two reasons. First, the centre left had an ambiguous position regarding the process of dealing with the past. The Socialist Party (PS), the major centre-left and most voted party in the first legislative elections of April 1976, did not oppose the process but was not enthusiastic of the revolutionary approach. They argued it was important to settle accounts with the past but this should be accomplished with respect for the democratic rule of law. For the Socialists, it was important to draw a line between the past and the present and to show that the methods of democracy were different from the methods of the authoritarian regime. In other words, had there not been a *coup* that opened the way for extreme-left parties to achieve a prominent role in the first year and half of the transition, the moderate left alone might have opted for a more reconciliatory approach, despite their antifascist origins.

Table 12.3 offers a sequence of the most important political events and laws that provided the legal framework for the implementation of the punitive transitional justice process. The table shows that until November 25, 1975, the focus was placed on retribution, even after the centrist parties received 64% of the vote in the first elections. At the time, the Communists and the Radical left were still in key positions in the provisional governments and inside the military political institutions. From then onwards, and even more clearly after the first legislative elections following the

Table 12.3 Sequence of the main political events and most important pieces of legislation for the punitive transitional justice process

Legislation	Origin	Legal measure	TJ
DL 277/74 (June 25)	Provisional Government	Dismissal of civil servants	Vetting
DL 398/74 (August 28)	Provisional Government	No *Habeas corpus* to those under military law	Trials
September 28, 1974	Rumors of demonstration organized by conservative forces ("Maioria silenciosa") The head of the JSN is put aside		
DL 621-B/74 (November 15)	Provisional Government	Suspension of political rights for those who held public office from 1926 to 1974	Lustration
March 11, 1975	Right-wing counter-coup attempt toppled by the left-wing military. Dissolution of the JSN and creation of the Council of the Revolution (CR)		
DL 123/75 (March 11)	Provisional Government	New criteria for the dismissal of civil servants	Vetting
DL 272/75 (June 2)	Council of the Revolution	Reopening of cases against members of the paramilitary militia	Trials
L 8/75 (July 25)	Council of the Revolution	Criminalization of political police officials and informants.	Trials
November 25, 1975	Coup attempt, toppled by the centre left and right Dismissal of left-wing members of the CR and new provisional government		
DL 729/75 (December 22)	Council of the Revolution	90 days' pardon	Trials
L 18/75 (December 26)	Council of the Revolution	Possibility of appeal and parole for those subject to L 8/75	Trials
DL 52/76 (January 21)	Provisional Government	Limits dismissals in the banking and insurance sectors	Vetting
DL 139/76 (February 19)	Council of the Revolution	Reintegration to those vetted from civil service	Vetting
April 25, 1976	Legislative elections		
DL 349/76 (May 13)	Council of the Revolution	Extenuating circumstances and lighter sentences for those subject to Law 8/75	Trials
DL 471/76 (June 14)	Provisional Government	Prohibits dismissals without just cause	Vetting

(continued)

Table 12.3 (continued)

Legislation	Origin	Legal measure	TJ
DL 825/76 (November 16)	Council of the Revolution	90 days' (cumulative) pardon	Trials
L 1/77 (January 12)	Parliament	Introduces changes to DL 349/76	Trials
R 64/78	Council of the Revolution	Unconstitutionality of article 3 of Law 1/77	Trials

Notes DL—Decree law; L—Law; R—Resolution
Source Own elaboration

approval of the new Constitution, in April 1976, the process was clearly reversed and a number of forgiving and extenuating measures were adopted.

Second, an analysis of the party manifestos of the Socialist Party shows that in 1974 the Socialists favoured the "restriction of political rights" of former regime collaborators. Yet, this was no longer present in their 1975 and 1976 electoral manifestos. Whereas initially the anti-fascist credentials of an important segment of the party founders led the party to support retribution, the strategy to become a mainstream party led it to detach itself from the remaining left-wing and extreme-left parties and to abandon retribution and even switch to a more 'forgive and forget' sort of position. Their progressive anti-Communist position can be observed in, for instance, their systematic attempts at putting an end to the Cultural Campaigns conducted across the country, allegedly by sectors of the military closely linked to the Communist Party.

The second reason why compliance with the democratic rule of law would probably have produced different results has to do with the historical context in which the process took place. As Sikkink claims, "by the 1960s, the basic institutions of the regional human rights system were in place in Europe, and NGOs were beginning to operate and create more public awareness about human rights" (2011: 36). On the other hand, "since there were so few precedents for these kinds of trials, the new [Greek and] Portuguese governments were inventing procedures as they went along" (Sikkink 2011: 34).

Four months after the *coup*, the Socialist Minister of Justice, who worked to implement the rule of law in the country, openly opposing revolutionary actions, set up the National Enquiry Commission (*Comissão Nacional de Inquérito*). The goal was to "inquire as to the basis of the complaints presented or documented regarding the abuse of power, violence against individuals or corruption committed between 28 May 1926 and 25 April 1974".[8] The Commission should collect evidence that would enable the Public Prosecutor to accuse those responsible for repression under the previous regime. However, according to statements from two of the commissions'

---

[8] Decree law 396/74, 28 August (DR Series I, 28.08.1974, pp. 952–954).

workers, it produced no results. In the few cases that reached the court, the defence argued the accused were merely complying with orders.[9]

12.2.3 Limited Judicial Role

The judiciary had a very minor role in the retributive process, despite what was said above. After the failure of the Commission of Enquiry, set to work in the framework of the Ministry of Justice in articulation with the Public Prosecutor, the trials were placed under military jurisdiction. This is said to have solved the issue of the time limit to preventive detentions—more than 1000 individuals awaited trial since April 1974. Military justice does not set limits to the time individuals can be placed under custody; hence it was seen as the best option to avoid setting them free without a trial. Had the judicial system intervened more, the officials of the political police who were under custody would have been released after 18 months. They would probably have escaped, like many did before and after the big wave of preventive detentions of April 1974.

As to the purge process, they were essentially administrative measures in the first phase, having become almost ad hoc decisions conducted 'wildly' by the workers themselves during 1975.[10] In the case of the restriction of political rights, the law did say that local tribunals would determine if a certain individual could be excluded from the list of those excluded, but there is little evidence of this having been the case. Hence, the issue was left to the military system of justice, the provisional governments, and even in the hands of the population, with some characteristics of vengeance more than justice.

Had the civilian judicial system had a more active role in the process, the outcome might have been very different, for two main reasons. First, when compared to all other ministries, the ministry of justice was the least vetted. Although the law determined that all those who had collaborated with the previous regime should be purged from their posts, it also stated that apart from the judges that had worked for the Plenary Courts or Special Military Courts[11] they were not to be removed from their posts under no circumstances.[12] This included several judges who had transitioned from the Plenary and Special courts to the regular judicial system. In addition, a first

---

[9] Ana Prata, interview with the author, Lisbon, 22.10.2016; Alberto Martins, interview with the author, Lisbon, 21.10.2016.

[10] We do not possess information on who had control over the implementation of the restriction of political rights imposed upon those who had collaborated with the previous regime.

[11] The Special Military Courts were created by the military dictatorship to try republicans armed rebellions on a somewhat ad hoc base. These courts, which were set up to try pro-democratic rebel officers, were transformed into the 'authoritarian judiciary' that until 1945 tried all 'political crimes'. The use of military courts to punish political crimes is a characteristic of many civilian dictatorships; however, in the case of Salazar's New State it was just one facet of the military presence within the authoritarian political system (see Pinto and Raimundo 2016).

[12] See note #5 above.

analysis of the situation by the first provisional governments concluded that the Public Prosecutor's office was as implicated as the whole judicial system (Rosas et al. 2008: 229). Even though in most other ministries, the purge process was partly carried out by the workers themselves—the so-called 'wild purges' (Pinto 2006)—in the case of the Ministry of Justice most purges were carried out from September 1974 onwards by a special commission called Commission for the Purge and Reclassification of the Ministry of Justice. Several judges were called upon to state their defence as they were suspects of having trouble adapting to the new democratic order. This included the last Ministry of Justice as well as other judges known to have been involved in political prosecutions. However, the process was slow and left out several judges who kept their jobs. By the end of 1974, "in a ministry with about 5,000 employees, only 59 proceedings were instituted (13 of the defendants were still being heard and 46 proceedings were completed" (Rezola 2015: 28).[13] This can be explained by a clear concern with the independence of the judiciary.

12.2.4 Left-Wing Bias

Despite the rapid institutionalization of the main Portuguese political parties following the *coup*, their position in the left-right continuum should not be regarded in a strict sense during the first years. Following the overthrow of the dictatorship, the political spectrum shifted to the left. This was due to several factors, namely the political radicalization caused by the presence of several extreme-left parties and the strategy of the Armed Forces Movement. "The MFA Program stated that only those who adhered to the MFA ideas were entitled to integrate themselves into the provisional governments. This was how the legitimacy of the resistance was established. In order to be worthy of respect, one had to demonstrate one's detachment from the New State (...) Political groups' legitimacy was dependent upon their commitment in fighting fascism" (Cervelló 1993: 191). Consequently, right-wing parties, having been founded during the revolutionary period, did not explicitly assume their true ideology. The radicalization made right-wing parties sacrifice "immediate material interests and (...) overcome momentary symbolic disadvantages to ensure their survival in the new political order" (Frain 1998: 77). This is well illustrated in the Constitutional drafts of the main political parties. As shown in Table 12.4, the way in which each party described the previous regime is very similar, from left to right. It is relevant that the longest description among the five belongs to the most right-wing party at the Constituent Assembly, CDS, precisely because they wish to emphasise their detachment from the previous regime. Regarding the description of the new (democratic) regime, the major difference is between the radical left's proposal and all others. From the Communists to the Conservatives, all parties declare their commitment with socialism and with the idea of establishing a society without classes. Certainly, right-wing parties did not believe in these ideals, but the fact that they

---

[13] Even though the process continued throughout 1975, figures are not available.

Table 12.4 Expressions contained in the Constitutional drafts of the main political parties (July 1975)

Party	Authoritarian regime	Democratic regime
UDP	"…the fascist beast"	"… the nationalization of all great capital and imperialist capitals (…), "maximum freedom of organization and mass revolutionary initiative"
PCP	"… the hated fascist dictatorship"	"… a socialist society without antagonistic classes based on the collectivization of the means of production and which will forever abolish the exploitation of man by man in Portugal"
PS	"… the fascist regime"	(…) socialism, understood as the democratic power of the workers, within the framework of the progressive collectivization of the means of production and of a regime of political democracy, with a view to the establishment of a classless society"
PSD	"…dictatorship, oppression and colonialism"	"… to build a fairer, freer, but fraternal society, from which all forms of oppression, exploitation and privilege must be abolished, corresponding to the ideals of personalist socialism"
CDS	"… 48 years of dictatorship (…) which relied on the means and processes that sustain any dictatorship, ruling without the people and against the people"	"… pluralism and democratic freedoms, social and community solidarity, valorization of initiative, rehabilitation of work, abolition of the proletarian condition, and primacy of labor over capital constitute, for the legitimacy of the Revolution, the guiding milestones in a society without classes, just and free, illuminated by the values of Christian humanism"

Source Constitutional drafts submitted in July 1975 by each political party represented at the Constituent Assembly. Available here: https://app.parlamento.pt/LivrosOnLine/Vozes_Constituinte/med01280000j.html

included it in their Constitutional draft shows how willing they were to align with ideas that they did not support just to be able to survive the radicalization period and succeed in the new regime.

Three good illustrations of this left-wing bias can be found in how political parties have tried to overcome the limitations imposed on former regime collaborators regarding their electoral participation. First, the leader of the Christian Democrats (PDC), who was co-opted from outside the party to increase its visibility, convinced the leadership that the party should sign the MFA/parties pact, which essentially committed all political parties to the (very left-wing) MFA program (Marchi 2012).

The PDC was a new and small party who claimed to stand for conservative anti-salazarist ideals, but in fact it comprised several old supporters of the regime. Their decision to sign the MFA/parties pacts represented a complete denial of their political program.

Second, in January 1976, a confidential document that circulated among members of the main Conservative party (CDS) contained a list of individuals who were not to be admitted as party affiliates: former single party leaders, leaders of the paramilitary militia, political police officials and informants, leaders of the regime youth and female organizations, members of government, all those who expressed anti-democratic behaviour while holding public office, among others. This showed that the party was aware of the difficulties it would face was it to present itself as a 'successor party' in the next elections. As Pinto argues, "a great effort was made to exclude from these parties any persons associated with the New State and to find leaders with democratic credentials" (Pinto 2008: 310).

Third, on the issue of vetting, again the Right became increasingly more vocal after the radicalization period. In 1977, the Socialists reintroduced the issue on the agenda with the goal of reassessing the democratic legitimacy of certain individuals who had collaborated with the previous regime. They argued for the need to maintain the vetting law adopted in 1974. Together, Conservatives and Social Democrats positioned themselves against what they considered to be a new vetting process when democracy should begin to consolidate itself. The Social Democrats argued that those who had been elected by the people after April 25 should be automatically considered rehabilitated; the Conservatives argued that the proposal would put a stop to the national reconciliation process. Following this discussion, the Socialists' project did not see the daylight.

Lastly, during the discussions to approve the new constitution, the Social Democrats' discourse on the issue of the trials reveals how strategic the party was. Were they to position themselves against the punishment of those responsible for repression during the previous regime, they risked being stigmatized and lose a segment of their recent electorate. Hence, they opted for issue avoidance, rather than taking the risk of positioning themselves in a way that would connect them with the old elite. In one of the rare occasions in which the Social Democrats expressed their views on the issue, one of the founders of the party argues: "the idea of adopting revolutionary measures to try officials of the PIDE/DGS was included in the MFA programme so, naturally, when the Social Democratic Party was created, those and other ideas contained in the programme were regarded by us as essential (…). Yet there may be discrepancies in how we view those trials" (cited by Raimundo 2015).

Had there not been a left wing bias, the punitive approach would be more difficult to achieve because right-wing and even centrist parties would probably have presented arguments against accountability mechanisms and they might even have been able to win a larger segment of the seats at the Constituent Assembly and been part of the provisional governments. This can be illustrated through two evidences. First, right-wing parliamentary parties changed their discourses once the revolutionary period came to an end. While they engaged mostly in issue avoidance during the first 18 months, they became more vocal when the extreme left was defeated. On one occasion, in October 1977, the Conservatives responded to a Communists' bill to forbid fascist parties, recommending that the prohibition be extended to all 'totalitarian' parties, implicitly suggesting that the Communist and the extreme-left parties should pay for their role during the transition.[14] In another situation, the Conservatives reacted to a bill proposed by the Socialists that sought compensation for victims of the *Estado Novo*, suggesting it should be extended to the victims of the transition. They were depicted as victims of the vetting processes, of persecution and forced exile, and of political radicalization. What is more, after the proposal was rejected and the Socialist's bill continued to the final vote, the Conservatives presented a vote declaration stating that they did not want to simply "vote against, but [to denounce the] political censorship and the whitewashing of our recent history."

The second reason why the outcome would have been different was it not for the left-wing bias rests in how the moderate forces within the MFA felt about the punitive measures. As explained by one of the members of the MFA, the military reproduced the ideological divisions found in the civilian elite:

> There were radicals who believed it was necessary to arrest and try immediately; however, the armed forces were very much divided on this matter. There was ... [a group] who demanded the trials. Basically, it was those who represented the PCP and the extreme-left. My opinion, which was shared by [the moderates] was that after the top hierarchies of the PIDE had fled the country, having been assisted by [the head of the JSN], with only the rabble remaining, there was no reason for keeping the trials. This would only keep the country agitated for many years. The trials would be, as they were, folklore with people shouting, "Death to the PIDE!" and, as such, a political mistake....[15]

Finally, the third reason why the outcome might have been difficult rests in the fact that there were several right-wing parties that disappeared during the radicalization period following the two coup attempts of September 1974 and March 1975. The Conservatives had even formed a coalition with the Christian Democrats, who in the meantime was prohibited to run for the 1975 elections after the second coup attempt.[16]

12.3 Conclusion

In the field of transitional justice, the most successful theory so far in explaining immediate retributive processes is the mode of transition to democracy (Huntington 1991; Olsen et al. 2010). Yet this explanation is unsatisfactory if we expand the temporal dimension beyond the transitional period, as some democracies that experienced other types of transition to democracy have been able to change their approach to the past by bringing it back onto the political agenda later on, such as Chile, for instance (Collins 2010; Raimundo 2012; Kim 2012).

---

[14] Project of Law 76/I: *Defesa da democracia* (DAR II série N°.2/I/2 Supl.1977.10.29 pág. 121-13).

[15] Miguel Judas, Interview with the author, Cascais, 23/07/2007.

[16] Decree-law 137-E/75, 17 March, Suspende a actividade política do Partido da Democracia Cristão, do Movimento Reorganizativo do Partido do Proletariado e da Aliança Operária Camponesa.

This chapter has shown that retribution in Portugal can be explained through a combination of four factors that, when considered together, were sufficient to produce the outcome. Our analysis shows: first, that the rupture with the past was an important factor contributing to the complete replacement of the previous elite, who might have otherwise tried to negotiate a non-punitive approach; second, that the revolutionary legitimacy was an important factor contributing to the approval of retroactive laws and swift dismissals, without which the democratic rule of law lacked the tools to punish the wrongdoers; third, that the limited role of the judiciary was an important factor that enabled the process to move without the obstacles that might otherwise be created by former regime accomplices in the judiciary; and fourth, that the left-wing bias was an important factor contributing to the strategic silence of the right, who might have openly opposed the process otherwise.

What we observe is that once the revolutionary legitimacy was replaced by democratic legitimacy, with the approval of the new Constitution and the formation of the first constitutional government, all other conditions also began to change: there was less concern with breaking with the past, there was a higher commitment to the democratic rule of law, and gradually the political spectrum became more balanced. This was not very distinctive from what happened in other second-wave democracies. In Italy, the clear victory of the Christian Democrats, in favour of forgetting and democratizing, was an important factor, as were the deep divisions among the Left. The Togliatti Amnesty, passed in June 1946, faced strong criticism, but Christian Democrats created a discourse based on the idea that the war against fascism between 1943 and 1945 and support for sanctions was suspicious and even anti-Italian and unpatriotic (Domenico 1991; Tarchi 2011). In Greece, which began its transition in 1974, the Social Democrats of the New Force were responsible for toning down the punitive process. "Karamanlis understood the destabilising effects of punitive policies when it affects large numbers of people; and second, he was aware that – at least until 1973 – most Greeks had not resisted the authoritarian regime" (Sotiropoulos 2011: 117). Similarly, in Portugal, in 1976, after the Socialists won the first legislative elections, a reintegration and reconciliation process began through which the most severe measures of the transition were reversed (Raimundo and Pinto 2014).

References

Aguilar, P. 2013. Judiciary involvement in authoritarian repression and transitional justice: The Spanish case in comparative perspective. *The International Journal of Transitional Justice* 7 (2): 245–266.
Antonakis-Nashif, A. 2016. Contested transformation: Mobilized publics in Tunisia between compliance and protest. *Mediterranean Politics* 21 (1): 128–149.
Capoccia, G., and D. Ziblatt. 2010. The historical turn in democratization studies: A new research agenda for Europe and beyond. *Comparative Political Studies* 43 (8/9): 968.
Cerezales, D.P. 2003. *O Poder Caiu Na Rua. Crise de Estado e Acções Colectivas na Revolução Portuguesa 1974–75*. Lisboa: Imprensa de Ciências Sociais.

Cervelló, J.S. 1993. *A Revolução Portuguesa e a sua Influência na Transição Espanhola (1961–76)*. Lisboa: Assírio & Alvim.

Collins, C. 2010. *Post-transitional justice: Human rights trials in Chile and El Salvador*. University Park: Penn State Press.

David, R. 2011. *Lustration and transitional justice: Personnel systems in the Czech Republic, Hungary and Poland*. Philadelphia: University of Pennsylvania Press.

De Brito, A.B., C. González-Enriquez, and P. Aguilar (eds.). 2001. *Politics of memory*. Oxford: Oxford University Press.

Di Palma, G. 1980. Founding coalitions in Southern Europe: Legitimacy and hegemony. *Government and Opposition* 15 (2): 162–189.

Domenico, R.P. 1991. *Italian fascists on trials, 1943–48*. Chapel Hill, NC: University of North Carolina Press.

Elster, J. 2004. *Closing the books*. Cambridge: Cambridge University Press.

Fassin, D. 2008. The embodied past: From paranoid type of politics of memory in South Africa. *Social Anthropology* 16 (3): 312–328.

Frain, M. 1998. *PPD/PSD e a Consolidação Do Regime Democrático*. Lisboa: Editorial Notícias.

Gibson, J.L. 2002. Truth, justice and reconciliation: Judging the fairness of amnesty in South Africa. *American Journal of Political Science* 46 (3): 540–556.

Hiblink, L. 2007. *Judges beyond politics in democracy and dictatorship: Lessons from Chile*. New York: Cambridge University Press.

Huntington, S. 1991. *The third wave: Democratization in the late twentieth century*. Norman: University of Oklahoma Press.

Kim, H.J. 2012. Structural determinants of human rights prosecutions after democratic transition. *Journal of Peace Research* 49 (2): 305–320.

Linz, J., and A. Stepan. 1996. *Problems of democratic transition and consolidation*. Baltimore: John Hopkins University Press.

Magalhães, P. 1995. Democratização E Independência Judicial Em Portugal. *Análise Social* 130 (1): 51–90.

Magalhães, P., C. Guarnieri, and Y. Kamisi. 2006. Democratic consolidation, judicial reform, and the judicialization of politics in Southern Europe. In *Democracy and the state in the New Southern Europe*. ed. R. Gunther, N. Diamandouros, and D. Sotiropoulos, 138–196. New York: Oxford University Press.

Mallinder, L. 2007. Can amnesties and international justice be reconciled? *International Journal of Transitional Justice* 1 (2): 208–230.

Marchi, R. 2012. As Direitas Radicais Na Transição Democrática Portuguesa (1974–76). *Ler Hsitória* 63: 75–91.

McAdams, D. 1997. *Transitional justice and the rule of law in new democracies*. Notre Dame: University of Notre Dame Press.

Morais, J.R. 2020. Quando as eleições não são para todos. As limitações dos direitos políticos nas eleições de 1975. In *As eleições de 1975. Eleições fundadoras da democracia portuguesa*, ed. F. Raimundo and J. Cancela. Lisboa: Assembleia da República.

Moran, J. 1994. The communist torturers of Eastern Europe: Prosecute and punish or forgive and forget? *Communist and Post-communist Studies* 27 (10): 95–101.

Nalepa, M. 2010. *Skeletons in the closet: Transitional justice in the post-communist world*. Cambridge: Cambridge University Press.

Offe, Claus, and U. Poppe. 2006. Transitional justice in the German Democratic Republic and in unified Germany. In *Retribution and reparation in the transition to democracy*, ed. J. Elster. Cambridge: Columbia University Press.

Olsen, T., L. Payne, and A. Reiter. 2010. *Transitional justice in balance: Comparing processes, weighing efficacy*. Washington, DC: United States Institute for Peace.

Pereira, A. 2005. *Political (In)justice: Authoritarianism and the rule of law in Brazil*. Chile and Argentina: Pittsburg University Press.

Pinto, A.C. 2006. Authoritarian legacies, transitional justice and state crisis in Portugal's democratization. *Democratization* 13 (2): 173–204.

Pinto, A.C. 2008. Political purges and state crisis in Portugal's transition to democracy, 1975–76. *Journal of Contemporary History* 43 (2). 305–332.

Pinto, A.C., and F. Raimundo. 2016. Violence, repression and terror in mass dictatorships: A view from the European margins. In *Palgrave handbook of mass dictatorships*, ed. L. Jie-Hjun and P. Corner, 105–117. London: Palgrave Macmillan.

Pion-Berlin, D. 1994. The Pinochet case and human rights progress in Chile: Was Europe a catalyst, cause or inconsequential? *Journal of Latin American Studies* 36 (3): 479–505.

Raimundo, F. 2012. Post-transitional justice? Spain, Poland and Portugal compared. PhD Dissertation, Department of Social and Political Sciences, Florence: EUI.

Raimundo, F. 2015. Strategic silence as a third way: Political parties and transitional justice. *Democratization* 22 (6): 1054–1073.

Raimundo, F. 2017. Justiça transicional e clivagem esquerda/direita no parlamento português (1976–2015). *Análise Social* 222 (1): 90–115.

Raimundo, F., and J.R. Morais. 2018. Justiça de Transição em Portugal: a Sequência e o Timing do Ajuste de Contas com o Passado. In *No Rastro das Transições: Perspectivas Sobre Memória, Verdade e Justiça no Cone Sul e no Sul da Europa, org*, ed. C.A. Gallo, 45–66. Pelotas: Editora Ufpel.

Raimundo, F., and A.C. Pinto. 2014. From ruptured transition to politics of silence: The case of Portugal. In *Transitional justice and memory in Europe (1945–2013)*, ed. N. Wouters. Cambridge: Intersentia Publishing.

Rezola, I. 2007. *25 De Abril. Mitos de uma Revolução*. Lisboa: Esfera Dos Livros.

Rezola, I. 2015. Transitional justice in the judiciary: Lessons from the Portuguese democratisation. *Studie Universitatis Cibiensis*. Series Historica xi: 15–35.

Rosas, F., et al. 2008. *Tribunais Políticos. Tribunais Militares Especiais e Tribunais Plenários Durante a Ditadura e o Estado Novo*. Temas e Debates.

Sczcerbiak, A. 2002. Dealing with the past or the politics of the present? Lustration in post-communist Poland. *Europe-Asia Studies* 54 (4): 553–572.

Sikkink, K. 2011. *The justice cascade: How human rights prosecutions are changing world politics*. New York and London: W. W. Norton.

Sotiropoulos, D.A. 2011. The authoritarian past and contemporary Greek Democracy. In *Dealing with the legacy of authoritarianism: The politics of the past in Southern European democracies*, ed. A.C. Pinto and L. Morlino, 109–124. London: Routledge.

Tarchi, M. 2011. Authoritarian past and democracy in Italy. In *Dealing with the legacy of authoritarianism: The politics of the past in Southern European democracies*, ed. António Costa Pinto and Leonardo Morlino, 39–54. London: Routledge.

Valenzuela, S. 1992. Democratic consolidation in post-transitional settings: Notion, process, and facilitating conditions. In *Issues in democratic consolidation: The new South American democracies in comparative perspective*, ed. Scott Mainwaring, Guillermo O'Donnell, and Samuel Valenzuela. Notre Dame: University of Notre Dame Press.

Welsh, H. 1996. Dealing with the communist past: Central and Eastern Europe experiences after 1990. *Europe-Asia Studies* 48 (3): 413–428.

Filipa Raimundo is Assistant Professor at the Department of Political Science and Public Policy at the ISCTE-Lisbon University Institute. She holds a PhD in Political and Social Sciences from the European University Institute, Florence. Her research interests include democratization, transitional justice and the quality of democracy. Her work has been published by journals such as Democratization, South European Society and Politics, and Mediterranean Politics and in edited volumes by Palgrave/Macmillan, Columbia University Press, and Interscientia.

Part IV
Transitional Time: Theoretical Approaches

Chapter 13
Transitional Justice: A Likely Story

Gabriel Rezende

Abstract In this paper, I explore the conceptual connections between transitology and transitional justice, focusing on Ruti Teitel's theoretical approach. Although transitional justice has brought about one of the most interesting critiques of the "transitional paradigm", it still relies on the same teleology of consolidation, i.e., the idea that normative stability is a goal to be achieved through elite pacts. I reject this view in favour of a transitional constitutionalism based on what I shall call a "genetic conception of justice".

13.1 Introduction

In 2009, when Paige Arthur published her famous essay "How 'Transitions' Reshaped Human Rights: A Conceptual History of Transitional Justice", a great number of practitioners and theoreticians were already convinced of the necessity to question transitional justice's liberal ideology (Nagy 2008). In constructing rules, principles, mechanisms, procedures and institutions based on an idealized image of Western democracies, transitional justice would have become an artificial set of remedies designed for a narrow understanding of violence. "Gender-based approaches" (for all, Rimmer 2010), "decolonial critiques" (Castillejo Cuéllar 2017) and "bottom-up studies" (McEvoy and McGregor 2008) are some of the rubrics that have been driving this critical effort since then.

However, Arthur's contribution goes beyond uncovering hidden ideological constraints in transitional justice. In reconstructing the history of the field, she explains why, in the late twentieth-century, the coupling of "justice" and "transition" succeed in congregating opposed political views, such as North-American neoconservatism and left-wing South-American human rights activism (Arthur 2009). Arthur

---

[1] Guilhot and Schmitter (2000) reject the idea that these lexicons form a coherent theoretical framework.

G. Rezende (✉)
Instituto Brasiliense de Direito Público, Brasília, Brazil

© Springer Nature Switzerland AG 2021
C. Paixão and M. Meccarelli (eds.), *Comparing Transitions to Democracy. Law and Justice in South America and Europe*, Studies in the History of Law and Justice 18,
https://doi.org/10.1007/978-3-030-67502-8_13

identifies a conceptual system that served as common lexicon both for theoretical discussions and practical endeavours.[1] Transitional justice, according to her, inherited the theoretical framework developed in the 1970s and 1980s by the so called "transitologists", a group of scholars interested in "understanding" the changes in political regimes across Latin America and, afterwards, in other regions of the globe. The word "understanding" should be enclosed in quotation marks because the "Transitions project", led by argentine political scientist Guillermo O'Donnel, also contained a performative dimension: it assumed, normatively, the desirability of democratic regimes, and intended to contribute to transitions in that direction.

Arthur judges the "transition paradigm" problematic in transitional justice for three main reasons. Firstly, the normative ideal of a transition to (liberal) democracy may be daunting to justice claims related to socio-economic issues: the main example would be the South African transition. Secondly, the conceptual framework designed for Latin American realities cannot be entirely applied to societies experiencing economic revolutions as in Eastern Europe (Arthur 2009: 369). Finally, justice claims may be hindered by transitions characterized by State failure, as for instance the transition from neopatrimonialism to democracy in sub-Saharan Africa.

Regardless of the validity of those claims, they point to a conceptual connection between transitional justice and transitology. In a very schematic way, transitology could be characterized by four key features, that we call here the "Thesis-T": (a) transitology renounces functionalist and structural explanations of political change, adopting an agency-based model that privileges political elites' behavior (Vitullo 2001: 54)[2]; (b) Instead of focusing on socio-economic constraints, transitology analyzes legal and institutional patterns that determine political change; (c) Democracy is thus defined as a very singular "pact", i.e., an agreement between a reformist elite in government and a moderate democratic opposition. This pact concerns future rules for the new regime, but also involves bargains aiming at some sort of political equilibrium. Reformists and moderates exclude therefore the more radical fractions of the political spectrum and present themselves as trustees of a future consolidated democracy[3]; (d) Transitions are periods of intense normative uncertainty and elites operate without a single and clear set of general rules and procedures. "Consolidation" means the end of this period of uncertainty.

We now understand why the term "transition" is so important. In its classical definition—"the interval between one political regime and another" (O'Donnell and Schmitter 1986: 6)—, this concept offers a fairly wide and indeterminate scope: it is abstract enough to be applied to different political realities. However, when read in light of the "transition paradigm", it functions as a magnet that attracts other concepts; particularly the one of "consolidation". Transitologists assume in general that, although transitions have a point of departure (the dissolution of an authoritarian regime), they do not have a necessary *denouement*.[4] And this is the very paradox

---

[2] For a critique of this elite-based methodology in social sciences, see Avritzer (2002).

[3] For an exceptionally clear example of this argument, see Huntington (1991: 165).

[4] The authors believe that transitions tend towards an uncertain "something else" (O'Donnell and Schmitter 1986: 3).

of transitology: transitions are both factually uncertain and normatively oriented towards democratic consolidation. Between the constative and the performative status of those claims, "transition" ends up being defined by "consolidation".

For no sooner we accept Thesis-T, than we meet the following argument: (a) transitions are a period of incertitude where rules and procedures are not well-defined or are not universally accepted; (b) consolidation is the moment where the political bargain among elites reaches stability and becomes the only set of institutional norms regulating political action; (c) therefore, consolidation is the outcome of a pact that brings transition to its completion.

There are obvious difficulties in working with this model. Besides its abstract character, Thesis-T seems to imply a low-intensity democracy. We are simply left with no explanation of how political legitimacy can be created out of the sole action of political elites. Over the years, researchers connected to the "Transitions project" have addressed this problem with more or less success.[5] One can argue, nevertheless, that it is precisely transitional justice that offers the best answer to it. Since its earliest formulations, transitional justice's measures presented limits to elite-sponsored pacts. The punishment of former state or state-sponsored criminality is probably the best example of how a normative input is designed to create wider social consensus. By virtue of their high payoff in political stability, transitologists often saw amnesties as key parts of elite pacts. Transitional justice shifts this perspective: questions of legal and moral rights overlap with the main goal of consolidation. "Punishment" and "impunity" may still divide opinions, but no one is authorized to simply dismiss justice claims as impediments to consolidation.[6]

Regardless of what we may consider as the right answer to the problem of punishment, transitions are neither a suspension of normativity nor a political dispute in a vacuum of rules and procedures. Consolidation cannot be achieved without reinforcing a general sense of respect for the rule of law. Normative claims are not only valuable contributions to a regime change, but also necessary properties of transitions. Pacts are not sufficient to stabilize democracies, for new normative environments depend on the kind of legitimacy created through practical rationality.

What are the main consequences of this new approach to transitional justice? In the next section, we shall sketch Ruti Teitel's theory of transitional justice, demonstrating how she corrects transitology by introducing something similar to a Thesis-JT. Then, we shall explain why this "correction" is unconvincing and in what sense transitional justice proceeds along the lines of a genetic conception of justice. This argument shall lead us to a complete revaluation of transitional constitutions and transitional constitutionalism. We shall conclude that the concept of "consolidation" should be rejected in favor of a "likely story": transitional constitutions as normative syntheses of past influx (the violence of the *ancien régime*) and project (societal transformation).

---

[5] O'Donnell (1992: 48) talks about a certain *desencanto* in what regards consolidation. Guilhot and Schmitter (2000) will enumerate the risks comprised in conflating consolidation and stabilisation.

[6] Clarifying her own position during the debates on punishment during transitions, Ruti Teitel stated that: "despite the moral argument for punishment in the abstract, various alternatives to punishment could express the normative message of political transformation and the rule of law, with the aim of furthering democracy". See Teitel (2000: viii).

13.2   Ruti Teitel's Transitional Justice

Ruti Teitel gives us privileged access to this discussion: she has not only coined the term "transitional justice" (Teitel 2008), but also established a theoretical framework that underpins the whole field. In that sense, her writings organize a dominant theory.[7]

According to Teitel, transitional justice is the justice associated with political transformation. Quoting, among others, O'Donnel and Schmitter, she uses the classical definition of the term "transition"—"transitional justice arises within a bounded period, spanning two regimes" (Teitel 2000: 6)—in order to move away from the vocabulary of "revolution". This seems to confirm Paige Arthur's thesis that transitional justice inherits the transitional paradigm. But there are also significant differences in Teitel's approach. After all, she explicitly criticizes transitology for focusing excessively on electoral procedures and other political criteria. In contrast, she demonstrates that law plays a fundamental role in transitions: legal systems determine the outcome of transitions, whilst being determined by it.

Teitel does not seek to negate Thesis-T; she offers instead a supplement to it. Call it Thesis-JT: (a) transitions are the result of elite-driven action that can subsequently acquire legitimacy; (b) legal institutions are quintessential to a successful transition; (c) pacts are possible, but they must incorporate a certain degree of justice, that is, pacts should sponsor the rule of law; (d) transitions are a time of fluid normativity.

This theoretical system is still informed by an action-based model that privileges elite behavior, and institutions continue to be regarded as the proper objects of observation—although focus is shifted to legal institutions. The main differences between Thesis-T and Thesis-JT lie in the last two criteria: the pact and the normative vacuum. In Thesis-JT, pacts are somehow limited by justice claims and transitions are no longer devoid of legal and moral obligations. Should we not conclude, then, that Thesis-JT negates Thesis-T? Should we not conclude that transitional justice raises a radical objection to transitology? In the remaining sections, we elaborate an affirmative answer to these questions.

Before we do so, we must explain why Teitel hesitates to move in this direction. The reason is her adherence to a teleology of consolidation. The rule of law, according to her, must be promoted in order to preserve the main goal of consolidating democracies. Let us go back once again to the problem of Criminal Justice and amnesties. Here is what Teitel writes on her famous 2000 book *Transitional Justice*:

> This trade-off of the balancing of perpetrators' political rights in exchange for support of the newly constituted union and for the aim of political stability mirrors punishment's more conventional goals of assuring ongoing rule of law. So it is that amnesties can advance the normative project of the political transition. (Teitel 2000: 54)

This quotation is particularly illustrative of Teitel's theoretical maneuver. The idea here is, roughly, that regardless of the content of existing pacts, and regardless of the design of further policies (memorials, purges, reforms), actors have to assure

---

[7] Teitel's work is a sort of standard liberal transitional justice and is often the attacked paradigm when it comes to critical transitional justice. See Pfeiffer (2015).

a certain level of commitment to the rule of law. This, of course, is not a static or idealized form, but rather a dynamic understanding of legality. Teitel constructs a theoretical dilemma: if rule of law, in standard legal philosophy, means adherence to "settled legal precedent", transitions impose an imperative of transformation. Both have to be balanced in order to reach democratic stability. In other words, rule of law is both the final goal of a successful transition and a constructive procedure where actors increasingly specify their understanding of legality.

Instead of dismissing the idea of "pacts", Teitel enlarges the political calculus of elites and incorporates the burden of restoring the "rule of law". Both punishment and amnesty, in our example, are valid results of a *trade-off* if they succeed in adding a normative component, or a normative message to it. In a way, Teitel solves transitology's fundamental paradox—transitions are contingent but democratic consolidation is the desirable goal—by providing a "regulative ideal"[8]: "[transitions] mean change in a liberalizing direction" (Teitel 2000: 10). In other words, consolidation now equals rule of law. There are at least two problems with this reasoning. Firstly, if "consolidation" and "rule of law" are now synonyms, only arbitrary criteria, developed within transitional processes, could define the end of transition. Secondly, one has to suppose a moment in time where the definition of the concept of legality cannot be further developed.

Is it possible to defend a constructive concept of rule of law and define transitions as bounded periods spanning two regimes? Teitel would think so. She assumes that an answer to this dilemma is possible along the lines of Thesis-JT—transitions are a normative flux, limited in time, tending towards a liberal stabilization of democratic legal institutions—: "a pragmatic balancing of ideal justice with political realism that instantiates a symbolic rule of law capable of constructing liberalizing change" (Teitel 2000: 215). We shall now analyze if this hypothesis is credible.

13.3 Distributing Violence

Transitional justice and transitology form a far less coherent body than Teitel is ready to admit. We demonstrate that transitional justice, if properly reconstructed, cancels out Thesis-T and Thesis-JT altogether. Our main disagreement with Teitel does not lie in the properties she assigns to transitional justice, but rather in the modality of this assignment. Those properties are causally irrelevant; they do not have causal powers to fully determine the outcome of transitions. Instead of focusing on whether law

---

[8] This is not in contradiction with Teitel's claim that Transitional Justice rejects a universal or ideal norm. In fact, she dismisses all universalism based on conceptual rigidity and abstract theories of justice. We use the term "regulative ideal" in a more kantian sense to designate principles that should be treated pragmatically. Without possible full knowledge of them, one can only postulate their existence as open horizons. A regulative ideal is a guide to action open to further specifications. That is how we read the following passage: "Transitional Justice begins by rejecting the notion that the move toward a more liberal democratic political system implies a universal or ideal norm" (Teitel 2000: 4).

contributes to the construction of a liberal regime, the relevant question is whether the autonomy of law and politics can be articulated as a shared horizon, or what we call a likely story. In simpler terms, we are interested in the possibility of opening the transition to new actors and new narratives. The autonomy of law means the possibility of using legal rules and legal principles to create unexpected articulations between the memory of the *ancien régime* and a project of societal transformation. We will take seriously Teitel's claim that the notion of "transitional justice" does not result in an abstract ideal, and show, contrary to her, that the concept of "consolidation" should be rejected.

One cannot explore Thesis-JT antinomical nature without referring to its self-defeating status. Here is our point of departure: transitions are normativity structured, i.e., justice claims can be formulated in terms of rights. According to Teitel, from this premise follows another: "Law is caught between the past and the future, between backward-looking and forward-looking, between retrospective and prospective, between the individual and the collective" (Teitel 2000: 6). This is transitional justice's most fundamental idea.

Borrowing the old vocabulary of phenomenology, we could say that this is a shift from a *static* to a *genetic* conception of justice. By "static conception of justice" we understand a priori possibilities, structures of validity at play in the constitution of the sense of justice. A "genetic conception of justice" investigates justice's conceptual unity as a temporal construct, as layers of sense sedimentation that are inescapably historical.[9]

Theories of justice are in general static, because they seek to identify justice's conditions of possibility in our practices or language games. Teitel believes that John Rawls' "justice as fairness" is such a theory. It comes as no surprise, nevertheless, that political liberalism represents for her a sort of paradigm. Teitel characterizes her approach as "constructivist" in reference to Rawls' "political constructivism" (Rawls 1993: 89–99): a gradual construction of political consensus through participants' own rational selection of principles. The difference, she argues, is that transitional justice is a less idealized version of these procedures. Instead of gradual construction of consensus, transitions cause a drastic normative change of perspective, leading to a change in what is considered politically possible or desirable (Teitel 2000: 196).

These discussions pertain to transitional constitutionalism. If we want to investigate the role of law during transitions, constitutions, the most dominant articulation of law and politics in modernity, should be placed at the center of our analysis. The problem, according to Teitel, is that constitutional theory is still informed by eighteenth-century political philosophy and is unable to capture the specificity of transitional phenomena. Modern constitutionalism would be predicated upon the ideal relation between revolutionary change and political foundationalism. This model would then define constitutions as the culmination of a liberal rupture with the *ancien régime*, as well as the founding element of a new political order.

---

[9] According to Husserl: "Only by virtue of this genetic Apriori does what was already said in advance become evident (and evident in its profounder sense): that, in what analysis uncovers as intentionally implicit in the living sense-constitution, there lies a sedimented 'history'" (Husserl 1969: 250).

Teitel, takes it that transitional justice corrects constitutionalism by introducing temporal digression, constitutive delay and gradual development. She is of course aware of the fact that twentieth-century literature on the topic has mainly evolved to admit constitutional changes other than the framing of a text and its ratification. Readers familiar with Bruce Ackerman's "constitutional moments" will recognize the idea of periods of high political consensus that transform passionate mobilization into "lasting legal achievements" (Ackerman 1989: 477). Yet Teitel's argument is more "transitological". She argues that foundationalists such as Ackerman create a false distinction between constitutional and ordinary politics. According to her, transitional constitutions are not necessarily driven by the irruption of popular sovereignty; they are often the result of elitedriven processes and gradual increments in legitimacy. In other words, constitutions follow Thesis-JT: "A transitional perspective helps to explain why in periods of political upheaval, even limited popular participation may well suffice to legitimate constitutional transformation" (Teitel 2000: 195). Stability is not only the main goal of transitions, but also its medium. "Transition" means a growing identification between a pact and the shared notion of rule of law in a given political community.

This is another example of the common gesture that we have seen throughout *Transitional Justice*. Although Teitel presents the resources for moving forward from transitology, she decides to reinforce the "transition paradigm": transitional constitutions become instruments in view of consolidation.[10] Still, assuming Teitel's premises, we may reach different conclusions. Let the genetic conception of justice inscribed both in constitutionalism and transitional justice be our Ariadne's thread here. Consider the following formulation of the problem by Teitel herself:

> The notion of transitionality has a number of normative implications. Within prevailing theory, constitutionalism is commonly understood as unidirectional, forward-looking, and fully prospective. [...] While the picture of a polis at constitutional point zero might have been appropriate for describing constitutionalism in the eighteenth century, in the late twentieth-century, constitutions associated with political change generally succeed preexisting constitutional regimes and are thus not simply created anew. (Teitel 2000: 196)

This co-implication of the practical rationality with retention and protention forms the core of transitional constitutions. This is what allows us to refer to a genetic conception of justice. Nonetheless, we are more skeptical when it comes to Teitel's claim that transitional justice brings a sort of correction applied to constitutionalism. It is not true that the latter has always been fully prospective and unidirectional[11]; this might not even be true of what Teitel calls the "prevailing conception of constitutionalism"—it is certainly incorrect to attribute this idea to Hannah Arendt (Teitel 2000: 193). From our perspective, transitional justice's merits lie rather in making explicit what remained implicit in the very notion of "constitution": a conception of justice that cannot do away with a distribution of violence.

---

[10] Teitel is adamant that other legal instruments are just as important as constitutions in view of consolidation (Teitel 2000: 196).

[11] See, for example, Sophie Wahnich's analysis of what she calls a "founding sentimental economy" during the French Revolution. Wahnich (2003).

We can illustrate that by an experiment in political constructivism. Suppose a rawlsian-like original position. This is a hypothetical situation where individuals have to decide upon principles of justice without having any knowledge of their own social class situation or their political status. Instead of admitting, as Rawls does, that the role of justice is confined to the distribution of values (rights and duties; material and immaterial values) produced in society,[12] we consider that justice also distributes political violence. Under the veil of ignorance, lack of information about social and cultural membership is coupled with an unawareness of one's belonging to a generation. Already for Rawls, many questions of justice arise between generations (environmental issues, for instance); this will be even more important to us, because transitional justice is mainly intergenerational. While the agreements reached in the original position are supposed to form, according to Rawls, a first rational consensus from which others may be derived, in our transitional justice thought-experiment participants understand that there can be no "original" or "foundational" act: the new political order is necessarily the heir of an *ancien régime*. It inherits a whole legal framework (statutes, precedents, doctrines) that may or may not be revisited; it inherits a body of public officials that may or may not be purged; it inherits crimes that may or may not be punished. Thus, participants' rational analysis of concurring theories of justice is not static, but genetic. They know that the a priori structure that determines their choice of principles is, in itself, historical. There is no ground zero in terms of normativity. Past political violence has to be identified, calculated, and then redistributed in the form of punishment, individual or collective redress, legal reform, memorials, purges, public excuses, etc.

Does this imply that participants will end up not choosing Rawls' famous two principles of justice? This is not the right question to be asked at this point. For besides the distribution of all the benefits of a given political association, we are interested here in the distribution of political violence. State-sponsored violence is a reality in every transition. What is the interpretative role of this assumption? If we are to propose a genetic conception of justice, rational participants in the original position need to admit that they might have been, at some point, persecuted and forced into exile; that they might have been tortured; that their grandsons and granddaughters might have been stolen and illegally adopted by other families; that they might have been sexually abused or been subjected to forced pregnancy; that they might have been disappeared.

Teitel is right in saying that transitional constitutions are ongoing constructivist experiments that *take time*. However, she is wrong in ascribing to it a "transitional" character, i.e., a transient, provisional, instrumental quality. A realist account may very well gather enough evidence about negotiations and pacts that have led to the drafting of a constitution; an idealist account may deplore the lack of either popular sovereignty or liberal institutions during the same process. But transitional justice should not be reduced to the realist-idealist divide. Instead of focusing on

---

[12] According to Rawls, the principles of justice "provide a way of assigning rights and duties in the basic institutions of society and they define the appropriate distribution of the benefits and burdens of social cooperation" (Rawls 1971: 4).

consolidation and the prospects for reaching it, a transitional justice account must respond to the normative openness of every transition. This is the reason why we prefer the term "genetic" to the term "constructivist". When we consider a genetic conception of justice, intrinsically tied to constitutionalism, foundations are caught amidst retention and protention, memory and project. Since we admit that the a priori structures of constitutional democracies are historical, we can only *re-create* its "constitutional moments". Transitional justice defies our understanding of what it means to begin something new, especially in the realm of normativity. Every original position, whether it is a thought experiment or not, has a presupposition. Here, we have to reconcile two different claims. On the one hand, foundations synthesize past influx: a constitution has to deal with past injustices and the heritage of the *ancien régime*. On the other hand, the foundation can only happen a posteriori. This seems anathema, but is actually perfectly logical: sense-unity is always open to further specification—Husserl calls it an "infinite task"—; therefore, the meaning of the founding principles, the meaning of the origin depends on an act of sense reactivation. The beginning is always the beginning of something that supersedes it: an intrinsically unending process of elliptical return (Husserl 1978).

In our opinion, Transitional constitutionalism successfully articulates these two claims. It assumes that justice involves a legacy of political violence that has to be constantly readdressed. This is true not only in virtue of potential new historical evidence (which is often the case with Truth Commissions and the disclosure of classified archives), but also in light of the perpetual redefinition of our principles, and of what counts as violence. Recent discussions about transitional justice and economic development, or transitional justice and environmental justice are good examples, whereby the subjects of justice claims are potentially redefined. Transitional constitutions defy the notion of "pacts" precisely because they are uncontrollable: they have no beginning and no end.[13] Their functioning has nothing to do with political stabilization (a pact among elites), but rather with the autonomy of Law (the possibility of publicly enunciating justice claims and redistributing past political violence).

13.4 A Likely Story

"Consolidation" is impossible: *constitutional democracy is transition.* Thesis-T and Thesis-JT are incompatible with the genetic conception of justice that transitional justice embraces. For the ideas of "elite pacts" and of a "bracketing of normativity" fail to account for the distribution of violence. There is no concept of consolidation which permits constitutions to be "consolidated": constitutions are, in our point of view, transitional constitutions.

---

[13] This is particularly clear in the jurisprudence of the Inter-American Court of Human Rights. Since *Barrios Altos v. Peru* the Court has repeatedly affirmed that self-amnesty laws, the quintessential modality of elite pacts, have no legal validity under international human rights law.

There are two ways of looking at the connection between law and consolidation and, therefore, there are two kinds of constitutionalists. The first one is close to the position held by Carlos Nino. In his book *Radical Evil on Trial*, Nino defined as "moral luck" the investigation and prosecution of human rights abuses committed during Argentinian dictatorship. According to him, the success of former President Raúl Alfonsín's policies depended on a very unstable series of factors that could have produced exactly the opposite effect: instead of reinforcing a commitment to the rule of law, punishment could have destabilized the transitional government. Nino then affirms: "this last caveat becomes all the more cogent once we realize that preserving the democratic system is a prerequisite for carrying out those very prosecutions and the loss of it is a necessary antecedent to massive human rights violations" (Nino 1996: 187).

The second kind of constitutionalist is well represented by Brazilian jurist Menelick de Carvalho Netto. In his 1992 book *A sanção no procedimento legislativo*, Carvalho Netto develops an interpretative model based on a normative brake with authoritarian constitutionalism. In other words, he believes that democratic constitutions can only produce normative meaning if they rightly address the authoritarian legacy spread throughout their correspondent legal order. Carvalho Netto's examples are not restricted to mass violence or political criminality: he also bears consideration to conceptual systems, legal frameworks, and past decisions that are implicitly anti-democratic. The aforementioned task of democratizing the legal order is seen as an infinite process, and constitutions are nothing but a "permanent becoming" (Carvalho Netto 1992: 294). Unlike transitional pacts, constitutions seek unity within a political project oriented towards social transformation. Rather than a compromise between elite actors defending their interests, constitutions are a common design that has to be constantly reactivated and re-articulated in light of present political circumstances.

When one is a constitutionalist of the second type, transitions represent projects, horizons of transformation. Without ever mentioning the word, Carvalho Netto defines transitional constitutions in the precise terms that we did here: pressure of antagonisms, interpretative openness, democratic response to the authoritarian legacy and transformative project. Consolidation, in that sense, is "becoming" or, in our own terms, "transition". This helps us clarify the title of our paper: "Transitional justice: a likely story". We are hinting at a famous passage of Plato's *Timaeus,* where the title character explains that a proper account of an object should be fashioned after the characteristics of that very object. If we are dealing with change and becoming (e.g., the physical world), our own speech, says Timaeus, is limited to a "likely story" (*eikôs muthos*), a plausible account (Plato 1929: 29c-4). Transitions are objects of that kind. However, our concern here is neither metaphysical nor epistemological. We are rather interested in the necessary connection between the normative and the narrative character of transitional constitutions. It is our contention that transitional constitutions acquire democratic legitimacy if and only if they socially articulate a convincing account of their own transformative project.

Only a "likely story" corresponds to that articulation. This is not to say that we negate the possibility of truth in history, especially when it comes to truth-seeking

processes and the right to truth. Once agains, our concern here is not epistemological, but normative. Constitutions are "likely stories" in the sense that they create
a reasonable account of normative change (a brake with authoritarian constitutionalism), one that is worth believing in. This account is not static: it is open to constant
re-actualization by its members. As in Carvalho Netto, the constitutional identity of
political communities that have faced transitions is marked both by the authoritarian
legacy and the transformative project: no positive dialectics can do away with this
tension. This should allow not only jurisprudence but also every interpreter of the
constitution to reshape justice claims and reinterpret the authoritarian vestiges in the
legal order. In other words, another "likely story" is always possible.

13.5 Conclusions

Once we assume that transitional justice is mainly concerned with a genetic conception of justice, the idea of "consolidation" becomes problematic. We argued that
this problem is all the more visible in transitional constitutionalism, where questions surrounding democratic legitimacy are intertwined with the transformation of
authoritarian legacies. Consolidation, however, presupposes a version of Thesis-T
or Thesis-JT in which elite pacts are seen as necessary instruments to overcome
periods of political turmoil and high normative contingency. Consolidation would
then be both the conclusion of the transitions and its main goal: relative stability
that respects the coordination efforts among elite actors. We have shown that this
idea is simply inconsistent with transitional justice, which states: (a) the autonomy
of law regarding any sort of pact; (b) the permanent possibility of re-actualizing
the relationship between the memory of the *ancien régime* and a project of political
transformation. We concluded that *democracy is transition to democracy*.

In her recent work, Ruti Teitel alludes to the conceptual difficulties that accompany
the term "consolidation". In *Transitional Justice and the transformation of constitutionalism*—a paper published originally in 2011 and later republished in *Globalizing
Transitional Justice: Contemporary Essays* (2014)—, Teitel recognizes in contemporary constitutional experiences a strong intertwinement with transitional justice's
main tenets, especially accountability. But the growing judicialization of transitional
claims, combined with the spreading influence of international tribunals, has resulted
in a phenomenon that has not been studied in *Transitional justice*: "transitional justice
postponed—often decades after the fact, particularly in the African continent, as well
as in parts of Latin America" (Teitel 2014: 188). Teitel sees in it an important discussion on the limits of the constitutional self (and national unity) during transitions.
She goes as far as asking:

> Can we still really speak of an independent understanding of transitional justice particular
> to moments of radical political change, when mechanisms associated with traditional justice
> become institutionalized as general obligations of accountability for the past, required as a
> matter of constitutional and/or international law? (Teitel 2014: 181)

Unfortunately, this question is never properly addressed by Teitel. We can see why: if we affirm that transitional justice is no longer limited to moments of radical political change, if we affirm that transitional justice processes can take place in apparently "consolidated" political regimes, then it is the concept of "consolidation" that has to be criticized. And this entails a critique of the whole legacy of transitology: a critique that Teitel does not seem inclined to elaborate.

References

Ackerman, B. 1989. Constitutional politics/constitutional law. *Yale Law Journal* 99 (3): 453–547.

Arthur, P. 2009. How "Transitions" reshaped human rights: A conceptual history of transitional justice. *Human Rights Quarterly* 31: 321–367.

Avritzer, L. 2002. *Democracy and the public space in Latin America*. Princeton: Princeton University Press.

Carvalho Netto, M.D. 1992. *A Sanção no procedimento legislativo*. Belo Horizonte: Del Rey.

Castillejo Cuéllar, A. 2017. *La ilusión de la justicia transicional: Perspectivas críticas desde el Sur global*. Colección general: Ediciones Universidad de los Andes.

Guilhot, N., and P.C. Schmitter. 2000. De la transition à la consolidation: une lecture rétrospective des *democratization studies*. *Revue française de science politique* 50: 615–631.

Huntington, S. 1991. *The third wave: Democratization in the late twentieth century*. Norman, London: University of Oklahoma Press.

Husserl, E. 1969. *Formal and transcendental logic*. The Hague: Martinus Nijhoff.

Husserl, E. 1978. *Origin of geometry*. Stony Brook: N. Hays.

McEvoy, K., and L. McGregor. 2008. Transitional justice from below: Grassroots activism and the struggle for change. In *Human rights law in perspective*, vol. 14, ed. K. McEvoy and L. McGregor. Oxford: Hart Publisher.

Nagy, R. 2008. Transitional justice as global project: Critical reflections. *Third World Quarterly* 29 (2): 275–289.

Nino, C.S. 1996. *Radical evil on trial*. New Haven: Yale University Press.

O'Donnell, G. 1992. Transitions continuities and paradoxes. In *Issues in democratic consolidation: The New South American democracies in comparative perspective*, ed. Scott Mainwaring, Guillermo O'Donnell, and Samuel Valenzuela, 17–56. Notre Dame: University of Notre Dame Press.

O'Donnell, G., and P.C. Schmitter. 1986. *Transitions from authoriarian rule: Tentative conclusions about uncertain democracies*. Baltimore: The Johns Hopkins University Press.

Plato, E. 1929. *Timaeus; Critias; Cleitophon; Menexenus; Epistles*. Cambridge, MA: Harvard University Press.

Pfeiffer, D. 2015. *Globalisierung und Vergangenheitsbearbeitung: Eine makrosoziologische Analyse von Transitional Justice*. Marburg: Springer.

Rawls, J.A. 1971. *Theory of justice*. Cambridge, MA: The Belknap Press of Harvard University Press.

Rawls, J. 1993. *Political liberalism*. New York: Columbia University Press.

Rimmer, S.H. 2010. *Gender and transitional justice: The women of East Timor*. London: Routledge.

Teitel, R. 2000. *Transitional justice*. Oxford: Oxford University Press.

Teitel, R. 2008. Transitional justice globalized. *The International Journal of Transitional Justice* 2 (1): 1–4.

Teitel, R. 2014. *Globalizing transitional justice*. Oxford: Oxford University Press.

Vitullo, G.E. 2001. Transitologia, consolidologia e democracia na América Latina: Uma revisão crítica. *Revista de Sociologia e Política* 17: 53–60.

Wahnich, S. 2003. *La liberté ou la mort: Essai sur la Terreur et le terrorisme*. Paris: Fabrique.

Gabriel Rezende teaches Constitutional Theory at the Instituto Brasiliense de Direito Público (Brazil). He obtained his doctorate in Philosophy at Université Paris 8 (France). He received a research grant from CAPES (Brazil) and wrote a thesis entitled "Droit et Normativité chez Jacques Derrida". He also holds a Master of Laws (LL.M) from the University of Brasília (Brazil). He is specialized in contemporary philosophy, legal philosophy and constitutional theory, with particular interest in transitional justice.

Chapter 14
Taking Transitional Justice Carefully: Multi-temporalities, Care, and Inclusion in Times of Transition

Douglas Antônio Rocha Pinheiro

Abstract This chapter goes back to the expression *justice in times of transition*, common in early reflections on the subject of the accountability of regimes that violate human rights, in order to criticize the chronocentric and chronormative attitude of current transitional justice. We say it is chronocentric because it usually operates with a view to linear chronological time, which is marked by a presentist hegemonic contemporaneity and whose boundaries as to past, future, and other alternative presents are rigidly built. It is chronormative because, by highlighting majoritarian life projects in democracy and rendering subaltern identities and experiences impossible, it strengthens the control over bodies initiated by the regime that violate human rights—and which transitional justice should overcome. As an alternative, a proposal is made for a transition to inclusion, which does not replace the goal of transition to democracy, but which renders it sensitive to constitutionalism, the right to difference, and non-linear and non-normative temporalities. To this end, we suggest a strategy of conjugating the ethics of justice and the ethics of care, which enables the integration of rules, rights, abstract procedures, and sets of principles with intersubjectivity, responsibility, specificity, and the accumulation of local experiences.

14.1 Introduction: Going Back to *Justice in Times of Transition*

The origin of a concept does not correspond to the origin of the social practices it describes. Of course, some of the characteristic features of any current concept may be found in past spaces of experience. However, historical methodology does not recommend that such previous practices be identified as part of a necessary archaeology of theoretical constructs that can only emerge by virtue of concrete conditions specific to, and temporally located in, contemporaneity. That is why it

D. A. R. Pinheiro (✉)
School of Law, University of Brasília, Brasília, Brazil
e-mail: darpinheiro@unb.br

© Springer Nature Switzerland AG 2021
C. Paixão and M. Meccarelli (eds.), *Comparing Transitions to Democracy. Law and Justice in South America and Europe*, Studies in the History of Law and Justice 18, https://doi.org/10.1007/978-3-030-67502-8_14

is possible to trace the existence of retributive and punitive practices adopted by political regimes in times of transition back to both the Athens of the fifth century B.C. (Elster 2004) and the post-World War II Nuremberg Tribunal (Teitel 2003). Still, it seems anachronistic to consider such experiences as prior examples of transitional justice, since this concept was not then available for social actors to use it as an instrument for meditating on the practices of the time.

This problem is not merely terminological. In many cases, the crystallization of a new concept reflects the identification of emerging demands or original solutions to the problems of a particular society. With regard to the notion of *transitional justice*, although it is hard to track its first conscious use—which may have occurred between the late 1980s and the early 1990s—the diffusion and recognition of its theoretical specificity has advanced significantly since the publication of *Transitional Justice: How Emerging Democracies Reckon with Former Regimes*, a full-length book edited by Neil Kritz in 1995. As Paige Arthur (2009) shows, the book has received several reviews and its visibility has put the incipient concept to the test. Its almost unanimously positive reception ended up proving its ability to synthesize the various convergent processes that occurred in the 1980s: the repositioning of the human rights movements, especially in Latin America, which were concerned with maintaining their relevance after the end of dictatorial regimes, and the changes in understandings of the transitional turn to democracy, which could be accomplished through legal-institutional reforms independent of a correspondent social-economic transformation.

At the time, the only voice that pointed out the reductionism of the concept was Timothy Ash's. For Ash, a historian, *transitional justice* did not comprise the different possibilities for dealing with the practices and narratives of fallen dictatorial regimes, and he preferred to use traditional German terms (*geschichtsaufarbeitung* and *vergangenheitsbewältigung*) that indicated complex, even contradictory alternatives for dealing with the past, which could, in turn, be ended, confronted, or overcome (Arthur 2009: 332). Ash had in mind the *Historikerstreit*, the debate conducted by intellectuals who, in the late 1980s, diverged over whether to maintain the duty of memory with regard to the horrors of the Holocaust or to seal off the past and start building a new national narrative. Because he followed this debate, Timothy Ash was able to see the complexities that could be concealed by a restrictive concept based only on the transition to democracy.

It happens, however, that there is another concealment that is hardly ever mentioned in the sanctioning of the expression *transitional justice*. The first widely-attended congress on the subject, organized in Salzburg in 1992 by Charter 77 Foundation, had as its theme "Justice in Times of Transition." The theme actually corresponded to the event organizers and their assistants' preferred expression for describing their activities, and then it ended up lending its name to an organization, the Project on Justice in Times of Transition, founded in the United States in 1993 (Arthur 2009: 329). At first, one may think that *transitional justice* and *justice in times of transition* are synonymous concepts, but their similarity is only admissible if the complexity of the second is reduced.

This simplification is similar to one suffered by Reinhart Koselleck in a specific translation for English-speaking contexts. Koselleck says that history can only exist as a discipline if it is capable of elaborating *eine Theorie der geschichtlichen Zeiten*, whose literal translation would be "a theory of historical times." However, in the 2002 English translation of his book *The Practice of Conceptual History*, with a preface by Hayden White, the "theory of historical times" gives way to the "theory of periodization," a change that probably occurred based on the assumption that historians only take an interest in plural times when they are arranged in a chronological succession of historical periods. This replacement is not innocuous. It eliminates the complexity of Koselleck's theory, which, in his approach to historical times, points to an overcoming of the linear narrative that rigidly limits the various units of time and seeks to freeze history through absolute continuities or discontinuities, boundaries for beginning and end, and pauses and fresh starts. In its place, Koselleck calls for multiple temporalities for the historian, with varied, overlapping strata that are characterized by different origins, durations, rhythms, and speeds. Thus, a theory of historical times would include not only structures of chronological succession, but also nonsynchronicities, unexpected events, and repetitions emerging from social processes of accumulation, changes with their own accelerations (Jordheim 2012).

The same gap perceived by Koselleck in historical theory studies seems to apply to *justice in times of transition*. Assuming transitional justice is a transition to democracy, it seems to arrange this experience in a linear march of progress that begins with a situation of oppression that is already overcome and advances toward a citizen society under construction. The expression *times of transition*, however, carries the mark of a reflective conceptual potential that ponders historical periods of consolidation of the institutional-legal democratic experience without depleting itself. *Times of transition* also enables both an analysis of the past, which cannot be confined to a single unit of time and, therefore, overflows into the present, and a criticism of the politics of time that rules out non-normative and minority temporalities through generic pacts standardized by international experience or scholars of the subject.

This chapter aims to explore that gap. To this end, it approaches, first, the limits of transitional justice as a chronocentric activity that operates from a specific presentist hegemonic contemporaneity with rigidly defined boundaries as to pasts, futures, and other alternatives for the present. Next, this chapter asks how a chronormative transitional justice fails its vocation, especially because it reinforces patterns of control over bodies that were initiated by a regime that violated human rights, precisely when those controls should be overcome. Lastly, it proposes a new trajectory to be followed by *justice in times of transition*, one that supplements the transition to democracy with a demand for inclusion to be accomplished through an ethics of care.

14.2 The Arrogance of a Single Present Time

There is a clear paradox between the temporality that is experienced by those who survived the violation of human rights perpetrated by states of exception and the politics of time that are usually adopted by practices of transitional justice. For survivors, trauma alters the perception of time. Many of them experience a kind of extra-temporality, a time of suspension outside of orderly social time, because of the unfinished identity cycles, the unanswered questions, the death narratives where the body is missing (Bueno-Hansen 2015: 15; Manrique 2003: 430). Others live in a synchronic temporal logic instead of diachronic chronological time because the past still overlaps the present (Bevernage and Lorenz 2013: 21)—an individual experience that is very similar to the palimpsestic character of time. The palimpsest reminds us of medieval parchments, which, after being first written on, were constantly erased in order to be used again, but which ended up keeping previous texts partially visible. Thus, palimpsestic time blurs the distance created between the periods of linear temporality, keeping the pasts in the present as a visible trace (Alexander 2005: 190). For that reason, Jean Améry (1980: 68), a survivor of Nazi concentration camps, said that the victim's resentment gives rise to two impossible desires—that of returning to the past and that of erasing the violations suffered—the consequence of which is a disoriented, distorted perception of time.

Transitional justice, on the other hand, needs to operate in linear chronological time. After all, it borrows its legitimacy from the power to deal with the past in an independent, impartial way, which is only possible when the regime that violated human rights no longer exerts power in the present, with the possibility exists for that regime to be perceived as a finished event in a historical time set in some past point on the historical axis. Evidence for this claim includes the fact that transitional laws or other measures that are adopted at the end of dictatorial regimes, but still within its alleged chronological period, usually constitute acts of self-amnesty, which—given that they are internationally censurable—only hold sway via some formal criterion of internal legality and a lack of subsequent political capital for their abrogation. Thus, if the boundary of the past time is not sufficiently delimited by those in charge of transitional justice, its operation may end up being considered partial to or as ratifying the violation it is supposed to judge. A linear notion of time is, therefore, the most appropriate for this case, as it permits the separation of the authoritarian past time that perpetrated atrocities from the democratic present time that promotes peace (Bueno-Hansen 2015).

In this process, the legal system is a strategically useful device. Since dictatorial regimes tend to be narrated retrospectively as illegitimate political expressions characterized by the total or partial suppression of the *rule of law*, the re-foundation of democracy during transition entails the establishment of a new legal system. This new legal system is simultaneously cause and effect of the rupture with the past, a separation that can happen in an far-reaching manner, if the Constitution itself is renovated, or in a restricted manner, if only infra-constitutional legislation goes through the purging process (McEvoy 2007: 417). Nonetheless, the legal system time will hardly be able to encapsulate the totality of past realities.

In many cases, such past realities continue along their ongoing trajectory, projected on the present time as a delay or as nonsynchronicities—a presence of the past that proves to be really destabilizing when it comes to violations of human rights that have not been suppressed by the new democratic order. However, even in such situations, the legal system plays a role. As Stan Cohen (2001) observed, one of the techniques governments use when questioned about their agents' illegal acts is that of *magical legalism*: the denial of the occurrence of state abuse based on the sole argument that legislation forbids it. Thus, for instance, the fact that torture has been legally condemned in the transition to the emerging democracy is enough proof that it does not happen anymore in the country's public security agencies.

The asynchrony of the linear time of transitional justice and the time of overlapping multi-temporal social realities is not totally derived from the legal system. Actually, it operates against the background of a social-political discourse that is informed by the two directions of the chronological time arrow. In one direction, the transitional rhetoric consigns to a past historical period all of the evils that may be ascribed to the State, thus making the present time a blank slate because the repressive past is absent. In the other, such a discourse points to a threatening, unidirectional future that lurks amid the present time with the *nunca más* (never again) warning, conditioning the alternatives of transition through a cause and effect relationship, as if the suppression of the recognized wrongs of the past were enough to ensure a promising future. Those stances seem to be strengthened even more by a regime of historicity that appears to privilege a certain presentism. These assertions are worthy of an explanation.

As to the past time narrative, the causal explanation of the origin of evil has always been problematic. In Christian theodicies, for example, the attempt to reconcile the existence of a creative God whose essence is incorruptible with the presence of evil in creation once required the juggling of arguments from various theology doctors. With the disenchantment of the world from religion, the philosophy of history filled the narrative void left by theodicies. However, if humanity were to undertake the protagonism of its own history, it would also become responsible for the suffering and atrocities it had experienced. In an attempt to exonerate most of humanity from the responsibility for evil and to reconcile a progressionist linear-temporal vision with a kind of social antagonism, the philosophy of history has ascribed this burden instead to a dominant, powerful, concrete enemy in each period, such as the nobility, the bourgeoisie, and the financial elite. Thus, a kind of narrative Manichaeism was created, opposing the good guys to the bad ones in the narration of the past (Bevernage 2015: 337–340).

Political rhetoric, which also seeks to exempt humanity from blame, has to deal with the problem of eliminating evil in the present. After all, by advocating that liberal democracy is the milestone for the end of history (Fukuyama 1992), toward which all political experiences would end up converging, it has become impossible to admit evil as something inherent to contemporaneity. Following that same logic, transitional justice has been conceived as a transition device to democracy, which is also considered its ultimate goal. This dominant politics, then, replaces the concrete enemy envisioned by the philosophy of history with a temporal Manichaeism, transforming the decontextualized, abstract past into the source of all evil and the concrete present into a mere victim. Under such a perception, a linear chronology is extremely apropos. Besides transforming the past into a temporalization of evil, all evil identified in the present is arbitrarily ascribed to the past and, therefore, inadmissible because it is anachronistic. Hate speech is considered "a thing of the past" and, as such, has to be banned (Bevernage 2015: 341–349). The past cannot be in the present, not even as a specter.

The banning of the presence of the past in the present does not emerge only from a post-historical rhetoric of liberal democracy. Most of historiography has been constructed on a logic of the irreversibility of the past and its current absence. This Western chronosophy relies on three pillars. First, the temporal metaphysics of the geometric point, which sees time as a linear continuity of unobtrusive moments in which the present does not have its own length, being instead merely a boundary that both separates and unifies the past and the future. The present, as an instant temporal point, becomes past as soon as it is consummate, and, as such, it cannot be reached or changed anymore. Second, this chronosophy relies on the perception that each temporality tends to gather and join all experiences together as a single collectivity. According to this tenet, all social manifestations in certain period—whether economic, political, scientific, religious—operate synchronically against the same temporal background, constituting a homogeneous block of time. Finally, as a consequence of the two previous pillars, the present time is the only contemporaneity. It is impossible for the past to anachronically span it (Bevernage 2008).

Paradoxically, the logic of time as the presence of the present and the absence of the past advocates and questions at once the legitimacy of transitional justice. As has been said previously, when the past is delimited by an impassable, irreversible boundary, this delimitation reinforces, politically speaking, the credentials of institutions acting as part of the transition to democracy and thus free from the influence of previous regimes that violated human rights. But such a notion of time does not afford theoretical grounds to the possibility of doing justice to the past. After all, judicial practice creates a reversible temporality in which the consummate wrongdoing stays totally in the present, and thus, it can be reversed or cancelled by the right decision (Bevernage 2008: 152). This is why Capograssi (1959) described the judge as the justice maker in relation to wrongdoing and the procedure as the possibility of "presentifying" the past in order to destroy, change, or reshape it. In this framing, therefore, justice would always imply a certain dose of anachronism (Bevernage 2008: 163). Denying this condition, then, is to deny the possibility of an appropriate justice that respects the various times of transition.

As to the future, the slogan "never again" has become a denunciation, a warning, and a promise in South America. A denunciation, for it has been associated, in some cases, with non-government initiatives of public, systematic exposure of the violations perpetrated by dictatorial regimes. In Brazil, for instance, the project "Brasil: nunca mais" [Brazil: never again]—led by both the Cardinal-Archbishop of São Paulo, D. Paulo Evaristo Arns, and the Presbyterian minister Reverend Jaime Wright—secretly investigated, from August 1979 to March 1985, the repressive dynamics of the Brazilian dictatorial period in order to identify political missing persons, executioners, and methods of torture employed at the time (Arquidiocese 1985). A warning, for the expression "never again" lent its name to some of the reports produced by truth commissions (Conadep 1984; CCDH 1999), reports that informed the State's accountability and the punishment of its executioners and signaled that future violations would be subject to the same public scrutiny. Finally, the reckoning with past atrocities implies the promise of a hopeful future, since the revelation of truth would allow people to follow different paths, open to new possibilities (Teitel 2014: 108).

However, the potential of "never again" as a warning and a promise when embraced by transitional justice has not been fully realized. In the first place, the prohibition of a repetition projected into the future does not take into account the past violent realities overlapping the present, which, despite being seen as anachronistic, bring about constant attacks against citizens' dignity. Another hazard is that, through the unidirectional projection of the future tragedy to be avoided, the present becomes conditioned to specific prevention measures based on how violence manifested itself in the fallen regime. There is a failure in perceiving that a future open to possibilities may mean either greater respect for or greater disrespect for human rights. Democratic experience is not immune to retrogression. Proof of this is the increase in social and family violence during transitional periods. Social groups or state apparatuses that are used to assaulting others during the repressive period tend to redirect their attacks. Thus, violence related to drug dealing activities or against vulnerable or non-normative groups, such as women, children, migrants, or sexual minorities, starts to increase, although it remains invisible to the projects conceived as part of transitional justice (Mani 2008: 259). Finally, the fear of repressive structures coming back may result in even greater complacency toward democratic structures, even when they reproduce situations of institutional violence.

The way transitional justice builds a certain kind of past and future may indicate that it operates under a regime of presentist historicity. According to Hartog (2012), the notion of a regime of historicity is a heuristic tool whose function is to better understand moments of crisis—showing how past, present, and future are articulated in given times and historical spaces—and to explain why certain narratives and temporalities end up being hindered. Presentism, in particular, puts temporal emphasis in the present, which is now seen as a situation of precariousness and as an advancement of life: a present time that excludes neither past nor future, but rather builds them in light of its own current needs. When transitional justice emerges in a moment of temporal crisis, it is subject to a kind of pressure that is twofold. On the one hand, there is the pressure of a narrow deadline to achieve its purpose; on the other hand, there is the pressure of achieving certain goals regarding the accountability of the fallen regime and the foundation of a new political order. Therefore, transitional justice experiences its own precariousness as something bound to end and its role as a catalyst for democratic experience. That is the reason why, when transitional justice functions, it ends up building the past and the future it needs— and it seems as if it does so at the expense of excluding nonsynchronicities, dim

and unpredictable futures, and temporalities that are unsusceptible to normalization. Such exclusions encompass bodies that carry themselves in different rhythms.
Chronocentric transitional justice becomes also chronormative.

14.3   The Normalization of Both Bodies and Times in Transition

The arbitrary domain carried out by dictatorial regimes does not confine itself to
state structures. The regimes' violation of human rights is not aimed only at those
who question the despotic government's legitimacy. In the process of social control
and normalization that accompanies a state of exception, all citizens' bodies must be
adjusted to the standard behavior expected by those in power, a pretense that does
not seem to be determined by the political-ideological background that supports
the regime, as is clear from two Latin American examples. In Brazil, the military
regime that was established in the period from 1964 to 1985 boasted about being anti-
communist. In its theoretical basis, there was the National Security Doctrine issued
by the *Escola Superior de Guerra* (ESG, the Superior War School), an institution for
high military studies that was created in 1949 in the mold of the U.S. National War
College. According to that doctrine, the greatest threat to national security was not
the classic war between nations, but the revolutionary war led by the internal enemies
of the State, who intended to undermine state power through the moral degradation
of society. Accordingly, in many of ESG's documents, there was a constant concern
over an alleged degeneration of youths' bodies by subversion, the major evidence
for which was free love, promiscuity, and homosexual orientation. Therefore, the
monopoly of power imposed censorship on social means of communication, targeting
not only political demonstrations against the government, but also moral expressions
considered deviant (Cowan 2007).

   In Cuba, on the other hand, the regime established by both Fidel Castro and
Ernesto Che Guevara in 1959 had a patent communist tinge. Ideologically situated
in opposition to the Brazilian dictatorship, the Cuban regime was also concerned
for society's morality. Guevara, aware that the island was seen as a destination for
sexual tourism, expressed his concern over the generation that had lived prior to
Fulgêncio Batista's regime, for it was not genuinely revolutionary and might pervert
new generations. So, the old generation would have to renounce the immoralities
of the past (Guevara 2004: 4). Guevara's mention of "the immoralities of the past"
gains further significance when it is contextualized. Between 1965 and 1968, the
Cuban government created the Military Units to Aid Production, or UMAP (*Unidades
Militares de Ayuda a la Producción*), which were forced-labor camps for the planting
and harvesting of sugarcane that became the destination for everyone who did not
fit the political regime's normative patterns (Guerra 2010). A specific UMAP was
created for homosexuals. At its entrance, one could read "Labor will make you men," a
slogan that adjusted the motto from the Nazi camps of Dachau and Auschwitz (*arbeit*

macht frei, or work makes one free) in order to express the alleged adjustment of sexual orientation (Martínez 2002; Madero 2016).

Hence, dictatorial regimes of different ideological orientations aim to normalize bodies, often in similar ways, and establish in this manner a single legitimate temporality. After all, time does not exist outside bodies. In fact, it shapes them according to its criteria (Freeman 2007). Both in a socially expressed temporality—such as that consolidated in calendars, time zones, and various other periodizations, including those that establish the length of a fiscal, tax, school or sports year—and in tacit social time—manifested in patterns that indicate the appropriate time to move out one's parents' home, raise a family or enter the work market—there is some normalization, some alleged naturalization of an asymmetric, arbitrary power that imposes a pattern to the rhythm of life. A judicial system that takes into account the various times of transition should be able to break with a normative temporality and make room for all of the asynchronous social rhythms in spite of the existing social chronormativity. However, it seems that, for many reasons, this inclusive attitude occurs infrequently.

The first reason is that transitional justice ends up reinforcing the difference between the public and the private spheres. This dichotomy is not neutral when it comes to gender, and the delimitation of both fields may vary depending on viriarcal interests. The public/private relation may have reciprocal implications and more fluid boundaries when citizens' patrimonial interests are at play, interests that were historically affirmed under the patriarchy. After all, the struggle to limit the confiscatory power of the State was at the origin of several bourgeois revolutions. Negative liberty was protected by a series of legal guarantees only because the topic gained ground in the public sphere. Therefore, the State's duty of abstention did not correspond to negligence toward the private sphere, but rather to recognition of the private sphere's power to impose limits. Nevertheless, the same public/private relation had its boundaries rigidly established when the domestic aspect of social relations was at stake. The family nucleus was excluded from political space. The dimensions of sexuality, household work division, and the family project were entrusted to the discretion of the *patria potestas*. The State was indifferent to the non-patrimonial aspect of the private sphere. For this reason, the second wave of feminism emphasized the idea that the personal aspect of individuals is also political, thus showing that domestic relations between men and women were not immune to the dynamics of power and, as an extension and reinforcement of gender inequalities created in the public plane, they should be included in the agenda of politically relevant debates (Pateman 1989; Okin 1998).

Therefore, transitional justice should be sensitive to the historical affirmation of the rights of women. However, times of transition do not tend to include the temporality of domestic relations, which still bear marks of the patriarchy. Despite the recognition of the horizontal efficacy of fundamental rights in several constitutional orders, the field of transitional justice is still dominated by a standpoint oriented toward the vertical relation established between state agents and citizens. In this respect, the temporality of the violence on streets, within state agencies of repression, or that perpetrated by public servants needs to be overcome, which would obviously encompass some of the violations suffered by women. But the temporality of the aggression suffered by women in a domestic environment, individually or collectively perpetrated by men and backed by the violence, omission, or morality of the State, ends up being neglected under the argument that it constitutes a private aggression (Aoláin 2006: 844). Accordingly, the intended transition to democracy does not erect an impassable wall against violent practices of the past because not all of them, especially those indirectly encouraged by the State, are subject to reckoning. Domestic violence remains, then, as a continuum, overflowing into the present and indicating that the judicial system also deserves a reassessment with regard to the dimension of the rhythm imposed on women's lives.

The second reason why transitional justice ends up adopting an exclusionary attitude is that it operates on a productive/reproductive temporality. The end of a repressive regime liberates several non-linear and non-normative temporalities that had been repressed before, which promotes a real asynchronous chaos. Right now, the various emerging rhythms, whether overlapping or opposed, compromise the national unitary discourse that synchronizes the bodies around a future project, drawing as much productivity as possible from them (Freeman 2010; Luciano 2007). Transitional justice, with the excuse of temporariness and a fixed, narrow deadline for its closing, ends up postponing the temporal babel until some future time while it supposedly settles accounts with the past. However, during this process, it builds a new agglutinating discourse characterized by accountability, forgiveness, or another form of re-establishing the social amalgam, a discourse that, in the end, will lead to the consolidation of democracy, a goal that starts to organize present efforts and temporalize bodies in a single synchronous rhythm again.

In addition, transitional justice falls into the reproductive futurism of politics, according to which every measure has as its parameter the alleged image of a future Child, who will be born, for whom battles are fought, and for whose sake measures are adopted in the present. This Child serves as a perpetual horizon, a phantasmagorical beneficiary of every political intervention at the expense of the living generation. In order that the nation's children and grandchildren *nunca más* (never again) be victims of violations similar to those suffered by the current generation, several measures are adopted and justified in the present. Thanks to this reproductive futurism, both the repeated human death drive—which is more perceptible with the fall of the dictatorial regime and the revelation of the atrocities perpetrated by it—and the lack of faith in that very futurity lose symbolic ground in the social substrate. Thus, the social fabric is not strained, but it remains close-knit because of a worldview that asserts hope as a sufficient value, even when it is propped against unachievable and irresponsible political chimeras (Edelman 2004).

The third driving force of chronormative transitional justice is related to the emphasis on the strict concept of violence to the detriment of a more comprehensive notion of arbitrary power. A dictatorial regime violates a great number of citizens' rights. The ascertainment of all crimes, the individuation of their respective executioners, their accountability, and the reparations to victims could result in the rendering of an endless and highly onerous lawsuit for the emerging democracy. This is why certain choices have to be made, and they normally rest on a certain spectrum of violations, especially those perpetrated through physical violence (Aoláin

2006). Aggression through psychological violence can also be included by enlarging the accountability circle. Explicit patrimonial damage—such as the confiscation of property—and the disruption of life projects suffered by the politically repressed—such as the prohibition of professional practice or compulsory dismissals—end up amounting to a larger spectrum of violations based on the exercise of arbitrary power, and these, too, can be compensated. But interferences in the life rhythms of non-combatant women related to those persecuted by the regime remain in the penumbra of invisibility. These women end up suffering closely the effects of a repressive regime, even when they decide not to take sides in armed conflicts. While their husbands, brothers or cousins fight, they need to give up their life projects in favor of maintaining their families, even if it means renouncing one's own country. After all, women and children compose the main groups in refugee camps. As a consequence of such conflicts, women tend to be more subject to forced displacement and hunger, even when they function as providers, because of insufficient and low-paying job opportunities. They are also subject to serving as non-remunerated caregivers of incapacitated combatants in their families, in addition to the overall responsibility of family reunification, which entails visits to detention centers, the location of relatives who were displaced and sent to other regions, and the search for information on missing people (Lindsey 2001). Transitional justice is hardly ever available for all these kinds of aggressions against women.

Interestingly enough, even when truth commissions want to break with chronormativity, they fall into it by neglecting the non-violent oppositional power of non-normative temporalities. The National Truth Commission in Brazil dedicated a full-length volume of its final report to violations perpetrated by the military regime (1964–1985) against specific groups, such as peasants and indigenous peoples. In the thematic report dedicated to homosexualities, there is a list of military charges that occurred based on the assertion that gender identities and non-normative sexual orientations were responsible for social degradation and that resulted in specific repressive actions, such as dismissals of gay diplomats, censorship of effeminate men in the media, and instances of criminalization suffered by transvestites, especially those who worked as sex professionals (Brasil 2014: 299–311). The report contains little information on other expressions of violence or resistance, arguing that military repression did not allow for the creation of human rights observers or organizations that could have made thorough social records of the violations—and, presumably, any attendant oppositions—suffered by homosexuals. However, there are well-documented non-normative forms of resistance, such as the *desbunde*, which—by avoiding the left/right polarization—questioned the State's normative pattern and created a counterculture movement characterized by non-partisan solidarity, sexual liberation, body pleasure, and, to a great extent, homosexuality (Dunn 2014). It was a clear form of opposition that was not even perceived as militant by the narrow temporality radar of transitional justice.

Finally, the way masculinities are usually viewed in the process of disarmament, demilitarization, and reintegration in the post-conflict era reinforces the normative nature of transitional justice. After all, a disarmament process that is apt to put an end to armed conflict and allow for the beginning of a transitional process may not mean a total exclusion of weapons in the public sphere, nor will such a process prevent the threatening potential that armament represents from being transferred onto the domestic sphere (Aoláin and Cahn 2009). Besides, the transposition of a military, guerrilla, or combatant *habitus* to a civil practice does not happen from top to bottom only via changes to bureaucratic institutions. Violent practices that corresponded to acts of bravery and heroism during the conflict are now seen as criminal by the emerging democracy, thus generating potential and dangerous masculine asynchronies. Demobilization in such a context may promote a sense of emasculation whose consequence, in a viriarcal tradition, will most probably be the reinforcement of manliness through violent practices against more vulnerable social groups. This logic does not reverberate equally in every man. In South Africa, for instance, this logic has tended to echo among those who live in a situation of marginalization and extreme poverty, which reveals an intersectional key to the overall understanding of the problem (Hamber 2007).

As to reintegration, the operation of transitional justice may be useful for overcoming gender stereotypes. A viable contribution to this arena is the formulation of public policies aimed at victims or combatants with a view to training them to perform non-violent social roles that bear certain respectability (Aoláin and Cahn 2009). To this end, the narrative pieced together by truth commissions must be compatible with that goal, and therefore, it cannot be woven only with the thread of violence. A narrative that presents other ways of fighting the regime—ways characterized by their emphasis on solidarity, on peaceful, and yet powerfully transformative, social arrangements—may be able to deconstruct the essence of the virile, aggressive man, and recognize other ways of constructing and living masculinity. This different view of non-hegemonic masculinities by transitional justice is not contrary to women's demands; rather, it reinforces them. After all, those women who had to rebuild their life projects and take on the role of providers in their families because of repression cannot simply revert to their previous condition of subordination when men are reintegrated into civil life or when persecuted militants come back home. It is not the mission of transitional justice to restore the pre-dictatorial past, but to lay the groundwork for a socially egalitarian future.

To this end, it seems apropos to go back to the insight about the initial significance of *justice in times of transition* in order to densify it. The existing multiple temporalities encompassed in this simultaneously provisional and fast-paced transitional interval would cease to be informed by a perception of time based solely on the present or by a normative pattern and would instead be informed by a new purpose, in addition to a democratic goal, and a new ethics, allied with the ethics of justice. The last section approaches these two points.

14.4 Conclusion: Social Inclusion and Carefulness During Transition

One of the objections posed to the conceptual limits of transitional justice identified by Arthur Paige (2009) is whether the final destination indicated by the transition can affect the kinds of vindications that are presented and acknowledged as valid. In other words, how one can identify the risks and possibilities of a transition to democracy whose implementation requires only legal-institutional reformation? The importance of the democratic purpose cannot be underestimated, especially when it comes to realities where sovereignty was exclusively in the hands of dictators or small elitist groups. While the battle for democracy is able to wipe out a dynamic of arbitrary power, it can also make do with replacing one centric, normative, and unpopular temporal parameter with another one in which the only difference is the popularity, that is, the consent of the majority. This solution does not bring about a legal system that takes into account all the times of transition.

Thus, democracy, as a final point of transition—an important goal that can legitimate and restore credibility to a politics that was previously discredited by repression—must be linked to a transitional goal of inclusion in a mutually constitutive way. Here, inclusion does not necessarily mean the social-economic transformation of classes subject to poverty and misery, since the narrow interval of transition can hardly carry out comprehensive changes. The goal of democracy should be to bridge the economic gap that prevents some of its citizens from having their basic needs met. But the goal of transition should be a guarantee of an inclusive and plural democracy, in which the various rhythms and temporalities of all bodies are given voice and opportunities for expression—to affirm their minority life projects in the public sphere and to give visibility, at the very place from which they speak, to the demands that deserve overriding attention.

A transition to inclusion requires a different perception of transitional times. A chronocentric transition that rigidly delimits the boundaries of the past turns a blind eye to, for example, asynchronous practices and experiences that, despite labeled as having been overcome, affirm their contemporaneity as difference. A chronormative transition that rigidly establishes the criterion of a certain *ethos* and temporal worldview denies the desires and identities of bodies that, despite being labeled as deviant, affirm their diversity as presence. Transitions that are not informed by inclusion maintain those groups that were marginalized by the old repressive regime on the outskirts of the emerging democracy. The transitional exclusion of the Quechua peasant women in Peru (Bueno-Hansen 2015) and lesbians, gays, bisexuals and transgenders (LGBT) in Serbia (McLeod et al. 2014) are examples of this situation, thus giving rise to an increasing demand for the *gendering or queering* of truth commissions and transitional justice (Bueno-Hansen 2010; Fobear 2014).

However, the recognition of several temporalities cannot be attained through an ethics that is exclusively informed by abstraction, neutrality, and objectivity. Carol Gilligan (1977, 1982, 1986) analyzed Kohlberg's cognitive development theory and demonstrated the existence of a "different voice" for the ethics of care. While the ethics of justice is based on rules and rights, formal and abstract patterns, and is characterized by a set of principles, the ethics of care is founded on the pillars of intersubjectivity and responsibility and has to do with concrete circumstances and pragmatic actions. Gilligan came across this different voice through her research on girls. Therefore, she was able to deconstruct Kohlberg's thesis that the development of feminine morals was inferior in relation to masculine morals, a conclusion Kohlberg could only have drawn because he was evaluating women according to a single pattern. But that different voice is not necessarily a female one. Rather, it reveals the existence of at least two moral perspectives capable of organizing the thoughts and feelings of both men and women, thus enabling them to develop different kinds of actions in public and private spheres. Both interact at various levels in the two distinct groups. However, in times of crisis and change, there are conditions that may enable the convergence of those two voices: that of justice and that of care (Gilligan 1982: 2).

Transitional justice operates in such times of crisis and change. With the knowledge drawn from concrete situations and debates that have taken place in several places around the world since the 1990s, a transitional standard has been gradually created, one that is informed by abstract and universally applicable principles elicited from International Law sources, even when such sources were only tangentially related to the topic of transition. The newfound closeness between transitional justice and International Law contributed to the vindication of a new and interdisciplinary field of study by its theorists, promoted an ethics of justice, and consolidated several procedures for accountability and processes for overcoming violations perpetrated in the repressive past (Bell 2009).

But the ethics of care has not been given the same heed. The voice that indicates the specificity of each dictatorial regime, the suppressed temporalities in each context, and the particular rhythm imposed by repression requires a kind of transitional justice that, without denying global accumulation, operates via a bottom-up system. To this end, the first requisite for cultivating an ethics of care is attentiveness, which is the ability to understand victims' needs from their own experiences (Tronto 2013: 34). From this perspective, hearing commissions can be potential generators of this process, for, besides their therapeutic purpose, they can reveal the transitional speed in each social stratum, how each group temporalizes the trauma(s) of violations, and the rhythm that should be applied to the process of re-founding democracy. Perhaps the achievement of a caring transition can restore the social fabric that was strained by repression, with no need for a nationalistic narrative dotted by violent symbols and warlike dates.

The combination of the ethics of justice with the ethics of care can clearly make transitional processes more complex. However, it is from this very densification that a more inclusive democracy can emerge, one that does not adopt the legitimacy of majoritarian time as a hegemonic pattern intending to be exclusive, but recognizes the discontinuities in the present that result from the breaches operated by different lived pasts and prospective futures and recognizes the right to identities and plural life projects that are guided by peaceful coexistence—in conclusion, justice that carefully takes into account the various times of transition.

References

Alexander, M.J. 2005. *Pedagogies of crossing: Meditations on feminism, sexual politics, memory, and the sacred*. Durham, London: Duke UP.

Améry, J. 1980. *At the mind's limits: Contemplations by a survivor on Auschwitz and its realities*. Bloomington: Indiana UP.

Aoláin, F.N. 2006. Political violence and gender in times of transition. *Columbia Journal of Gender and Law* 15 (3): 829–849.

Aoláin, F.N., and N. Cahn. 2009. Gender, masculinities and transition in conflicted societies. *New England Law Review* 44: 101–123.

Arquidiocese de São Paulo. 1985. *Brasil nunca mais: um relato para a história*. Petrópolis: Vozes.

Arthur, P. 2009. How "transitions" reshape human rights: a conceptual history of transitional justice. *Human Rights Quarterly* 31: 321–367. https://doi.org/10.1353/hrq.0.0069.

Bell, C. 2009. Transitional Justice, interdisciplinarity and the state of the 'field' or 'non-field'. *The International Journal of Transitional Justice* 3: 5–27. https://doi.org/10.1093/ijtj/ijn044.

Bevernage, B. 2008. Time, presence, and historical injustice. *History and Theory* 47: 149–167. https://doi.org/10.1111/j.1468-2303.2008.00444.x.

Bevernage, B. 2015. The past is evil/evil is past: On retrospective politics, philosophy of history, and temporal manichaeism. *History and Theory* 54: 333–352. https://doi.org/10.1111/hith.10763.

Bevernage, B., and C. Lorenz. 2013. *Breaking up time: Negotiating the borders between present, past and future*. Göttingen: Vandenhoeck & Ruprecht.

Brasil. 2014. *Comissão Nacional da Verdade. Relatório: textos temáticos*. Brasília: CNV.

Bueno-Hansen, P. 2010. Engendering transitional justice: Reflections on the case of Peru. *Journal of Peacebuilding & Development* 5 (3): 61–74. https://doi.org/10.1080/15423166.2010.566611431450.

Bueno-Hansen, P. 2015. *Feminist and human rights struggles in Peru: Decolonizing transitional justice*. Urbana: University of Illinois Press.

Capograssi, G. 1959. *Opere*, vol. 5. Milano: Giuffrè.

CCDH (Comisión Chilena de Derechos Humanos). 1999. *Nunca más en Chile: síntesis corregida y actualizada del informe Rettig*. Santiago: LOM Ediciones, Fundación Ideas.

Cohen, S. 2001. *States of denial: Knowing about atrocities and suffering*. Cambridge: Polity Press.

Conadep. 1984. *Nunca Más: Informe de la Comisión Nacional sobre la Desaparición de Personas*. Buenos Aires: Editorial Universitaria de Buenos Aires.

Cowan, B.A. 2007. Sex and the security State: Gender, sexuality, and "subversion" at Brazil's Escola Superior de Guerra, 1964-1985. *Journal of the History of Sexuality* 16: 459–481. https://doi.org/10.1353/sex.2007.0073.

Dunn, C. 2014. Desbunde and its discontents: Counterculture and authoritarian modernization in Brazil, 1968-1974. *The Americas* 70: 429–458. https://doi.org/10.1353/tam.2014.0037.

Edelman, L. 2004. *No future: Queer theory and the death drive*. Durham, London: Duke UP.

Elster, J. 2004. *Closing the books: Transitional justice in historical perspective*. Cambridge: Cambridge UP.

Fobear, K. 2014. Queering truth commissions. *Journal of Human Rights Practice* 6: 51–68. https://doi.org/10.1093/jhuman/hut004.

Freeman, E. 2007. Introduction. *GLQ: A Journal of Lesbian and Gay Studies* 13(2–3):159–176. https://doi.org/10.1215/10642684-2006-029.

Freeman, E. 2010. *Time binds: Queer temporalities, queer histories*. Durham, London: Duke UP.

Fukuyama, F. 1992. *The end of history and the last man*. London: Penguin Books.

Guerra, L. 2010. Gender policing, homosexuality and the new patriarchy of de Cuban Revolution, 1965-70. *Social History* 35: 268–289. https://doi.org/10.1080/03071022.2010.487378.

Guevara, E. (Che). 2004. *Pensamiento y acción: Selección de escritos y discursos*. Buenos Aires: Nuestra Propuesta.

Gilligan, C. 1977. In a different voice: Women's conceptions of self and of morality. *Harvard Educational Review* 47: 481–517. https://doi.org/10.17763/haer.47.4.g6167429416hg5l0.

Gilligan, C. 1982. *In a different voice: Psychological theory and women's development*. Cambridge: Harvard UP.

Gilligan, C. 1986. Reply. *Signs* 11 (2): 324–333. https://doi.org/10.1086/494226.

Hamber, B. 2007. Masculinity and transitional justice: An exploratory essay. *The International Journal of Transitional Justice* 1: 375–390. https://doi.org/10.1093/ijtj/ijm037.

Hartog, F. 2012. *Régimes d'historicité: Présentisme et expériences du temps*. Paris: Points.

Jordheim, H. 2012. Against periodization: Koselleck's theory of multiple temporalities. *History and Theory* 51: 151–171. https://doi.org/10.1111/j.1468-2303.2012.00619.x.

Lindsey, C. 2001. *Women facing war*. Geneva: International Committee of the Red Cross.

Luciano, D. 2007. *Arranging grief: Sacred time and the body in nineteenth-century America*. New York, London: New York UP.

Madero, A.S. 2016. "El trabajo os hará hombres": Masculinización nacional, trabajo forzado y control social en Cuba durante los años sessenta. *Cuban Studies* 44: 309–349. https://doi.org/10.1353/cub.2016.0016.

Mani, R. 2008. Dilemmas of expanding transitional justice, or forging the nexus between transitional justice and development. *The International Journal of Transitional Justice* 2: 253–265. https://doi.org/10.1093/ijtj/ijn030.

Manrique, N. 2003. Memoria y violência: la nación y el silencio. In *Batallas por la memoria: Antagonismos de la promesa peruana*, ed. Marita Hamann, Santiago Maguiña, Gonzalo Portocarrero, and Víctor Vich, 421–433. Lima: Red para el Desarrollo de las Ciencias Sociales en el Perú.

Martínez, S.E. 2002. Las estrellas más brillantes. Maricones y hombres nuevos en el cine de la Revolución: Cuba 1961-1993. *Orientaciones: Revista de Homosexualidades* 3:103–124.

McEvoy, K. 2007. Beyond legalism: Towards a thicker understanding of transitional justice. *Journal of Law and Society* 34: 411–440. https://doi.org/10.1111/j.1467-6478.2007.00399.x.

McLeod, L., J. Dimitrijević, and B. Rakočević. 2014. Artistic activism, public debate and temporal complexities: Fighting for transitional justice in Serbia. In *The arts of transitional justice: Culture, activism, and memory after atrocity*, ed. Peter D. Rush and Olivera Simić, 25–42. New York: Springer.

Okin, S.M. 1998. Gender, the public and the private. In *Feminism and politics*, ed. Anne Phillips, 116–141. New York: Oxford UP.

Pateman, C. 1989. *The disorder of women: Democracy, feminism and political theory*. Stanford: Stanford UP.

Teitel, R.G. 2003. Transitional justice genealogy. *Harvard Human Rights Journal* 16: 69–94.

Teitel, R.G. 2014. *Globalizing transitional justice: Contemporary essays*. New York: Oxford UP.

Tronto, J.C. 2013. *Caring democracy: Markets, equality, and justice*. New York, London: New York UP.

Douglas Antônio Rocha Pinheiro is Professor of Law at the University of Brasília, Brazil. Former Professor of Law at the Federal University of Goiás—Brazil (2008–2016). He obtained his J.S.D and his LL.M from the University of Brasília. He has been a visiting researcher at University of Florence (Italy) and University of La Rioja (Spain). His main research interests are constitutional history, queer legal theory, and interdisciplinary studies in law.

Chapter 15
Time and Legal Change: Some Methodological Remarks on Italy's Transition to Democracy

Massimo Meccarelli

Abstract This chapter focuses on Italy's struggle to hold Fascism to account between 1943–1946 within the complex framework of the nation's transition to democracy after World War II. This historical turn will be taken as an example of a specific regime of temporality, one in which the conjunctural features of time exercise an attributive force over legal issues. Responding to the demand for justice was an unavoidable step in the aftermath of the dictatorship, and the manner in which this issue was handled qualified some long-term solutions that were absorbed into the democratic legal order. The tension between restorative justice and national appeasement will be considered on two analytical levels: normative framework and legal debate. The concluding remarks will propose some methodological considerations on the importance of transitional time for historical research, with ascriptive time also being examined in general terms.

15.1 Introduction

"Today […] when one says that Italy has been (or may still be going) through a revolution, one is asking for abuse […]. Even at the Constituent Assembly, the proof that a revolution has taken place […], the word 'revolution' rings false, and it is good etiquette not to utter it" [1]. These were the words with which the great Italian jurist and member of the Constituent Assembly Piero Calamandrei opened a well-known article (Calamandrei 1947: 959). With effective rhetoric, he stated a basic fact that was both a warning and counsel for those who were shaping Italy's fledgling democracy. After the end of Fascism and World War II, a Referendum in

---

[1] "A dire oggi […] che in Italia c'è stata (e forse non è finita) una rivoluzione, c'è da farsi maltrattare […]: perfino alla Costituente, dove la dimostrazione che una rivoluzione è avvenuta è data […] la parola "rivoluzione" dà un suono falso: ed è regola di buona creanza non pronunciarla".

M. Meccarelli (✉)
Department of Law, University of Macerata, Macerata, Italy
e-mail: massimo.meccarelli@unimc.it

© Springer Nature Switzerland AG 2021
C. Paixão and M. Meccarelli (eds.), *Comparing Transitions to Democracy. Law and Justice in South America and Europe*, Studies in the History of Law and Justice 18, https://doi.org/10.1007/978-3-030-67502-8_15

June 1946 irreversibly sanctioned a constitutional change by turning the country into a republic. This revolution, however, could not be completed, as it was held back by political conflict within the democratic front and by lingering reactionary forces. It was, therefore, exposed to the risk of being usurped and quashed.

Rereading Calamandrei's quote, it is interesting to see how this "revolution" paradoxically, yet unavoidably short-circuited. Although it succeeded in marking a discontinuity with *history*, it needed *time* to be fully accomplished. Italy, too, needed time, a transition period, to come to terms with its past; this time was also an obligatory step, a test and an operational condition of revolutionary plans for the future.

This chapter deals with this dominance of time over legal change. Historians and jurists tend to consider time as an indicator, a measuring instrument which allows the law to be observed as it interacts with other social objects (Searle 1996) along the diachronic sequence of historical events. In these terms, time is external to the law; it performs a *descriptive* function.

This chapter, however, considers the relationship between time, the law and history from a different point of view. It dwells upon a specific regime of temporality, one in which the conjunctural features of time exercise an attributive force over legal issues. It is a condition of time that performs an *ascriptive* function, a *time that influences the content of the law*, and is where the law occurs.

In theoretical, as well as in historical terms, the main hypotheses on attributive time are the ones that affect the law's *condition of permanence*. There are some legal concepts that are built on this premise. Customary law, abrogation and constituent power are all examples in which time sets the legal rules and regulations. Nevertheless, there are also examples of ascriptive time that influence the law, but they do so differently, as they determine the value and legitimacy of a legal rule or regulation by forcing it into a *condition of impermanence*. This is the case for "transition".

Post-war Italy provides a fascinating historical context for this subject. Within the political and legal turn to democracy (Cau 2016a; D'Ottavio 2016; Pombeni 2017), which had to deal with an open and dramatic demand for justice (Stonebridge 2011; Sebald 2004), the issue of transition becomes central. European culture was faced with a perpetually slippery world ("un monde perpétuellement glissant") (Febvre 1946: 3) and a broken past that could not be reassembled. The "angel of history", to recall Walter Benjamin's visionary image (Benjamin 2014: 80), was being pushed towards a future, but his face was still turned towards the past; he strove to recompose the shattered, but could not avoid being driven forward.

In situations such as these, legal solutions are put in place to deal with any contingency, as well as to support and enable the structural change and long-term reform of a political and legal order. In Italy's case, however, age-old problems, namely the "crises" of the State (Romano 1910; Capograssi 1959), of statutory law (Carnelutti 1937; Cesarini Sforza 1936; Lopez de Oñate 1942; Calamandrei 1996) and of legal science (Del Vecchio 1934), were inserted in renewed form within the framework of that change. Debate has focused on these issues since the early twentieth century (Grossi 2011; Stolzi 2016; Cau 2016b), but the fall of Fascism and the subsequent political and legal scenario represented a further stage in this debate. Contingency, future planning and long-term transformation processes were all linked to the problem of Italy's transition to democracy and all of them are examples of attributive force being exerted upon temporal condition.

Within this complex framework, the struggle to hold Fascism to account between 1943–1946 deserves special attention. In many respects, it might seem only a minor aspect of Italy's wider transition to democracy, as the main problem would prove to be the drafting of its Republican Constitution. Nevertheless, responding to the demand for justice was an unavoidable step in the aftermath of the dictatorship (Mihai 2010; Portinaro 2011; Paixão 2015; Fornasari and Wenin 2015). Moreover, the manner in which this variable was handled qualifies the long-term solutions that the democratic legal order undertook.

The following pages look at the issue of Fascism's accountability on two analytical levels—normative regime and legal debate—in order to make some general methodological considerations on the importance of the transition for historical research.

15.2 The Accountability of Fascism Between Restorative Justice and National Appeasement: The Normative Framework

Italy's approach to bringing Fascism to account was consistent with that in other parts of Europe (Franzinelli 2018) and involved a series of measures (Nubola 2016; Caroli 2020; Vassalli 2001) that alternated between criminalization and clemency.

The main measure was Legislative Decree no. 159 of July 27 1944, entitled "Sanctions against Fascism". In continuity with Royal Decree no. 29/B of December 28 1943, issued after the end of the Fascism, Decree no. 159 envisaged the barring from Italy's public administration of those who had held leading positions in the Fascist party. The most important part, however, regarded punishment for acts perpetrated by its members, which the decree described as "crimes". The decree also punished collaboration with the German enemy, as well as any support for the re-establishment of a Fascist regime. Further measures included the establishment of a High Court of Justice (*Alta Corte di giustizia*) to try these crimes (Colao 2015: 179). Finally, the political amnesties issued during the Fascist regime and their effects were revoked. The decree no. 159 contained other restrictive measures, such as being barred from public office or political rights being withdrawn, which could also be applied to acts which, though not included among the crimes provided for in the decree, were committed "for Fascist reasons" and were contrary to "the rules of righteousness or of political probity". Without going into detail, these measures were exceptional and in contrast with the legal tradition based on the principle *nullum crimen nulla poena sine lege*.

With the end of the war, two decrees were issued that continued these anti-Fascist policies: Legislative Decree no. 195 of April 26 1945, which punished "Fascist activity" after Italy had been liberated and prevented the reconstitution of the Fascist party and "Fascist" political activity. Similarly, Legislative Decree no. 149 of April 26 1945 continued measures such as withdrawal of political rights, barring from public office, and even imprisonment "for politically dangerous Fascist militants", even when the alleged acts were not actually a crime.

Other exceptional measures concerned jurisdiction. Legislative Decree no. 142 of April 22 1945 established Extraordinary Courts (*Corti straordinarie di assise*) to try crimes envisaged by Articles 5 and 3 of Decree no. 159 of 1944, including collaboration with the German troops and the organization of Fascist squads for acts of violence and devastation. A few months later, as a consequence of the end of the war and the country's reunification, Legislative Decree no. 625 of October 5 1945 returned to these issues in a bid to reorganize these courts. The extraordinary courts were replaced by Special Sections of the Courts of Assize (*Sezioni speciali delle Corti di Assise ordinarie*), and the High Court of Justice established in 1944 was abolished (for a description of the High Court and its activity, see Liuzzi 1945; Maroni 1947). The system was again reorganized in 1947, with the Special Sections of the Courts of Assize being abolished and the jurisdiction for the above crimes being handed to Italy's Courts of Assize.

However, alongside these decrees to punish Fascist crimes, a range of major clemency measures were also introduced, to pardon those who had been imprisoned under Fascism. Between 1944 and 1949, more than twenty amnesties came into effect (Nubola 2016: 58–59) covering an assortment of crimes (e.g. military[2], financial, fiscal, black market trading of food (*reati annonari*)[3], social conflict[4]); two of them were expressly devoted to political crimes.

Royal Decree no. 96 of April 5 1944 and Legislative Decree no. 719 of November 17 1945 introduced an amnesty for all crimes that "had been committed before October 28 1922 or during the Fascist regime in the fight against Fascism, or to defend oneself against Fascist prosecution, or to escape from Fascist repression" (Art. 1). In his report presenting the decree, the Minister of Justice Palmiro Togliatti explained that it was "an act of *restorative justice* for which society is indebted" to those who had broken the law "to counter Fascist tyranny". It was intended "to encompass any criminal act that had its immediate and direct motive in anti-Fascist action" (Togliatti 1945: 472, 1946a, 1946b).

As can be seen, the government's acts of both repression and clemency between 1943 and 1945 were inspired by restorative justice. From 1946, however, its policies were inspired by another purpose and clearly changed. Rather than "restoring justice"

---

[2] For example, Decree no. 132 of March 29 1946; Decree no. 92 of March 1 1947.

[3] For example Decree no. 11 of June 24 1946 (Remission of sanctions for violation of the rules on currency and the gold trade); Decree no. 24 of June 27 1946 and Decree no. 25 of June 27 1946 (Remission of sanctions on tax matters and amnesty for financial crimes); Decree no. 32 of February 9 1948 (Amnesty for common political crimes and crimes in trade of foods); Decree no. 138 of February 28 1948 (Amnesty for financial crimes).

[4] Decree no. 513 of June 25 1947 (Amnesty for crimes perpetrated over agricultural disputes).

to the anti-Fascists, the government promoted broad pacification between winners and losers in an attempt to contain the effects of its anti-Fascist policies in the immediate post-war period (Nubola 2016: 58–59; Colao 2011: 484–487).

The key measure was Legislative Decree no. 4 of June 22 1946. It was a controversial amnesty for common political and military crimes issued by Togliatti (Franzinelli 2006; Colao 2015: 185–186), the same minister who had instigated a programme of restorative justice in favour of anti-Fascist activists only one year earlier.

This new approach was brought about by a change in the political and institutional landscape. On July 2 1946, Italy voted to make the country a republic in a referendum. As a consequence, a Constituent Assembly was elected with a mandate to write a new constitution. Starting from the observation that "with the passage from a monarchy to a republic, a new period in the life of the united Italian State had begun", Togliatti explained that it was now a priority to give a sign of "pacification and reconciliation to all good Italians", even to those who had supported the dictatorship (Togliatti 1946c: 708. See also Berlinguer 1946: 484; Pilotti 1947: 21; Funaro 1947: 62).

Thus, the new clemency law covered "a large number of political crimes", including those "committed in collaboration with the German invader". It had a wide-ranging impact on the previous anti-Fascist measures, as it was designed to revise the original objective of restorative justice for the victims of Fascism and to promote a "new background of unity and harmony" (Togliatti 1946c: 711).

The introduction of amnesties to promote national appeasement also inspired additional clemency measures that were not directly related to Fascist crimes. They included Provisional Head of State's Decree no. 460 of May 8 1947, an amnesty for crimes whose proceedings or sentences had been suspended due to the war (Gullo 1947a; De Francesco 1947; Cordone 1947); Provisional Head of State's Decree no. 513 of June 25 1947, concerning crimes committed over agricultural disputes (Gullo 1947b); and Presidential Decree no. 32 of February 9 1948, which ushered in an amnesty for political crimes in a bid to supplement "the acts of clemency previously granted" (Grassi 1948: 153).

This new reconciliatory framework, however, did not spell an end to the criminalization of Fascism. One example was Law no. 1546 of December 3 1947, which was entitled "Norms for the Repression of Fascist Activity and Activity Aimed at the Restoration of the Monarchy". A report by the Constituent Assembly Commission (*Commissione per la Costituzione*), which wrote the law, presented it as a continuation of Law no. 195 of April 26 1945 (see above) and an act that deemed "Fascist activity a crime" in order to defend "the new democratic and republican Italy" from "the dangers of a return of Fascism or the emergence of movements or parties that reproduce the essential features of that Fascist party" (Bettiol 1947). It is noteworthy that this law was temporary, with Article 11 stating that it was to remain in force until December 31 1953, after which its provisions were to be introduced permanently into the criminal justice system. The ban on reconstituting the Fascist party was also reiterated in the Constitution of 1948 by the XII Transitional and Final Disposition and by the related legislative Act no. 645 of June 20 1952, which comprised "Norms for the Implementation of the XII Transitional and Final Disposition (first paragraph) of the Constitution".

If analysis is limited to this framework alone, some useful conclusions can still be drawn about the attributive nature of this transition period. All of the above-mentioned measures are the result of contingency in that they were responses to a specific political phase, one that witnessed a shift in strategy from transitional justice for reparation to transitional justice for reconciliation. Despite this, however, they illustrated a unitary regime of legality, in which punitive and clemency norms were mutually complementary. The introduction of amnesties to mitigate the effects of emergency repression was by no means new to Italian legal history, as in other criminal emergencies (Meccarelli 2011; Colao 2011), clemency measures introduced a balance that created a systemic circularity to ensure exceptional criminal law was "compatible" with ordinary criminal law.

The management of the transition period, at least in normative terms, can thus be said to have played a role in shaping Italy's future legal order, even though it was part of contingency measures. The manner in which restorative justice and appeasement were combined at institutional and judicial levels to provide justice for Italy's political past (see Meniconi in this volume) highlights the extent to which the transition laid the foundations for future democratic life. Moreover, it served as a time in which issues that fuelled the legal debate could emerge.

It should not be forgotten that the legal regimes introduced during this time were emergency measures, far removed from the concept of criminal law laid down by liberal legal culture. It was, however, precisely that liberal legal culture to which the political project for democratization, at least in criminal legal issues, looked to define its fundamental principles and to build a new constitutional order. Consequently, the transition may have contributed to uncovering a number of problems and to raising issues on which the debate on democratic Italy's criminal system would focus. The next section dwells briefly on this aspect, before concluding with some methodological considerations.

15.3   Issues and Problems of the Criminal-Law Debate on the Transitional Measures

The punishment of Fascism and collaborationism, along with the related amnesties, was a major issue for Italy's jurists and judges, as they felt called upon to provide a sustainable interpretation for a body of laws that they saw as obscure and contradictory (Granata 1946; Vitale 1946; Loasses 1947a; Serena Monghini 1947; Leonelli 1948; Jemolo 1945). Consequently, they believed it was their duty to put forward reforms, a belief that surfaced in explicit passages from the opening speeches of the Supreme Court's judicial year (Pilotti 1945: 25–34; Pilotti 1946: 2–3, 20–26; Pilotti 1947: 18–23; Macaluso 1948: 17–20). This issue has been covered by numerous articles for major legal journals, such as *La giustizia penale*, *La Rivista penale*, *Archivio penale* and *Il Foro italiano*, as well as by a range of monographs (e.g. Angeloni and Santoni-Rugiu 1946; Fortunio 1946; Guarnieri 1946; Lener 1946; Meucci 1946; Vassalli and Sabbatini 1947, Sotgiu 1950).

One major example is the works of Giuliano Vassalli, an anti-Fascist militant who was imprisoned during the dictatorship. He was also a brilliant young jurist who, in his long life, would become one of Italy's most important criminal lawyers, as well as Minister of Justice and President of the Constitutional Court. Between 1945 and 1947, he wrote an article about the case law for the crimes of collaborationism, which was published in several issues of the journal *Giustizia penale* and then compiled in a single volume with a selection of amnesty studies (Vassalli and Sabbatini 1947).

Although Vassalli's article dealt with a legal regime linked to contingency for an exceptional period in history, it sought to provide a "reasoned exposition of the principles" laid down by the Supreme Court (*Corte di cassazione*) in order to "give a legal definition" to the crime of collaborationism (Vassalli 1945: 2). On this basis, he intended to establish where this crime lay "in the system of our criminal laws" (Vassalli 1946: 65). In short, his approach consisted in studying the exceptional measures and how they fitted into Italy's criminal system, taking into account the constraints built into the framework of categories and fundamental principles that must govern a criminal system (see also Vassalli 1947a, 1947b, 1947c, 1948).

This approach is also found in other authors, who tended to read these norms "through the most fundamental legal principles" (Granata 1946: 159) and therefore took into account the features which, in their opinion, should have been included in the fledgling Republic's criminal law system (Jemolo 1945; Battaglini 1947; Berlinguer 1946; Angeloni 1947; Peluso Cassese 1948; Carnelutti 1948; Ebner 1948). It is also noteworthy that after the passing of Decree no. 159 of July 1944, eighteen jurists signed a manifesto by Arturo Carlo Jemolo against eschewing the foundations of modern criminal law when seeking to punish Fascism (Giannetto 2003: 64; Colao 2015).

The legal debate on various aspects of the issue showed that holding Fascism to account was the first major hurdle to overcome in the broader operation of building a criminal legal system for democratic Italy. By way of example, we should briefly examine the issues addressed by articles published in the two main specialized criminal-law journals: *Giustizia penale* and *Rivista penale*.

An initial problem was posed by those norms, which described the crimes unclearly and vaguely. This led to uncertainty, as well as to excessive judicial discretion, thus reducing the effectiveness of the guarantees expected from the definition of a crime by statutory law. Lawyers attempted to contain the problem by interpreting these exceptional norms within the principles of the ordinary legal system (Vassalli 1946: 67; Liuzzi 1945: 346–347) and by devising new categories, e.g. the distinction between *norma penale interpretativa* (an interpretative criminal norm), *norma incriminatrice di estensione* (a norm that extends an existing criminal norm) and *norma di rinvio* (a norm that refers to an existing criminal norm). This was a hermeneutical exercise steered by a deliberate intention to tie the vague content of the exceptional norms to clearer Criminal Code norms that afforded the proper guarantees.

Another major issue, as mentioned above, was to ensure justice against Fascism without infringing the principle of non-retroactivity of criminal law (Jemolo 1945). This was an urgent problem for a legal culture that had made the fundamental principle of *nullum crimen nulla poena sine lege* the cornerstone of every theory on the State's right to punish. Jurists, therefore, had to take a complex hermeneutic approach that took into account the case law on such measures (Vassalli 1945: 5; Mirto 1946; Battaglini 1948a; Battaglini 1948b; Carnelutti 1948; Pace 1947), emphasising some aspects of the law in which legislators had been careful not to completely overturn the prohibition of retroactive application.

Art. 3 of Decree no. 159 of July 27 1944 referred to norms on "crimes against the powers of the State", in order to retroactively punish acts against anti-Fascist political dissent during the dictatorship. These norms were in the Criminal Code of 1889, which had been in force during the Fascist regime until the enactment of a new Criminal Code in 1931. Likewise, with reference to "crimes against the loyalty and defence of the State" committed after Fascism, in particular, after September 8 1943, when the armistice with the Allied Forces was signed, the Italian High Court of Justice argued (Vassalli 1945: 5; Liuzzi 1945: 346; Mirto 1946: 680; Carnelutti 1948: 29–30) that Art. 5 of Decree no. 159 of July 27 1944 and Art. 1 of Decree no. 142 of April 22 1945 did not provide for new crimes with retroactive effect, but specified and adapted crimes already provided for in Articles 241–243 of the Criminal Code and in Articles 51, 54 and 58 of the Military Criminal Code of War (Colao 2015: 183–184).

Although some jurists were not persuaded by interpretations of this kind, they considered anyway the importance of the principle of non-retroactivity; thus, they interpreted this law in a manner which could save both the principle and the exceptional measures. Vassalli's theory was that "the effectiveness of the statutory law in relation to time is a matter that falls within the discretionary power of the legislator"; as a consequence, only the judge is obliged "to comply with the new law even if it has retroactive effect". The principle of non-retroactivity constitutes a constraint on the legislator only when it is provided for by a higher constitutional norm (Vassalli 1945).

This last remark draws our attention to a third major issue within the debate, namely whether these exceptional criminal laws were constitutionally lawful. Since the nineteenth century (Fioravanti 2009: 98–104; Cau 2016a), Italy's legal system had had no form of judicial constitutional review, meaning that checks on whether statutory law complied with the constitution was not a duty of the Judiciary. It was thus up to Legislative power to establish whether normative measures were constitutional. Jurists, as well as Italy's Supreme Court judges (Macaluso 1948: 15), successfully took advantage of this legal tradition (Vassalli 1945: 4; Iaquinta 1948: 757–758) to defend the retroactive application of punishments against Fascism. At the same time, however, they seemed to realize that criminal law could be steered by the Constitution, an approach that would be used much later on (Sbriccoli 2009: 658–664).

Jurists also found themselves having to discuss a whole host of criminal-system related issues when dealing with the special measures against Fascism. One was the regimes of the "ius superveniens" in matters under ordinary and military jurisdiction, an issue that arose with the abolition of the infamous *Tribunale speciale per la difesa dello Stato*, a Special Court for the repression of political dissent (see the July 27 1946 ruling by the Third Section of the Supreme Court and the commentary in Battaglini 1947). Further issues were related to: crimes against the State (Vassalli 1946; 1947d); the presumption of innocence (the exceptional norms provided for presumptions of guilt *iure et de iure*; Vassalli 1947a: 583; Mirto 1946: 681–688[5]); the relevance of intention when the crime was committed and the "material causality of the crime" (Mirto 1946: 688; Battaglia 1945: 52–55; Liuzzi 1945: 349–350; Delitala 1946; Risso 1946a; Risso 1948; Marinario 1948); mitigating circumstances (Battaglini 1946); amnesties (Granata 1946; Vitale 1948; Sabatini 1947; Montalto 1948 [6]); foundations of the right to punish (Sant'Angelo 1947). All of these problems are of a general nature, but they emerged while the measures against Fascism were being interpreted and as Italy made its transition towards democracy, thus turning them into an opportunity for reflection on the categories upon which the criminal system was based. The transition was not viewed as a parenthesis while democratic criminal law was being planned; on the contrary, it became an opportunity to contribute to shaping Italy's new legal order.

This aspect should be observed in greater detail because it marks a change in attitude within Italy's legal culture. Under Fascism, legal science had settled on a formalistic methodological approach, known as the *indirizzo tecnico-giuridico*, which, despite being based on the construction of legal dogmas, took a neutral position with regard to axiological choices made by the legislator (Sbriccoli 2009: 635–649).

In this case, the transition and its contradictions pushed jurists towards a return to the law's original commitment to society and thus to the idea that it should act as a "guide" rather than an "instrument" for legislative options within criminal law (Vassalli 1947b). As mentioned above, a real and conscious rethinking of criminal law based on constitutional principles only began to take root in Italy in the mid-1960s, sometime after the transition phase. However, the 1940s debate on holding Fascism accountable showed some early evidence of a civil reawakening among Italian criminal lawyers, who were committed to building a new criminal-law system for democratic Italy.

---

[5] *Rivista Penale* devoted special attention to this problem in volume LXXI, 1946, which collects contributions by Bettiol 1946; Delitala 1946; Petrocelli 1946; Grispigni 1946; Saltelli 1946; Manzini 1946. Moreover, it reissued an 1880 article by the great jurist Francesco Carrara (Carrara 1946). *Rivista penale* printed other articles on the subject the following year (Funaro 1947; Ottolenghi 1947).

[6] *Rivista penale* devoted special focus to this subject in issues LXXI, 1946 and LXXII 1947 (Vitale 1946; Pittaluga 1946; Risso 1946b; Vitale 1947; Augenti 1947; Pintacuda 1947; Loasses 1947b).

15.4   Concluding Remarks

In conclusion, below are some general reflections on the repercussions of what has been observed so far on a historiographic and methodological level. Focusing on an ascriptive time, such as a transition period, has provided a deeper insight into the complex osmosis of temporal regimes (Bevernage 2012; Paixão 2015; Cau 2016a; Pombeni 2016), which overlap and intertwine as they seek to establish the relationship between past, present and future. This configuration, which could be considered an underlying issue that affects the perception of historical time in general (Ricoeur 2000: 449–535; Hartog 2015; Lorenz and Bevernage 2013; Paixão 2013), surfaces during the transition as *Jetztzeit* (Benjamin 2014; Desideri 2014: 334), the key issue, one which shapes the legal and political order.

More specifically, in historiographical terms, the study of transitional time takes at least three levels of analysis into account. The first regards *legislative options* and aims to understand the regulatory regimes that the introduction of transitional legislation has helped to shape. The second is *judicial practices* and studies what manner of solutions transitional justice has produced (Meniconi 2012: 260–263; Focardi and Nubola 2015; Bernardini 2017; Bolzon and Verardo 2018) and to what extent it contributed to shaping the democratic turn. It also looks at the effects transitional justice produced on the governing class after the end of Fascism, with one example being the problem of barring former leading Fascists from democratic Italy's public administration and judiciary (Melis 2003; Meniconi 2017; Portinaro 2011; Galimi 2014). The third is *legal discourse* and involves carrying out studies on the extent to which the attributive force of the transition brought to light fundamental legal issues for criminal law and to what extent this changed the way that jurists approached their task.

On a methodological level, studying the attributive function of time also implies a change in the analytical categories used to observe and understand historical phenomena. In hermeneutical terms, the conceptual dyads that emphasize the contrast between the commensurable profiles of the time factor—such as continuity/change, tradition/modernity, crisis/stability, or even transition/revolution—are of lesser importance. In this case, however, other dyads, that enable (seemingly) non-commensurable time-factor profiles to relate - such as continuity/modernity, tradition/change, transition/crisis, transition/emergence, transition/construction, transition/circulation and transformation/exception -, are of primary analytical importance.

Studies of ascriptive temporality tend to give greater prominence to the synchronic profiles of legal experience, as they consider time to be more than a neutral, one-dimensional platform. In this light, a reading of this attributive moment in history and its relationship with the law, allows us to observe how legal configurations are produced beyond their abstract configuration as legal dogmas and to associate them more clearly with the contexts that explain their *raison d'être*. In other words, it is not a matter of exploring the meaning of juridical configurations by placing them in the abstract context of the "system" (outside of time); on the contrary, their meaning should be explained by looking at the ascriptive factors that produce them.

This approach returns legal configurations to their original meaning and value and restores their relativity, thus opening them up to critical re-examination. In short, ascriptive time seems to be particularly fertile ground for research on legal history and theory, since it facilitates the removal of dogmatic and atemporal scaffolding when reflecting on the questions that reality poses the law. These observations also suggest how important it is for legal history to understand complex and contradictory processes, such as a transition to democracy, when time, which affects the regimes of impermanence of law, is a key factor in determining legal change.

References

Bernardini, G. et al. (eds.). 2017. *L'età costituente. Italia 1945–1948.* Bologna: Il Mulino.

Bevernage, B. 2012. *History, memory, and state-sponsored violence: Time and justice.* New York, London: Routledge.

Bolzon, I., and F. Verardo. 2018. *Cercare giustizia. L'azione giudiziaria in transizione.* Trieste: Istituto regionale per la storia della Resistenza.

Caroli, P. 2020. *Il potere di non punire. Uno studio sull'amnistia Togliatti.* Napoli: Edizioni Scientifiche Italiane.

Cau, M. 2016a. Constitutional Lore in Transition: Italy and Germany Post-1945. In *The historiography of transition. Critical phases in the development of modernity (1945–1973)*, ed. Paolo Pombeni, 168–182. New York: Routledge.

Cau, M. 2016b. Forme novecentesche del discorso sullo Stato e la sua crisi. In *Spazi politici, società e individuo: le tensioni del moderno*, eds. Christoph Cornelissen and Paolo Pombeni, 285–314. Bologna: Il Mulino.

Colao, F. 2011. Il volto della nazione nelle amnistie politiche. In *Grazia e giustizia: figure della clemenza fra tardo Medioevo ed età contemporanea*, eds. Karl Härter and Cecilia Nubola, 477–484. Bologna: Il Mulino.

Colao, F. 2015. I processi a Rodolfo Graziani: un modello italiano di giustizia di transizione dalla Liberazione all'anno Santo. In *Nei Tribunali. Pratiche e protagonisti della giustizia di transizione nell'Italia repubblicana*, ed. Giovanni Focardi and Cecilia Nubola, 169–220. Bologna: Il Mulino.

Desideri, F. 2014. Apocalissi profana: Figure della verità in Walter Benjamin. In *Angelus Novus. Saggi e frammenti*, Walter Benjamin, 307–339. Torino: Einaudi.

D'Ottavio, G. 2016. Democracy in transition: The development of a science of politics in Western Europe after 1945. In *The historiography of transition. Critical phases in the development of modernity (1945–1973)*, ed. Paolo Pombeni, 183–198. New York: Routledge.

Fioravanti, M. 2009. *Costituzionalismo. Percorsi della storia e tendenze attuali.* Bari-Roma: Laterza.

Focardi, G., and Nubola, C. (eds.). 2015. *Nei Tribunali. Pratiche e protagonisti della giustizia di transizione nell'Italia repubblicana.* Bologna: Il Mulino.

Fornasari, G., and Wenin, R. 2015. La giustizia di transizione. In *La persecuzione dei crimini internazionali. Una riflessione sui diversi meccanismi di risposta*, eds. Gabriele Fornasari, Roberto Wenin, and Emanuela Fronza, 47–64. Trento: Università degli studi di Trento.

Franzinelli, M. 2006. *L'amnistia Togliatti. 22 giugno 1946. Colpo di spugna sui crimini fascisti.* Milano: Mondadori.

Franzinelli, M. 2018. La punizione del collaborazionismo nell'Europa occidentale. In *Cercare giustizia. L'azione giudiziaria in transizione*, eds. Irene Bolzon and Fabio Verardo, 41–65. Trieste Istituto regionale per la storia della Resistenza e dell'Età contemporanea nel Friuli Venezia Giulia.

Galimi, V. 2014. Circulation of models of Epuration after the Second World War: from France to Italy. In *Dealing with wars and dictatorships. Legal concepts and categories in action*, eds. Liora Israel and Guillaume Mouralis, 197–208. Berlin: Springer.

Giannetto, M. 2003. Defascistizzazione: legislazione e prassi della liquidazione del sistema fascista e dei suoi responsabili (1943–1945). *Ventunesimo secolo. Rivista di studi sulle transizioni* 2: 53–90.

Grossi, P. 2011. Lo Stato moderno e la sua crisi (a cento anni dalla prolusione pisana di Santi Romano). In *Rivista trimestrale di diritto pubblico e procedura civile* LXI: 1–22.

Hartog, F. 2015. *Regimes of historicity. Presentism and experiences of time.* New York: Columbia University Press.

Lorenz, C., and B. Bevernage. 2013. *Breaking up time negotiating the borders between present, past and future.* Göttingen: Vandenhoeck & Ruprecht.

Meccarelli, M. 2011. Outside the society: Political emergency, widening of the penal system and regimes of legality in the late nineteenth century. In *Beyond the statute law. The "grey" government of criminal justice systems,* eds. Luigi Lacchè and Monica Stronati, 21–45. Macerata: EUM.

Melis, G. 2003. Note sull'epurazione dei ministeri, 1944–1946. *Ventunesimo secolo. Rivista di studi sulle transizioni* 2: 17–52.

Meniconi, A. 2012. *Storia della magistratura italiana.* Bologna: Il Mulino.

Meniconi, A. 2017. La magistratura nella storia costituzionale repubblicana. *Nomos. L'attualità nel diritto* 1: 1–19.

Mihai, M. 2010. Transitional justice and the quest for democracy: A contribution to a political theory of democratic transformations. *Ratio Juris* 23 (2): 183–204.

Nubola, C. 2016. Collaborators and clemency measures in Italy after the II World War. In *The historiography of transition. critical phases in the development of modernity (1945–1973),* ed. Paolo Pombeni, 56–72. New York: Routledge.

Paixão, C. 2013. Tempo Presente e Regimes de Historicidade: Perspectivas de Investigação para a História do Direito. In *As Formas do Direito. Ordem, Razão e Decisão (Experiências Jurídicas antes e depois da Modernidade),* ed. Ricardo Marcelo Fonseca, 77–87. Curitiba: Juruá.

Paixão, C. 2015. Past and future of authoritarian regimes: Constitution, transition to democracy and amnesty in Brazil and Chile. *Journal of Constitutional History* 30(II): 89–105.

Pombeni, P. 2016. Transition and its phases: Thoughts on some issues raised. In *The historiography of transition. Critical phases in the development of modernity (1945–1973),* ed. Paolo Pombeni, 1–19. New York: Routledge.

Pombeni, P. 2017. Ricostruire lo Stato, progettare il futuro. Alle origini del momento costituente. In *L'età costituente: Italia 1945–1945,* ed. Giovanni Bernardini et. al., 329–350. Bologna: Il Mulino.

Portinaro, P.P. 2011. *I conti con il passato. Vendetta, amnistia, giustizia.* Milano: Feltrinelli.

Ricoeur, P. 2000. *La mémoire l'histoire, l'oubli.* Paris: Seuil.

Sbriccoli, M. 2009. *Storia del diritto penale e della giustizia.* Milano: Giuffrè.

Searle, J.R. 1996. *The construction of social reality.* London: Penguin.

Sebald, W.G. 2004. *Storia naturale della distruzione.* Milano: Adelphi.

Stolzi, I. 2016. Immagini della crisi e ruolo delle fonti: un'ipotesi di lettura. In *Parlamento e Storia d'Italia. II Procedure e politiche,* eds. Vicenzo Casamassima and Andrea Frangioni, 253–262. Pisa: Edizioni della Normale.

Stonebridge, L. 2011. *The judicial imagination.Writing after Nuremberg*: Edinburgh, Edinburgh University Press.

Vassalli, G. 2001 Formula di Radbruch e diritto penale: note sulla punizione dei delitti di Stato nella Germania postnazista e nella Germania postcomunista: Milano, Giuffrè.

Sources

Angeloni, G.C. 1947. Diritto penale e ricostruzione sociale. *Giustizia penale,* LII(I): 177–183.

Angeloni, R., and M. Santoni-Rugiu. 1946. *Ricostruire la giustizia.* Carabba: Roma.

Augenti, G.P. 1947. In tema di rinuncia all'amnistia. *Rivista penale* LXXII: 35–39.

Battaglia, A. 1945. Osservazioni sul delitto preveduto dall'art. 3 del Decreto legislativo luogotenenziale 27 luglio 1944 n. 159. *Giustizia penale* LI(II): 49–54.

Battaglini, E. 1946. Osservazioni in tema di successione di leggi penali. *Giustizia penale* LII(II): 26–27.

Battaglini, E. 1947. Sulla efficacia dello "jus superveniens" in tema di competenza. *Giustizia penale* LII(II): 244–247.

Battaglini, E. 1948a. Una questione di diritto transitorio sui limiti della giurisdizione militare. *Giustizia penale* LIII(III): 246–252.

Battaglini, E. 1948b. *La irretroattività della legge penale nella nuova costituzione*. Milano: Il foro padano (Estratto da *Il foro padano*, 5, 1948).

Benjamin, W. 2014. *Tesi di filosofia della scienza*, (trad. it. di *Geschichtsphilosophische Thesen*, 1940). In Id., *Angelus Novus. Saggi e frammenti*. Torino: Einaudi.

Berlinguer, M. 1946. Incongruenze e iniquità dell'amnistia. *Giustizia penale* LI(II): 484–487.

Bettiol, G.M. 1946. Eccezione alla regola "in dubio pro reo". *Rivista penale* LXXI: 297–299.

Bettiol, G.M. 1947. *Relazione della sottocommissione sul Disegno di legge presentato dal Consiglio dei Ministri nella seduta del 17 marzo 1947*, Seduta del 23 ottobre 1947, Relatore Giuseppe Maria Bettiol. Atti parlamentari, Assemblea costituente n. 10-A, Commissione per la Costituzione.

Calamandrei, P. 1996. La crisi della legalità (1944). In Id., *Costituzione e leggi di Antigone. Scritti e discorsi politici*, 3–11. Firenze: La Nuova Italia editrice.

Calamandrei, P. 1947. Restaurazione clandestina. *Il Ponte* III(11–12): 959–968.

Capograssi, G. 1959, Riflessioni sull'autorità e la sua crisi (1921). In Id., *Opere*, I, 151–387. Milano: Giuffrè.

Carnelutti, F. 1937. La crisi della legge (1929). In Id., *Discorsi intorno al diritto*, 162–182. Padova: CEDAM.

Carnelutti, F. 1948. Abrogazione del reato di collaborazionismo. *Rivista penale* LXXIII: 28–41.

Carrara, F. 1946. Eresie giuridiche. Presunzioni "iuris ed de iure" in criminale (1880). *Rivista Penale* LXXI: 291–296.

Cesarini Sforza, W. 1936. La crisi delle fonti, *Archivio giuridico 'Filippo Serafini'* XCV: 18–43.

Cordone, G. 1947. Osservazioni sull'articolo 1 del Decreto di amnistia 8 maggio 1947 n. 460. *Rivista penale* LXXII: 782–788.

De Francesco, A. 1947. Note interpretative sull'art 1 D.L. 8 maggio 1947 n. 460. *Rivista penale* LXXII: 775–781.

Del Vecchio, G. 1934. La crisi della scienza del diritto. *Archivio Giuridico 'Filippo Serafini'* XCI: 5–21.

Delitala, G. 1946. Il reato vien meno se fa difetto la volontà. *Rivista penale* LXXI: 297–302.

Ebner, G. 1948. Tribolati trapassi. L'ultima disposizione dell'art. 103 della Carta costituzionale e il diritto processuale penale transitorio. *Rivista penale* LXXIII: 665–675.

Febvre, L. 1946. Face au vent: manifeste des Annales nouvelles [À nos lecteurs, à nos amis]. *Annales. Économies, Sociétés, Civilisations* 1(1): 1–8.

Fortunio, T. 1946. *La legislazione definitiva sulle sanzioni contro il fascismo. Delitti fascisti, epurazione, avocazione. Commento, dottrina, giurisprudenza*. Roma: Nuove edizioni Jus.

Funaro, F. 1947. Sentenze di morte dei Tribunali straordinari e reato di omicidio. *Rivista penale* LXXII: 53–62.

Granata, L. 1946. Primi lineamenti giuridici dell'amnistia politica. *Massimario Penale* 1: 159–162.

Grassi, G. 1948. Relazione del Ministro Guardasigilli sul decreto legislativo 29 gennaio 1948 n. 28, concernente la delegazione per la concessione di amnistia e indulto. *Rivista penale* LXXIII: 153–154.

Grispigni, F. 1946. Interpretazione autentica e non fattispecie di responsabilità oggettiva. *Rivista penale* LXXI: 303–306.

Guarnieri, F. 1946. *I delitti del fascismo: commento alle disposizioni contenute nel titolo I del d. L. Lt. 27 luglio 1944, n. 159*. Roma: Scuola Tipografica Artigiana.

Gullo, F. 1947a. Relazione del Ministro Guardasigilli al Decreto del Capo provvisorio dello Stato del 8 maggio 1947 n. 460. *Rivista penale* LXXII: 707–709.

Gullo, F. 1947b. Relazione del Ministro Guardasigilli al Decreto del Capo provvisorio dello Stato del 25 giugno 1947 n. 513. *Rivista penale* LXXII: 710–711.

Iaquinta, A. 1948. Della ultra-attività delle leggi eccezionali penali per il controllo delle armi e del sindacato di costituzionalità su di esse. *Giustizia penale* parte II: 754–760.

Jemolo, A.C. 1945. Le sanzioni contro il fascismo e la legalità. *Il Ponte* 1: 277–285.

Lener, S. 1946. *Diritto e politica nelle sanzioni contro il fascismo e nella epurazione dell'amministrazione.* Roma: La civiltà cattolica.

Leonelli, L. 1948. Amnistia e reati annonari. *Giustizia penale* LIII(II): 492–495.

Liuzzi, F. 1945. Bilancio dell'Alta Corte. *Rivista penale* LXX: 345–352.

Loasses, C. 1947a. Come si fanno le leggi in Italia, *Rivista penale* LXXI: 1184–1187.

Loasses, C. 1947b. Non contro l'amnistia ma contro l'abuso e la svalutazione dell'amnistia. *Rivista penale* LXXII: 140–149.

Lopez de Oñate, F. 1942. *La certezza del diritto.* Roma: Tip. Consorzio nazionale.

Macaluso, G. 1948. *Discorso per l'inaugurazione dell'anno giudiziario, del 5 gennaio 1948 dell'Avvocato generale della Corte suprema di cassazione.* Roma: Società anomia editrice.

Manzini, V. 1946. Presunzione relativa. *Rivista penale* LXXI: 306–312.

Marinario, F. 1948. Elemento psicologico del reato di collaborazione. *Rivista penale* LXXIII: 1143–1144.

Maroni, L. 1947. Relazione sul lavoro giudiziario dell'Alta Corte di giustizia presentata dal Presidente dell'Alta Corte alla Presidenza e al Ministro di grazia e giustizia. *Rivista penale* LXXI: 294–298.

Meucci, G.P. 1946. *Il delitto di collaborazionismo col tedesco invasore.* Libreria Editrice fiorentina: Firenze.

Mirto, P. 1946. Collaborazionismo presunto?. *Giustizia penale* LI(II): 677–692.

Montalto, P. 1948. Contro l'inflazione delle amnistie. *Giustizia penale* LIII(II): 187–190.

Ottolenghi, G. 1947. Collaborazione presunta e responsabilità obiettiva. *Rivista penale* LXXII: 923–928.

Pace, G. 1947. *Su una nuova teoria generale del diritto transitorio.* Milano: Vallardi (estratto da *Rivista di diritto commerciale*, XLV, 1947, parte I).

Peluso Cassese, G. 1948. L'amnistia del febbraio 1948 e le leggi annonarie. *Giustizia penale* LIII(II): 489–493.

Petrocelli, B. 1946. Necessità di valutare il comportamento per la determinazione della norma violata. *Rivista penale* LXXI: 312–313.

Pilotti, M. 1945. La giustizia e la ricostruzione nazionale. Discorso per l'inaugurazione del Procuratore generale presso la Suprema Corte di cassazione. *La Cassazione penale: rivista di dottrina, giurisprudenza e legislazione* 1: 9–23.

Pilotti, M. 1946. La giustizia e la ricostruzione nazionale Discorso per l'inaugurazione dell'anno giudiziario 1946 del Procuratore generale presso la Suprema Corte di cassazione. *Rivista penale* LXXI: 1–32.

Pilotti, M. 1947. L'amministrazione della giustizia e la riforma costituzionale. Discorso per l'inaugurazione dell'anno giudiziario 1947 del Procuratore generale presso la Suprema Corte di cassazione. *Rivista penale* LXXII: 1–34.

Pintacuda, S. 1947. La rinunzia all'amnistia. *Rivista penale* LXXII: 40–46.

Pittaluga, M. 1946. Questioni sull'amnistia. *Rivista penale* LXXI: 648–655.

Risso, L. 1946a. Il rapporto di causalità in reati di collaborazionismo. *Rivista Penale* LXXI: 1098–1100.

Risso, L. 1946b. In tema di amnistia. *Rivista penale* LXXI: 761–765.

Risso, L. 1948. La coazione morale nel collaborazionismo. *Rivista penale* LXXIII: 49–52.

Romano, S. 1910. Lo Stato moderno e la sua crisi. *Rivista di diritto pubblico* 3: 98–114.

Sabatini, G. 1947. L'amnistia politica. In *Il collaborazionismo e l'amnistia politica nella giurisprudenza della Corte di cassazione,* Giuliano Vassalli and Giuseppe Sabatini, 521–561. Roma: Edizioni "La giustizia penale".

Saltelli, C. 1946. In tema di collaborazione presunta. *Rivista penale* LXXI: 484–486.

Sant'Angelo, G. 1947. L'amnistia come causa estintiva della pretesa punitiva. *Giustizia penale* LII(II): 641–662.

Serena Monghini, A. 1947. La crisi della giustizia penale in Italia, *Rivista penale* LXII: 867–873.

Sotgiu, G. 1950. *Il delitto politico.* Roma: Croce.

Togliatti, P. 1945. Relazione del Ministro Guardasigilli al Decreto legislativo luogotenenziale del 17 novembre 1945 n. 719. *Rivista penale* LXX: 472–473.

Togliatti, P. 1946a. Circolare del Ministro guardasigilli del 3 dicembre 1945 n. 3120, applicativa del Decreto di amnistia del 17 novembre 1945 n. 719. *Rivista penale* LXXI: 155.

Togliatti, P. 1946b. Intervento alla seduta dell'Assemblea costituente del 22 luglio 1946. *Rivista penale* LXXI: 1048–1049.

Togliatti, P. 1946c. Relazione del Ministro Guardasigilli sul Decreto Presidenziale 22 giugno 1946 n. 4. *Rivista penale* LXXI: 707–714.

Vassalli, G. 1945. La collaborazione col tedesco invasore nella giurisprudenza della Sezione speciale della Cassazione. *Giustizia penale* L(II): 1–15.

Vassalli, G. 1946. La collaborazione col tedesco invasore nella giurisprudenza della Sezione speciale della Cassazione. *Giustizia penale* LI(II): 65–86.

Vassalli, G. 1947a. La collaborazione col tedesco invasore nella giurisprudenza della Sezione speciale della Cassazione. *Giustizia penale* LII(II): 577–592.

Vassalli, G. 1947b. Intorno all'art. 2 della legge sulle sanzioni contro il fascismo. *Giustizia penale* LII(II): 663–680.

Vassalli, G. 1947c. Intorno al fondamento giuridico della punizione dei crimini di guerra. *Giustizia penale* LII(II): 618–626.

Vassalli, G. 1947d. Sul soggetto attivo nei reati di collaborazione col nemico. *Giustizia penale* LII(II): 128–132.

Vassalli, G. 1948. La collaborazione col tedesco invasore nella giurisprudenza della Sezione speciale della Cassazione. *Giustizia penale* LIII(II): 128–132.

Vassalli, G. and Sabbatini, G. 1947. *Il collaborazionismo e l'amnistia politica nella giurisprudenza della Corte di Cassazione: diritto materiale, diritto processuale, testi legislativi.* Roma: Ed. della "Giustizia penale".

Vitale, N. 1946. Contro l'amnistia. *Rivista penale* LXXI: 1054–1074.

Vitale, N. 1947. In difesa dell'amnistia. *Rivista penale* LXXII: 1049–1056.

Vitale, N. 1948. Ancora contro l'amnistia. *Giustizia penale* LIII(II): 855–860.

Massimo Meccarelli is Professor of Legal History at the University of Macerata (Italy), and affiliate researcher of the Max Planck Institute for European Legal History (Frankfurt am Main). He was visiting professor at: Universidad Autónoma de Madrid, Johann Wolfgang Goethe-Universität in Frankfurt am Main, Universität Wien, Universität Luzern. He is author of several works on history of legal thought, history of justice, historiography and methodology of legal history. Most recently research interests: law and diversity, legal pluralism, constitution making process, time and law, law and humanities.

Chronology

ARGENTINA

March 1976	Coup d'État initiated a military dictatorship called *Proceso de Reoganización Nacional*
October 1983	Raúl Alfonsín's election as President.
December 1983	*Comisión Nacional sobre la Desaparición de Personas* (CONADEP) was instituted and published *Nunca Más* report, which registered the practice of assassination, disappearance, tortures, and kidnapping of babies during the dictatorship.
December 1985	Trial of the military juntas (*juicio de las juntas*) that convicted five out of nine military officials that integrated the juntas that governed the country during the dictatorship.
December 1986/ June 1987	Approval of the "impunity laws" (*Ley del Punto Final* - Law n. 23.492, de 1986 - and *Ley de la Obediencia Devida* - Law n. 23.521, de 1987) that prevented perpetrators of human rights violations from being held accountable for their crimes.
December 1994	Law for economic reparation of victims of enforced disappearance and of political detention and their relatives (Law n. 24.411/1994).
April 1998	Beginning of "trials for truth" (*juicios por la verdad*), which were judicial proceedings that aimed at gathering evidence and establishing the truth about the dictatorship's violations, especially against victims of enforced disappearance.

© Springer Nature Switzerland AG 2021
C. Paixão and M. Meccarelli (eds.), *Comparing Transitions to Democracy. Law and Justice in South America and Europe*, Studies in the History of Law and Justice 18, https://doi.org/10.1007/978-3-030-67502-8

August 1996	Beginning of the trial before the *Audiencia Nacional de España* for crimes committed by Argentine military
March 2001	First declaration of nullity of the impunity laws (*Ley del Punto Final* and *Ley de la Obediencia Devida*) by a federal judge.
September 2003	Annulment of the impunity laws by Congress (Law n, 25.779/2003) and reopening of judicial cases of criminal persecution for human rights violations.
March 2004	Recovery of the building where the *Escuela de Mecanica de la Armada* operated, one of the main detention and disappearance centre.
June 2005	Judicial declaration of unconstitutionality of the impunity laws (*Ley del Punto Final* and *Ley de la Obediencia Devida*) by the Supreme Court (case *Simón Julio y otros*)

BRAZIL

March 31, 1964	Military troops march from Minas Gerais to Rio de Janeiro, initiating the events that would lead to President Jango's overthrowing.
April 9, 1964	First Institutional Act (a decree laying the legal foundations of the dictatorship) enacted.
April 11, 1964	Castello Branco, an officer of the Brazilian Army, elected president in an indirect election held by Congress.
October 27, 1965	Institutional Act n. 2 enacted. Dissolution of the existing political parties and adoption of a bipartisan system. End of direct elections for president.
October 3, 1966	Costa e Silva, also an officer of the Brazilian Army, elected president in an indirect election.
March 15, 1967	The 1967 Constitution comes into force. The constitutional text, originally drafted by the Executive branch, was submitted to Congress and eventually modified. Congress, however, was forced to deliberate in a stringent procedure previously defined by the Executive branch.
December 13, 1968	Institutional Act n. 5 enacted. Among other prerogatives, the Act granted the president the ability to adjourn Congress (and take over legislative powers) at any time, to freely remove individuals from office and suspend their political rights, and to arbitrarily declare federal intervention in the state and local government, replacing governors and mayors at will.

1973	The Inter-American Commission on Human Rights recognized in its Annual Report the violation of human rights in the case of Olavo Hansen (Case no. 1683), a union leader who was arrested, tortured and murdered by Brazilian state agents. In another case, related to three anonymous complaints about the existence of 12 thousand political prisoners in Brazil and the practice of torture and rape, it stated that the Brazilian government imposed difficulties on the investigation (Case no. 1684).
October 27, 1978	The family of the journalist Vladimir Herzog managed to obtain a judicial decision which not only recognized the falsehood of the suicide version and the state's responsibility for Herzog's death but also admitted, in broader terms, that the Brazilian state practiced the torture of political prisoners.
August 28, 1979	An Amnesty Law was adopted which allowed the release of political prisoners from jail and the return of exiled activists (Law 6683/1979)
January–April 1984	Street demonstrations for elections for President of Brazil (Diretas Já)
February 1, 1987–October 5, 1988	National Constituent Assembly and enactment of the 1988 Federal Constitution
December 4, 1995	A law was adopted which created a commission (Special Commission on Political Deaths and Disappearances) to recognize State responsibility for deaths and disappearences, to grant financial compensation to their families, and to work for locating the remains of the disappeared (Law 9140/1995).
November 13, 2002	A law was adopted which created a commission (Amnesty Commission) to grant reparation to victims of political persecution (Law 10.559/2002).
June 2003	A decision was issued in a civil action initiated in 1982 by the families of those disappeared in the Araguaia Guerrilla, which ruled that the Brazilian state must identify the location of the graves and present to this court all the information about the operations related to the Guerrilla.
April 2010	The Brazilian Supreme Court decided that the amnesty in favor of perpetrators of gross human rights violations could be preserved.
November 2010	The Inter-American Court of Human Rights delivered its merits decision in the Araguaia Guerrilla case, ruling that the amnesty in favor of perpetrators of gross human rights violations contradicts the American Convention on Human Rights.
May 2012	The National Truth Commission was established, on the basis of a Law adopted in 2011 (Law 12.258/2011).

CHILE

September 1970	Socialist Party candidate Salvador Allende wins Chile's presidential election, heading the Popular Unity coalition
September 11, 1973	A violent coup deposes President Allende, initiating a repressive right-wing military dictatorship headed by General Augusto Pinochet
November 25–28, 1975	Founding meeting of Condor in Santiago, Chile, with the participation of representatives from Argentina, Bolivia, Brazil, Chile, Uruguay and Paraguay
September 11, 1980	A new, authoritarian, Constitution is 'ratified' by a fraudulent plebiscite
October 5, 1988	A second plebiscite narrowly rejects conceding eight more years in power to Pinochet, meaning open elections would be held.
March 11, 1990	After Chile's first free elections in 17 years, centrist Christian Democrat candidate Patricio Aylwin became president, representing a 17-party centre left coalition, the "Concertación".
March 4, 1991	Chile's first Truth Commission, the National Commission on Truth and Reconciliation ("Rettig Commission"), reported on grave human rights violations and acts of political violence committed during the dictatorship. Totals, updated in 1996 and 2005, came to stand at 3,216 individuals killed or disappeared.
May 1995	Supreme Court upholds criminal verdicts dictated against DINA's high-ranking officers Manuel Contreras and Pedro Espinoza Bravo for the 1976 murder of exiled politician Orlando Letelier in Washington DC
1998	Domestic criminal complaints naming Pinochet directly are admitted, for the first time, to the investigation stage (in January.) In October, Augusto Pinochet is detained in London, under the terms of an international arrest warrant requested by Spanish judge Baltazar Garzón
November 17, 2004	The first domestic human rights case criminal case verdict explicitly recognising dictatorship-era "kidnappings" as enforced disappearance, sentenced former secret police chief Manuel Contreras to a prison term
November 28, 2004	Chile's second truth commission, the National Commission on Political Imprisonment and Torture, "Valech Commission", published its report, naming almost 29,000 survivors of dictatorship-era political imprisonment and torture

2009–2010	Gradual introduction of national human rights infrastructure including a National Human Rights Institute, Museum for Memory and Human Rights, and (later) a Human Rights Subscretariat in the Justice Ministry.
October 2019	Major social unrest, met with disproportionate police violence, threatened Chile's carefully cultivated image of success and stability. Political elites grudgingly conceded the need for a new Constitution. A plebiscite on whether to open a process for Constitutional replacement, initially scheduled for early 2020, was postponed, due to the COVID pandemic, until October 2020
October 25, 2020	Plebiscite on constitutional replacement: an overwhelming majority (78.24%) of voters supported opening a process to draft a new Constitution, and opted for a fully popularly-elected, gender-parity body as the method. Just over 50% of the eligible electorate took part in the vote. The draft, due in 2022, will then be subject to approval in a second plebiscite.

ITALY

October 28, 1922	Rise of Fascism to power
November 25, 1926	Issue of the Act n. 2008: measures against political dissent and establishment of a Special Court to prosecute political crimes (Tribunale speciale per la difesa dello Stato)
July 10, 1940	Entry into the World War II
July 25–26, 1943	Destitution of Benito Mussolini as a Chief of the Government and Fall of Fascism. new government for the Kingdom of Italy headed by General Pietro Badoglio;
September 8–10, 1943	Armistice between Italy and Anglo-American Allies; Self-organisation of resistance forces for the liberation of Italy from German control
September 23, 1943	Institution of the *Repubblica di Salò*, the new fascist State headed by Mussolini in the northern Italy occupied by German Army
June 4–9, 1944	Allies enter in Rome. Enforcement of a New Government headed by Ivanoe Bonomi, composed by antifascist representants of the Committee of National Liberation
July 27, 1944	Decree n. 159 - Law for the epuration of fascist collaborators and leaders
April 22, 1945	Decree n. 142 - Institution of Special Courts against Fascism crimes
April 25, 1945	End of the World War II in Italy

June 2, 1946	Referendum to choose the State form between Monarchy and Republic; birth of the new Republic
June 25, 1946	First session of the Constituent Assembly
June 22, 1946	Amnesty for the crimes committed during the war by fascists and members of the resistance forces (a.k.a. Togliatti Amnesty)
January 1, 1948	New Constitution of the Republic of Italy

PORTUGAL

April 25, 1974	Around 400 middle-rank military stage a *coup* against the authoritarian regime leading to the resignation of the dictator, Marcelo Caetano, and the dissolution of the regime
April 26, 1974	Decree law 173/74 grants amnesty for political crimes and similar military crimes and allows individuals dismissed from their jobs for political and ideological reasons during the authoritarian regime to seek reintegration
June 25, 1974	Decree-law 277/74 determines civil servants should be purged from their jobs if their behaviour is not aligned with the new democratic framework
November 15, 1974	New electoral law, decree law 621-A/74, imposes political rights restrictions to those who held public office positions or worked for regime institutions from 1926 to 1974
March 11, 1975	New decree-law 123/75 introduces an amendment to the purge law to cover individual behaviour prior to the breakdown of the 'fascist' regime
July 25, 1975	Law 8/75 determines all workers and informants of the former political police are to be tried for belonging to a terrorist organization
February 19, 1976	Decree-law determines those who were purged from their jobs in 1974-1975 may have their situation reassessed and be reintegrated in their jobs
April 10, 1976	New Constitution approved
April 25, 1976	First free and fair legislative elections
October 25, 1976	The first trial of former political police workers and informants takes place in a military court

PARAGUAY

May 4–7, 1954	Coup d'état by General Alfredo Stroessner inaugurates South America's longest dictatorship, which would last until 1989.

February 2–3, 1989	Internal power struggles within the ruling Colorado Party leads Army General Andres Rodriguez to topple dictator Stroessner in a coup d'état
December 22, 1992	Discovery by Judge Agustín Fernández and human rights activist Martin Almada of the so-called "Archive of Terror," in the Lambaré outskirts of Asunción
September 12, 1996	Law 838/96 provides for reparations to survivors and/or relatives of victims of disappearances, torture, executions, and illegal detention committed during the dictatorship.
October 2004	The Truth and Justice Commission begins its mandate to investigate past horrors and its final report is submitted in August 2008

SPAIN

July 18, 1936	Outbreak of the Civil War
April 1, 1939	End of the Civil War
April 1964	Commemoration of "XXV Años de Paz" (25 years of "Peace")
November 20, 1975	Death of Dictator Francisco Franco
October 15, 1977	Amnesty Law
December 29, 1978	Spanish Constitution
February 23, 1981	Failed Coup d'etat
December 2003	Beginning of public policies of memory by Catalan Government
December 26, 2007	Spanish Ley de "Memoria Histórica"
February 27, 2012	Decision on Garzón case by Tribunal Supremo

URUGUAY

June 27, 1973	A military-backed coup by President Juan Maria Bordaberry shuts down Parliament and inaugurates twelve years of dictatorship
March 1, 1985	Transfer of power from the military regime to President Julio Maria Sanguinetti of the Colorado Party, who had been previously democratically elected in November 1984
March 8, 1985	Parliament sanctions Law 15.737, a general amnesty for political prisoners
December 22, 1986	Parliament enacts Law 15.848 known as "Expiry Law," which shields military and police officers from prosecution for dictatorship's human rights violations

March 1989	The Peace and Justice Service (SERPAJ) releases its "Uruguay: Never Again" report on the human rights violations committed during the dictatorship
August 2000	Creation of the Peace Commission, which submits its final report in April 2003
September 2005	Establishment of legal category of "absent due to enforced disappearance"
March 2009	First criminal sentence dictated for dictatorship-era crimes (*Adalberto Soba et al.* case)
September 2009	Law 18.596 acknowledges the systematic practice of state terror between 1968 and 1985, and awards reparations to victims and/or their relatives.
February 2011	*Gelman vs. Uruguay* condemnatory verdict by the Inter-American Court of Human Rights
October 27, 2011	Parliament derogates the Expiry Law
July 8, 2019	The First Assize Appeals Court of Rome, Italy, condemns on appeal 24 former civilian, police, and military officers from Uruguay, Chile, Bolivia, and Peru for 38 murders committed by Operation Condor.

Index

© Springer Nature Switzerland AG 2021
C. Paixão and M. Meccarelli (eds.), *Comparing Transitions to Democracy. Law and Justice in South America and Europe*, Studies in the History of Law and Justice 18, https://doi.org/10.1007/978-3-030-67502-8

Lightning Source UK Ltd.
Milton Keynes UK
UKHW021002240822
407764UK00005B/586

9 783030 675042